Georgian London

Georgian London

Into the Streets

LUCY INGLIS

VIKING
an imprint of
PENGUIN BOOKS

VIKING

Published by the Penguin Group

Penguin Books Ltd, 80 Strand, London WC2R ORL, England
Penguin Group (USA) Inc., 375 Hudson Street, New York, New York 10014, USA
Penguin Group (Canada), 90 Eglinton Avenue East, Suite 700, Toronto, Ontario, Canada M4P 2Y3
(a division of Pearson Penguin Canada Inc.)
Penguin Ireland, 25 St Stephen's Green, Dublin 2, Ireland (a division of Penguin Books Ltd)
Penguin Group (Australia), 707 Collins Street, Melbourne, Victoria 3008, Australia
(a division of Pearson Australia Group Pty Ltd)
Penguin Books India Pvt Ltd, 11 Community Centre, Panchsheel Park, New Delhi – 110 017, India
Penguin Group (NZ), 67 Apollo Drive, Rosedale, Auckland 0632, New Zealand
(a division of Pearson New Zealand Ltd)
Penguin Books (South Africa) (Pty) Ltd, Block D, Rosebank Office Park, 181 Jan Smuts Avenue,
Parktown North, Gauteng 2193, South Africa

Penguin Books Ltd, Registered Offices: 80 Strand, London WC2R ORL, England

www.penguin.com

First published 2013
001

Copyright © Lucy Inglis, 2013
The moral right of the author has been asserted

Set in 12/14.75pt Bembo Book Mt Std
Typeset by Palimpsest Book Production Ltd, Falkirk, Stirlingshire
Printed in Great Britain by Clays Ltd, St Ives plc

A CIP catalogue record for this book is available from the British Library

ISBN: 978-0-670-92013-6

www.greenpenguin.co.uk

For Richard, with love
'The web of our Life is of a mingled Yarn'

Contents

List of Illustrations

Endpapers: Mary Roque's map of London, 1766, showing the boundary of the City of London (© Museum of London)

In the text

Plates

SECTION ONE – BLACK AND WHITE

SECTION TWO — COLOUR

Preface

I do not pretend to give a full account of all things worthy to be known, in this great city, or of its famous citizens . . . but only the most eminent which have occurred to my reading or observation.

Thomas de Laune, *The Present State of London* (1690)

Fourteen years ago I arrived in London to work for an antiques dealer. The city fascinated me, its history hanging in the air like a salty tang. My days were spent amongst eighteenth-century objects, from milk jugs to gold boxes. Who had made them? Where did they live? What were their lives like? In looking for answers I found tales of men, women, children, wealth, crime, poverty, the erotic, the exotic and the quiet desperation of the mundane.

Monarchs, politicians and aristocrats grab the historical limelight, but the ordinary people were my quarry: the Londoners who rode the dawn coach to work, opened shops bleary-eyed and hung-over, fell in love, had risky sex, realized the children had head lice again, paid parking fines, cashed in winning lottery tickets, fought for good causes and committed terrible crimes. Behind their stories, I saw modern London emerge between the Restoration of Charles II and the arrival of Queen Victoria on the throne.

One Sunday, in the summer of 2009, I stood on the steps of St Paul's Cathedral and listened as the bells called to worshippers and tourists alike. People loitered chatting, or climbed the steps and went inside. I imagined this clamour was almost exactly the same as it had been three centuries ago. I recorded it on my telephone and walked home.

For years I had dragged my husband to churchyards, houses, demolition sites, public monuments and hidden memorials, telling him the stories of people long dead: cabinetmakers, slaves, domestic servants, weavers, chimney sweeps and prostitutes. Back at home I played him the recording, my precious moment of shared experience with Londoners of the past. His dry recommendation was to start blogging the tales I had accumulated and what I believed about Georgian London (perhaps hoping to deflect my endless enthusiasm on to the miasma of the World Wide Web). The blog gained instant traction as it explored relationships, crime, literature, disability, personal hygiene, jobs, sexuality, charity, sport and shopping. This book has sprung from its loins, a tribute to the people of the eighteenth-century city and testimony to the eternal feeling that if I could just run fast enough through London's endless archives I will catch them, grasp their coat-tails and make them tell me everything about being a Georgian Londoner.

Introduction

Much of this book is concerned with the minutiae of daily life in Georgian London, during the years between 1714 and 1830. It was an extraordinary period in the city's history, but its foundations lay in the latter half of the seventeenth century, when four defining events shaped the psyche of Londoners. The first was a question of government, followed by a terrifying epidemic and a devastating fire. The last was a matter of religious identity.

Our story begins in the winter of 1659. The country was poor, and disheartened by civil war. It was the time of the Commonwealth, when England was a republic under Oliver Cromwell's Rump Parliament, the 'hind' or leftovers of government from the war. But now Cromwell was dead. In December, gangs of youths took to the streets of London, pelting soldiers with rocks. These were not street children but the city's teenage apprentices, feared since medieval times for their propensity to riot when aggrieved. Their protest was put down at sword- and gunpoint, but it was the start of a series of public displays of unrest, where the watermen wore the badges of the old King and urchins made bonfires and burned mock 'rumps' in the streets. The republic's days were numbered.

Charles Stuart, son of the executed King, had been exiled in The Hague, and was waiting to return to power. He was proclaimed King in his absence on 8 May 1660, and 'Bow Bells could not be heard for the noise of the people'. The Quaker Daniel Baker reprimanded citizens for their enthusiastic celebrations, calling the city an 'Impudent Harlot, thou whorish Blood-thirsty Mistress of abomination'. But London's royalist pamphleteers styled Charles as a phoenix rising from the ashes of the republic. He arrived in London on 29 May, his thirtieth birthday. He was welcomed to the City of London by the Lord Mayor before processing along the Strand to Westminster. Such were the crowds that it took him seven hours to cover the distance, a little under two miles. Accompanying him were 'above 20000 horse and foot, brandishing their swords, and shouting with inexpressible joy; the ways strewed with flowers, the bells ringing, the streets hung with tapestry, fountains running with wine'. John Evelyn the diarist recalled how he had 'stood in the Strand and beheld it, and blessed God'.

The Restoration returned colour and fun to London. The theatres, closed by the Puritans, reopened and were soon full every night. Before the Restoration of Charles II London had lacked the money to grow, or else had been held back by cautious monarchs who prohibited building, fretting that the city might become unmanageable. It remained a medieval city of narrow streets and courts, a jumble of gables crowded too close together to be either comfortable or sanitary. However, Charles did not fear expansion and London soon began to grow. Then came the twin horrors of the Plague of 1665 and the Great Fire of 1666. In little over a year, a fifth of London's population lay below the earth. Above it, four-fifths of the City was ashes.

The Plague killed approximately 100,000 Londoners over the summer of 1665. Amsterdam had been devastated the year before, and London knew it was only a matter of time before the disease arrived. It began in April, when the first fatality was recorded. The initial outbreak was in St Giles-in-the-Fields, a poor area near Tottenham Court Road. Many who died there went undiagnosed and unrecorded, for no one in London understood that the rod-shaped plague bacterium, *Yersinia pestis*, was carried by London's black rats. Rats were, after all, part of city life. Plague rapidly made 'a great impression of fear on the hearts of men' because of its unpredictability and the devastation it wreaked on the body. There were no set signs, and some died suddenly with no symptoms at all. Others suffered terribly with fever, or large black buboes growing in the lymph nodes of their groin or throat, followed by organ failure and seizures. It was hot and airless in the cramped streets; the numbers of dead rose and no one knew where the sickness would strike next. London was gripped by terror.

By the summer, anyone who could leave London had gone. Shops and taverns were closed, the streets empty. Priests, doctors and some officials, including Samuel Pepys, remained – as did a few hardy residents. Many of those who stayed behind were servants abandoned by their fleeing employers. The superstitious carried 'charms, philtres, exorcisms, amulets' to protect themselves. On 1 July, the Mayor and Aldermen of the City published a more practical set of emergency procedures for each parish to follow. Plagued households were shut up by the watchmen with all the occupants inside. Daniel Defoe recorded that some died simply of fear, watching the sufferings of their family. In the event of a death, a searcher – usually a poor old woman – was sent in to investigate. The watchmen granted them access to the house and they had to diagnose the dead, 'as near as they can'. Any surviving members of the household had to stay in the house for twenty-eight days, relying on food passed through windows by friends. The friendless starved.

By September, the death toll had hit 7,000 a week. The Lord Mayor ordered London's cats and dogs to be exterminated as a misguided precaution against the spread of the disease: 'they talked of forty thousand dogs, and five times as many cats; few houses being without a cat'. Free from predators, the toxic rat population boomed. Londoners ventured out only when necessary, often returning sick. A clergyman named John Allin and his brother had decided to stay in London. Early in that deadly September, John's brother went out one morning. When he returned he found a 'stiffnesse under his eare, where he had a swelling that could not be brought to rise and breake, but choacked him; he dyed Thursday night last'. That week, with the deaths at their peak, Allin wrote of the 'dolefull and almost universall and continuall ringing and tolling of bells'.

The 'dead carts' rumbled through the empty streets, piled high with bodies. As they approached the drivers tolled a handbell and called, 'Bring out your dead!' Few were prepared neatly for the grave. Plague pits were dug, several around Aldgate and Cripplegate, where the dead were to be buried at least six feet deep. Those expectant holes in the ground had a great effect upon the living. John Allin was distressed by the one he could see from his bedroom window, and at the height of the deaths Defoe remembered how 'people that were infected and near their end, and delirious also, would run to those pits, wrapt in blankets or rugs, and throw themselves in'. The drivers and the 'buriers' became hardened to the sufferings around them. One driver, named Buckinham, was whipped and imprisoned for driving through the streets shouting, 'Faggots, faggots, five for six-pence' then holding up the corpse of a child by the leg.

Then, just as Londoners feared extinction, the spread of the disease slowed as autumn cooled the city. It seemed that more victims were surviving. They 'sweated kindly', their buboes burst and could be drained. Families still fell sick, but then they recovered, sometimes without the loss of even one life. The worst had passed. By spring 1666, most of those who had left the city returned to their homes, and the King and his court were back in St James's. The disease would linger on in some slums through another blazing summer, but life returned to normal with remarkable speed. London had survived. Or so it seemed.

In the early hours of 2 September 1666, in Seething Lane, Samuel Pepys and his wife, Elizabeth, were woken by their maid, Jane, to tell them of a fire she and the other maids had seen in the City. He got up, put on his nightgown and went with Jane to look but, as he recorded in his diary, 'thought it far enough off; and so went to bed again and to sleep'. He rose again around seven and after getting dressed, 'Jane comes and tells me that she hears that above 300 houses have been burned down to-night by the fire we saw, and that it is now burning down all Fish-street by London Bridge'. Perturbed, Pepys walked to the Tower of London and watched the progress of the fire. He went down to the river and took a boat to get a perspective from the water. The Steelyard, a four-acre area of light industry, ware-houses and housing now covered by Cannon Street Station, was already burning fiercely and people had begun to evacuate their homes on a large scale. Public order broke down as people looked for someone to blame. London's foreign population, particularly the French element, were targeted that day. A fourteen-year-old West-minster schoolboy, William Taswell, remembered seeing a blacksmith who met 'an innocent Frenchman walking along the street, [and] felled him instantly to the ground with an iron bar'. His brother told him he too had seen a Frenchman 'almost dismembered' in Moor-fields because the mob thought he was carrying firebombs. It was a box of tennis balls.

Samuel Pepys continued to traverse the city, watching the progress of the flames. The cramped, high buildings were 'so very thick thereabouts' that their gables leaned towards each other and allowed the fire to spread across the roofs unchecked. The wind had got up 'mighty high and [was] driving [the fire] into the City; and every thing, after so long a drought, [was] proving combustible, even the very stones of churches'. Pepys was called to see the King, who told him to go and order the Lord Mayor to pull down the houses in the path of the fire 'every which way'. The Mayor was found in Canning Street, 'like a man spent, with a handkercher about his neck'. He had responded too late to stop the fire. Pepys took to the water again. Everywhere people were loading the contents of their homes on to the small Thames cargo boats, known as 'lighters'. He watched the fire from the river, nearly overwhelmed by smoke, and his face 'almost burned with a shower of firedrops'. That night, sitting in an alehouse at Three Cranes Wharf, Samuel and his wife saw the flames above the city, 'an arch of above a mile long: it made me weep to see it'.

In the morning, Monday, they began to pack up their own house. While Samuel's household laboured to save their belongings, London's other famous diarist, John Evelyn, had come up from Deptford to see the 'Great Fire'. By the time he saw the city, from Southwark, the alehouse Samuel and Elizabeth had sat in the night before was gone. Nor was the Lord Mayor, Thomas Bloodworth, anywhere to be seen. Instead King Charles's brother, James, the Duke of York, arrived in the City, marshalled groups of firefighters and ordered the demolition of whole streets. The fire continued to spread. The Royal Exchange, the glory of Elizabethan London, burned through the late afternoon.

On Tuesday, the garrison stationed at the Tower took decisive action and blew up all the houses on the eastern limit of the City, halting the spread of the fire in that direction. High on Ludgate Hill, St Paul's began to burn. Evelyn reported 'the melting lead [from the roof] running down the streets in a stream, and the very pavements glowing with fiery redness, so as no horse, nor man, was able to tread on them'. He recalled how, throughout the City, 'the fall of towers, houses and churches was like a hideous storm'. To the west, James and his men had hoped the Fleet Ditch would provide a natural fire-break. Yet the wind still blew hard and dry from the east and, as they watched, the fire leapt the ditch and arrived on Fleet Street. Then they ran.

That evening the wind died abruptly. The firebreaks held. On Wednesday morning, Pepys roamed the city, seeing widespread devastation in Moorfields where he walked, his 'feet ready to burn', and watched people huddled amongst their possessions on the scrubland. On a much smaller scale, he observed the destruction of medieval London. He picked up, as a souvenir, 'a piece of glasse of [the sixteenth century] Mercer's Chappell in the streete . . . so melted and buckled with the heat of the fire like parchment', and was upset to see 'a poor cat taken out of a hole in the chimney, joyning to the wall of the Exchange; with, the hair all burned off the body, and yet alive'. That night, there were whispers that the French and Dutch were rising, to take over the enfeebled City, but nothing happened. For the first time since Sunday, Samuel lay down and 'slept a good night'.

On Thursday morning, the fire burned only in localized patches. Young William Taswell, equipped with his sword and helmet, walked into the City along the Strand and then Fleet Street. Number 55 now marks the westernmost limit of the fire. The ground almost scorched his shoes, the heat coming up from the pavements so fiercely. He stopped on the Fleet Bridge for a rest, so hot he was worried he might faint. He explored the ruins of St Paul's, dodging falling masonry and putting twisted pieces of metal from the molten bells in his pockets. Against the east wall he found the corpse of a woman who had taken shelter there, 'whole as to skin, meagre as to flesh, yellow as to colour'. The number of deaths recorded in the Great Fire was low, but there is no accurate figure which would take in people such as this woman, shackled prisoners, invalids and the elderly living alone.

As the fire died, the need to find someone to blame became urgent. Frenchman Robert Hubert, 'a poor distracted wretch', was executed for starting it, but the culprit turned out to be baker Thomas Farynor of Pudding Lane who had failed to extinguish his oven properly. The fire had destroyed over 13,000 homes, 87 churches, a cathedral, and

St Paul's Cathedral destroyed by the Great Fire, engraving by
Wenceslas Hollar, 1666

most of the City's public buildings. Charles II invited plans for
rebuilding. John Evelyn and Christopher Wren sent in designs featuring orderly streets and broad piazzas within a clearly delineated
border. But it was too late for that; the citizens of London were
already in a frenzy of rebuilding, sifting the charred remains of their
homes, marking out boundaries and sourcing building materials.

The Great Fire shaped London like no other single event until the
Blitz of 1941. *Sisymbrium irio*, a bright-yellow mustard plant, flowered
everywhere over the blackened ruins of the city. It became known as
London Rocket, and returned in 1941 to colonize the wreckage.

After the Great Fire, many moved west and settled in the medieval
streets off Holborn. Others began to build in the fields of Soho using
brick, making the buildings less flammable. London was changing
rapidly, transformed by private enterprise and the need for commerce.
In two years, London had lost one in five of the population and over
400 acres of warehousing, shops and homes. The servants who had
been cast aside as plague descended were now in demand, as were construction workers. Gideon Harvey estimated 'in the four years after the
Fire of London there was earned by tradesmen, relating to building

only, the sum of four million, one million per annum'. Using relative earnings comparisons this equates to a total of approximately £7 billion today.

London was changing – not only physically, but socially. Theatre and literature were becoming more bawdy, and libertines such as Charles Sedley and John Wilmot, Earl of Rochester, became the poster boys for a more relaxed sexual morality. Actresses appeared on stage for the first time, in both female and male roles. Their glamorous lifestyles, rich lovers and their defiance of previously strict gender 'rules' scandalized and inspired a city emerging from the grip of Puritanism.

Whatever his personal feelings on religion, Charles II navigated a careful course around the subject. London was a staunchly Protestant city but, populated by practical and mercantile people, it accommodated many religions for the sake of commerce. Of these, only Catholicism was barely tolerated. Partly, this was a case of bitter experience: the burnings of Protestants in Smithfield in 1555 by Catholic Queen Mary Tudor had not yet faded from the collective memory. Ordinary Roman Catholics were banned from celebrating Mass, from taking public office and teaching children.

In February 1685, Charles suffered a fit and a gradual decline. His brother, James, the Duke of York, was a Catholic who made no secret of his faith. Four days after Charles fell ill, when it had become clear he would not recover, James cleared the King's bedroom of everyone but a few sympathizers before bringing in Father John Huddleston. Huddleston had helped Charles escape from Cromwell's Roundheads over thirty years before. The King, whose lucidity was questionable, was received into the Catholic Church. There is no evidence that this was against his will. His last words concerned his 'Protestant whore', Nell Gwynn, when he implored James, 'Let not poor Nelly starve.'

The Duke of York took the throne as James II. He ruled for only four years, a short reign filled with political strife during which he became increasingly dependent on his Catholic advisers. In 1688, his daughters, Anne and Mary, conspired with his son-in-law, the Dutch Prince William of Orange, to depose him.

The crisis came when, in June 1688, James II's wife gave birth to a son. The English throne now had a Catholic male heir. Meanwhile, Princess Anne wrote to her sister, Mary, wife of William of Orange, 'the Church of England is, without all doubt, the only true Church'.

In November, William, Prince of Orange, invaded England at Torbay and marched towards London. Anne fled in the middle of the night with her best friend, Sarah Churchill. James was shocked by the desertion of his daughter. He was also suffering from severe and debilitating nosebleeds, further undermining his authority and confidence. He had already sent his wife and infant heir to France and realized he too must flee. He took a boat from Westminster to Vauxhall. While crossing over he is alleged to have dumped the Great Seal of the Realm into the Thames, washing his hands symbolically of the responsibilities of the throne. It was recovered sometime later by a waterman.

James only got as far as Faversham before being recognized by some sailors, who detained him until a company of guards from London arrived. They had no choice but to take him back to the city, however reluctant both sides were. Yet as William advanced from the west, James's time was running out. William arrived outside London in December. He offered James the chance to leave, and the King took it (perhaps all too mindful of the fate of his father). He joined his wife and son in France and lived out his days as a guest of the Catholic Louis XIV. He died in 1701. His removal from the throne became known as the Glorious Revolution of 1688. The 'glory' lay in its lack of bloodshed, and in the returning of a Protestant to the English throne.

Parliament quickly curtailed the powers of the monarchy. William was a Protestant, but men were changeable and London had 'found by experience that it is inconsistent with the safety and welfare of this Protestant kingdom to be governed by a papist prince', as later expressed in the Bill of Rights, passed on 16 December 1689. The Catholic question would remain a constant flashpoint in Georgian London. There was an abiding suspicion, ignorance and prejudice, which often erupted into violence.

Restoration, Plague, Fire, Revolution. These four events set the stage for the transformation of London during the Georgian years.

They created tremendous opportunity, prompted the arrival of waves of economic migrants, and enabled the making of a new city upon an ancient one. When Samuel Pepys ventured out into a smoking wasteland that Friday in September 1666, his London held only half a million people. This figure remained relatively steady until the end of the seventeenth century. Then, in the second decade of the eighteenth century, London began to grow. There was a building boom; coal imports and beer production rose. But it was followed by a sudden stall until the 1750s, when London emerged from stagnation and hurtled outwards in all directions. By 1831, the city had a population of 1,654,994. The landscape had solidified first into brick and then into stucco, as the outlying marshes and green fields were slowly eaten up by speculative builders in a 'mad' attempt to 'roof all the county of Middlesex with tiles'. In little more than 150 years, London was to change from a charred medieval city to capital of the world. On a fine summer's day in the reign of George IV, Cyrus Redding walked up Primrose Hill to contemplate the city and saw 'royalty, legislation, nobility, learning, science, trade, and commerce, concentrated before me in a mightier whole than had ever before been in the history of the world; and its fame and glory had gone forth and been felt in the most remote corners of the earth'.

This city, and the empire which it controlled, was founded by merchants, bankers, diplomats and eccentric aristocrats. It was consolidated by their sons and daughters on wharves and in shops. Artisans and artists furnished every type of house and public building. Traders kept one hand on their *copie-books* and their eyes on the ever-widening horizon. At the edges were the rent boys and hot-air balloonists, dognappers, immigrants, life models and journalists. Attendant on everyone were the hawkers, the prostitutes and the scavengers – London's underclass. It was to each of these characters that the city belonged, and this book is a tour of *their* streets. It is set out in chapters which reflect each distinct area and tell the stories of the people and events which defined their character during the Georgian period. Some of these were villages now engulfed by the metropolis, such as Marylebone, and some were miniature housing estates, such as St James's, south of Piccadilly. Many of these areas retain their Georgian personality. Even now, the City is still full of office workers, Mayfair remains muted and smart, Soho is still creative and Hackney can be dangerous after dark. Above all, this book is about Georgian Londoners, their occupations and preoccupations, secrets, peccadilloes, crimes and pastimes. Less has changed than you might think.

1. The City

Viewed from the circular Golden Gallery at the summit of St Paul's Cathedral, London spreads in every direction, an endless suburbia spawned by the railways. From the same vantage point at the beginning of the Georgian period, the limits of London were clear.

The cathedral sat at the heart of the rebuilt City, its dazzling white exterior already attracting a patina of dirt by the time the first service was held in December 1697. Around it, the shops and houses thrown up on the razed earth were low and neat, the ridges of their roofs orderly, built to the new post-fire regulations. They ranged from the solid palaces of merchant princes to the hastily erected cheap dwellings of Aldersgate and Cripplegate, packed with porters, day labourers and watermen. The streets were wider and cleaner than before the Great Fire. All around, the myriad spires of rebuilt parish churches poked up above the new tiles, echoed across the river by the many windmill sails rising from the mist of low-lying Southwark. Through the white haze over the water spiked a forest of masts, waiting to unload their cargoes. Warehouses lined the north bank. The names of their wharves are ancient and evocative: Puddle Dock, Broken Wharf, Queenhithe and the Oystergate.

To the east, lions roared hungrily in the Tower menagerie. Beyond lay the shanty towns and marshlands of Wapping where, at the beginning of the nineteenth century, the new docks began to form – over ninety acres of enclosed water which would transform east London. In the distance, the meadows of Hackney and Bethnal Green beckoned to Londoners on sunny days. To the west, the nave of the cathedral pointed down Ludgate Hill and over the Fleet River towards the court. Fleet Street was the main thoroughfare towards London's second city, Westminster. The Fleet was little more than a broad and dirty ditch crossed by a flat bridge to Fleet Street on the other side and the Strand beyond. Today, the Strand is full of pub chains, coffee shops and dull outlets selling mediocre greetings cards. Then, it was taverns, shops full of bibles and pornography, and even the odd elephant. Covent Garden and Soho were visible as a cluster of chimneys and rooftops, some old, some new. Just further west, before the parks and palaces of the court, Charing Cross formed the transport hub for the West Country. Georgian Mayfair and Marylebone were still pleasant fields, but soon the builders were due to arrive. To the north are the hill villages of Hampstead and Highgate, twin peaks in the chalk and clay of the Thames Valley. Summer boltholes and weekend retreats, they were the sophisticated rural outposts of a busy metropolis.

Three hundred and sixty-five feet below the Golden Gallery, the streets of the City still follow their medieval lines. Then, as now, this was where the wealth of London was generated. Wholesale warehouses held the precious cargoes brought in from the wharves, to be picked over by dealers. The City was an engine for the creation of wealth. From the moment rebuilding started, the Square Mile began to move from a medieval place of merchants and merchandise, to a place of moneymen and speculators, insurance offices and clerks. Money was the preoccupation of the City and those who worked within it, and here our story begins.

St Paul's Cathedral: the heart of the City

When Gideon Harvey put an estimate of a million pounds per year on the rebuilding of the City after the Great Fire, it seemed a gargantuan sum. In all likelihood the true figure was far higher. The figures involved in the construction of the new St Paul's Cathedral alone were huge. It was the longest ongoing project in the rebuilding, a masterpiece amongst the hastily constructed new housing and shops.

A cathedral dedicated to St Paul has been the centre of the City of London since AD 604. On 27 August 1666, John Evelyn recorded in his diary how he and Dr Christopher Wren had attended a meeting of the clergy, City officials and 'several expert workmen' to discuss how the medieval St Paul's might be rescued. They found it 'ill-designed

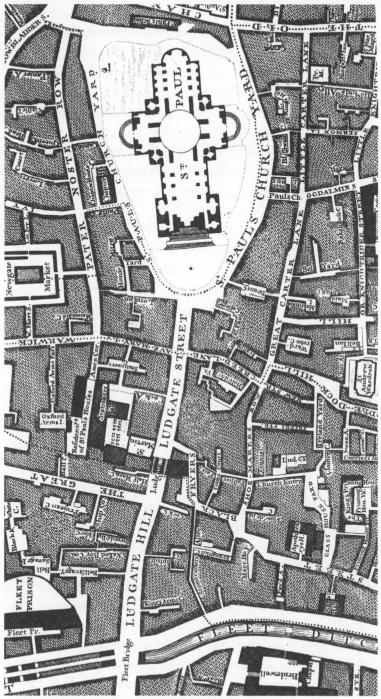

St Paul's and surrounding area, detail from John Roque's map, 1745

and ill-built from the beginning' and the structure 'much torn with age and neglect'. Wren and Evelyn favoured a new church altogether, with a 'noble cupola, a form not as yet known in England, but of wonderful grace'. Just over a week later, the cathedral Wren had wished to rebuild was a burned-out shell. For Christopher Wren and the many men and women who would work upon both the church, and the rebuilding of the City, it was a peerless career opportunity.

New building regulations were introduced in 1667, with Wren and Robert Hooke, amongst others, responsible for drawing up new construction guidelines. Private housing was restricted to a small number of types, constructed according to strict rules: grand merchants' houses, buildings fronting the main roads and, finally, smaller shops and houses in alleys and courtyards. They were to be of stone, with wooden window frames recessed so that they would not catch fire easily. The plans for the new buildings were not beautiful, but they were sensible, 'without hovels, without ill-planned, ill-executed temporary buildings, and without slums . . . jutties, bulks, projecting shopfronts and water-pipes gouting onto passersby'. The muddled old City would not be recreated.

The City had become a vast builder's yard, full of masons and scaffolders. New houses and shops were flung up by carpenters, bricklayers, even glaziers. By 1675, over 8,000 homes had been rebuilt. Often, they conformed to the new rules, but not to high standards of construction. Workmen flooded in from the countryside, ready to take advantage of the high wages offered by Londoners desperate to get their businesses operational and a roof over their families' heads. Strict rules governing apprenticeships and the right to work in the City meant that, in theory, an artisan had to be bound to a master in his trade for seven years before obtaining his 'freedom' to work. The Great Fire changed all that, and demand suddenly exceeded supply. Workers were drafted in from all the provinces of Britain and Europe.

St Paul's would benefit from some of these foreign workers, although the core building team remained English. Almost immediately, high walls were built around the St Paul's site to keep out the curious. In September 1667, a group of masons were paid to abseil over the ruin, knocking down anything they thought might be in danger of falling. Against Wren's advice the clergy spent the equivalent of half a million pounds shoring up the ruin and creating an ill-advised temporary choir in the unstable West End. Soon afterwards, it fell in.

From then on, a core group of twenty to thirty labourers worked on the building under Wren's supervision and that of his assistant, Edward Woodroffe, an experienced and highly capable surveyor. The men were expected on site at 6 a.m. in summer, clocking in at the Call Booth which stood roughly where the drinking fountain stands today on the south side of Cannon Street. They continued to work until noon and took their lunch on-site. An oversized hourglass sat in the yard, making sure they didn't waste any time. The end of the afternoon shift at 6 p.m. was marked by the ringing of an old bell, rescued from the rubble and put in a frame for the purpose.

Some of the old church proved impossible to dismantle, including the vast leaning pillars of the West End. They were eleven feet across and cemented in place by the heat of the fire. Wren had to resort to gunpowder. He made careful calculations as to where the hole should be dug in the north-west corner, where a particularly stubborn pillar would not come down. A pine box of gunpowder was lowered into the hole, trailing a wick which was protected by lengths of cane until it was out of the hole, and then a trail of powder was poured along the ground. Bricklayer Thomas Warren was paid extra to light the trail and run for cover.

Wren's calculations had been so careful that not only did Thomas make it safely back, but the 18lbs of gunpowder shifted an estimated 3,000 tons of masonry and saved thousands of man hours. The success of this experiment led his assistant to try it. A pillar exploded, sending a piece of masonry straight across the churchyard and through the upper floor of a bookshop where some women were at work. No one was hurt, but the accounts of St Paul's list two months' worth of repairs to the bookshop for the summer of 1672, and Wren was ordered not to have gunpowder used on the site again.

It took almost eight years of continuous work to prepare the site, dig the new foundations and sort the good stone from the ruined.

The first stone of the new cathedral was laid in June, when Wren marked out the centre of the dome and stood upon it. Not wanting to leave his spot to find a marker, he asked one of the workmen to find him a large flat stone. Legend has it that this stone was one of the old tombstones of St Paul's, engraved with a single word: RESURGAM. The same word (Latin for 'to rise again') is now seen over the South Door, beneath the phoenix representing the King, the rebirth of the cathedral and the City itself. The idea of resurrection seems to have been important for Wren, as the main axis of the new cathedral lines up exactly with the sunrise on Easter Sunday 1675, the year the groundwork for the new building was finished.

Once the foundation stone was laid, the masons moved in. They would work continuously on the cathedral for the next twenty-two years, a remarkably short amount of time to finish such a church. The Portland stone which forms the main building material of St Paul's arrived by boat from Dorset, before being lifted by cranes on to the wharves south of the cathedral. Sheds for the masons were constructed over the whole site, and a blacksmith was on hand to sharpen or mend any tools which became blunted or broke. Other sheds contained what were known as 'tracing floors', where parts of the plans could be carefully drawn out to scale and the cut stone placed on top of the chalk outlines to see if they would fit together correctly before they were lifted into place. During this time, in 1691, it appears that Christopher Wren was inducted into the Masonic Lodge of St Paul's Churchyard. Freemasonry was slowly moving away from craft-based mutual support groups towards speculative information-sharing and networking for gentlemen. Whilst Wren was no doubt welcomed in as 'the boss', there was little of the secrecy which began to enclose the organization only a few decades later. Discussion of religion and politics was strictly forbidden, and the emphasis was on gaining new knowledge. In the 1690s, Masonic lodges were drawing on the rapid advances in scientific and mathematical ideas to apply this new 'natural philosophy' to their professions. Lectures were given on 'true, useful and universal science' for the education of the members, models were built and experiments carried out in a fraternal environment. Fraternity was one of the long-standing traditions of the City, seen clearly in the parish system and in the medieval trade guilds, the livery companies. As parish officers, freemen of their chosen trade and, increasingly, Masonic brothers, the citizens of London were used to contributing to the community in a number of ways which cemented neighbourhoods, offering both social promotion and protection in times of hardship. Helping others paid dividends.

Whether all the men working on St Paul's were Freemasons is impossible to know. They were, however, at the cutting edge of their professions. Wren employed John Longland, a master carpenter, to make sure all went to plan. Huge amounts of timber were used; soft- and hardwoods were soon piling up on the three nearby wharves. The softwoods came from Christiania (Oslo), Dram and Fredrikstad, and the hardwoods came from British forests. A running joke was that the Baltic timber merchants warmed themselves handsomely on the Great Fire. Timber was not only used as scaffolding, but in the construction process. It forms the internal structure of the dome. When viewed from the inside, you are not seeing the interior of the dome visible from the outside, but a dome built below it. In between the two is another cone-shaped dome made of brick, which supports the Golden Gallery right at the top. From the outside what one sees is a dome created from timber and covered in lead sheeting. In 1711, the dome was finished and a 76-year-old Wren was hauled up in a basket to inspect the quality of the work.

As the church came into being, the interior became a priority. St Paul's is full of miraculous oddities executed by London artisans. Sir James Thornhill, painter and father-in-law of William Hogarth, painted the famous scenes on the inside of the cupola. John Evelyn looked through the window of a 'mean' cottage in Deptford and saw a man carving a wooden model of Tintoretto's *Crucifixion* by the light of a candle. That man was Dutch-born carver Grinling Gibbons, skilled in both stone and wood, who would go on to produce most of the work in the choir. French Huguenot Jean Tijou was responsible for the ironwork. The south-west tower holds a brass pineapple at the very top. It was made by iron foundress Jane Brewer in 1708, by which time the cathedral had been conducting services for almost a decade. Brewer was not the only woman to work on the cathedral; the accounts record 'Sarah Freeman, Plumber', 'Widdow Pearce, Painter' and 'Anne Brooks, Smith'. They were not labourers but business-women, working at the top of their professions.

The final bill for St Paul's was £736,752 2s 3¼d, putting over 75 million modern pounds into the pockets of London manufacturers and workmen and women.

Paternoster Row: the library of the City

Crouched on the north side of St Paul's churchyard was Paternoster Row. It was the bookselling centre of London from the Middle Ages to the Blitz of 1940–41 when it was bombed out of existence with the loss of more than one million volumes. With only literature and music available for home entertainment, books and publishing were lucrative businesses for those who had an eye for what would sell. Start-up costs were relatively low, and a small efficient business could do well. As literacy spread during the late seventeenth century, and as trade became more international in the eighteenth, the ability to read – if not to write – became far more important.

Printing shops were family affairs, like most eighteenth-century businesses. Two presses in each shop were standard. Each press took two people to work it. A compositor handled the typesetting, work-ing alongside the master and often his wife, apprentices and servants. A handbook designed to help parents choose a career for their child shows the variety of work available, and also the high standards of language skill required in a 'youth' who might do well in the book trade.

> A Youth designed for a Compositor ought to have a tolerable Genius for Letters, an apt Memory to learn the Languages: He must under-stand Grammar perfectly; and will find great Advantage in the course of his Business if he understands *Latin* and *Greek* . . . The Spirit of Writing that prevails now in England, and the Liberty of the Press, has given Employment to a great Number of Hands in this Branch of Business, which had arrived of late Years to a great Perfection.

Masons, carpenters and manual labourers were all respected as core workers, but at the beginning of the eighteenth century there was a rapid increase in demand for literate young men of all classes to serve as apprentices. Nor was any of the work in a printing shop too physically demanding for women, provided they had the skill with language. Unlike most of the other London trades, women were not barred from becoming 'freemen' of their chosen trade, so they could work within the City walls without prejudice. Elinor James was the widow of printer Thomas James but published a broadside under her own name circa 1715, titled *Mrs. James's Advice to All Printers in General* and stating, 'I have been in the element of Printing above forty years, and I have a great love for it.' During her printing career Elinor published around fifty pamphlets. Some transcripts of speeches she gave, including *Mrs. Elinor James's Speech to the Citizens of London at Guild-Hall* (1705), show that she was not only politically active as a publisher, but also as a speaker. She addressed everyone from the King down with what she believed was the correct way to carry on. More than once, Elinor's efforts would land her in Newgate 'for dispersing scandalous and reflecting papers'.

Elinor's achievements as a polemicist pamphleteer mean that her fame was relatively short-lived, but other City printers are still with us. Thomas Longman, founder of today's educational publisher Pearson Longman, had a keen eye for new literature, an acute business sense and the ability to handle tricky authors. Born in Bristol, Longman was apprenticed in the City and married his master's daughter. In 1724, he took up the premises of the Black Swan and the Ship in Paternoster Row, and went into business on his own account. He purchased the stock and buildings of William Taylor, the publisher of Daniel Defoe's *Robinson Crusoe*. Soon after this, Longman embarked on one of the Enlightenment's greatest printing endeavours.

In the intellectual crucible of late seventeenth-century Europe, texts on science, astronomy, philosophy and the natural world proliferated, but many were too specialized for the ordinary reader. In 1704, John Harris produced *Lexicon Technicum*, but it rambled and lacked an index, rendering it unsearchable. Someone needed to produce a concise guide to this new knowledge. The need to categorize information is a constant modern theme (the Wikipedia experiment is the most recent and certainly the largest attempt in history).

Ephraim Chambers was born in Kendal in 1680. Gifted but poor, he was apprenticed to a London mechanic, 'but having formed ideas not at all reconcilable to manual labour he was removed from thence and tried at another business'. This attempt also failed and 'he was at last sent to Mr Senex, the globe-maker'.

Senex globes are now prized for their astronomical accuracy (although his maps are equally prized for showing California as a large island). Ephraim Chambers was no ordinary apprentice; Senex, a man from Shropshire turned Royal Society Fellow and Freemason, was only two years older than his charge, making Chambers one of London's oldest apprentices at the age of about thirty-four. Ephraim spent his time studying, and a friend noted that he left the apprenticeship 'a very indifferent globe-maker'. Instead, he had decided he was going to write 'the best Book in the Universe'.

It was a huge undertaking and, in 1728, his *Cyclopaedia* appeared. Chambers laid out his considerable aspirations for the book on the title page: 'Cyclopaedia, or, An Universal Dictionary of Arts and Sciences'. He died in 1740, still working on another edition. There were rumours of trouble amongst the collection of publishers who had undertaken to produce the massive *Cyclopaedia* but the only one mentioned specifically after Ephraim's death is Longman, who 'in particular used him with the liberality of a prince and the tenderness of a father'. It is surely no coincidence that Longman's of Paternoster Row would go on to publish Samuel Johnson's Dictionary, in 1775, which did for words what the *Cyclopaedia* had attempted to do for art and science.

Society as a whole was becoming more literate, and it was not only aided by the rise of books. In 1680, William Dockra had introduced his 'New and Useful Invention, commonly term'd the PENNY POST'. A letter brought to the Post Office at 8 a.m. could be delivered across London by 10 a.m., or would be on its way out of town on one of the six Post Roads. Throughout the Georgian period, the Post Office was overseen by the Treasury and comprised a small elite group of supervisors: John Evelyn worked hard to get the country offices in order; Francis Dashwood campaigned to get rid of boys on ponies with messenger bags, replacing them with horses and carts; and William Pitt the Elder recorded the necessity of disinfecting mail coming in from certain foreign locations.

The eighteenth century saw the emergence of letters as something not only for the elite classes, but for everyone. Writing equipment had become cheap enough for those of even the lowest social classes to obtain, and the Post allowed them to convey their thoughts, ideas and hopes to distant hands and eyes. Ink pigment and quills were hawked about the streets by specialist pedlars. The very poor burned wool and pounded it into a black powder. The best quill was the third feather in from a goose's wing. Right-handers preferred a quill from the left wing of the goose as they curve more comfortably over the hand. A rare left-hander used the right wing feathers. Most paper was made from bleached rags which had been pressed into sheets: it was durable and provided a decent surface for the scratchy pens. This paper was purchased in 'quires' from stationers and bookshops, which would produce, when carefully cut or torn as directed, sheets of a size acceptable to the Post, costing one penny each to send.

The importance of the postal system, and the literacy it fostered, was an integral part of the business of London itself, increasing the influence of London across the country and the wider world. Londoners could rely upon the rapid dispatch, but also receipt, of information. Far-flung thinkers enjoyed serial literature by post, which encouraged the regular publication of ongoing stories that would reach a peak with Charles Dickens. Serials were snapped up by eager hands in London, but also anticipated by villagers all over the country and serving soldiers across the world. Business letters were travelling between London and China on a regular basis by the 1720s. The barely literate wives of sailors addressed their letters to husbands on ships, with the current guesstimate of which dock they might be in, and a return address on the front if 'ye ship be gone'.

From 1760 onwards, the Post Office was also responsible for introducing the rest of the country to the London media, by the franking and distribution of a large amount of the London press. Whilst the government was becoming increasingly aware that it could not control the press, it could – through the Post Office – control its distribution. It franked and sent out the newspapers which were most supportive and least inflammatory to those 'who keep coffeehouses, that they might be furnished with them gratis'.

With the expansion of the Post Office, a clerical office culture was born. The compositors of the early eighteenth-century printing houses were educated young men from grammar school backgrounds, but by the mid-eighteenth century orphanages had realized they could find work for literate boys and girls much more quickly than for those with manual skills. In 1784, the Post Office was worth £196,000. Thirty years later, it was worth over a million. In 1829, the Post Office moved to beautiful new buildings, designed by Robert Smirke, and situated in St Martin's Le Grand, just north of St Paul's Cathedral. It would remain there for almost a century, the culture of letters becoming ever stronger, but its roots would remain in the busy and ambitious mercantile 'middling' community of the eighteenth century.

London's ancient markets: Smithfield, Billingsgate, Leadenhall and the Fleet

Elsewhere in the City, away from the noisy construction site of St Paul's and the bookish Paternoster Row, basic cash and commodity transactions continued as they had done for centuries. Smithfield Market, bounded on one side by the vast St Bartholomew's Hospital, is an ancient livestock market and, today, the last surviving wholesale market in the City; Daniel Defoe was convinced it was, 'without question, the greatest in the world'.

Smithfield was also the setting for Bartholomew Fair, a four-day spectacle held in September, where Ned Ward watched women compete in handstand races in 1703, although he did note they were wearing men's breeches underneath their skirts. He and his friend also stopped at a cookshop, fancying some roast meat for which the area was so famous, but:

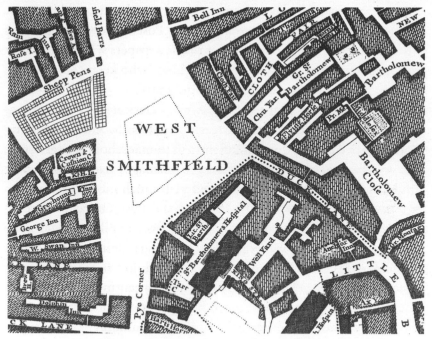

Smithfield Market, detail from John Roque's map, 1745

. . . no sooner had we entered this suffocating kitchen, than a swing-
ing fat fellow, the overseer of the roast to keep the pigs from blistering,
who was standing by the spit in his shirt, rubbed his ears, breast, neck
and arm-pits with the same wet-cloth which he applied to his
pigs . . . we defer'd our eating till a cleanlier opportunity.

William Hone visited in 1825, at the end of the fair's heyday. He
recalled small stalls, selling

. . . oysters, fruit, inferior kinds of cheap toys, small wicker baskets
and other articles of trifling value . . . One man occupied upwards of
twenty feet of the road lengthwise, with discontinued wood-cut
pamphlets, formerly published weekly at twopence, which he spread
out on the ground, and sold at a halfpenny each in great quantities.

There were constant calls to ban the fair, due to the rowdiness; but
it was an institution. It was finally suppressed in 1855.

From all over England, livestock was driven into Smithfield and kept in five acres of pens before being sold either for meat or for breeding. The noise and stench must have been overwhelming. Edward Jay, Essex livestock breeder of the 1750s and 60s was one of the more unusual Smithfield characters: he was 'no more than three feet and a half high, had not any joint at his knees, and was entirely straight to his hip-bone. He had only one arm and hand with which, however, he could make a pen and buckle his shoes without stooping.' Livestock breeders trading in and out of Smithfield would often avail themselves of farmers with land on the edges of London and have their stock fattened in purpose-built enclosures. These enclosures, many situated near Islington, had high walls made of earth and stacked cow horns; they were planted with grass, with a narrow gate allowing entrance or exit. The pasture inside became lush and was regularly irrigated. It could then be let out at a high price to cattle dealers, or to innkeepers who kept carriage horses, for resting and fattening up animals. When the livestock was in prime condition, the best price could be had at Smithfield.

Once purchased, the livestock was driven through the streets

Smithfield market scene, with St Bartholomew's Hospital beyond the animal pens, engraving after Pugin and Rowlandson, 1811

towards its final destination, either a backyard or a slaughterhouse. The main areas for butchering animals were near Smithfield, or on Pudding Lane to the east. These areas, which had been centres for wholesale butchering since at least 1300, were specifically set up to receive large quantities of animals. In the middle of the eighteenth century, annual numbers were around 74,000 cattle and over half a million sheep.

In the slaughterhouses animals were stunned by a blow, hoisted and then bled to death. Sometimes this happened in small cellars beneath butchers' shops as other animals waited, penned in corners. Most of the butchered meat went out to Clare Market, near Covent Garden, which was London's largest retail meat market, and where the gangs of butchers' apprentices were feared for their tendency to fight with knives. Cattle and sheep were skinned of their valuable hides in another set of buildings, and these fresh hides went out to special wholesalers who sold them to tanners – the closest on St John Street, just outside the City limits.

Since medieval times it had been customary for London's wholesale butchers to remove their waste down to piers on the Thames, where it was loaded into boats, taken out to the middle of the river at low tide and tipped in. Other unsaleable parts were disposed of on London's laystalls, which were boxed-in rubbish tips dealt with by the parishes, who employed scavengers to clean the streets. Sometimes the butchers disposed of their waste in the sewers, where it coagulated just beneath the pavement in piles of sweating gore, damming the legitimate flow of human excrement to the Thames. Disposal into drains and sewers was eventually banned, and there were high fines which were rarely enforced (probably due to the unsavoury nature of investigating the crime). Added to this were the rivers of urine from cattle and sheep pens as well as dairy yards, which Londoners had to navigate as they walked the streets. In warm weather, the smells from the sewers and the fetid pens enveloped the area in a fug of animal stench.

Two other markets which remained open for the whole period between the Restoration and the Regency were Billingsgate and Leadenhall, both of which were inside the City limits and were open to traders and the public alike. Billingsgate had long been established just east of London Bridge, where an inlet allowed fishing boats to dock out of the traffic. Like Smithfield, it was an ancient market with permanent shops and stalls which had sprung up around the dock, growing so numerous that it became a constant unregulated market. The modern architecture and geography of that area of the City disguises what would have been a steep descent down to the river, like a ravine into which one was obliged to venture to get to the water with its huddle of fish stalls and shops.

There were many little places to eat oysters fresh off the boats. German visitor Sophie von La Roche had never eaten an oyster before she visited London in 1788, but after watching the oysters being unloaded at Billingsgate, she was persuaded to sample them in one of the inns by the market.

> The cubicles were neat, the tables were laid with white cloths, and there were delightful wicker-chairs to sit in. A fisherwoman with a basket of oysters, a youngster with lemons and a small basket containing bread, plates and knives followed immediately after us . . . I liked them very much.

This charming set-up would please anyone who likes an oyster today, as would the image of the Billingsgate fishwives who peddled their stock in the inns and on the streets. Described even as 'boisterous', these

> . . . crying, wandering, travelling creatures carry their shops on their heads, and their storehouse is ordinarily Byllingsgate or Ye Brydge Foot . . . They set up every morning their trade afresh. They are easily furnished; get something and spend it jovially and merrily. Five shillings a basket and a good cry are a large stock for them.

Each 'cry' was particular to the seller, and prospective purchasers would have listened out for their favourite. These women specialized in selling eels, herring, white fish, crabs or other small shellfish. They announced their stock daily, with shrimp and other moieties sold by measuring them out in third-of-a-pint pewter tankards, the larger items by piece – a practice still found in some pubs today.

Leadenhall was one of the oldest London markets and was much

like a farmers' market today, with small stalls selling a variety of seasonal produce. Strawberry and soft fruit sellers were everywhere
during the summer months. This was a trade dominated by women,
pretty girls in particular, who spent a great deal of time making 'pot-
tles', the eighteenth-century version of a punnet: thin wicker cones
with a loop handle, into which they packed their wares. The vegetable man and his donkey or 'little moke', its back laden with panniers,
was a common sight. There was no fixed cry for the vegetable seller,
as his shouts varied with his stock, which would include 'collyflow-
ers', asparagus, potatoes, carrots, beans, peas, parsnips, leeks and
turnips. More exotic fruits and goods were also sold at these markets,
including home-grown and imported oranges, lemons, and Spanish
and French onions. Other street traders included the mouse-trap
man, the water carrier, the knife grinder, the ink seller, the muffin
man, egg girls and earthenware sellers.

The Fleet Market emerged when the Fleet River was covered over
in 1736. The river was a symbolic boundary, and those who came and
went over the busy Fleet Bridge regarded it as the real gate to the
City. It rose on high ground to the north near Kenwood House in
Hampstead and flowed down to the City, running along what is now
Blackfriars Bridge Road in a wide stream before joining the Thames
where the foot of Blackfriars Bridge now stands. The stream was
navigable for a stretch, and it provided a useful place to get out of the
busy traffic of the Thames.

Once a 'fleet' and fast-flowing river, by the middle of the seventeenth century the Fleet waterway was silted up. Christopher Wren
and Robert Hooke oversaw a project to reopen it, boarding out the
banks and creating a deepish navigable channel again, this time with
commercial potential. For three and a half years, lighters were filled
with silt and rubbish at each low tide by men standing in the filth
and digging, filling wheelbarrows and baskets. It was completed,
finally, in the autumn of 1674 at the stupendous sum of £51,000,
roughly the equivalent of £5,730,000 now. But one major problem
was that no one had stopped the residents upstream throwing their
rubbish into the river, and by the early Georgian period the Fleet
River had become 'a mere sluggish and plague-breeding sewer' once

more. In an attempt to solve the problem, the river was bricked over in a piecemeal fashion; by the 1730s, much of it was underground. The size of the sewer, and the amount of rubbish in it, was revealed by *The Gentleman's Magazine* in August 1736, when it reported:

> A fatter boar was hardly ever seen than one taken up this day, coming out of the Fleet ditch into the Thames. It proved to be a butcher's near Smithfield Bars, who had missed him five months, all which time he had been in the common sewer, and was improved in price from ten shillings to two guineas.

The area had been popular with medieval religious houses, such as the Carmelites and the Dominican 'black friars', but by Wren and Hooke's time the banks were lined with warehouses. Upriver, close to where Holborn Viaduct now stands, was Holborn Bridge. The valley was steep and therefore avoided by heavy carriages and wagons when possible. Horses were often trapped beneath their load which had overtaken them, or fell to their knees on the ascent out of the dip, unable to haul their burden. The houses built near and upon Holborn Bridge were medieval slums which had escaped the Great Fire. A letter featured in *The Times* described how the 'rear of the houses on Holborn Bridge has for many years been a receptacle for characters of the most daring and desperate condition'.

The Fleet and some of the streets around it fell into an ancient City 'Liberty'. Liberties were geographical and historical hangovers from the religious properties, and exempt from City laws. So, in a curious twist of fate, the Fleet was a place where ordinary laws could be flouted. The river – or, as it became known, 'the Ditch' – was bounded on the eastern side by what was known simply as 'The Fleet', a prison which was seven centuries old when it was finally demolished, in 1846. From the late thirteenth century it was a debtors' prison, where people could be incarcerated by order of their creditors for very small amounts of debt. Many prisoners took lodgings in the streets included in the Liberty, from where they continued to live relatively normal lives. Foreign workers could also work there and ignore the City's need for an apprenticeship and consequent 'freedom', with many of them congregating in the lodgings around The Blew Boot pub. Various bylaws made prosecution of Fleet clergy impossible, even for conducting big-amous or over-hasty wedding services, and so the Liberty of the Fleet became the Las Vegas wedding chapel of London.

There, it was possible to walk in off the street and be married legally, at very little cost. By the 1740s, more than half of all London weddings were celebrated within the Fleet's boundaries, where houses and shops displayed 'the frequent sign of a male and female hand enjoined with "Marriages performed within" written beneath'. It was possible to walk in, sign and get out in under fifteen minutes, as the mammoth number of records for the period show: over a quar-ter of a million in fifty years. Marrying 'at the Ditch-side', as it is called on some certificates, might not have been romantic but it was fast, fuss-free and didn't require parental consent. Local pubs, such as the Belle Savage, held set-price receptions.

In 1753, Lord Hardwicke's Marriage Act was passed, bringing in rules regarding parental consent for those under twenty-one, and stricter guidelines for the reading of the banns, the issuing of licences and the church celebration. The Liberty of the Fleet was not exempt. The regulations did not come into force until sundown on 24 March 1754, at which point the Fleet Chapel recorded 'near a hundred pair had been joined together' in a single day.

Hardwicke's Marriage Act coincided with the end of the Fleet as an open river, and its reincarnation as a market. The Fleet was silting up again, slowly rolling a 'large tribute of dead dogs to Thames'. This time the City of London wasn't interested in spending a fortune dig-ging out a stinking ditch which would only be impassable again within another few decades. The water was unfit for consumption or bathing, and was so filthy and muddy that it had become a health hazard. It was decided that the river would be totally bricked over, thus creating not only a large and handy sewer, but also a wide piece of open ground on which a market was to be constructed. But it would take until the completion of Blackfriars Bridge in 1769 for the majority of the river to disappear beneath the bricks. In the winter of 1763, the Ditch claimed its final victim, but not through contagion or drowning. A drunken barber from Bromley fell in and, before he could clamber out, died frozen upright in the mud.

The wharves and warehouses

Along the river, the City warehouses acted as a crowded market, selling exotic goods to middlemen, a 'mighty mass of brick, and smoke,
and shipping, Dirty and smoky'. Many different types of goods
arrived in the Port of London, and from the carriage charges levied
to take them from the wharves it is easy to see that products such as
calico, tobacco, rice, figs, sugar, wine, currants, olive oil, cheese and
cream of tartar (used in industrial quantities as a metal cleaner and
known as 'argol') were readily available. Alum came from the Middle
East, or the north of England, and was used both in cloth dyeing and
as a deodorant. Other goods included perishables, exotic manufactured products, and diverse animal products such as tortoiseshell and
whalebone, essential to the London fashion industry.

Whalebone, in particular, was a much sought-after commodity, as it
was essential to the better class of 'stays' – the corsets worn by almost
every woman. The baleen to oil ratio of any catch was calculated at
about 1:20, but with over half the income coming from the baleen
(from the mouth of the whale), this was the prized asset. England was
unique in that stays were worn by very young children in the hope of
preventing deformities and encouraging good posture: girls remained
in them until maturity, and boys until they were 'breeched' or went
into trousers aged about six. Only the poorest children went stay-less.
Women of low status wore stays sewn by seamstresses, who fashioned
them from brown linen or leather and stitched them with packthread.

The Throgmorton Street area, in particular, was known for its
'Bone-Shops' where bundles of expensive finished and steamed
whalebone could be purchased. When Madame du Bocage visited, in
1750, she observed that, 'The women use no paint and are always
laced.' Elizabeth Ham recorded tight-laced corsets of the period as
'very nearly purgatory'. The ever-fashionable Georgiana, Duchess of
Devonshire, featured them in her novel of 1778, *The Sylph*, writing,
'my poor arms are absolutely sore with them; and my sides so
pinched! But it is the "ton"; and pride feels no pain.'

It wasn't only vanity which claimed a proportion of the City's whalebone supply. A small but significant proportion of the population suffered with bone disease and hernia, making corsets an essential piece of everyday wear. Stays or corsets were also fashioned for the correction of scoliotic spines and dropped shoulders. Alexander Pope, who suffered with tuberculosis of the bone, wore one for most of his life.

As people grew richer, the trade boomed and the demand for whalebone grew. Most whaling ships pitched up at Howland Great Dock in Rotherhithe, later known as Greenland Dock, where the stench of rendering whale carcasses was not inflicted on the city. The dealers descended upon the ships and examined the catch, and the whalebone was removed for sale to warehouses near Three Cranes Wharf, where it was laid out carefully on the floor, with aisles between for the merchants to wander up and down and make their choice. Other floors held elephant ivory, cochineal beetles or natural sponges – all luxury items.

Once purchases had been made, they needed to be transported. London had a highly developed logistics system by the 1720s, run by the Guildhall, off Cheapside. All vehicles wanting to carry goods in the City of London had to purchase an annual licence which, when each part of it was added up, came to over £2. No driver was to be under sixteen years of age. A one-way traffic system operated in the Thames Street area to facilitate the loading of goods without chaos: the carts, when empty, had to enter it via one set of nominated streets, to the east, and exit via another set, when laden, to the west. One-way systems were in place by around 1720. Carts and wagons had 'stands' (just like taxi ranks today) where they were allowed to wait for work, and each employer had to take the first cart or wagon in the queue. Being overloaded was an offence, and long lists of what comprised a load – such as 'three bales of Aniseeds' or 'six barrels of Almonds' – give an insight into the goods being transported. 'Three puncheons of prunes' was a small load, and nineteen hundredweight of cheese a mere half-load. Any cart or wagon found unattended, or 'standing', resulted in a fine of five shillings for the first offence, ten shillings for the second and twenty shillings for every offence after that. Constant abusers would have their vehicle taken to 'the Green-Yard', near Cripplegate, to be 'impounded and kept, until the Owner thereof shall have paid the Penalty incurred, and the Charges of impounding and detaining every such Cart, Car, or Horses'.

For smaller purchases, weighing up to 56lbs, licensed porters were on hand for hire. Strong, hardy men, they carried goods back through the streets. Two porters were permitted to carry double the weight; regular and often impromptu wagers were held to see how quickly they could make it to their destinations. Handbooks for shopkeepers and clerks were published with comprehensive entries of which carriers took goods where: goods could be sent to Chipping Norton through Powers at the White Horse, in Cripplegate, or to South Wales through Edwards at the Castle and Falcon, in Aldersgate. In 1768, twenty-two coaches per day left London for Bristol, all of them available to take small purchases and passengers. The detail involved in such tradesmen's guides reveals the complexity and volume of the London commodity trade. As the century progressed, the guides became larger and more detailed as trade continued to grow. Yet the City's rich trade in goods was being rapidly eclipsed by the trade in money itself.

The Bank of England and the Stock Exchange: the emerging financial centre

Threadneedle Street is associated with the Bank of England and the Stock Exchange. But it also has a hidden history: it was home to both the French Church and one of London's oldest synagogues.

The French Church was the church of the Huguenots, the Protestant people of France. As Nonconformists in a Catholic country, they had long been under pressure to convert. The Threadneedle Street Church was founded in 1550, when a group of Huguenot merchants arrived in London. They were Calvinists, coming predominantly from the educated classes, including the lower nobility. They banded together in communities that appear to have been based on similar interests and friendship, but they gave themselves a military hierarchy. Samuel Pepys described one of their relaxed services in 1662: 'In the

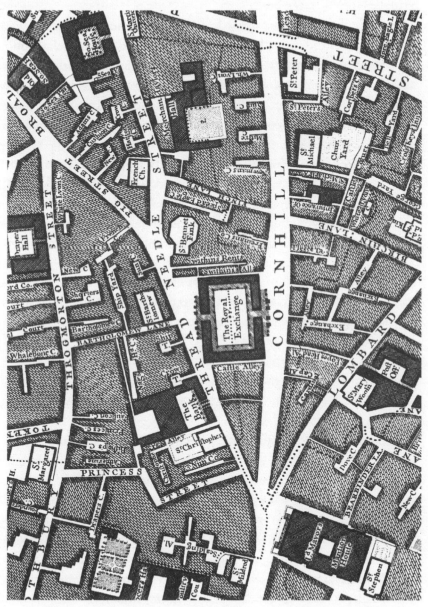

The Bank of England and Royal Exchange, showing the Mansion House, the French Church and South Sea House, detail from John Roque's map, 1745

afternoon I [went] to the French Church here in the city, and stood in the aisle all the sermon, with great delight hearing a very admirable sermon, from a very young man.' The Threadneedle Street Church burned down in the Great Fire but was rapidly rebuilt, and by the beginning of the Georgian age the descendants of the original founders were already powerful figures in the City.

Only a stone's throw from the French Church, and right in the heart of what would become the financial district of the City, was a Sephardic Jewish synagogue. It was illegal to be Jewish in England after the Edict of Expulsion, passed by Edward I in 1290. Jews continued living in London, but in secret. Outwardly, they pretended to be Spanish Catholics but three ancient City synagogues remained active: Old Jewry, Threadneedle Street and Gresham Street.

On 17 December 1656, a group of openly practising Jews of London purchased a house in Creechurch Lane for a synagogue, with a total capacity of 85 men and 24 women. The following year, a piece of land was purchased at Mile End for a Jewish cemetery, the first Jewish broker was officially admitted to the Royal Exchange, and the first Jewish names appeared in the Denization Lists, akin to having an 'indefinite leave to remain' visa. The official admission into the Royal Exchange was little more than a token gesture, for people of all backgrounds and religions traded freely there: 'the Jew, the Mahometan, and the Christian transact together . . . and give the name infidel to none but bankrupts'.

London's early Jewish community was made up mainly of Sephardic Jews of Levantine descent, in small family units, often specializing in the trade of exotic goods. The Ashkenazi Jews of Germany and eastern Europe, who came later, comprised swathes of people from the very rich to the very poor, with larger families and a broader selection of vocations. In 1692, the Ashkenazim were present in large enough numbers to open a synagogue of their own in Duke's Place, near Aldgate. They termed themselves 'the German Jews' and saw themselves as distinct from 'the Portuguese Congregation' of the Sephardic Jews.

King William III had been ably assisted in matters of war and finance by Solomon de Medina who, in 1700, was the first Jew to be knighted in England. When, in 1698, Rabbi David Nieto formed a committee to raise money for a new synagogue, de Medina was the largest contributor by a healthy margin. Some land in Plough Yard was purchased on a lease of sixty-one years for the Bevis Marks Synagogue. (Bevis Marks may sound like a person but it was the street Plough Yard opened on to, and was only a short distance from the Duke's Place synagogue.)

On 12 February 1699, the committee signed an agreement with Joseph Avis, Quaker and builder, for the building of a synagogue on Bevis Marks at a cost of no more than £2,750, which is the equivalent of four and a quarter million pounds now. The Quakers were the largest Nonconforming religious denomination in the same area, traditionally living around Lombard Street. Queen Anne showed her approval of the collaboration by donating a roof timber – a symbolic gesture, corresponding with the Jewish requirement to maintain a head covering in the sight of God. In 1702, the Bevis Marks synagogue was dedicated. Avis returned all monies left over from the works, stating that he would not profit from building a religious house.

In 1723, a law was passed allowing Jews to hold title to land. This was a major step forward and led to the 'official' opening of a third synagogue, in Magpie Alley, Fenchurch Street, known as the Hambro synagogue. The Jewish Naturalization Act was passed in 1753, which meant that Jews could become naturalized English citizens after seven years in the country. It was dubbed 'The Jew Bill' and was repealed the following year due to massive street protests. Things calmed down, and London's Jewish community carried on as before – commercially present, yet socially invisible.

Despite being marginalized citizens, who clung tenaciously to 'foreign' lifestyles, the French and Jewish communities of the City are crucial to the history of the Bank of England. Just as English monarchs had traditionally turned to Jewish moneylenders before the Edict of Expulsion, William III turned to some of London's richest men in the early 1690s. He was waging a war in the Low Countries and was desperately short of cash. The Bank of England was founded in 1694, to supply this need, and became such a part of the British identity that when the first commuter omnibus service started in 1829, running from Paddington to the City, its destination was given only as 'The Bank'. These days, we have lost the definite article and the same destination, whether by bus or Tube, is known simply as 'Bank'.

During the late seventeenth century, banks were private and it was up to the customer to choose which man he trusted enough to deposit his money with. Child's Bank, Hoare's and Coutts & Co., are three of the earliest and most famous. Their founders – Francis Child, Sir Richard Hoare and John Campbell – were all goldsmiths and bankers, used to buying in and storing quantities of bullion to fashion their wares. Their promissory notes were known as Running Cashes and functioned like a banknote. These men were prominent and trusted, but it was thought that London needed an official bank, such as those in Amsterdam or Germany.

A group of City merchants stepped up who believed they could raise a million pounds to start a new bank. A significant number of these men were Huguenots, including their leader, John Houblon, whose family had made their money in shipping. The million pounds would go to the state, and the newly created Bank of England was to reap £65,000 interest for its investors annually, and in perpetuity. Thus, in one swift Act of 1694, the National Debt was created.

In the chapel of Mercers' Hall in Poultry, a Book of Subscriptions was opened for ten days at the end of June, allowing the citizens of London to invest in the new bank. At the end of this short period, 1,267 people had subscribed and Houblon was elected first Governor.

The Great Seal of the Bank bore the image of Britannia, with her spear and her leg boldly on show, which had appeared on the coins of Hadrian and Antoninus Pius in the second century AD. No more was heard of her until after the Restoration when, in 1667, Charles ordered a Britannia medallion to be struck to commemorate the Peace of Breda, which ended the Second Anglo-Dutch War. His own likeness, on the front, was captured from a drawing done by candlelight, by 'Mr Cooper, the rare limner', whilst John Evelyn held the candle. Charles decided that Britannia should feature on the reverse, and that the Duchess of Richmond should sit as the model. The reaction to the Duchess of Richmond was so positive that she began to appear on the halfpennies and farthings issued soon after. As Samuel Pepys recorded, her face is 'as well done as ever I saw anything in my whole life, I think; and a pretty thing it is, that he should choose her face to represent Britannia by'.

Two years later, during the Great Recoinage of 1696, Britannia came to symbolize the new standard of English money. Old, fake or clipped coins had become a huge problem. England had minted most of its coins in the Royal Mint near the Tower since around 1279, with the high-value denominations in gold and sterling-standard silver. These coins had a set value, but they stayed in circulation for a long time. Over the decades, the bullion prices changed, so the real value of the metal was either lower or higher than the face value of the coin. If the value was lower, it was cheaper to 'buy' coins and make them into silver dishes, spoons and forks than it was to buy the bullion to make them. So coins were removed from circulation. At the same time, the price of bullion on the Continent rose and clever merchants shipped English coin to Europe, where it was purchased and melted down. By the 1670s, John Evelyn recorded that there were not enough coins around to pay for simple household items and food. This provided the perfect opportunity for fakers. As long as no one looked too closely, and simply continued to pass the money around the system, it *was* worth the face value. Daniel Defoe always attempted to hand over any fake money first, but made sure he had the right amount of genuine money in his pocket in case he was caught. When nineteen-year-old Isaac Newton made lists of his 'sins', at Whitsuntide 1662, along with stealing, 'punching my sister', 'falling out with the servants' and 'having unclean thoughts' was 'striving to cheat with a brass halfe crowne'. A less than promising start for the man who would become Warden of the Royal Mint. Passing off the fake coin was so widespread that the shopkeepers – who were supposed to destroy any fake coin that came their way – often passed it on, and a secondary trade in fake money sprang up alongside the bullion trade. The making of fake money was a skilled job: there were dies to carve, and striking coins from hard mixed metals was not easy.

Those further down the currency chain often turned to coin clipping. The edges of Britain's modern coins are milled to prevent this crafty exercise, but in the early Georgian period plenty of old, worn coins were swimming about in the system, their fine edges ripe for trimming and polishing back up. It was so prevalent that fakers even clipped their forgeries to make them appear more convincing. Coin clipping allowed poor but daring people to build up enough shavings to take to a smelter and have changed for money. The smelter had to be in on the act, but he was just another component of a complicated network, with one foot either side of the law. Coinage offences were taken very seriously by the courts: women caught clipping were supposed to be burned, and the men were hanged (although this wasn't regularly enforced).

With so many fakes and devalued coins around, it was no wonder William III decided, in 1696, to give English money a makeover through recoinage, effectively revaluing the pound. Anticipating the demands of recoinage upon available bullion reserves, the Bank of England decided it needed to appoint 'a fit person who understands gold and silver'. That man was Moses Mocatta, a partner in the firm Mocatta and Goldsmid. Moses Mocatta and his family worshipped at the Bevis Marks Synagogue and had strong ties with the Amsterdam bullion community. He established a repository near the Bank, known only as 'The Warehouse', where vast quantities of gold and silver bullion were kept. The early bullion trade was supplemented by the issuing of promissory notes, which were an instant and somewhat alarming success. Because Bank of England notes were payable instantly upon presentation and because the Bank's credit was so good, Bank of England notes became an easy target for forgers. In 1724, the Bank thought it had found a solution. The Huguenot Henry Portal made high-grade paper at Bere Mill in Hampshire. This paper, when watermarked, was very hard to fake. The Bank began printing large numbers of notes for fixed sums, whereas previously they had been filled out for the sum specified by the customer. In 1725, the first modern banknotes appeared. The Portals still make the paper for all English banknotes.

The commissioning of the new banknotes came when the Bank was formalizing its structure. It became clear that the Bank needed both consolidating and securing; in the late 1780s, Sir John Soane was appointed as the architect of a new building in the Classical style. From then until 1833, the Bank was slowly transformed into an enormous strongroom.

This transformation was both symbolic and real: the Bank had become a vast and wealthy institution, on its guard against theft and fraud. Clever forgers had caught up, and were making copies of the Portal banknotes. Many were caught, including Mary England. She and her husband, James, were arrested in January 1814 for circulating forged Bank of England notes. The penalty for forgery itself was death, but the Bank decided not to prosecute James for forgery. He promptly skipped out and boarded a ship. Mary was left, with her four children, facing prosecution for possessing forged notes. She was tried at the Old Bailey in February, and was sentenced to be transported for fourteen years. They were confined to Newgate Prison until the ship was full enough with other prisoners to sail.

By April, she had pawned all the family's clothes and, in desperation, she wrote to the Bank, asking to be excused for troubling them, but: 'I have Been so Unfortunate as to be in Newgate on Account of the Bank Business'. The Bank sent her an allowance of 10s 6d per week until she was transported. She applied to the Bank again, from on board the convict ship *Northampton* sitting at Deptford, asking for a lump sum for her family's new life. Her letters are annotated by a bank employee: 'Mr Kaye to pay her ten pounds.' Mary signed for the money on board ship four days later, and the *Northampton* left England soon after that. That the Bank of England took pity on her reveals the complex attitudes to philanthropy and wealth during the Georgian period.

The change of the Bank of England from early modern money warehouse to a financial temple began both from within and without. Sadly, little of Soane's original exists today. It was largely demolished in the 1930s, when Herbert Baker was charged with bringing the buildings up to date. The destruction of Soane's work was described by Nikolaus Pevsner as an 'architectural crime'. The Bank of England, dealer in money, looks south across the road to the Royal Exchange. Since Thomas Gresham built the Exchange in 1565, it had housed London's trade in commodities and was where native and foreign merchants gathered to conduct their business. Their trade was based on real commodities – such as spices, cloths, furs and gold – but things were changing. Just as the Bank of England became a reality in 1694, others, in the small coffee houses of Exchange Alley on the south side of the Royal Exchange, were starting to deal in what would become known as 'stocks' and 'shares'.

The coffee houses of Exchange Alley and the South Sea Bubble

The elite cabal of the Bank of England had opened a book in Mercers' Hall for ordinary Londoners who wanted to invest. Investment was becoming increasingly appealing to the emerging middle classes who, for the first time, due to international trade and the boom in the City were finding themselves with spare cash. The rise in newspapers meant foreign and financial news was more easily circulated, and in London a particular type of venue hosted a class of men on the make: coffee houses.

Coffee houses were as numerous in Georgian London as they are now. They were places for men to gather and obtain news. Then, as now, many business meetings were conducted there. Coffee, although condemned initially as 'Mahometan gruel', suited their purpose better than wine, as it did not dull the senses. Although alcohol was available at most coffee houses, the atmosphere was one of professional sobriety. The 'Turkey merchants' had long been familiar with coffee, having been given it on their trips abroad, where it was served by their hosts 'in little China dishes, as hot as they can suffer it; black as Soot and tasting not unlike it'. The purging nature of hot, strong coffee was soon seized upon by London's quack health writers and in no time at all it was used to cure anything from the gout to period pain. Its stimulating effects were purported to sharpen the brain for commerce.

London's first coffee house was opened in 1652, in a shed on St Michael's Alley, by Pasqua Rosée, a Greek born in Sicily who had come to London as a servant. In the same year he published an advertising flyer, *The Vertue of the Coffee Drink*, advertising his coffee as 'a simple innocent thing, composed into a drink, by being dryed in an oven and ground to powder and boiled up with spring water'. Rosée asserted coffee had medicinal benefits, but it also gave imbibers the advantage of staying sober during business hours. His shed became known as The Turk's Head, owing to his dark appearance and the fact that he used his own likeness as the shop sign. More coffee houses were springing up in the area; by the time Rosée disappeared from London in uncertain circumstances, coffee houses were part of the street scenery, even if they weren't welcomed by everyone. One early coffee house proprietor, John Farr, was prosecuted by his neighbour because his business created an offensive smell, but by 1663 there were 83 licensed coffee houses in London, almost all of them near the Royal Exchange. They tended to specialize in a clientele with particular commercial interests in the Baltic or Levantine trade; they would carry the pertinent newspapers, and write up on chalkboards the news of ships about to dock or depart. Just how important these coffee houses were to City trade is seen in their rapid spread: almost 500 of them had appeared by the time George I was crowned in 1714.

The coffee houses represented an important mixture of common business and intellectual interests, sobriety and socializing. A large selection of newspapers were part of coffee house culture from the start, and thus patrons could keep up with all the latest domestic and foreign happenings. The papers were often complemented by a small selection of books, such as that offered by Walsal 'the Coffee-man against Cree-Church in Leaden-hall-Street' who kept 'a Library in his Coffee-Room for his Customers to read'. Sometimes the library was run by the coffee house owner's wife; these collections became some of the first lending libraries in London. Thus with their themed interests, their emphasis on business and their congenial surroundings, the coffee houses became an acceptable place for men of almost every culture and faith to be seen in, particularly those who otherwise would not venture into taverns or alehouses.

By 1690, there were at least 100 companies selling stocks that were traded in London. Their value fluctuated according to the news that came and went along the international information routes: the ships coming and going from London's docks. News of lost cargoes, huge hauls, diseased crews and delays for repair were brought back by thousands of vessels, both large and small. The coffee houses employed boys to go to the mouth of the Thames, wait for news and watch for ships. Then they would report back their findings, which would be displayed on a board behind the bar. Entry to the coffee house cost a penny, with the coffee, newspapers and current news included. Suddenly, literacy came to mean not only an increased chance of employment but also the ability to grasp fleeting opportunities from information displayed in the coffee houses. The entrepreneurial self-improving men the coffee houses attracted resulted in these establishments being nicknamed 'Penny Universities'.

Investment trading suffered an early setback with the great fiasco of the South Sea Bubble in 1720, which changed the nation's attitude to investing in stocks for the rest of the Georgian period. The South Sea Company was founded in 1711 and operated using money from government bonds. These bonds paid a low return, so Robert Harley, the Lord Treasurer, offered to exchange the government bonds for stock in the South Sea Company. This would then give a greater return, as the company was operating so profitably.

In 1719, the South Sea Company wished to purchase more of the government debt, and so the company issued more shares for this purpose. To get people to buy the shares, agents were sent out amongst the traders in the coffee houses of Exchange Alley, spreading rumours of massive trading opportunities in the South Seas, with huge profits to be had. The names of prominent politicians who already held shares were freely circulated. The share price shot up from £128 in January to £550 at the end of May. In June, the government passed the Joint Stock Act to regulate the formation of such companies, but this only gave further impetus to the galloping rise in the already established South Sea Company, with the share price nearing £1,000 in August.

It couldn't last, and the sheer volume of selling triggered a fall which snowballed into a crash. By the time the year was out, the price was back down to near its original level. Many were ruined. Ordinary Londoners came to fear the trade in stocks, often preferring to buy a ticket for the increasingly popular public and private lotteries instead. The instability of the market became the subject of cartoons, songs and popular literature, and stockbrokers, known as 'jobbers', came to be seen as shady and unreliable.

Yet Londoners had got a taste for investment, and throughout the century the coffee houses remained centres of specific trades. Lloyd's coffee house on Tower Street was a place where shipping merchants discussed insurance for their ships and cargoes. Soon the insurance deals began to dominate, and what had started in the coffee house became the Lloyd's of London Insurance Market, finally moving to the Royal Exchange in 1774 as the Society of Lloyd's. Jonathan's, perhaps the most famous of all the London coffee houses, was opened by Jonathan Miles in 1680 and became one of the leading coffee houses for men who speculated in stocks and shares. Along with Garraway's, it was frequented by City businessmen, although the 'quality' was thought to be better at the latter. John Castaing, a Huguenot broker who spent a lot of time at Jonathan's, began to write up stock prices, bullion prices and exchange rates in 1698, publishing the sheet on Tuesdays and Fridays as *The Course of Exchange and Other Things*. Castaing's prices were relied upon by many of the coffee houses in the City. His exchange rate was commonly used, and the publication continued for almost a century. Jonathan's coffee house burned down in 1748, ending an era. A new Jonathan's was built without delay, supported by various brokers, and soon took on the name of the Stocks Exchange. The coffee house was close to the site of London's original livestock market, the Stocks Market. The two were soon combined, and the London Stock Market was born, where many a man traded 'whose great ambition is to ride over others, in order to which, he resolves to win the horse, or lose the saddle'.

London's first zoo: the Tower of London

As the City moved increasingly towards its modern identity, one corner of it remained obstinately ancient. The Tower of London, sitting right on the eastern edge of the City for centuries, was still a political prison and an armoury. But at the beginning of the eighteenth century, it was also a popular tourist destination. Occasionally it housed political prisoners, but by the seventeenth century it was already a valuable income-generating attraction.

It was traditional for foreign dignitaries to make gifts of the exotic creatures of their kingdoms to the countries they visited. Britain acquired a polar bear from Norway in 1252. He was at first allowed to roam about the Tower of London, but when he became huge his keeper was given a muzzle and a chain and they were sent to spend their days outside, fishing and bathing in the Thames, apparently happy in each other's company. By the time England had begun to squabble over a fair proportion of the globe under Elizabeth I, the animals were arriving thick and fast, with some, at times, being quartered in the empty moat. Elizabeth improved the menagerie and had it opened to the public on high days and holidays. In 1603, James I overhauled the menagerie again, providing much larger cages for the animals, and running water 'for the Lyons to drinke and wasche themselves in'. He also installed a viewing gallery so that visitors could look down upon them in safety.

During the Georgian period, the Tower contained up to eleven lions at any one time. The male lions were regarded as the tamer, and Samuel Pepys records going to the Tower on 11 January 1660 to see 'Crowly, who is now grown a very great lion and very tame'. When young, all the lions were allowed out to play in the Tower grounds, much to the amusement of the visitors, who patted and played with them. The Duke of Sussex was particularly fond of a brother and sister who had been fostered by a goat, and he often went to see them. Also kept in the Tower were oddities such as cats and dogs born with more or fewer legs than they should have had. Ned Ward was unimpressed with such spectacle and thought:

> . . . they should take as much care to feed the poor human cripples who were born with all their legs, and have lost one half in the nation's service . . . were it as uncommon a thing to see a soldier or a sailor with but one leg, as 'tis to see a dog or a cat with no more than two, no questions but they would live as well and be taken as much notice of as these are.

In 1704, John Strype produced his new edition of Stow's *Survey of London*, and the menagerie was then said to contain six lions, two leopards, three eagles, two Swedish owls (both called Hopkins), two 'Cats of the Mountains' and a 'Jackall'. In 1728, when Gertrude Savile visited the menagerie, the lioness had given birth and the cubs had been taken away because: 'They say if they did not take them from the lyoness, she would kill them upon any thing that frighted her . . . getting them from her she, to save it, took one in her mouth & gave it too kind a squeeze; kill'd it.' Gertrude watched the surviving cubs being nursed in a room by the fire, and she also played with other adolescent lions in a room where they were free to run around.

In 1729, the cost of entry to the lions was threepence, a figure that rose to ninepence by the end of the century. Dead cats and dogs were used to supplement the feed of the big cats, and free entry could be had for anyone bringing one of either. In 1741, the guide to the Tower included an introduction to the lion Marco, his wife, Phillis, and their son, Nero. The lions roared with hunger at dawn, a sound which echoed throughout the east of the City and outside the wall. Their feed consisted of eight to nine pounds of raw beef daily, excluding any bones and any dogs or cats. On Sunday, the Tower was closed to visitors, and the keepers noted that the lions would often roar all day until someone came and paid them some attention.

There were also tigers. Dicka was recorded as a cub in 1741. Leopards such as Willa, 'hunting-leopards' (as cheetahs were known), lynx and ocelot were also recorded. Visitors agreed that the ocelot was the prettiest cat, but that the cheetah was the most affectionate. The cheetahs were led about the grounds on leashes in pairs for exercise and as a spectacle. In the same year, the first educational guidebook to the menagerie was introduced, aimed at children: 'The wild creatures that are shewn are all kept in strong dens, so that you need not be under any fear of danger from them.' The guidebook also included information on the animals' diets.

> Lions, Tigers, Panthers and Leopards, are fed sheeps heads and plucks [offal] twice a day, of which a Lion eats four or five in a day; but Leopards, Panthers, and Tigers, are much fonder of raw dogs-flesh. They drink as often as they please. Usually several times in a day; each having a stone trough in his den.

By the time the guidebook was published, exotic animals were no longer the creatures of myth and legend. Surveys conducted in London between the 1730s and 1750s by George Edwards and Eleazer Albin show that ownership of unusual pets was spread across the social classes, with around a third owned by the artisan classes, including Mr Bradbury the apothecary with his mongoose, Mr Scarlet the optician with his jerboa, and Mrs Kennon the midwife with her ring-tailed lemur and marmoset. It's impossible to know if they flourished in their domestic settings, but some seem to have defied early deaths long enough to become treasured companions. Back in the menagerie in the 1750s, the big cat cubs survived into adulthood. However, the keeper of the King's animals, John Ellys, made an arrangement that the surgeon John Hunter was to have first refusal on the bodies of all the menagerie animals, so that they might be dissected.

In about 1767, John Wesley visited the Tower with a flute player, requesting that the man play for the animals whilst he watched for any sign of a soul. Animals that did not show any such response included the dangerous grizzly bear, Old Martin, who was an old man by 1823 but still regarded his keepers as 'perfect strangers'. Old Martin died in 1838, allegedly over a hundred years old, but he was probably Old Martin mark two or three. Other dangerous animals included the hyena and the jackals. The disconsolate solitary mongoose was made happy by the addition of a friend, and the two slept together, interlacing 'their limbs and tails in a singular fashion' so that each could see over the other's back, 'and like that fall comfortably asleep'.

The School of Monkeys lay in an outer yard near the Lion Tower. In 1753, the guidebook issued a warning about one of the baboons who had become expert in throwing missiles and would 'heave anything that happens to be within his reach with such Force as to split Stools, Bowls and other Wooden Utensils in a Hundred Pieces'. One young baboon was deemed unfit for polite company as 'by his Motions when Women approach him, [he] appears to be lecherous to a surprising Degree'. The monkeys were not a huge success, and were removed in 1810 for 'one of them having torn a boy's leg in a dangerous manner'.

There was usually an Indian elephant in the menagerie. They were largely judged to be inferior to a dog or a horse in understanding, yet they were observed to play by spraying things with water from their trunks. Mr Cops, one of the better keepers at the Tower, was convinced of their 'wisdom'. Quite how they found out that elephants are 'fond of wine, spirits and other intoxicating articles' is best consigned to the past, but the elephant rations contained a gallon of wine daily.

Kangaroos and emus wandered about freely in the grounds. The Royal Park at Windsor had quite a stock of roaming kangaroos, and they were breeding successfully at the Tower before 1820. An aside in an account of the Tower menagerie of this period notes that there were various parklands around England where kangaroos were present in some quantity.

My favourite account of an animal in the Tower is from the 1820s, when a zebra was recorded in the menagerie. Zebras are stubborn, and remain wild under all but the most confined circumstances. The Tower zebra had retained her character, suffering the indignities of her confined state with a tolerably good nature, provided she got her reward.

> The subject of the present article, which has now been about two years in the Menagerie, will suffer a boy to ride her about the yard, and is frequently allowed to run loose through the Tower, with a man by her side, whom she does not attempt to quit except to run to the Canteen, where she is occasionally indulged with a draught of ale, of which she is particularly fond.

The menagerie was much improved by Mr Cops, and during his tenure it became clear that it was no longer acceptable to house animals in such conditions as the Tower afforded. The menagerie housed 280 creatures by 1832. It was closed in 1835, when the animals formed the basis of the collection for London Zoo in Regent's Park.

2.   The Margins

The City represents the heart of Old London, and it remained the hub of the growing metropolis. At the beginning of the Georgian era it was newly built and cleaner than it had ever been, full of ideas and urgency. And money. If the people were not sophisticated, displaying only commercial taste, they were solid and prosperous.

We now leave the tightly packed mercantile streets, smelling of fish, whale oil, animals and coffee, and head for the lawless urban sprawl outside the walls; the haunt of restless apprentices, homosexuals and forgers, writers, refugees and rebels. A place where anything might happen.

As early as the reign of Elizabeth I, London had 'got a great way from the streame [of the Thames]'. Living outside the City rapidly became an attractive option for many, particularly merchants who wanted grand gardens rather than enclosed courtyards, artisans whose trades required space and freely running water, and those who could not afford to live in the Square Mile. However, from the moment the urban sprawl began to creep round the eastern walls of the Tower it became a place for poor immigrants and the marginalized.

The jagged arc of the City boundary begins in the east, beyond the Tower. Up against the Tower of London was the church of St Katharine and its associated hospital. In 1598, the historian John Stow described it as 'pestered with small tenements' and wrote that there was a large number of 'strangers' living there. St Katharine-by-the-Tower and St Botolph-without-Aldgate hold a significant amount of records for baptisms and burials of black members of the local community during the eighteenth century. Their entries are annotated with 'Black' or 'Blackamoor'. In May 1827, St Katharine's was pulled down so that the area might be redeveloped as part of the new London docks. More than a thousand small tenements were cleared to make way for the docks, displacing over 11,000 inhabitants with compensation only for freeholders.

The first of the docks was to sit immediately in the space the church had occupied for seven centuries.

Just north of St Katharine's was 'Rag Fair', the nickname for Rosemary Lane 'where old clothes and frippery are sold'. A later account reveals:

> There is no expressing the poverty of the goods, nor yet their cheapness. A distinguished merchant, engaged with a purchaser, observing me look on his with great attention, called out to me, as his customer was going off with his bargain, to observe that man, *For*, says he, *I have actually cloathed him for fourteen pence.*

On 14 February 1756, *The Public Advertiser* recorded that Mary Jenkins, a second-hand clothes dealer in Rag Fair, had sold a pair of breeches to a woman 'for sevenpence and a pint of beer'. In the pub, the purchaser found eleven Queen Anne gold guineas and a banknote dated 1729 sewn into the waistband. The woman was apparently illiterate, and she sold the banknote to another customer for a gallon of 'twopenny purl' (a powerful mixture of hot beer, sugar, ginger and gin) before being told that the note's value was £30. Elsewhere:

> Jews used to go about the streets with bags full of wigs, crying out, 'A dip for a penny.' . . . It would happen that the man fished up a wig too big or too small, or a black-haired man got a red wig, or the reverse; or a most outrageous fit, in which no decent citizen or artisan could appear.

The Rag Fair would migrate to what became known as Petticoat Lane, where by the Victorian period there were 'between two and three miles of old clothes . . . it is a vista of dinginess, but many-coloured dinginess, as regards female attire'.

Nearby, in Goodman's Fields, house numbers were introduced to London in 1708. However, London continued to work on a system of large and elaborate signboards and descriptions, such as 'At the Naked Boy and Three Crowns Against the New Church in The Strand'. To the north and west, the Huguenot refugees invaded the earlier textile-making settlement, sticking close to the charity of their mother church in Threadneedle Street and their soup kitchen, 'La Soupe'. Where

Broadgate passes Liverpool Street Station and becomes Norton Folgate, the City's jurisdiction ended; the area had been a place to find cheap lodgings since Christopher Marlowe took a room there. At the beginning of the period it was a scraggy patchwork settlement but by the end was occupied by more commercial buildings. It is still a discordantly odd area now, pummelled by heavy traffic, dotted with gritty nightclubs and cornershops where all the biscuits are out of date. To the west of Norton Folgate were the huge open spaces of Moorfields, perhaps the most symbolic of all of east London's open spaces.

Through Aldgate and Bishopsgate passed the roads to Whitechapel and Shoreditch, taking rural traffic at the beginning of the period and suburban commuters at the end. Between them ran Houndsditch, just outside the City walls where 'dead dogges were there laid or cast' for centuries. Further west was Bethlem Hospital, crouched upon the southern edge of Moorfields. Commonly known as Bedlam, it was where the insane poor were housed. Moorfields itself played host to the City's leisure time as well as her protests, and acted as a refuge during times of terror. On its western edge was Grub Street, where poor scribblers huddled in frozen garrets and broadsheets fluttered on washing lines, drying in the wind. 'On lines stretched from tree to tree, slips of ballads fluttered in the breeze.'

At Cripplegate there were noisy coaching inns, such as the Catherine Wheel and the Bell, which catered for all classes of customers in their warren-like interiors. Clerkenwell played host to the artisan as goldsmiths, horologists and cabinetmakers set up workshops around the Green. Many were poorly paid pieceworkers, exempt from the apprenticeships enforced within the City. Holborn was where the richest merchants had moved a century earlier to build large houses strung out along the road. Behind them were courts and fields, mixed with large gardens that were getting ever smaller as the weight of population encroached. Most of the houses were by now subdivided into cheap tenements. Behind lay Chick Lane, a street of brothels and shops selling second-hand goods and clothes.

To the south-west Lincoln's Inn Fields and Temple acted as London's universities, full of bright and affluent young men away from home. In the late seventeenth century, it became a small town of regular squares and passages with gardens opening on to the river, gulls wheeling overhead. Solidly middle class in both occupation and occupant, it was not immediately apparent that the Inns were busy haunts of prostitution and, sometimes, violence. Between Temple and the City was Alsatia, also known as the Liberty of Whitefriars, named after the white clothing of the Carmelites who had once inhabited the area. It was a 'dull, narrow, uninviting lane sloping from Fleet Street to the river . . . a debtors' sanctuary and thieves' paradise, and for half a century its bullies and swindlers waged a ceaseless war with their proud and rackety neighbours of the Temple'. Close by was the Bridewell Prison. Originally a palace for Henry VIII, it had been given over to the correction of 'disorderly women', and soon Bridewell became London's byword for prison.

These ragged margins of the City did not remain for long. The Georgian period saw them appear, flourish in their extraordinary ways and then die as London leached into the surrounding villages.

The 'motley assemblage' of Moorfields

Moorfields is gone, much of it hidden beneath the vast Barbican complex whose myriad water features recall something of the marshy swamp concealed beneath. For Moorfields was a moor. It was boggy, and a danger to those who did not know their way around it in the late seventeenth century. It was so wet that Stow spoke of the necessity for 'Cawswaies' across it. The Moor Fields lay half in and half outside the City boundary. This marginality defined the area's role in the London subconscious of the eighteenth century.

The idea that Moorfields was outside the accepted order of things was reinforced by the presence of Bethlem Hospital, the oldest hospital in the world to deal specifically with mental disturbance. It has lived in four places since it took in its first mentally ill patients in 1357: in a priory where Liverpool Street Station stands now, in Moorfields, then Southwark from 1815 and, finally, Beckenham. Whilst the priory with its individual cells had been useful for confining inmates separately, it was oversubscribed and in a poor state of repair.

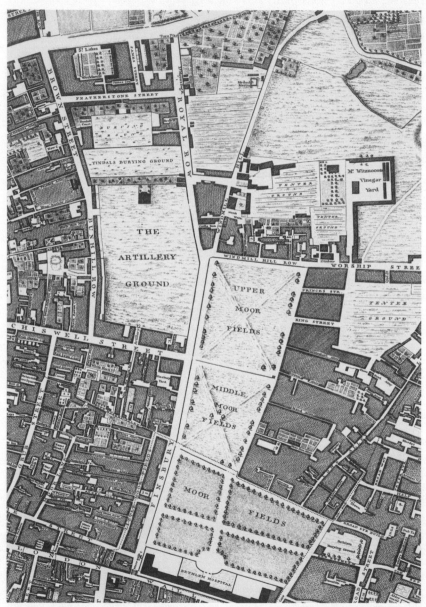

Moorfields and the Artillery Ground, detail from John Roque's map, 1745

The new building, designed by Robert Hooke, was built at the southern edge of Moorfields. It was far more like a sanctuary than a prison, and Hooke's plans showed a distinct care for space, light and recreational areas for the patients. Over the door were two sculptures by Caius Gabriel Cibber, of 'Raving' and 'Melancholy Madness', now in the Victoria and Albert Museum. These sculptures signified the distinction made at the time between the insane 'incurables' and depressive 'curables'. Those born with severe mental deficiency but largely passive natures were classed as 'idiots'. 'Moral insanity' was an acceptable euphemism for syphilis or trauma resulting from distressing experiences as a street prostitute.

From its opening in 1676, tours of the new building could be had for a penny a time, and people came to watch the 'ravers'. There was a resident apothecary, and physicians visited during the week. The men of the Monro family served as doctors at Bedlam during the Georgian period and improved care in over a century of attendance. They exchanged shackles for straitjackets, and fitted cork or India rubber flooring to cells. Numbers indicate there were above 200 patients, plus around 80 criminally insane prisoners who were kept separately. Exceptionally violent or criminally insane patients were still fettered, in some cases wearing only blanket tunics. If they continued to soil bedding, they were given only straw to sleep on. Almost every patient had a carer, but men were sometimes put in charge of female patients and there were accusations of abuse. In the middle of the century, the Monro regime made attempts to protect female inmates, particularly if they were 'Lewdly Given', by confining them 'to their Cells and no persons Suffered to come to them but in Company with one of the gallery Maids'.

In 1751, St Luke's mental hospital 'for the Reception of Lunatics' opened opposite Bedlam. It was run by William Battie, a progressive mental health practitioner and strong critic of the Monros. In 1758, he published his *Treatise on Madness*. 'Madness,' he began, 'though at present a terrible and very frequent calamity, is perhaps as little understood as any that afflicted Mankind.' He went on to attack the Monros and their madness monopoly at Bedlam. Battie, who invited medical students to come and see him work at St Luke's, criticized the 'few

select Physicians' who 'keep the cases as well as the patients to themselves'. His theories are free of the black and white approach the Monros
had taken to madness. He believed 'uneasiness is so interwoven in the
frames of mortals' that madness might come to affect anyone, not only
the defective or morally flawed. John Monro responded instantly, with
a publication priced at half that of Battie's, and opening with:

> Madness is a distemper of such a nature, that very little of real use can
> be said concerning it . . . My own inclination would never have led
> me to appear in print; but it was thought necessary for me, in my
> situation, to say something in answer to the undeserved censures,
> which Dr. Battie has thrown upon my predecessors.

Monro tackles Battie's rebukes ably, but the impact is somewhat lost
when he extols the virtues of emetics as a cure for madness, using
ipecacuanha to dislodge the 'phlegm' from the body. Only once the
phlegm was removed could purges and bleeding drain the residual
toxins the patient harboured.

In 1770, John Monro put a stop to Bedlam being used for the
amusement of the paying public. Not everyone in Bedlam was an
incoherent lunatic, though; some inmates were both lucid and per-
suasive, such as James Tilly Matthews. Matthews was admitted in
1797 and is believed to be the first fully documented case of paranoid
schizophrenia. He was a Welsh tea merchant who became obsessed
with the idea that a gang of espionage 'experts' had set up a magnetic
'Air Loom' at London Wall and were brainwashing the citizens of
London, including major politicians. As a patient Matthews was
charming, but he was detained for the rest of his life and died in 1815.
His death coincided with the removal of Bedlam to Southwark, the
same year the Parliamentary Committee was set up to investigate
abuses of the madhouse system.

The constant presence of Bedlam, followed by St Luke's, on the
edge of Moorfields reinforced the area's association with madness
and marginality. It was also where the City of London's crowds congregated, either as protagonists or spectators. It was a popular place
for the apprentices to meet, bring their lovers, play football and other
sports, and to gather in large numbers when they felt threatened or

put upon by the government, foreign workers, their masters or changes in commercial practice. In particular, the weavers of Spital-fields held protests there against cheap Irish labour encroaching on their business. The government was not above making its presence felt, and on 14 July 1709, Richard Steele recorded in the *Tatler* that the Artillery Company, which had its headquarters on the eastern side of Moorfields, had been observed 'carrying out exercises through the northern part of the City near Moorfields . . . to the astonish-ment of the residents'. The government's fear of crowds, and the need to assert a sometimes sinister authority, was followed up by the Riot Act of 1714, which declared any gathering of twelve or more people illegal and punishable by law.

Moorfields had cheap housing and ready access to water, and by the time the Artillery Company was making its presence felt there was a 'motley assemblage' of men and women trying to scrape a liv-ing. The surroundings were less than salubrious: for centuries the laystalls (dunghills) of the City had been located in the southern part of the area. Then small shops 'began to spring up on the outskirts of the Moor . . . tenanted by botchers', many of whom made wheeled walking frames known as 'go-carts' for children and the elderly and infirm. Spinning Wheel Alley was given over almost entirely to the go-cart trade. Physical sports such as wrestling and cudgel-play were practised on the open ground. Tenants of the poorest housing included 'jobbing tailors, and renovators of old clothes, always ready to leave their shop boards and to join in the scuffles which went on before their doors'. Under trees planted across the lower part of the moor were stalls of second-hand booksellers, where antiquaries rum-maged. The poor writers and the constant threat, or promise, of violence defined the area.

Building was getting under way in the north, and the parish church of the newly created parish of St Luke's was opened in 1733. The citi-zens worked on getting rid of the laystalls and installing tree-lined walks. These walks were not always used for the pleasant perambula-tions their planners had intended, and one in particular was notorious. The walk running along the boundary between Upper and Lower Moorfields also marked the border between the area officially within the City (Lower), with all its rules, and the area outside (Upper), which was unregulated and known as Sodomites' Walk. All the different cruising areas of London have their own 'specialities', and Moorfields was what would become known as 'rough trade'. Moorfields may have been the place where this term originated, as Sodomites' Walk was the destination for those seeking congress with workers in the 'rough trades' such as coal-heaving and the river trades. Sodomites' Walk was officially removed in 1752, when the wall separating Upper and Lower Moorfields was pulled down 'as it was a Screen for Thieves and the most obnoxious persons'. These were the same persons who 'have frequented that Place for many Years, and debauch'd the Morals of 'Prentices and other unguarded Youth'. Another local haunt of both London's youths and those who might seek to debauch them was the Perilous Pond, a dangerous bathing hole near Old Street. In 1743 it was transformed into the Peerless Pool, London's first proper outdoor swimming pool, measuring 108ft by 170ft and used as a skating rink in winter. The Peerless Pool is gone, but Sodomites' Walk is marked by the south side of Finsbury Square – so it is still possible to walk along it, if the fancy takes you.

The 'motley' nature of Moorfields was seen again in 1750, when London experienced a series of earthquakes. At noon on Thursday 8 February, those sitting in the Chancery Courts felt a severe jolt, those in Lincoln's Inn watched their furniture move, and a lamplighter was forced to cling to his ladder in Gray's Inn.

The usual round of pamphlets and sermons was soon on the way regarding divine disgruntlement against the sinful nature of Londoners. Between 10 and 13 February, *The London Evening Post* published a scientific explanation with no mention of the geological implications of sin. John Wesley, however, was having none of it; he dismissed any 'natural explanation', for clearly 'God is himself the Author, and sin the moral cause, of earthquakes'.

It is likely that the earthquake would have been forgotten by busy Londoners soon enough had not, on Thursday 8 March, exactly a month after the first quake, a second one struck. It was little more than a tremor, estimated at having a magnitude of 3.1 (whereas the first earthquake has been estimated at 4.1), but London was in uproar.

The Jacobite Rebellion of 1745, droughts and cattle shortages caused by a bovine 'plague', as well as the resulting high prices, had all been features of the previous decade. The country was going to the dogs, in a biblical handcart.

On 16 March, the Bishop of London, Thomas Sherlock, wrote an open letter to his people. It was published in large numbers as a pamphlet. It warned against scientists, whom he termed 'Little philosophers'. These men saw 'a little, and but a very little'. It was a straightforward rebuke to the people of London for their ungodly ways, and it sold in reams. The Church wasn't giving away the word of God, even in such spiritually challenging times.

Church sermons spoke of London as the 'headquarters of wickedness' and deemed the earthquake a lesson. Bandwaggoners at every level saw money to be made from the earthquake: pamphlets and news-sheets abounded, and lectures were given. All this contributed to a general feeling of panic.

Then, like a match to kindling, a 'lunatic lifeguardsman called Mitchell' began to walk around London crying a prophecy that London would suffer a huge earthquake on 8 April. The city would be flattened.

Londoners began to clear out. They went to family in the country, or took a holiday. For those unable to leave it was clear that the feeling on the streets was tense. The clergy lambasted the people for cowardice. A man with a foot in each camp was Roger Pickering, pastor of a Dissenters' church and a Fellow of the Royal Society. On 5 April, he published a sermon ordering Londoners to remain, and take their medicine.

> I *adjure* you, by the *Interest* of that *Gospel* you profess, by the *Credit* of that *Faith* on which you rest your Souls, that, with *humble Hearts*, but with *Christian Confidence*, in your respective Stations ON THE SPOT where *Providence* had place you, YE WAIT the WILL OF GOD.

But Londoners had been told for over a month that earthquakes buried both the good and the guilty. Horace Walpole recorded, on the evening of 7 April, that in the past three days '730 coaches have been counted passing Hyde Park Corner with whole parties removing into the country'. That night, everyone who feared for their lives the coming day cleared out either to Moorfields or Hyde Park, to take shelter on the open ground. Some took their carriages and slept in them. Others pitched makeshift tents and windbreaks. Moorfields had become the place of refuge on the edge of the City once again. The following morning, after the earthquake had declined to make an appearance, the Moorfields refugees crept back to their undamaged homes and got on with life, no doubt feeling both relieved and foolish.

Close to Moorfields, Bunhill Fields burial ground holds the graves of many religious Dissenters, such as George Fox, founder of the Quaker movement, John Bunyan, the Baptist preacher, as well as that of Susannah Wesley, the mother of John Wesley. The area hosted Wesley's open-air preaching, and it was just outside Aldersgate, on 24 May 1738, that he noted in his journal how he 'felt his heart strangely warmed' at a Lutheran service. A memorial outside the doors of the Museum of London now marks the spot. Wesley worked mainly amongst those who did not attend established churches, and he drew many followers from the dispossessed through his inclusive style of worship. He first occupied a disused foundry just off City Road for his Methodist meetings, but by 1777, he had enough subscribing followers to commission George Dance the Younger to design the City Road Chapel, still in existence. He wrote extensively, not only on religion but also about scientific and medical breakthroughs, and his ideas would have informed his congregations. Through his preaching and writing he embraced members of the community who felt distanced from the rich members of the City churches. He often preached in Moorfields, gathering large crowds.

By the 1770s, the role of Moorfields as open ground for playing, protesting and preaching was declining. In 1777, Finsbury Square was built on some of the drier ground, and the parish of St Luke's was rapidly growing to cope with a burgeoning population. By the final quarter of the eighteenth century, Moorfields was surrounded on all sides and shrinking; but in 1784, it would have one last hurrah as London's premier space for the people.

In 1766, Henry Cavendish's new work on hydrogen had led scientists and madcaps all over Europe to experiment with balloon flight. The concept of little hydrogen balloons for amusement or communication purposes wasn't new, but it took a series of adventurers to prove that man could take flight. The most famous of all of these were the Montgolfier brothers whose balloon ascended in Paris in 1783. The following year, the ballooning bug hit London.

Vincenzo (or Vincent) Lunardi came to England as a diplomat, but he was obsessed with the idea of flying. He was a dashing 22-year-old and was determined to gain royal permission to 'demonstrate' a manned balloon flight with the help of his partner, George Biggin. This was to take place on the Artillery Ground near Moorfields, in September 1784. The almost impossible number of 200,000 people turned out to see this demonstration, including the royals and a healthy chunk of the nobility.

Lunardi made everything dramatic and packed his cat and dog into the basket with him for company before releasing the tethers, whereupon the balloon rose 'with slow and gradual majesty into the air' to the disappointment of 'the splenetic' doubters. 'He appeared composed, and as the balloon went up, bowed most gracefully, and calmly waved his flag to the admiring and wonder-struck spectators.' It wasn't all glamour, though: the cat got sick and was let out when the balloon touched down briefly in north London before Lunardi finally landed near Ware, to a very surprised reception.

Lunardi bonnets, fans and garters became all the rage, and the charming Italian had quite a fan club. The balloon went on show in the Pantheon on Oxford Street, the great hall of public entertainment designed by James Wyatt, which stood on the plot now occupied by Marks & Spencer. Thousands came to visit Lunardi's balloon, displayed in the Pantheon's rotunda, and aerostatic science became the wonder of the age. Allegedly, after seeing a balloon on Hounslow Heath in 1784, Horace Walpole predicted that the whole heath would become 'the harbour of the skies' – predicting, if not quite prophesying, the arrival of Heathrow. The sense of potential these first balloon ascents created was huge: visible, exciting proof that the world was changing, and almost anything was possible.

After Lunardi, Moorfields would no longer hold the massing crowds and soon disappeared under housing of the meaner Georgian sort, in addition to workshops and cookhouses. In 1800, it was the site of an illuminating case of dognapping, illustrating the diversity of the area, when a man venturing into an establishment for a bowl of soup was surprised to find his missing and 'much-lamented' bull terrier, Cesar, there under another name. The owner of the cookhouse, Mr Day, explained that the dog, named Charles, could not possibly be Cesar and was, instead, the produce of the costermonger's dog, Lover of Smut, and the lamplighter's dog, Rose. Charles had been born in Moorfields on the premises of a 'horse-boiler' and raised by a carter, before being purchased for one guinea by Mr Day. Eventually, it emerged that Mr Day had, in fact, purchased the dog from Charley, 'the milk-man from over the water'.

By the time of Cesar's restoration to his rightful owners, Moorfields had largely disappeared beneath urban development. It would remain densely populated by the poorer classes before being comprehensively flattened during the Second World War.

Grub Street: home of 'ye poets, ragged and forlorn'

The geography of Moorfields and Bedlam is now hidden, but both were linked inseparably with the legend of Grub Street, particularly during the early part of the eighteenth century. To live and work in Grub Street as a writer, either in reality or metaphorically, meant literary prostitution. It was a poor street running from St Giles-without-Cripplegate (the church still standing in the Barbican complex) north to Chiswell Street, in Clerkenwell.

The Moorfields book and ballad sellers were in place by the Restoration, but it was to be a different generation of writers who would create the Grub Street legend. There are many who could lay claim to being 'the first' writer of Grub Street, but there are few who could do it with as much authenticity as Daniel Defoe, born the son of a Presbyterian butcher in Fore Street in the scrubby parish of St Giles, Cripplegate, the parish which covered the bottom half of Grub Street.

Defoe would go on to become one of the most important political writers of his day, working for Robert Harley and his Tory faction as the first 'spin doctor'. His big breakthrough came in 1701, with his poem 'The True-Born Englishman', which satirized the John Bull ideal of the pure-bred Englishman, harking back to his early days amongst the outsiders and immigrants of Cripplegate.

> Thus from a mixture of all kinds began,
> That het'rogeneous thing, an Englishman . . .

Grub Street publishers, unlike their Paternoster Row colleagues, specialized in topical publications and, sometimes, smut. Elizabeth Nutt ran a cluster of shops in the Royal Exchange where she sold her more respectable stock, such as Swift's *Tale of a Tub*. She was also listed as a 'Mercury-woman', printing cheap and often seditious or salacious ballads in Grub Street; in the 1730s, she was printing pornography there, aided by her daughters.

In *The Dunciad*, Alexander Pope's Goddess of Dullness lives 'near Bedlam', meaning Moorfields and the Grub Street area, from where she and her agents bring disrepute, vulgarity and imbecility to London. His placement of the seat of Dullness was no mistake. Pope viewed the cheap output of poor literature as one of the chief agents of what he saw as society's decline.

This attitude did not change over the course of the Georgian period. It became set in literary history when Samuel Johnson, in his dictionary, defined Grub Street as 'a street near Moorfields, much inhabited by writers of small histories, dictionaries, and temporary poems'.

Delarivier Manley (1672–1724) was one of London's first writers for a political party, but she wasn't popular with everyone. Pope slammed her most popular work, *Secret Memoirs and Manners of several Persons of Quality, of Both Sexes, from the New Atalantis, An Island in the Mediterranean*, published in 1709, as a piece of transient scandal. In 1711, Manley decided she was retiring, tired of wading 'through Seas of Scurrility' and 'the Filth they have incessantly cast at me'. She didn't retire, of course, and in 1714 – when again she wrote that she might give it all up, as politics was 'not the business of a Woman' – she was also writing her six volumes of political allegories, six political pamphlets and another nine issues of the *Examiner*. Manley was a plain woman, unlucky in love and reclusive, but she carved out a successful career in the masculine realm of political writing as queen of the Grub Street hacks.

Clerkenwell: clocks, cabinets and confinement

Close to Grub Street was an unusual building which would house one of perhaps the most famous publications of Georgian London: *The Gentleman's Magazine*. St John's Gate, which had been built in 1504 as the house entrance to the Priory of the Knights of St John, is the traditional entrance to Clerkenwell from the south. The gate soon fell into secular use; in the early 1700s, it was Hogarth's childhood home during the years when his father ran a coffee house there, after which Edward Cave took it on as a house. Cave began *The Gentleman's Magazine* in 1731, featuring the gatehouse on the front of each issue. The magazine provided Samuel Johnson with his first regular writing job and went on to be one of the most influential 'human interest' publications of the eighteenth century. The gate was also where Johnson's pupil and friend David Garrick gave his first theatrical turn in London.

For many years during the eighteenth century, part of the gate also served as the local watch house, and Clerkenwell seemed to have more than its fair share of prisons, with the Clerkenwell Bridewell, New Prison and later Coldbath Fields. Land was cheap and the proximity to the Old Bailey meant it was convenient. The space available in Clerkenwell was also attractive to trades such as furniture making, which required workshops as well as storage space. Those who employed large numbers, such as metalworkers, watch- and clockmakers, also found Clerkenwell very suitable for their purposes, and soon a large artisan community was built up around the Green, where Fagin and the Artful Dodger taught Oliver Twist to pick pockets.

Local metalworkers included silversmiths, such as the Bateman family, headed up by the matriarch Hester who after the death of her husband, in 1760, pulled herself up from being an illiterate widow to a formidable businesswoman. Her workshop represented the zenith of small family firms during the eighteenth century.

Metalworking, clockmaking and cabinetmaking are trades which used piecework from the earliest times, and required plenty of both natural light and water. The clock- and watchmaking trades, in particular, required men to turn out small parts, usually the same one over and over again, with great precision. The piecework system meant they were paid according to how many they produced. Others were responsible for the assembly, and eventually it was only the employer's name which was engraved or stamped on the mechanism and case. In 1798, of the 11,000 men living in Clerkenwell, 7,000 were watchmakers.

John Harrison, the man who created the first reliable marine chronometer and solved the longitude problem in 1761, took up residence first in Clerkenwell's Leather Lane and then in Red Lion Street, just to the west. Here he worked tirelessly, with the help of the government, to produce a timepiece which would accurately place a ship at sea. Harrison's overriding and long-term obsession was often regarded as something of a joke, but his work enabled British ships to undertake vast journeys with confidence. Despite his borderline reputation Harrison contributed immeasurably to securing the British Navy's dominance of the oceans during the Age of Sail.

'All manner of gross and vile obscenity' in Holborn

Holborn was one of London's oldest roads, and much of it escaped the Great Fire. The large houses built in the Tudor period for merchants wanting to leave the City smoke had long since been divided into apartments leased by students at the Inns of Court, or poorer families clubbing together for the rent. The underworld which had occupied the Holborn Valley (where the Viaduct stands now) was forced out by the Fleet River improvements, and began to move west. Other residents included the brothel keepers of Chick Lane, and taverns of the lowest sort. Men who were happy to pay for their company could obtain partners both female and male, and the Holborn area was known for its gay subculture.

The Georgian period in London saw the development of modern gay sexuality. Men and women identified themselves as homosexual

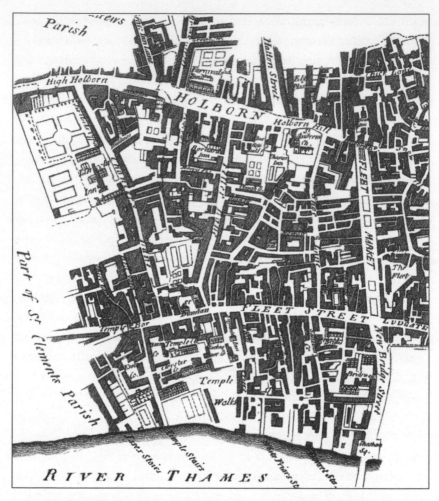

Holborn, Lincoln's Inn and Temple, showing the Fleet Market built over the
Ditch, and The Fleet prison, detail from John Royce's map, 1790,

and succeeded, to varying degrees, in establishing a network of
friends, acquaintances, locations and establishments which served
their sexual needs. The 'typical homosexual of the eighteenth century was a respectable tradesman rather than a fashionable libertine',
and the vast majority of people who lived gay lives in London were
ordinary men and women.

The Buggery Act, as it was known, had been passed in 1533 by
Henry VIII, making the 'detestable and abominable Vice of Buggery

committed with mankind or beast' punishable by hanging. It was, however, rarely brought to court. After the Restoration, literature on the act of sodomy proliferated, largely due to licentious poetry by the new breed of libertines, such as John Wilmot, Earl of Rochester. 'Sodomy' became taboo – the act of the debauched and diseased – and just as there were groups which protested against the low morals of the theatres and alcohol, the Society for the Reformation of Manners was established in 1690. The group went around forcibly shutting pubs, taverns and coffee shops on Sundays. By 1701, there were almost twenty spin-off societies in London. They set up a network of busybodies known as Reforming Constables, four in each ward of the City, and two in each parish outside. It was their responsibility to act as hubs of knowledge, finding out information about those who offended decency and keeping a tally of evidence. These 'sly reforming hirelings' rose to have a quasi-legal power within the community, and it behoved everyone to keep on their right side. Their first victim was Sea Captain Edward Rigby, in 1698, who had picked up a young man at the fireworks on Bonfire Night and was later entrapped by the boy and members of the Society. Rigby was sentenced to stand in the pillory at Charing Cross and Temple Bar. He also had to pay a fine of £1,000 and spend a year in prison, but he was not executed.

By the early eighteenth century, the Society was actively targeting gay cruising grounds. In 1707, in a ten-day campaign, they succeeded in arresting over forty men suspected of being active sodomites. The fear of accusation created a brisk trade for blackmailers, who ingratiated themselves with their targets before informing them that they would report them to the Society if they did not pay up.

At the same time, molly houses had become a fixture of the London male gay scene. They were essentially pubs or taverns catering for a gay clientele rather than gay brothels, although sex often took place on the premises. During the 1720s, there were at least twenty active molly houses in London. In February 1726, on a Sunday evening, the constables gathered for a raid on the molly house of one Margaret, or 'Mother Clap', in Field Lane, Holborn. Margaret Clap was married to John Clap, who ran a nearby pub but rarely visited her coffee house. In many rooms of the coffee house were beds for the use of the clientele, at a price, although they all made use of the large central room for drinking and dancing to fiddle music. There was also a 'marrying room', where men could be 'blessed' before having sex.

In the early hours of that Monday morning, forty homosexual men were arrested, taken to Newgate and held for trial. Significantly, none were discovered having sex, although some were found in a state of undress. For those arrested, there were fines, imprisonments, time to be spent in the pillory and three hangings. The raid on Mother Clap's house was prompted by a customer-turned-informer, Mark Partridge, who had fallen out with his lover and who decided to take the Society on a tour of London's molly houses. The prosecutions themselves were facilitated by a thirty-year-old prostitute named Thomas Newton. Newton decided to visit Mother Clap in gaol to pay her bail. There he was apprehended by two constables who coerced him into becoming an informer. It appears there were few corners of gay London Newton was not familiar with, and he was very effective for the Society, particularly when used as a familiar face to entrap men cruising in Moorfields, along Sodomites' Walk.

> I was no stranger to the Methods they used in picking one another up. So I takes a Turn that way, and leans over the Wall. In a little Time a Gentleman passes by, and looks hard at me, and at a small distance from me, stands up against the Wall, as if he was going to make Water. Then by Degrees he sidles nearer and nearer to where I stood, 'till at last he comes close to me. - *'Tis a very fine Night*, says he. *Aye*, says I, *and so it is*. Then he takes me by the Hand, and after squeezing and playing with it a little (to which I showed no dislike), he conveys it to his Breeches, and put his Privities into it. I took fast hold, and call'd out to Willis and Stevenson, who coming up to by Assistance, we carried him to the Watch house.

William Brown, the married man apprehended by his penis, was indignant at being arrested and responded to questioning with, 'I did it because I thought I knew him, and I think there is no Crime in making what use I please of my own Body.' His defence echoed the words of the philosopher John Locke, who posited that, 'Though the earth, and all inferior creatures, be common to all men, yet every man had a property in his own person: this no body has any right to but himself.' Despite Brown's high-minded assertion of his right to use his own body as he wished, he was sentenced to stand in the pillory, where he was pelted with rotten eggs, dead cats and turnip tops.

The men involved with the trials of 1726 were working men: cow keepers, a milkman, an upholsterer, an orange-seller. Around half were married or were known to have fathered children, but a clear minority were self-identifying prostitutes or practising homosexuals. The trials brought homosexuality out into society. It may not have been discussed in 'polite' company, but there was no getting away from it. On 7 May 1726, the front page of the *London Journal* featured an exposé of London's major cruising grounds:

> ... the nocturnal Assemblies of great Numbers of the like vile Persons at what they call the Markets, which are the Royal-Exchange, Moorfields, Lincolns-Inn Bog-houses, the South Side of St James's Park and the Piazzas of Covent Garden, where they make their Bargains, and then withdraw into some dark Corners to *indorse*, as they call it, but in plain English to commit Sodomy.

The remains of Gibbon's Tennis Court off Vere Street, Lincoln's Inn, after the fire of September 1809

The societies died out in the 1740s, as the fashion for moral reform faded, but towards the end of the Georgian period the Holborn area saw one last gay scandal with the White Swan affair. The White Swan was a tumbledown pub in Vere Street, now obliterated by Kingsway. It stood near Gibbon's Tennis Court, an old real tennis court which had become an increasingly down-at-heel theatre. The area was edgy, with most of the residents taking advantage of the cheaper, older housing.

On 8 July 1810, the Bow Street Police raided the pub. Twenty-seven men were arrested on suspicion of sodomy and attempted sodomy. The Swan had been going for less than six months, established by two men, Cook and Yardley, but it already had a considerable following. Cook and Yardley had furnished their establishment for its purpose.

> Four beds were provided in one room - another was fitted up for the ladies' dressing-room, with a toilette, and every appendage of rouge, &c. &c. . . . The upper part of the house was appropriated to youths who were constantly in waiting for casual customers; who practised all the allurements that are found in a brothel, by the more natural description of prostitutes. Men of rank, and respectable situations in life, might be seen wallowing either in or on beds with wretches of the lowest description.

Amongst the regulars at the White Swan were: Kitty Cambric, a coal merchant; Miss Selina, a runner at a Police Office; Black-eyed Leonora, a drummer; Pretty Harriet, a butcher; Lady Godiva, a waiter; the Duchess of Gloucester, a gentleman's servant; the Duchess of Devonshire, a blacksmith; and Miss Sweet Lips, a country grocer.

> It is a generally received opinion, and a very natural one, that the prevalency of this passion has for its object effeminate delicate beings only: but this seems to be, by Cook's account, a mistaken notion; and the reverse is so palpable in many instances, that Fanny Murry, Lucy Cooper, and Kitty Fisher, are now personified by an athletic barge-man, an Herculean coal-heaver, and a deaf tyre-smith.

Black-eyed Leonora, the drummer – who stands out amongst this motley crowd – was most likely Thomas White, a sixteen-year-old drummer in the Guards. Thomas was one of the youths who stood and waited in the upper part of the house. He was a great favourite amongst the 'more exalted' visitors to the house, 'being an universal favourite, was very deep in the secrets of the fashionable part of the coterie'. Poor Thomas, who wasn't even at the White Swan on the night of the raid, was too quick to confess under pressure and was executed after almost a year in prison. With him died a man called John Hepburn, aged forty-six, who had procured Thomas White's services. White was prosecuted as the giver, rather than the receiver, which made it almost impossible for the court to avoid the death sentence when the jury found him guilty. White's execution was a social event: 'A vast concourse of people attended to witness the awful scene. The Duke of Cumberland, Lord Sefton, Lord Yarmouth, and several other noblemen were in the press-yard.'

The Duke of Cumberland had avoided a homosexual scandal by a razor-thin margin in June 1810, when his servant was found with his throat sliced. He had threatened to out his master after catching the Duke and his valet 'in an improper and unnatural situation'. Perhaps Cumberland was one of White's 'fashionable' guests. We will never know. Of the other twenty-five, only six were found guilty and they were pilloried and imprisoned, including Cook the landlord. Yardley seems to have got away with the whole thing. The White Swan affair raised the public ire, and *The Times* reported that the convicted men suffered at the hands of a mob 'chiefly consisting of women, with tubs of blood, garbage, and ordure from their slaughter-houses, and with this ammunition, plentifully diversified with dead cats, turnips, potatoes, addled eggs, and other missiles, the criminals were incessantly pelted to the last moment'. They ended their hour 'completely encrusted with filth' and by the time the cart got them back to Newgate the wagon was 'so filled with mud and ordure as to completely cover them'.

The death of Thomas White was a sad end to a period of increasing awareness and toleration of homosexuality. Prosecutions had declined and the Enlightenment brought a different way of thinking regarding homosexuality. Sodomy was no longer simply something one 'did', but part of the wider picture of being a homosexual. By 1785, in his essay *Offences Against One's Self*, Jeremy Bentham advocated the decriminalization of homosexuality, as it 'might as well be said that the taste a man has for music is unnatural'.

Thomas Chatterton: faker, forger or genius?

Thomas White's death at seventeen had a tragic Romanticism which echoed the death of another Holborn seventeen-year-old, also named Thomas. In 1770, Thomas Chatterton took poison in a Holborn garret, gaining in death the reputation as a poet that he had sought in life. 'He was a prodigy almost without equal in the history of literature', and no other Romantic poet produced work of a comparable quality at such a young age. Yet the best of Chatterton's poems were fakes. He had written them, but pretended they were the work of Thomas Rowley, a fifteenth-century monk, and that he had discovered them in the church of St Mary Redcliff in Bristol, where he had grown up.

Thomas was apprenticed as an attorney's clerk at fourteen. His friends described him as slight, fair and scruffy, with large grey eyes. He was regularly caught writing poetry, which was then flung into the fire as punishment. Undeterred, he continued to contribute to the local papers and, despite his youth, acquired the reputation of something of a ladies' man.

He wrote to Horace Walpole, enclosing some of the work of Thomas Rowley. Ever the avid correspondent, Walpole answered by return, but when he showed Thomas Rowley's manuscripts to a friend they were denounced as fakes. Walpole felt taken in, having assumed from the assured tone of Thomas's letters that he was an adult antiquarian and not an apprentice clerk.

Equally, when Thomas Chatterton received Walpole's letter, he was hugely disappointed in his hero. After all, he had only sent the esteemed author samples of old poetry, making no claims for them. Nor had he asked for money, or advancement, and was bitterly upset by Walpole's patronizing advice to stick to his day job. Despite this setback, Thomas was soon writing political satire for the London press, gaining contacts and a route to London. Already, he had threatened to commit suicide if he was not able to pursue a career in writing. Those around him became alarmed by his threats, including his master, who cancelled his apprenticeship indenture and let him go. 'Farewell Bristolia's dingy piles of brick,' Thomas wrote as he left. He went to live with his cousin Mrs Ballance, in Shoreditch. The young boy who lodged with him would remember how 'not with-standing his pride and haughtiness, it was impossible to help liking him'. He also remembered that Thomas barely ate and rarely slept, sitting at the window all night to read instead.

Mrs Ballance was confused by her manic young cousin. She had once called him 'cousin Tommy' and was most upset when he had got into a temper and 'asked her if she had ever heard of a poet being called Tommy'. As insufferable as Thomas was, he had talent. Within two months of arriving in London, his work was published in the *Middlesex Journal*. He wrote elegies for the dead mayor and kept a tally in the back of his notebook: 'Am glad he is dead by: £3 3s 6d.'

He left Shoreditch, taking up residence in the garret of 29 Brooke Street, Holborn. His landlady was Mrs Angel and over the next weeks she would live up to her name, watching out for her young tenant as he grew ever thinner. He wrote like a dervish: short stories, skits, a long poem about indecent exposure and some others on Africa. He received a commission to write a *burletta* for Marylebone Gardens, and was paid five guineas for a comic piece about marital strife between Juno and Jupiter.

August fell upon London, and with it the lull of the long vacation. Thomas had not been paid for much of his work. He was also suffer-ing from venereal disease. Mr Cross was the Holborn chemist who passed the time of day with Thomas in the slow afternoons. He pressed Thomas to eat a meal with his family, but the young poet would not, except once taking a share in a barrel of oysters Mr Cross opened on the counter in an attempt to entice him. Mrs Angel, upon realizing that Thomas had not eaten to her knowledge for two to three days, asked him to share her dinner, but again he refused and went up to his garret. On the following morning, 24 August, she found him dead, having taken arsenic in water. He was covered in his own vomit and torn scraps of paper.

The verdict of the inquest was 'suicide by reason of insanity' and he was interred in the burial ground of Shoe Lane workhouse, but the legend of his thwarted genius had already begun. Many thought Horace Walpole instrumental in Thomas's death. Twelve years later, in 1782, the weight of public pressure had become so great that he felt a guilty need to publish his entire correspondence with the young poet over four issues of *The Gentleman's Magazine*. He concluded, 'all of the house of forgery are relations'.

Fakery, or falsehood, was a growing preoccupation throughout the eighteenth century. Fake coin was an ever present problem, but the very notion of what was real became pressing in the collective mind. Chatterton's work sits on the cusp of the Augustan pursuit of the rational nature of Truth, and the Romantic vision of the Truth of Beauty. He would influence both William Blake and Samuel Taylor Coleridge. Keats was devoted to him. When Horace Walpole died, he had collected eighteen volumes of scrapbooks of press clippings on Thomas. In an unguarded moment Samuel Johnson admitted that 'it is wonderful how the whelp has written such things'.

Lincoln's Inn Fields: bog-houses and The Beggar's Opera

Just south of Holborn, Lincoln's Inn Fields is now occupied by those practising law, but during the eighteenth century it had a more varied set of residents and a dangerous edge. It was built to designs by Inigo Jones and 'affords in its central enclosure one of the largest and finest public gardens in London, and in point of antiquity is perhaps the oldest'. The square itself sat between Covent Garden and the official border of the City, running down Chancery Lane. It encompassed the spectrum of London life: rich and poor, drama, art and science.

The original houses in the New Square were grand and imposing, but it had a bad reputation. John Gay, in his poem *The Art of Walking the Streets of London* warned readers in 1716:

> Where Lincoln's Inn's wide space is railed around,
> Cross not with venturous step; there oft is found
> The lurking thief, who, while the daylight shone
> Made the walls echo with his begging tone . . .

Beggars, and muggers posing as beggars, had been a problem in the square from the outset, as Londoners made their way to and from the City using the square and garden as a short cut. On the west side, in a stand of trees, was London's most famous bog-house, a public lavatory and the site of illicit engagements, as well as sexual-encounters-turned-muggings. The paths leading across the open space were where the beggar's crutch

> . . . which late compassion mov'd, shall wound
> Thy bleeding head, and fell thee to the ground.

Beggars were a constant preoccupation in Georgian London, and Lincoln's Inn Fields was shorthand for a beggar's haunt. Some of them were real, such as Scarecrow, 'who disabled himself in his right leg, and asks alms all day to get himself a warm supper and a trull at night'; and some were but beggarly fictions. The gardens were railed early specifically to prevent rough-sleepers. (Even now, centuries later, Lincoln's Inn Fields is one of the main locations for the feeding of the homeless. After dark, trucks catering to all denominations pull up and dispense food aid to dishevelled characters who flit in and out of the square.)

It seems more than coincidence that John Gay's 'Newgate pastoral' *The Beggar's Opera* premiered at the Lincoln's Inn Theatre, in 1728. The theatre had previously been a real tennis court, but was then taken over by the Rich family and rebuilt for staging dramas. The success of *The Beggar's Opera*, which ran to sixty-two consecutive performances, made 'Rich gay and Gay rich'. The opera, a comic English version poking fun at the fashion for Italian opera, starred the characters Polly Peachum and her roguish lover, Macheath the high-wayman, who would become staples of eighteenth-century literature and popular culture.

As the century progressed, Lincoln's Inn Fields continued to be populated by wealthy householders and poor vagrants. The arrival of the architect John Soane and his family, in 1782, when he bought Number 13 signalled that the square was on the up. He went on to buy Number 14 and integrate the two as his wealth and ambition increased. Almost all of John Soane's major works have been swept

away, giving him an almost mythical status amongst the great architects of the eighteenth century. Yet Soane was not universally
approved of during his lifetime, and his ruthless pursuit of success
and perfectionism made him unpopular.

The son of a 'common bricklayer' from Berkshire with a 'feverish
thirst for fame', John Soane rose to become one of London's premier
architects and art collectors. His houses, on the north side of the
square, were given over to collections of Greek and Roman marbles
and funerary urns, as well as Gothic affectations and contemporary
pictures, including Hogarth's 'Rake's Progress'. Soane was remarkable in the way he combined all types of architectural styles, some
Classical and some contemporary. His fascination with matters
funerary was reflected in his favourite room in his home, which was
based on a tomb and admits only an eerie crepuscular light. He relied
extensively on coloured glass to create odd light effects, and Mrs
Soane even dyed their net curtains with turmeric to complete the
effect of a house caught in a time warp. Soane was also a pioneer of
central heating, which he installed in his home together with hot
showers. Such modern thinking and dramatic effects did not always
win him friends, one commentator writing in the *Morning Post*:

> I presume you haven't lately passed through Lincoln's Inn Fields, oth-
> erwise I think you would have animadverted on a new-fangled
> projection now erecting on the Holborn side of that fine square. This
> ridiculous piece of architecture destroys the uniformity of the row
> and is a palpable eyesore.

But Soane's star was in the ascendant, despite his apparent unpop-
ularity and some bad misjudgements. He was appointed Professor of
Architecture at the Royal Academy, which had decreed that com-
ments or criticisms of living artists were not to be allowed in lectures.
Soane couldn't help himself, and he attacked his young competitor
Robert Smirke for the 'glaring impropriety' of his designs for the
new Covent Garden Theatre. The audience was shocked, and began
to hiss. Soane defended himself: 'It is extremely painful to me to be
obliged to refer to modern works.' The subsequent fallout led him to
suspend his lectures.

Such small matters, however illuminating, were not part of Soane's grand plan. When his sons disappointed him by not wanting to follow in his footsteps, he conceived the idea to gift his house and collection to the nation; in 1833, he obtained an Act of Parliament to do so. A comprehensive guidebook of the house by John Britton stated, in 1827, that it had not been 'adapted for spectacle and display but constructed from the beginning as an architecture of spectacle and display, a theatre of effects'. By leaving his house as a museum 'in perpetuity', Sir John Soane (as he would become) prompted some to 'wonder what sort of perpetuity he imagined? Was he thinking of a hundred or a thousand, or a hundred thousand years? A hundred would show him a prudent man, a thousand a vain man, and any longer term, a megalomaniac.' He was probably all three. Sir John Soane's house is still preserved by that Act of Parliament, and can be visited today.

Temple and the Inns of Court: London's seat of learning

The variety of residents in Lincoln's Inn Fields was an exception in an area of London otherwise dominated by the law. It lies just to the west of Chancery Lane, which is the spine of legal London. At the head is Gray's Inn, on Holborn. At the base nearest the river sit Middle and Inner Temple, inside the City limits. Outer Temple lay outside the City limits and was gradually phased out. Thus, the Inns of Court straddle the City boundaries, but they are a settlement quite apart from both the City and Westminster.

During the Elizabethan period the Inns flourished, becoming a busy camp of young men all eager to learn the law and to acquire the polish of London life. Law was not only a functioning machine but a web of theory to be moulded in the best way to serve both the people and the state. Each of the Inns had a hall for communal eating, a chapel for worship and a library for reference. Surprisingly, they offered relatively little instruction in the law; boys who wanted to learn it took private tuition. Without a formal structure of education and with no qualifying exam (introduced in 1852), getting called to the Bar was as much about personal charm and intellect as it was about knowledge of the law and ethical soundness.

During the eighteenth century, two men emerged from the Inns of Court who were utterly different, yet together saw the emergence of the 'modern' system of British legal representation. They made important advancements, not only for themselves but for the profession and for the state. They were also both outsiders who made their way up the system through a combination of hard work and intellect.

Thomas Erskine was the youngest son of the Earl of Buchan. Beautiful and clever, he had gone to sea at fourteen after a basic grammar school education in Scotland. The sea wasn't to his taste, so he raised enough money to buy a commission in the army. Aged twenty-two, he met James Boswell, who would later record that the young officer 'talked with a vivacity, fluency and precision so uncommon, that he attracted particular attention'. This fluency and ability led Thomas to consider a legal career. He put his name down at Trinity College, Cambridge; three years later, he obtained a degree without attending lectures. Meanwhile, he installed his young wife in Kentish Town with their growing family, so that his annual allowance of £300 could be eked out, whilst he studied law. By the summer of 1778, Erskine had been called to the Bar and his charm and intelligence brought in the cases thick and fast. He soon gained a reputation as a liberal intellectual who believed in freedom of speech and the press, taking on cases in which he and his clients emerged as the victors owing to his mastery of 'the art of addressing a jury'. In 1792, he defended Thomas Paine when he was charged with seditious libel after the publication of the *Rights of Man*. Although he was unsuccessful in this case, Erskine famously lectured barristers on the need to take on even unpopular and risky cases.

Erskine came to prominence through charm and oration whilst assisting Lloyd Kenyon, who was the opposite of his young protégé. Born in Wales in 1732, he served his term drudging for an attorney, learning the rules of Chancery law. He was called to the Bar young, in 1756, but couldn't get any work because he was no good as a public speaker and had few contacts. He was appointed Master of the Rolls, which is the right-hand judge serving the premier judge, Lord Chief

Justice. In this position, he was in charge of the tedious but important arm of Chancery law, something he was eminently trained for. His work became the benchmark others strove to follow. Four years later, he succeeded the Earl of Mansfield as Lord Chief Justice, a post he held until his death. He was hugely admired as a judge, and played the perfect counterpart to the charming persuader his assistant had become by being patient, full of knowledge and 'of the most determined integrity'.

A career in law during the eighteenth century was random and opportunistic, but Erskine and Kenyon represent the best of it – and also the emergence of our modern court systems and the move towards trial by jury.

Erskine and Kenyon are fine examples of the sort of men the Inns were producing during the eighteenth century, but not all their colleagues were quite so diligent. The area of the Inns was an affluent one, and there were large groups of young, privileged men with time on their hands, who enjoyed all that the area had to offer. The Royal Society had moved here in 1710, when Isaac Newton negotiated the purchase of a small house in Crane Court just north of Fleet Street. Samuel Johnson lived nearby, in a house which is now a museum in his memory; his local pub, The Cheshire Cheese, is still standing. Mrs Salmon's Wax Works stood near the entrance to Middle Temple, where one might see waxworks of kings and queens, and where an automated waxwork of 'Old Mother Shipton, the witch, kicked the astonished visitor as he left'. On the south side of the road near Temple Bar was the favourite coffee house of the young men of the Inns, called Nando's.

Between 1710 and 1712 a group of young men, mostly in their late teens and early twenties, would use Nando's as a focus for their violent gangs, called the Mohocks. The Mohocks were active throughout the year, mainly along Holborn and the Strand and in Westminster. They drank heavily, smoked marijuana and tried to act like the savages they took as their namesake.

Marijuana was in use as a recreational drug in London from the late seventeenth century. Robert Hooke lectured on it at the Royal Society in 1689/90 and noted that it rendered the user

... unable to speak a Word of Sense; yet is he very merry, and laughs, and sings ... yet is he not giddy, or drunk, but walks and dances ... after a little Time he falls asleep, and sleepeth very soundly and quietly; and when he wakes, he finds himself mightily refresh'd, and exceeding hungry.

Hooke obtained his score from a sea captain in a coffee house, no doubt along with many others.

The Mohocks committed acts of street violence on both men and women, but although their victims appear randomly chosen, the damage inflicted was not. Watchmen were badly beaten and women humiliated. Two women were stabbed through the lower lip, perhaps in a bizarre piercing ritual.

When caught, the men were all young 'gentlemen' and often associated with the Inns of Court. Bail was set at hundreds of pounds. The ringleader of the 1712 violence was thought to be Lord Hinchingbrooke, but his arrest did not stop him becoming a Member of Parliament the following year. Some of those arrested for involvement in the violence were later called to the Bar.

Students didn't only learn the law, but also dancing and fencing and various other social skills thought necessary. In 1744, a court case at the Old Bailey recorded the trial of Ann Duck, born in 'Little White Alley, Chancery-lane, the Daughter of one Duck, a Black, well known to many Gentlemen in our Inns of Court, by teaching them the Use of the Small Sword, of which he was a very good master'. Ann went on to teach young men the use of the small sword too, but as a prostitute.

As a community of young affluent men, the Inns of Court were a natural magnet for prostitutes of the better sort. The ward of Farringdon Without contained over seventy bawdy houses – more than half the City's brothels in the early part of the century. There was speculation that educated young women who had fallen on hard times ventured into longer-term agreements with the students, flitting in and out of Temple or Lincoln's Inn with their faces masked. Common prostitutes also sought keepers amongst the students and barristers, such as the 'luscious' Miss Sh——rd:

. . . a most pleasing *pupil* of *pleasure*, and perfectly competent to the instruction of those who desire to be announced *Students* of the *mysteries of Venus*. She is about 20, and a single guinea will content her . . . [she] has several City friends, and lawyers from Gray's Inn and Temple.

And so, even the respectable legal engine of London hosted gangs, drug takers and prostitutes, making many barristers not so far removed from those who sat in the dock.

At the beginning of the eighteenth century, the margins of the City were little more than a varied combination of hotchpotch urban overspill, but soon the old houses and brothels were swept away in a frenzy of building and rebuilding. Only Temple and the Inns of Court remain almost unchanged since the early eighteenth century, when a new London had already run away westwards along the Strand.

3.   Westminster and St James's

Westminster is London's second city. Since the twelfth century, it has been the seat of government and of the sovereign. By 1700, it was far from the grand administrative centre we know now. It was a small settlement which had grown up around ancient palaces, religious houses and a school. Whitehall Palace, built by Cardinal Wolsey and appropriated by Henry VIII, was the sprawling home of the civil service until it burned down in 1698 after a maid left sheets drying too close to the fire. Inigo Jones's Banqueting Hall was the only building to remain intact. The opportunity to rebuild to any coherent plan was missed, as John Gwynne, the man whose grand plans for London came to nothing, observed: 'why so wretched a use has been made of so valuable and desirable an opportunity of displaying taste and elegance in this part of the town is a question that very probably would puzzle the builders themselves to answer'.

Nearby, the medieval Palace of Westminster sat by the river and was used for the two Houses of Parliament. Today, Parliament Square is a jostling roundabout, with police in high-visibility clothing restricting access to only the chosen few. But in the eighteenth century, Parliament struggled on with an increasingly shabby and dilapidated set of buildings surrounded by open ground and mixed housing, much of the latter dating from the Middle Ages. The faded grandeur of the palace and the nearby poverty was revealed nowhere more starkly than just behind Westminster Abbey. Beyond a smattering of new streets were the slums and ugly open ground of Tothill Fields, where boys played football and pigs rooted in the cinder heaps. It was a dangerous area, and Westminster School, whose pupils had included Christopher Wren and John Locke, was not immune to the atmosphere. In the autumn of 1679, a group of 'Gentleman Schollars' were tried for kicking to death a bailiff who had entered the school to make an arrest. 'After some mature consideration of their Youth

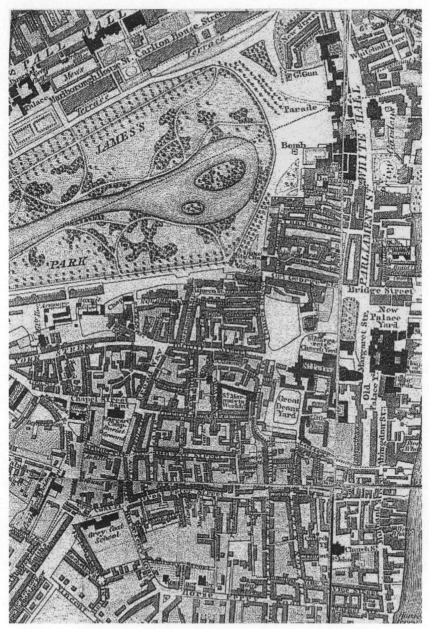

Westminster, detail from John Greenwood's map, 1827

and Quality' they were let off, but the young scholars were a constant presence in the taverns and eating houses around the school, where they mixed with every type of Londoner. Near the school, a slum on Pye Street became known as The Devil's Acre. The palace and the abbey were no more than 'a stately veneer for the hovels crouching behind'. From these 'labyrinths of lanes and courts and alleys and slums, nests of ignorance, vice, depravity and crime' issued forth Westminster's underclass.

The poorest women of this slum sifted the cinder heaps for anything still worth burning. Some were also the lowest class of prostitute, the filthy scarecrows of caricature, with ragged and toothless mouths. Many were dependent upon charity, and St Margaret's workhouse was one of London's oldest. St Margaret's is the official church of the

'Love and Dust', by Thomas Rowlandson, 1788, a
caricature of paupers on Tothill Fields, Westminster

Houses of Parliament. The associated workhouse moved locations through the century but the institution in Little Almonry pioneered maternity care in the 1740s, offering courses in midwifery at vastly reduced rates for women who were to work amongst the local poor. They were taught alongside the young male students, who paid handsomely for their lessons and would go on to lucrative careers as 'man-midwives'. The contrast of rich and poor in the area meant the Members of Parliament were reminded constantly of their duties to the less fortunate members of society. They had only to walk out of the Palace Yard to see the cinder-women and infants scavenging on the Tothill laystalls. Gaggles of poor children trailed behind an older brother or sister, left in charge while parents worked. On a Saturday in 1762, in a run-down alley near Tothill Fields, Mary Flarty left her toddler Jerry with five-year-old Anne Ellison. The alley had no traffic, and seemed safe for young children. Jerry tried to use the special low seat for youngsters in the communal privy, and fell into the cesspit. Although the community rallied immediately to retrieve the boy, Jerry was already dead. Cesspits, wells and carriage wheels were all waiting for a moment's inattention.

The government's awareness of the social problems of poverty was growing. Urban poverty was becoming more obvious and pressing as the population increased. Riots, though often attached to political causes, were usually closely linked to empty bellies. The greatest of these, the Gordon Riots, where Parliament was attacked by a rampaging mob, made London realize it needed a police force. Although many in the government saw the police as little more than a standing army, they realized by 1780 that without a police force London would be ungovernable. With greater organization came bigger and better prisons, built on new designs. Nearby, to the west, was Millbank, home of the horse ferry and 'so called from a mill on the bank of the river'. There the forbidding Millbank Prison was built in 1821, to a design by philosopher Jeremy Bentham. It was a terrifying labyrinth in which even the warders got lost, and the prisoners used the bizarre acoustics to communicate between cells. It held large numbers of prisoners waiting for transportation; for many years, a prison hulk lurked on the river outside.

Behind Westminster, open land lay undeveloped as far as Knights-bridge. When Charles II came to the throne, in 1660, he chose to live in St James's Palace and left behind the medieval architecture, slums and cinders of Westminster for the countryside. He created the Arcadian St James's Park, with water features and walks. He also created a demand for new housing of the smartest sort, resulting in the development of St James's Fields. This was housing for London's most fashionable, including rich foreign visitors in temporary lodgings. When the business of the day had been dispensed with, including the coffee house visit and parliamentary business:

> . . . the evening is devoted to pleasure; all the world get abroad in their gayest equipage between four and five in the evening, some bound to the play, others to the opera, the assembly, the masquerade, or musick-meeting, to which they move in such crowds, that their coaches can scarce pass the streets.

These 'new rich' were not entirely self-serving. As in Westminster, there was a growing awareness of the division between rich and poor. The spectre of poverty was never far from even the grandest doorstep, and even the palaces admitted chars to do the washing. The cheek-by-jowl relationship of Westminster and St James's nurtured some of the country's most remarkable men and women. Thinkers, politicians and fashionistas all congregated in this rapidly growing district, the polite area of London, so different from the City's mercantile origins.

Providing for the urban poor: the Workhouse Act

After the Reformation, Protestant England used local parish officials to distribute part of the land tax as charity, uniting Church and State in providing for the poor. The Poor Law of 1601 meant that to obtain parish charity an individual had to belong to that parish. Belonging was not as simple as taking up residence: poor would-be settlers were often removed by parish officers, and it was a widely held belief that the Poor Law gave those living in poverty an incentive to continue their breadline existence without working.

Vagrancy was a preoccupation of the Middle Ages, when decent citizens feared tinkers, pedlars and other itinerant workers. Their estrangement from community ties was seen as a threat to society, and they were associated with decayed morality and petty crime. Yet as the country entered the modern era, migration became essential. Seasonal workers, domestic servants and those simply wishing or needing to find employment gravitated towards towns – London, in particular. 'Settlement' in a new parish was gained through a complicated system of qualification. By 1700, settlement could be gained through birth, marrying into the parish, serving an apprenticeship there, working there for a year or serving as a parish officer.

In the medieval period, when towns were small and prosperous, poverty was more a rural phenomenon, experienced when crops failed, or murrains killed off the livestock. The system of poor relief which emerged in the mid-sixteenth century concentrated on taking care of the sick or those who were old and infirm with no one else to care for them. But as towns, and particularly London, grew in the late seventeenth century, urban poverty – unrelated to seasonal highs and lows – became part of the landscape. St Margaret's parish had built workhouses in Tothill around 1624, to house the old and infirm but not the able-bodied poor, who were supposed to be able to shift for themselves.

Urban poverty was often more desperate than rural poverty because urban life was more dependent upon money. In the countryside, foraged food and wood for fuel were available, even if in short supply. Those who paid rent paid it quarterly, or exchanged their labour for housing. In the rapidly growing London of the eighteenth century, however, people rented rooms by the month, week or even day. The available fuel was coal, which cost money. Food was brought into the capital and retailed. In order to appear employable, particularly in service, clean linen and tidy clothes were essential. Life in London was expensive.

Appearing poor was a thing to be avoided at all costs. John Loppenberg was a servant in Westminster and later St James's who used to go to the ponds at Paddington early in the morning to wash his linen:

I was ashamed to be seen doing it by any body, because it was torn and ragged. I went to one Pond, and saw People there, so I went to another . . . I hung my Shirt up to dry, and walked to and fro while it was drying, and saw two Men walking about; I threw the Shirt from me least they should laugh at me.

John Loppenberg was typical of many London servants who lived on the edge of respectability and were always in fear of 'being out of a place'. People arrived from overseas, or elsewhere in Britain, because they were following an employer. Should they fall on hard times and throw themselves on the mercy of a parish within that year, the overseers were perfectly within their rights to move them along – by force, if necessary, though this happened relatively rarely.

The Season, stretching from March until the end of July, saw peak demand for employment in Westminster and St James's. Anyone with pretensions to fashion or business was in town for those months, requiring servants, washerwomen, errand boys and porters. They also provided work for shoemakers, tailors, prostitutes and thieves. In the hard winter months, when working the streets was impossible, and there was less demand for jobbing servants, workhouse numbers rose by up to 25 per cent.

In wealthy London, the urban workhouse developed rapidly after the Workhouse Act of 1723. The Act meant, in brief, that in order for the destitute to claim parish charity they had to enter the workhouse and 'work' for the good of the parish. 'Outdoor relief' (payments made to people so that they could remain in their own homes) was available, but this didn't help people like John Loppenberg if they were to lose both their job and accommodation at the same time. But workhouses did acknowledge the new developments in medicine and social welfare. There were wards for pregnant women, as well as labour wards, wards for the sick, the healthy, same-sex wards and rooms for the married. Inmates wore uniforms bearing the parish badge. Unmarried mothers were sometimes made to wear yellow gowns. Those who behaved badly had to wear special uniforms or distinctive badges.

As the century progressed, workhouses became more developed and more socially conscious; they were no longer housing just the disabled, infirm and aged, but men and women who had fallen on hard times, as well as their attendant children. In 1817, St Martin-in-the-Fields workhouse admitted two-thirds adults and one-third children. The women made up 60 per cent of the adult population and stayed on average for six weeks, two and a half days. In contrast, the men averaged two weeks and six days. It is clear to see that there was a pattern: it was easier for men to get back on their feet. A third of the women of childbearing age who were admitted were in the later stages of pregnancy, and alone.

Being in the workhouse was undesirable, but it wasn't seen as a punishment. For many of the poorest families it was viewed as a temporary solution to the temporary problem of destitution. They could, and did, leave when they thought they would be able to make their own way again. It was often far harder to get into the workhouse than it was to get out. There are instances of non-parish women in labour and victims of industrial accidents being turned away. For the duration of their stay inmates had to submit to rules on sobriety, smoking and visitors. Sometimes children were taken in alone, during periods of parental absence or inability to provide care. Sometimes wives and children were taken in when the wife was sick, and the husband would visit once or twice a week whilst continuing to work, trying to get the family back on their feet.

Workhouses not only provided food and shelter, they were also where medicine and care could be found. Soon after the Workhouse Act, many workhouses introduced separate infirmaries. St Sepulchre's installed 'an oven' in which to heat inmates' clothing to kill pests, and this was also offered as a public service to the parish poor outside the workhouse.

Towards the end of the eighteenth century, more and more people had to move to towns to find work, gain skills and better themselves. The young men and women who left their rural backgrounds to take up offers of work in London had no safety net other than friends or family already there. If it didn't work out, they were faced with a long trudge home or a scramble to find other employment. In 1796, Matthew Martin opened his Mendicity Enquiry Office at 190 Piccadilly. His idea was simple, but effective: he produced 6,000 numbered tickets, each promising the bearer threepence upon its presentation at the Office. To earn their 3d the bearer had to submit to an interview which Martin had devised in order to shed light upon both the causes and conditions of the increase in desperate poverty in London.

In under eight months, he filled dozens of volumes with the stories of over 2,000 adults and their 3,000 dependent children. He excluded 600 individuals who would not consent to being labelled as beggars. What emerges is that the vast majority of Martin's poor were single mothers. The numbers are telling: 192 men to 1,808 women. Martin concluded that men were stronger than women, with more resources. Occasionally employers kept women on through illegitimate pregnancies, but we cannot estimate how many there might have been. Above all, a woman was likely to be thrown into a state of advanced or abject poverty by the burden of children for whom she received no support. Martin's Mendicity Studies are one of the few to make transparent how large the poor female population was.

In addition, the new theories of Thomas Malthus and Jeremy Bentham were alarming Londoners. Contrary to what they had always thought was a declining population, Malthus told them that soon there wouldn't be enough food to feed the burgeoning poor. Bentham's utilitarianism promoted the greatest good for the greatest number. Quasi-charitable bodies were formed in the early nineteenth century, such as the Society for the Suppression of Mendicity, in 1818. The Duke of York was the Patron, the Duke of Northumberland the President, and the officers included four marquesses, eight earls and Matthew Martin. Its philosophy was concerned with the economics of poverty and sifting the 'deserving poor' from the 'vagrants', much in the same way as we now have the political touchstones of 'hard-working families' and 'benefit scroungers'.

For the first three decades of the nineteenth century, it was increasingly apparent that something must change. In 1832, a Royal Commission determined that the old system was outdated and not up to the task in hand. In 1834, the Poor Law Amendment Act ushered in a new era. The workhouses became something to be feared: they were to be run on the cheapest terms; food was of poor quality and in short measure; rules were draconian. Miserable and scanty, there was little of charity about them. The old workhouses, designed as a temporary prop to support the lowest classes and thus the city itself, had a humanity to them. In the same way that the 1832 Reform Act enfranchised London's new middle classes, the 1834 Poor Law Amendment Act further disenfranchised her poor. Poverty became a numbers game.

Westminster Bridge: lotteries and the Jernegan cistern

Much of the debate surrounding poverty centred on public funds. Public money was historically associated with the parishes, and used on a local level. Urban improvements such as street lighting and paving were initially funded by householders on a street-by-street basis, further adding to the variety of London's landscape. As the city grew, it became clear that it needed infrastructure. But where to find the money?

The generation of public funds, and how to spend them, was a puzzle. The story of Westminster Bridge is an example of just how confused the government had become: in the late 1730s, they held a series of lotteries to build the bridge.

London Bridge connected the City to Surrey in the south, but Westminster had no crossing of its own besides 'the ancient Horse-ferry between Westminster and Lambeth'. The need for a bridge was pressing, and an Act was passed, as noted in *The London Gazette*, 'for building a bridge cross the River Thames, from the New Palace Yard in the City of Westminster, to the opposite Shore in the county of Surrey'. Plans were called for and, in 1736, put out to tender amongst the engineering community. But money for construction was the real sticking point. Around half the money was raised by a series of five lotteries, one of which offered as first prize the largest known surviving piece of English silver, the Jernegan cistern.

Henry Jernegan came from a family of Catholic gentry and started out as a banker. He acquired Littleton Pointz Meynell as a client. Meynell was a gambler. His wins were mammoth, his losses likewise. When he was winning, Jernegan made attempts to divert his client's capital into works of art in solid silver. This helped Jernegan mitigate his

losses through commission, and made sure his client had money in commodities. In 1730, Jernegan and Meynell decided to create the biggest
wine cistern ever. The cistern holds sixty gallons and is formed from
over a quarter of a ton of silver. A piece of silver weighing more than a
quarter of a ton takes time to make, and when it was finished, so was
Meynell. Jernegan was stuck with an enormous white elephant.

The government was still short of money for the building of Westminster Bridge. Jernegan petitioned Parliament, where he explained
that he had 'designed and made a silver cistern, acknowledged to excel
anything of the kind hitherto attempted, but that four years later, the
cistern remained on his hands notwithstanding his best attempts to dispose of it to foreign princes'. In desperation, he offered the cistern as
first prize in a lottery in aid of funds for the bridge. In exchange, he
would take a cut of the ticket sales in an attempt to recoup some of his
losses. A Dorset farmer won first prize but, there being little call for a
rococo silver bathtub in Dorset, he sold it. By the following year, it was
in Russia in the collection of Regent Anna Leopoldovna. Perhaps
Jernegan's error was in trying to dispose of it to foreign princes, rather
than to a princess. It remains in the Hermitage Museum, the largest
extant piece of antique solid silver in the world.

The lottery over, the government put in the rest of the money to
ensure that Westminster Bridge would become a reality. The maze of
narrow slum alleys around the southern end of King Street was cleared
to make way for the road to the bridge, and it finally opened on 18
November 1750. It was hailed as 'a very great ornament to our metropolis, and will be looked on with pleasure or envy by all foreigners. The
surprising echo in the arches, brings much company with French horns
to entertain themselves under it in summer.' Alcoves over each pier
were designed to offer shelter in bad weather, but pessimists feared
they 'might be used by robbers and cut-throats who, if it were not for
the special guard of 12 watchmen and the high balustrades, might set
on unwary travellers and push their bodies into the river'.

Bodies in the river were a continual concern, and the addition of
the high balustrades 'was to prevent the suicide to which the English
have so strong a propensity, particularly in the gloomy month of
November'. Despite the balustrades, Westminster Bridge claimed its

fair share of suicides, most of them nameless and seen only as a tumble of clothing and a brief impact with the water, then recovered later somewhere downriver. One London visitor who narrowly avoided meeting a watery end on Westminster Bridge one gloomy November night is not usually famed for his melancholy temperament.

Giacomo Casanova had arrived in London in 1763 with plans to start his own lottery and to see his illegitimate daughter, who lived in Soho Square. He took a house on Pall Mall and a mistress before he became infatuated with the young courtesan Anne Marie Charpillon. La Charpillon was most particular about her customers and determinedly had a headache whenever Casanova called. On one visit, however, he found her beneath her hairdresser and promptly smashed the place up. He returned to Pall Mall, pulled on his greatcoat, filled the pockets with a large quantity of lead shot and walked towards the river. He remembered walking slowly because of the immense weight he was carrying in his pockets. Standing on the bridge and summoning his courage, he was interrupted in his thoughts by young Welbore Ellis. Welbore was twenty-eight, and a cheerful soul. He remarked that Casanova looked glum and offered to take him for a drink and something to eat. Casanova refused and said he wanted to walk, so Welbore walked with him, in the end guiding him to a tavern where he paid a young woman to strip naked and dance the hornpipe to amuse him. Welbore's intervention probably saved Casanova's life; he didn't return to Westminster Bridge. Instead, he bought a parrot and taught it to say, 'Mademoiselle Charpillon is more of a whore even than her mother,' before leaving it at the Royal Exchange to impart this knowledge to passers-by.

Westminster Hall and the Court of the King's Bench: *'Let justice be done, though the heavens fall'*

Westminster Hall dates from the latter part of the eleventh century, and 'was formerly made use of by the kings, &c., for feasting, and as a room to relieve the poor'. Its 'length is two hundred and seventy feet; the breadth seventy-four'. The remarkable roof dates from the reign of Richard II and is 'most curiously constructed, and of a fine species of *gothic*'. In the late fifteenth century, the Court of the King's Bench made its home there, along with trinket shops and the bookstalls run by Westminster School. Outside was a sundial inscribed: *Be Gone About Your Business*. 'It is said the dial-maker sent his lad to ask for the inscription, but an irascible old bencher ordered him away with "Be gone about your business!" Thus the lad told his master this was the desired inscription.' Later, coffee sheds grouped around the North Door, and in a building nearby Mr Waghorn's coffee house became a popular destination. Waghorn's had a large balcony overlooking 'the House of Peers', which was packed on days of holidays and processions. In the gatehouse of Westminster Hall was a small prison, one of many secure places dotted around London where people could be confined.

The dangers and injustices of eighteenth-century prison life are apparent in the case of Mary Ferril, an inmate of the gatehouse, in 1720. She accused fellow prisoners Edward Wooldridge and John Nichols, of St Margaret's Westminster, of raping her. In court she testified, 'At about two a Clock in the Morning . . . they both forced her . . . one stood at the Door while the other lay with her.' That Wooldridge and Nichols had both had sex with Mary was not disputed, since both men 'as soon as they were up the next Morning, bragg'd that they had lain with the little Woman above Stairs'. That it had been a demeaning and possibly abusive encounter for Mary was not in question, but the court heard she was in the gatehouse for beating her mother and verbally abusing a Justice of the Peace, and that she had worked as a prostitute when she and her husband hit hard times. One witness 'said that she was a Fool of a Woman that could not take a Stroke without telling her Husband . . . The Jury considering the whole Matter, Acquitted them.'

Although being violent, abusive and a part-time prostitute had not helped Mary's case, a key failing was that the incident had taken place in her cell in the prison. Most successful rape prosecutions in London during the eighteenth century involved abduction. Unlawful detention had been a preoccupation of English identity since Magna Carta. The later evolution of habeas corpus is one of the central tenets of the legal system. John Locke continued this theme when he asserted the freedom of each man or woman to 'own' their own body.

Infringements upon personal physical freedom were taken seriously by the law, making abduction a grave offence. In the muddled complications of many rape accusations, it was a concrete fact.

In the 1757 trial of Daniel Lackey for the rape of Christian Streeter, the fact that she went with him willingly from the Hercules Tavern near Westminster Bridge to his lodgings in Ryder Street, in St James's, was vital to his acquittal. In 1797, when 37-year-old John Briant was tried for the rape of fourteen-year-old milkmaid Jane Bell on a summer's evening in Green Park, the physical manner in which he stopped her crying out and forced her away from the cows into a secluded 'hollow' was dwelt on as much as the rape itself. They were discovered by unemployed housemaid Sarah Scott, who berated Briant for a 'rascal' and said that he should avail himself of a willing prostitute rather than 'a child'. She 'laid hold of him; I collared the man' and it was through her intervention that Briant was brought to trial. Despite Briant's previous good character, and the many witnesses who appeared for him in court, Scott's evidence along with Jane Bell's clear testimony of how she was abducted and subsequently raped were enough to secure a guilty verdict. Briant was sentenced to death.

That rape cases even came to court was a reflection of the legal system – for defendants, prosecutors and their representatives. Throughout the eighteenth century, the conviction rate in rape cases stood at about 17 per cent on average, reflecting the belief that access to the courts and legal redress for ordinary people was a basic function of eighteenth-century law.

In Westminster Hall, lawyers sat in booths and gave succinct advice to anyone who could pay them for a few minutes. These men were often depicted as grasping, but it allowed ordinary people to consult a lawyer at a fixed price. The courts sat in open view in another part of the hall, making decisions on matters both petty and great. Although England had a great legal tradition by the Middle Ages, the eighteenth century saw law and philosophy combine to create laws which recognized modern sensibilities. Dedication to a cause, stamina and debate could – and did – change society.

At the turn of the eighteenth century, there was concern about the status of slaves arriving in England from the Colonies. In 1690, John

Locke stated in his *Second Treatise of Government* that it was a basic right 'not to be subject to the inconstant, uncertain, unknown, arbitrary will of another man', reflected in the courts' approach to rape cases. Yet Locke owned shares in the Royal African Company, which traded in slaves and wrote the 110th Statute of South Carolina: 'Every freeman of Carolina shall have absolute power and authority over his negro slaves, of what opinion or religion soever.' In 1729, the Yorke–Talbot legal ruling decreed that slaves did not become free on English soil. In 1772, the Somersett ruling changed everything.

In 1765, surgeon William Sharp treated Jonathan Strong, a slave beaten to the point of losing an eye and then abandoned in the street by his master, David Lisle. When Strong had recovered, Lisle reclaimed him as property. Granville Sharp, William's brother, engaged in a legal battle to free Strong, and lost. Sharp became an advocate for the rights of slaves and, in 1772, masterminded the test case of James Somersett. Somersett had arrived in England as the property of Charles Stewart, a Boston customs official, and was baptized in St Andrew's Holborn early in 1771, with three godparents standing for him. When he wished to leave Stewart's employment, he was abducted and put on a ship for Jamaica. Sharp arranged for the case to come to court and published pamphlets which garnered public interest. The presiding figure was Lord Mansfield, a moderate and educated man. At his home, Kenwood House in Hampstead, lived his illegitimate mixed-race grand-niece, Dido Elizabeth Belle.

Mansfield was heavily criticized by the pro-slavery community for being influenced by 'a Black [Dido] in his house which governs him and the whole family'. Thomas Hutchinson, Governor of Massachusetts, went to dinner with the family and noted in his diary that:

A Black came in after dinner and sat with the ladies and after coffee, walked with the company in the gardens, one of the young ladies having her arm within the other. She had a very high cap and her wool was much frizzled in her neck, but not enough to answer the large curls now in fashion. She is neither handsome nor genteel - pert enough . . . He calls her Dido, which I suppose is all the name she has. He knows he has been reproached for showing fondness for her - I dare not say criminal.

Mansfield tried to persuade Stewart to settle by selling Somersett to his godparents, but neither side was having it. Both parties were determined to see the law decided once and for all. Mansfield ruled that habeas corpus applied to anyone in England, even if they originated elsewhere. He was aware of the significance of his ruling, stating, '*Fiat justitia ruat caelum*,' or, 'Let justice be done, though the heavens fall.' It was the beginning of the end of slavery, though it would take many more years for the abolitionist movement to triumph. Londoners everywhere discussed and debated the position of slavery within a 'free society'. The Westminster Forum, one of the premier debating societies, posed the same question over many years and, increasingly, invited 'ingenious Africans' to speak at debates, inquiring:

> Can any political or commercial advantages justify a free people in continuing the Slave Trade? A NATIVE OF AFRICA, many years a Slave in the West-Indies, will attend . . . and communicate to the audience a number of very remarkable circumstances respecting the treatment of the Negroe Slaves, and particularly of his being forcibly taken from his family and friends, on the coast of Africa, and sold as a Slave.

Mansfield had made slavery on English soil difficult, but not impossible. When he died, in 1793, he made sure to 'confirm' Dido's freedom in his will. The trade in unpleasant racist pamphlets continued, using the Somersett case as an excuse to pontificate upon 'the negroe cause', but for the ordinary people in Westminster, and throughout London, integration was the new reality.

Living happily in Westminster, above his grocery, was Ignatius Sancho. He was born either on a slave ship or in Greenwich. The Duke of Montagu saw Sancho on Blackheath and brought him home to amuse his wife, Lady Mary. She died in 1751 and left him with a year's salary and a £30 annuity. Sancho promptly fell to women and cards. However, after an 'unsuccessful contest at cribbage with a Jew, who won his cloaths', he appears to have given up gambling. He returned as a valet to his old employer's son-in-law, George Brudenell, who had assumed his wife's name for himself and their children, in 1749, to prevent it dying out. When his father-in-law died, George was created the 1st Duke of Montagu, reviving the title in 'the second creation'. George

Brudenell inherited the mantle of John Montagu in more ways than one, and he continued the latter's charity towards the somewhat hapless Sancho. Whilst in George Montagu's employ, Sancho married Ann Osborne, a young woman of 'West-Indian origin'. By 1773, he was crippled by gout and could no longer work for the Duke, who set him up with a freehold in Westminster and a small grocery.

He was a prolific letter writer and one written to Laurence Sterne, in 1766, gives a neat picture of his life: 'I am one of those people who the vulgar and illiberal call "Negurs".' Also in 1776, he wrote of the slave trade 'it is a subject that sours my blood'. Sancho loved music and published three collections in his lifetime, making him Britain's first native black composer. After his death, a collection of his letters was published, full of the trivia of eighteenth-century life and also one of its landmarks: in the summer of 1779, he hoped that the family dog, Nutts, would not catch fleas in the heat; and in September of 1780, he wrote to his friend Mrs Cocksedge that he had cast his 'free vote' in the election of that year in favour of Charles James Fox. Ignatius Sancho was the first recorded black voter in Britain.

When he died, in December of that year, *The Gentleman's Magazine* featured the first known British obituary of a black individual, recording simply: 'In Charles-str. Westminster, Mister Ignatius Sancho, grocer and oilman; a character immortalized by the epistolary correspondence of Sterne.' There was no mention of his race. It was Joseph Jekyll who, in 1782, published a biography of Sancho along with an edition of his letters, and coined the phrase which would immortalize the Westminster butler and grocer as 'the Extraordinary Negro'.

The Houses of Parliament: 'A man can never be great that is not popular, especially in England'

The British government operated from the old palace of Westminster in a series of cramped and dilapidated rooms, as outdated as the system which filled them with MPs. Busy debating societies advertised in the papers, calling politically minded citizens to taverns and coffee houses to pick apart foreign policies and domestic matters.

'Sedition' became an ever greater preoccupation as the government, if not King George III, began to realize their powers over the ordinary people had limits. The right to vote, so long the preserve of a few free-holders, was, as a result of the property boom, becoming the right of many independent Londoners. Parliament would evolve rapidly during the eighteenth century to cope with changes in society and the wider world as Britain established an Empire. Within Westminster, three events would act as catalysts for change in the old system: the John Wilkes affair, the Gordon Riots and the election of 1784.

Political corruption was endemic for most of the eighteenth century. Even those who entered Parliament with the most altruistic of motives often utilized the ancient system of rotten or pocket boroughs to secure their seat. These boroughs were constituencies in which the vote could be influenced. In many rural areas this was tolerated, where social ties or allegiances to local landowners held sway, but London was a city of independent traders. Men voted as they saw fit, and were proud of it; few had a landlord looking over their shoulder as they cast their vote. By the middle of the eighteenth century, many realized that the political system as it stood was unsatisfactory and did not reflect the way the city and the nation was growing and changing. One man, John Wilkes, would highlight many of the deficiencies of the British government.

Born in Clerkenwell in 1725, Wilkes was the son of a distiller. Physically he was unappealing, cross-eyed and with a severe underbite. This did not dissuade him from making the pursuit of women one of his foremost concerns. After a short-lived and unsuccessful marriage, he settled in London with his daughter, Polly, and a year later had bribed himself into a seat in the House of Commons, as Member of Parliament for Aylesbury.

While Wilkes' disadvantages in the looks department did not hamper his success with women, they did hamper his success as a speaker in the House. In 1762, he turned to the written word to express his political opinions. On 5 June, he began to publish the anti-Scottish magazine *The North Briton* anonymously. The following year, he used issue 45 to attack the King's speech for the opening of Parliament. It had been written by Lord Bute, a Scottish minister popularly associated with Jacobitism. Even the number 45 was symbolic, evoking the Jacobite Rebellion of 1745. The attack on the King was too thinly veiled. On 26 April, the government put out a warrant to find and arrest the anonymous author of *The North Briton*. Four days later, John Wilkes was arrested and taken to the Tower of London. His house was searched and his papers confiscated.

The government had made a huge mistake. Wilkes, despite his sly appearance and financial incontinence, was popular. He was also canny. He argued that his arrest was unlawful and that as an MP he could not be arrested for libel. When he was taken from the Tower to Westminster Hall to plead his case, he was accompanied by cheering crowds yelling the rallying cry which was to become a London legend: 'Wilkes and Liberty!'

It was clear that a gulf was opening up between the courts of Westminster and the government. Wilkes was released on 6 May, and won £1,000 in damages against the government for trespass. This could not, however, plug the holes in his finances.

John Wilkes was not only in financial trouble but also incapable of keeping himself out of mischief. As soon as he was free, he began to print *The North Briton* as a collected volume, seeing it as a useful way to bring in some money. He also printed a small number of copies of a poem he had written, for limited circulation amongst his friends. This poem was a spoof of Alexander Pope's *Essay on Man*, entitled *Essay on Woman*, and began with the line, 'Awake, my Fanny!' It goes downhill from there.

The poem was read out in the Lords. In the Commons, Samuel Martin called Wilkes a coward, and the two fought a duel in Hyde Park the next morning. Wilkes took a shot to the groin and for some time was dangerously ill. Realizing the game was up, he escaped to Paris on Christmas Eve 1763.

He was expelled from the House of Commons, tried by Lord Mansfield in his absence, and found guilty. But Paris was not for a man like Wilkes. For one thing, he didn't have deep enough pockets and was soon at risk of being arrested for debt. In February of 1768, he returned to London and was voted into the seat of Middlesex, prompting more cries of 'Wilkes and Liberty!' from his electorate.

Wilkes, however, was still facing sentencing for the guilty verdict Mansfield had passed on him after he fled to Paris and, despite the crowds' efforts, he was sent to prison in Southwark.

On 10 May 1768, Parliament was opened by the King. A huge crowd gathered outside the King's Bench Prison with the expectation of 'returning' Wilkes to the Commons. He was, after all, still an MP. The army was waiting. Shots were fired and seven were killed, including the son of a farmer working nearby. It was instantly dubbed the 'St George's Massacre'.

In February 1769, the House of Commons expelled Wilkes again. What followed, when his seat fell vacant, would see the start of the movement for parliamentary reform begin in earnest. At the election to replace him, Wilkes' name was on the papers. The votes came in, and the people returned him. The House of Commons then decided that he was ineligible to be returned as an MP, and held another election. He was returned again. And again, in April 1769. Two days later, the House of Commons declared the election void and installed Colonel Henry Lawes Luttrell as MP. The people shouted for reform.

The City, ever defiant of Westminster, chose Wilkes as Alderman for the ward of Farringdon Without, close to his Clerkenwell roots. The City petitioned the King, calling his ministers corrupt. The petition was ignored. When a second, bolder petition was also disregarded, the people knew that the government was not acting in the interest of the nation.

In the meantime, John Wilkes became one of the twenty-six City magistrates and, as such, was more involved in the application of day-to-day law than ever. He went on to become Sheriff, and then Lord Mayor. During the 1770s, he also supported the reporting of business from the Houses of Parliament, which had previously been banned. Politics were increasingly in the public domain, and this was seen clearly during discussion of what became popularly known as 'The American Question'.

America's Declaration of Independence in 1776, so soon after Britain had ceded substantial foreign territories to end the Seven Years War, was a huge blow to the natural optimism of London, many of whose citizens earned a living by trading with American friends and family. Amongst societies, the press and in many ordinary homes there was constant debate on the subject: 'Would it not be advisable for the legislature of Great-Britain to treat with the American Congress on terms of reconciliation?' asked *The Gazetteer* on 18 January 1776. The declaration echoed John Locke's ideas and even quoted directly from his *Second Treatise of Government*. America was annexed to Britain yet seen as a land apart, one of unlimited opportunity and conflicting, often flexible values. As Samuel Johnson wrote, 'How is it that we hear the loudest yelps for liberty among the drivers of negroes?'

The middle-class Westminster debating societies went into overdrive in the taverns surrounding Parliament. The Declaration of Independence was seen not so much as a definitive break but a step along a long road. Interest in matters American continued unabated amongst the middle classes. Many felt let down, believing that agreement could have been reached with America were it not for the stubbornness of George III.

Recourse to government by the educated citizen was seen increasingly as a right. But in the latter part of the eighteenth century, the vulnerability of the shabby old Parliament buildings became alarmingly apparent. For almost a week during the summer of 1780, London was gripped by a violent and drunken mob, raging against the Papists Act of 1778 which aimed at returning Catholics to public life. After the passing of the Act, rumours began to circulate that there were 20,000 Jesuit priests hiding in Bankside, waiting for the word from Rome, upon which they would blow up the banks of the Thames and flood the city. Another rumour was that a team of Benedictine monks had disguised themselves as chairmen in order to poison all the flour in the borough. No one bought any bread for days, until it was tested publicly upon a dog.

Lord George Gordon was a London-born nobleman of Scottish extraction. He was charming, articulate and intense, but the Gordons 'were, and are, all mad'. This included their choice of wives, and Gordon's mother was famous in Edinburgh for 'galloping madly down High Street on the back of a capering pig'. Gordon got into Parliament by having the pocket borough of Ludgershall bought for him at the age of twenty-two. He emerged as a great speaker, but he criticized all the parties and was unpopular in the House of Commons.

Inflamed by the Protestant cause, Gordon proposed that London's Protestants meet him in St George's Fields on Friday 2 June, at ten o'clock in the morning. Then they would proceed to the Houses of Parliament, to deliver a petition against the Act. The day dawned hot, and the numbers were massive: in excess of 50,000. They arrived early to sign the petition, which was made of strips of parchment; as each one was filled, a tailor began to sew them together. Gordon arrived almost an hour late, having struggled through the crowd. It was sweltering, and Gordon couldn't make himself heard above the masses. He soon gave up, pushed back through the crowd and was rescued by a friend who drove him off towards the House of Commons. The crowd followed, with the rolled-up petition carried like a carpet.

Fifteen-year-old Frederic Reynolds and his best friend, the young Duke of Bedford, were pupils at Westminster School. They bolted their lunch and came out to get a look at the protest. They saw protestors 'occupying every avenue to the Houses of Parliament, the whole of Westminster Bridge and extending to the northern end of Parliament Street'.

Coaches arrived carrying members to the House of Lords. The crowd took leave of its senses. Lord Bathurst was an old man and Lord President of the Council, but this did not prevent him being pulled from his coach, punched and smeared with filth from the road. Lord Stormont's coach was destroyed in the road, and he took a sustained beating. Lord Mansfield had the windows of his carriage smashed in, and the protestors tried to pull him out by his hair; his wig came off in their hands. It was only by the bravery and cunning of his coachman that he got into the House unscathed. Old Lord Ashburnham was so badly beaten that those in the crowd with a remaining sense of decency lifted him over their heads and passed him into the House.

MPs heading for the Commons were treated somewhat better, but a few were unlucky. Welbore Ellis, who had 'saved' Casanova some years before, was struck viciously across the face with a horsewhip, leaving him pouring blood as he pelted into the Westminster

Guildhall pursued by more than thirty men before skittering over the roof to the next-door building.

Not enough magistrates could be found to control the mob. In the House of Commons, a disgruntled group of men were waiting to hear Gordon speak. The parchment petition was brought in and put on the floor. For the next six hours, the House debated; and then, at eight in the evening, they voted. One hundred and ninety-eight MPs had fought their way into the House of Commons on that day. Only six voted with Gordon.

The violence outside escalated as this news reached the mob. Just after nine o'clock, the Foot and Horse Guards arrived to 'release' the captive MPs. Rather than having an intimidating effect, the soldiers were pelted with stones and filth.

As darkness fell, a mob including many street children and prostitutes converged in Lincoln's Inn, then headed to the nearby chapel of the Sardinian Ambassador. Minutes later, the interior of the chapel was ripped out and burned in the street. In the following days, the uproar swept through Soho, Moorfields and Holborn. Irish Catholics were targeted, including one silk weaver whose house was torn down, a bonfire made in the fields and his collection of caged canaries placed on the top. One distressed bystander offered money for the canaries but was knocked back and told that they were 'Popish birds and should burn with the rest of the Popish goods'.

Newgate and The Fleet prisons were liberated, setting free in excess of 1,600 convicts. Gangs roamed the streets, requesting money with menaces. The poet William Cowper saw the fires across the city and wrote, 'London seemed a second Troy.'

At dawn on Wednesday morning, 7,000 soldiers of the Home Counties militia marched into London. With the arrival of the army, the violence petered out. 'Such a time of terror you have been fortunate in not seeing,' Samuel Johnson would write to Mrs Thrale. The official death toll was low – some 210 deaths – but those who had been piled on to a barge beneath Blackfriars Bridge and cast off into the fast waters of the Thames remained uncounted. Gordon was arrested for treason. His luck held long enough for Lloyd Kenyon and Thomas Erskine to be appointed to defend him, and he was acquitted. He disappeared into a Birmingham slum, where he was found some months later living as an Orthodox Jew, having been circumcised and taken the name Yisrael bar Avraham Gordon. Eventually, he was committed to Newgate on other charges. There he kept strict observance of Jewish religious law and was allowed to turn his room into a synagogue on the Jewish Sabbath. He seems to have suffered from a form of holy anorexia, becoming ever more devout and thin until he was carried off by gaol fever aged forty-two. A sad end for a deeply engaging, deeply eccentric man.

The Gordon Riots left their mark upon London. As people began to write up their memories of those terrible days, they wondered if such an event were not the product of a conspiracy, 'the effect of Accident or Design?' But by whom, and to what end, none could say. The mini-militias which had sprung up across neighbourhoods were at once admired and distrusted. Whilst such vigilante groups had worked well in the ill-lit and cramped quarters of London half a century earlier, they were not so welcome in Enlightenment London. The endless wrangling over the need for a properly funded police force, such as the French had, was brought up by the House of Lords, and eventually resulted in the introduction of the Metropolitan Police in 1829.

The historian Edward Gibbon called the rioters the 'scum' who had 'boiled up to the surface in the huge cauldron'. But they had achieved what Westminster's many active pub and coffee house debating societies full of concerned citizens could not. The riots led to a widespread questioning of how urban communities functioned and how they should be administered or controlled. As importantly, they raised questions about the identity of Londoners: who they were, what they believed and what they would do when the rules were suspended, even temporarily.

The Gordon Riots made it relatively easy for George III to get rid of Lord North and Charles James Fox. The King appointed the 24-year-old Tory, William Pitt, as Prime Minister. Fox, however, was determined not to give up. Shambolic and charismatic, he wore blue coats and buff trousers like George Washington's troops. He also gambled and drank, and had widespread support in all the social classes. The King loathed him and thought him responsible for leading his son the Prince of Wales, later the Prince Regent, astray.

The general election was fiercely contested, but no more so than in Westminster. Fox and Pitt spent thousands, exchanged personal insults and engaged their friends to canvass for them. Fox's canvassers included the Prince of Wales and Georgiana, Duchess of Devonshire. 'She gets out of her carriage and walks into alleys—many feathers and fox tails in her hat,' wrote a disdainful Lady Boscawen. It was even reported that she was exchanging a kiss for the promise of a vote. Fox was returned for Westminster by a slender margin, but the result was delayed for over a year by legal challenges. William Pitt became Prime Minister and immediately put forward a Bill to reform the electoral system, but it was rejected. Finally, in 1832, the 'Act to amend the representation of the people in England and Wales', otherwise known as The Great Reform Act, began to improve the fairness of the electoral system.

As the Georgian period came to a close, politics remained an enduringly mysterious art. In the best parliamentary tradition, a Londoner attending the House of Commons debate one evening noted that, having inquired as to which was the politician he had come to hear speak, he was directed to a man 'sitting cross-legged and cross-armed; his hat on a head resting on a sunk doubled-in chest'. For many others, politicians had emerged as a separate breed, as the *Morning Herald* asked, 'Have the people more reason to believe that the present opposition to Government proceeds from a sincere regard for the interest of the nation, or a desire only to get into power?'

The Parliament buildings became even more run-down, and Sir John Soane was brought in to modernize them. However, a fire in an unattended stove, on 16 October 1834, set light to the flues beneath Black Rod's dais and resulted in an almost comprehensive destruction of both Soane's new buildings and the old Palace. Westminster Abbey and St Margaret's church were untouched, but only a lucky change in wind direction, along with a colossal effort by spectators and the London Fire Brigade, saved Westminster Hall. That night, an army captain, George Manby, was injured in an accident with a fire engine, but what he saw inspired him to invent the first modern fire extinguisher. The London Fire Brigade's famous 'firedog', Chance, was also there and rode in on the engine before running up and down the lines, barking at the flames.

J. M. W. Turner stood on the banks of the Thames, filling a sketchbook. It was a memorable night and one deeply symbolic to the onlookers: the capital of a nation in the grip of parliamentary reform watched as the old Houses of Parliament were destroyed.

St James's Village: 'ye dwellings of Noble men and other Persons of quality'

The development of St James's Square and the surrounding area was under way soon after the Restoration. Charles II had chosen to live in St James's Palace, close to the fresh air and countryside of which he was so fond. Henry Jermyn, Duke of St Albans, was the man who began to build on St James's Fields, south of Piccadilly. He was 'a man of pleasure . . . and entertains no other thoughts than to live at ease', perhaps the ideal qualifications for a man who was to design a miniature village for London's wealthiest families. The first residents included the King's ex-mistress Mary 'Moll' Davis. Elizabeth Pepys called her 'the most impertinent slut in the world', which is no doubt how she came by the £1,800 she paid for the property, aged twenty-nine. Jermyn had Christopher Wren design a local church, St James's Piccadilly, and a market for the residents, located just to the west of the Haymarket.

St James's proximity to the palaces and to Westminster meant it was much in favour with those who played a part in court and political life:

Those who have offices, places or pensions from the court, or any expectations from thence, constantly attend the levees of the prince and his ministers, which takes up the greatest part of the little morning they have. At noon most of the nobility, and such gentlemen as are members of the house of commons, go down to Westminster, and when the houses do not sit late, return home to dinner or visit their clubs. Others that are not members of either house, and have no particular business to attend, are found in the chocolate-houses near the court, or in the park.

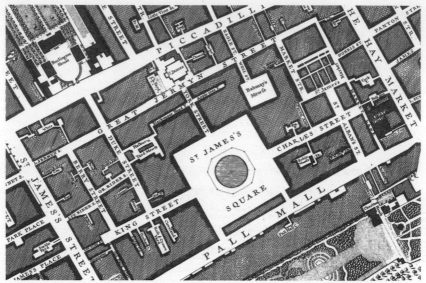

St James's Square and the surrounding streets and market, detail from John
Roque's map, 1745

St James's market was like any other London exchange, although the
rougher edges of some of the traders could cause offence, as Tobias
Smollett observed when he saw

> . . . a dirty barrow-bunter in the street, cleaning her dusty fruit with
> her own spittle; and who knows but some fine lady of St. James's par-
> ish might admit into her delicate mouth those very cherries which
> had been rolled and moistened between the filthy, and perhaps ulcer-
> ated, chops of a St. Giles's huckster?

Smollett's caricature, though amusing, is just that. But the market
was full of real people too. William Border slept for years in a hayloft
in the market. He was nicknamed 'The Doctor' by the local community, known to the nightwatchmen and given free ale at the local
pubs. In the 1730s, Richard Albridge, who was referred to even by his
friends as an 'idiot', was working in the market. He was treated brutally by the other boys who 'black his face, and carry him about in a
basket, and then throw him out in the kennel to wash him'. In 1732,
Richard stabbed a spiteful colleague who stole the roll he had just
buttered for himself. The thief was known and disliked amongst the

stallholders for being cruel and particularly unpleasant to the retarded but gentle porter. He taunted Richard with the roll, they tussled and then Richard, still holding his knife, stabbed him. The stallholders trooped into the Old Bailey to defend him. He was found guilty of manslaughter and branded on the hand.

Around the market, fine streets sprang up, built for London's richest men and women. New ideas about domestic space meant magnificent interiors were created for entertaining. With lunches, tea and card parties, women dominated aristocratic households in a way not seen before. Gentlemen had the refuge of their clubs to retreat to. Some, such as the Athenaeum and the Travellers Club, cultivated members with similar interests, but the earlier ones, such as White's, Brooks's and Boodles – all based on St James's Street – were based around the gambling aristocracy. The betting books of White's and Brooks's were legendary Any wager could be laid on any challenge, from the outcome of the American Revolutionary War to who would get gout first. Gambling amongst the upper classes rose throughout the eighteenth century; by the 1780s, it had reached a near epidemic level. Pamphlets protesting against it appeared regularly. Popular feeling was that the ruling class, who theoretically held a moral authority, should know better. Gaming itself was also changing: sociable partnership games, such as whist, were giving way to high-stakes, antisocial, player-versus-banker games, such as faro. What had been a luxurious pastime for people with money to spare was suddenly becoming an addiction.

Many of the social elite had made dynastic or financially advantageous marriages, which were threatened by this addiction. In other classes of society, cohabitation was becoming relatively common, if not necessarily accepted. In 1776, the *Morning Chronicle* featured the debate: 'Is not the cohabitation of an unmarried man and woman, though attended with harmony and fidelity till death, an immoral connection?' For the aristocracy, their marriages, barring death, were difficult and costly to unravel. The threat to property and lineage meant that even the unhappiest of many landowning couples lived separate lives rather than seek divorce. But the English were coming round to divorce 'as a remedy for a state of things which is making, and is bound to make, a man wretched for life; nor is he debarred from the joy of living happily with another woman whom he loves'.

One major cause of trouble both at home and at the gaming tables was immoderate drinking. Consuming alcohol was seen as manly, particularly amongst the ruling elite, and teetotallers were rare. Charles James Fox, William Pitt the Younger and the Prince Regent all qualified as alcoholics for a large part of their lives. Berry Brothers, the wine merchant, which was one of the many shops in the area catering for the rich, still stands on St James's Street. It was not only a supplier but also a meeting place, and aristocratic visitors used the huge hanging scales to determine their own weights. William Pitt liked to get weighed there, as did Lord Byron. The poet was rakish and glamorous, but with his club foot making exercise difficult he was also aware of his 'morbid propensity to fatten' and watched his weight obsessively. He slimmed by fasting and swimming, and his dramatic weight fluctuations were recorded by the Berrys. In 1806, they noted his weight at 13st 12lbs. But by 1811, he had starved himself beneath the 9st mark. His obsession worried his friends, but he would not be dissuaded, telling them, 'I maintain that more than half our maladies are produced by accustoming ourselves to more sustenance than is required for the support of nature.' He may have been right, but he was also accustomed to large amounts of alcohol – white wine being his diet drink of choice.

As the century progressed and wealth increased, the cultivation of taste became a fashionable preoccupation. In 1766, James Christie opened his Great Rooms on Pall Mall and held a sale of ordinary household goods. But his aspirations were much higher, and soon he was specializing in high-quality pictures. Viewing the latest sales became a fashionable pastime. As art became a widespread hobby amongst the rich, there were increased calls for a national gallery. In 1824, the National Gallery crept into existence at 100 Pall Mall, in the home of John Julius Angerstein. Angerstein was a hugely successful Lloyd's underwriter, his bonds becoming the byword for trust and reliability. Art was his passion. He was painted by Sir Joshua Reynolds and Sir Thomas Lawrence; he purchased works at auction and supported emerging British artists, such as Turner. When he died, in

1823, the final destination of the collection was a matter of some speculation. During a debate

> . . . it was remarked that the collection of Mr. Angerstein would be sold in the course of 1824, and if not looked after would very probably go out of the country. Mr. Agar Ellis thereupon announced his intention of moving for a grant for the purchase of this and other collections for the formation of a National Gallery.

After a very brief residence at 105 Pall Mall, the National Gallery finally got a home of its own in Trafalgar Square, on the site of the Royal Stables.

In the time it had taken for Angerstein to build his collection, St James's had changed. The old oil street lights had gone, along with their smelly lamplighters who were

> A set of greasy fellows redolent of Greenland Stock . . . employed to trim and light these lamps, which they accomplished by the apparatus of a formidable pair of scissors, a flaming flambeau of pitched rope and a rickety ladder, to the annoyance and danger of all passers-by.

These had been replaced by gaslights, which were demonstrated on Pall Mall by lighting pioneer Frederick Albert Winzer, in 1807. They were such a success that the London and Westminster Gas Light and Coke Company was formed; by New Year's Eve 1813, gaslights had spread through the streets of Westminster and St James's and over Westminster Bridge.

St James's Park: 'mingling in confusion with the vilest populace'

St James's Park was the social centre of the area, bordered to the north by The Mall, where 'the ladies look'd like undaunted heroes, fit for government or battle, and the gentlemen like a parcel of fawning, flattering fops'. To the south, Birdcage Walk 'took its name from the cages which were hung in the trees'. To the east stood Horse Guards Parade Ground, where young shoeblacks, the 'Blackguards', waited to clean the boots of soldiers for a copper. It wasn't only the soldiers who benefited from their numbers but also those who liked to be well turned out on their visits to the smart set 'where the women are so very careful about their clean and white floors'. St James's Park and Green Park had milk stalls, where the cows were milked to order, a practice that would continue until 1905. The popular nature of the park was commented upon as 'the public walk of London and open to all, and it's a strange sight, in fine weather, to see the flower of the nobility and the first ladies of the Court mingling in confusion with the vilest populace'.

In 1725, George I brought to the park what Jonathan Swift sarcastically termed *The Most Wonderful Wonder that ever appeared to the Wonder of the British Nation*, more commonly referred to as 'Peter the Wild Boy'. Peter was found by George I's huntsmen near Hamelin (the Pied Piper's sinister little town). He was about fifteen and could 'not articulate a single syllable'. He was wild and hairy, with long broken fingernails. George sent 'Peter' to England as some sort of pet, with ideas of transforming him into the perfect human. He could be seen in the park, walking with his keepers. To César de Saussure, an observer in St James's Park, Peter's clothes 'seemed to hinder his movements', and he would not keep his hat upon his head, but continually threw it upon the ground. César also confessed, 'He frightened me.' For the intellectuals of Georgian London, Peter emerged from the forest into the storm of early eighteenth-century debate about the nature of self. For some, like Daniel Defoe, he was evidence of a man without a soul. For others, he was proof of the blank slate of human nature, reliant wholly upon nurture.

The likely reality was that Peter had ceased to develop mentally at a young age and was abandoned in the Hamelin forest when puberty and sheer size made him unruly and difficult to care for. For a time, his royal patrons in England hoped he might benefit from an education, but he failed to learn even the rudiments of written or spoken language. Eventually, his tutor, the polymath Dr John Arbuthnot, gave up on him. He was still a celebrity, and William Kent painted him amongst other members of the royal court on the east wall of the staircase of Kensington Palace (where he remains today). In reality, Saussure noted that Peter 'could not be taught good manners, and he had to be removed'. He was 'retired' to a farm near Northchurch, in Hertfordshire, with a Crown pension for his care. He liked music and gin, and was given to absconding when the opportunity arose. After making it to Norwich, he was fitted with a leather collar upon which was embossed: 'Peter, the Wild Man of Hanover. Whoever will bring him to Mr Fenn, at Berkhamsted, Hertfordshire, will be paid for their trouble.' Peter was cared for by the Fenn family until he died, in his seventies. He saw three Kings occupy England's throne, living at the expense of each of them. Peter's main patron was George II's queen, Caroline of Ansbach. Yet despite her kindness to poor retarded Peter, Caroline loathed the fact that the populace were allowed access to St James's Park, and she decided it would be better as a private garden for the palace. She inquired of Prime Minister Robert Walpole what this might cost, to which he replied 'only three crowns', meaning hers, her husband's, and their son's. She decided to leave the park open to the public.

As the century progressed, the park became the place to be seen. In the 1740s, Robert Skinner, who was 2ft 1in tall, and his wife, Judith, who was an inch taller, could be seen in their miniature carriage. It was 'no larger than a child's chaise, drawn by two dogs, and driven by a lad of twelve years old, attired in a purple and yellow livery'. They made their money exhibiting themselves throughout Westminster. They were married after Robert saw a newspaper advertising a 'little woman' of 2ft 2in tall, to be exhibited in London. He hotfooted it to the capital to propose. Judith accepted, and they were married in St Martin-in-the-Fields Church one week later. They were quite the characters about town, being described as 'very good-looking, perfectly straight and well made, witty, intelligent and jocose'.

The park was not always a safe place. In 1790, Ann Porter of St James's Street was accosted by a man. He was smartly dressed, but spoke to her using 'gross and obscene language' and even struck her across the head. As Ann ran back towards her house, he caught up with her and stabbed her through her skirts, giving her 'a dangerous wound on her right thigh, of the length of nine inches, and the depth of four inches'. Frightened and shocked, Ann didn't realize the extent of her injury, which was the worst the man had inflicted in what emerged as a two-year spree. The press fixed instantly on the case, and 'The London Monster' was born. There were other victims, often sisters and usually beautiful, whom he accosted and spoke to 'in a shivering sort of voice, expressing some thing that is unintelligible, and when he speaks, speaks a most horrid language to them, talks of drowning them in their blood'. His hunting ground was St James's and the park. His sexual fixation, known as 'piquerism' – stabbing sharp objects into the hips and thighs of women in pretty clothes – meant he was compelled to continue until he was caught.

In June 1790, Ann was sure she saw her attacker in St James's Park. Her companion, a Mr Coleman, followed and accosted him. Renwick Williams, aged twenty-three, protested his innocence in the Old Bailey; the trial was a farce, and Williams had to be retried. During the retrial it turned out he had an alibi for one of the attacks, and the witness statements were contradictory, but he was still convicted and served six years. Intriguingly, the attacks stopped when he was off the streets.

The roughness and bustle of the park were added to by the public sedan chair rank. In 1634, Sir Saunders Duncombe took a fourteen-year licence in Westminster to provide sedan chairs to the public; they would remain popular for the next 150 years. Sedan chairs were legal on both the pavement and the roads, so were used to avoid the traffic wherever it was necessary. The smart set often complained about the public chair rank in the park: it was open to the air, and the leather chairs got soaked through in bad weather, making them smelly and unwholesome. Irishmen dominated the chair business through their size, strength and willingness to labour hard. Carrying a person of around ten stone through the streets, even with a light public chair, worked out at a load of around 100lbs per man. Still, the bearers of London were generally regarded to be the best by continental visitors, as they were agile enough to overcome most obstacles, as well as remarkably rapid. Swiss visitor César de Saussure wrote, in 1725, 'the bearers [go] so fast that you have some difficulty in keeping up with them on foot. I do not believe that in all Europe better or more dexterous bearers are to be found; all foreigners are surprised at their strength and skill.' He records being knocked over four times

1. William Hogarth, 'Noon, 1738', showing a London street scene including a Huguenot congregation exiting a church service

2. St Martin's Le Grand, the site for the new Post Office, engraved by J. Bailey, published 1815

3. The Jernegan Cistern. Goldsmith/banker Henry Jernegan commissioned this monumental cistern from Frederick Kandler in 1734

4. Coffee pot made by the silversmith Paul de Lamerie for fellow Huguenot Sir John Lesquesne, 1738

5. 'A Paraleytic Woman' by Théodore Géricault, 1821, produced as a print by Charles Hullmandel, Rodwell & Martin

6. A view of Marylebone Pleasure Gardens, c. 1755

7. Dockhead, Bermondsey, showing the notorious slum of Jacob's Island, *c.* 1813

8. Castle's Shipbreaking Yard opposite Baltic Wharf, Millbank. This collection of naval artefacts was later destroyed in the Blitz.

9. The Yard of the Oxford Arms Inn, with St Paul's Cathedral in the background

10. Capper's Farmhouse being slowly consumed by Heal's, Tottenham Court Road, 1913. Note the furniture-packing crates on the right

11. 'The Tower of London', from an engraving by William Miller after J. M. W. Turner, 1832

12. 'New London Bridge, with the Lord Mayor's Procession Passing Under the Unfinish'd Arches', after Thomas Hosmer Shepherd, 1827

13. 'Southwark Bridge from Bank Side', after Thomas Hosmer Shepherd, 1827

14. 'Wapping Old Stairs', from *The Miseries of London,* by Thomas Rowlandson, 1812

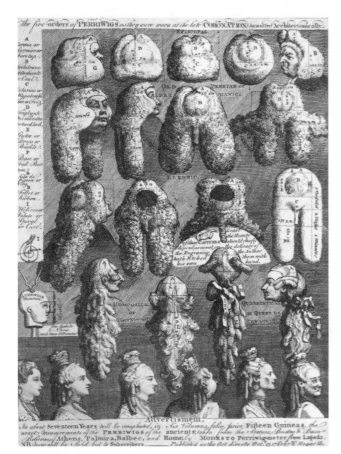

15. 'The five orders of Perriwigs as they were worn at the late Coronation measured Architectonically', William Hogarth, 1761

16. 'The Fellow 'Prentices at their Looms, Representing Industry and Idleness', William Hogarth, 1747

by sedan chairs during his visit to the capital. Bearers were regularly fined for cursing loudly in the street, and they were notorious fighters and Romeos, probably much in demand for their stamina. As the city grew, sedan chairs faded. In 1791, Horace Walpole wrote that 'the breed of chairs is almost lost, for Hercules and Atlas could not carry anybody from one end of this enormous capital to the other'.

At the west end of the park, away from the rowdy chair rank, was the house of the Duke of Buckingham, later purchased for George III and Queen Charlotte. The house was desirable for the 'fine garden and terras, from where there is a prospect of the adjacent country'. The Royal Family eventually relocated to Buckingham House; its refurbishment as a palace did not meet favour with everyone, and by the end of the Georgian period many felt the royal residence and the park had lost their earlier 'country in the city' appeal. For a start, Charles II's Dutch canal was 5ft 1in below the surface of the Thames at high tide, 'thus the water, once admitted to this ornamental reservoir, cannot again flow out, but stagnates' and therefore stank in 'sultry' weather. If the old landscaping was proving unpopular, so was Edward Blore's new design for Buckingham House (now Palace) so close to Charles's canal: 'the verge of this puddle has been chosen whereon to expend above a million sterling in the erection of a bedlam-like building as a royal residence'.

The 'fashionable herb': tea and philanthropy

The exclusive residents of St James's were not only occupied with traditional upper-class pursuits. The growing fashion for tea and all-female tea parties was often used for the benefit of the many private charities springing up in Georgian London.

Tea had been in London since at least 1659, when 'theire ware also att this time a Turkish drink to be sould, almost in evry street, called Coffee, and another kind of drink called Tee'. Writing in his diary on 25 September 1660, Samuel Pepys noted that he 'sent for a cup of Tee (a China drink) of which I had never drunk before'. At that stage, tea was sold in the coffee houses. But it soon became the feminine alternative to coffee, which some women regarded as harsh and unhealthy. *The Women's Petition Against Coffee* of 1676 complained that coffee had reduced Englishmen to 'meer Cock-sparrows' and claimed that: 'Never did Men wear greater breeches, or carry less in them of any Mettle whatsoever.' This the writer attributed to 'nothing more than the Excessive use of that Newfangled, Abominable, Heathenish Liquor called COFFEE'. Tea, on the other hand, was considered as healthy and refreshing. During the 1680s, tea was regarded as a ritual at court, and a mark of taste and social status amongst courtiers. Soon, other reasons for drinking it besides an overt way of displaying wealth and discernment were found, and a traveller to India in the 1690s found tea 'very convenient for our Health, and agreeable to the Habits of our Bodies'.

Samuel Johnson described himself as 'a hardened and shameless tea-drinker' who barely let his kettle cool before brewing up again, but he represents one of the few male voices claiming a tea addiction. The association with women did not go down well with tea's detractors. They did not see non-alcoholic tea as the drink of true Englishmen, asking, 'Were they the sons of tea-sippers, who won the fields of Cressey and Agincourt, or dyed the Danube's streams with Gallic blood?'

Tea was difficult to obtain. It is easily tainted by the smell of other cargo and so must be carefully packed for transportation. One thing that definitely wouldn't taint the tea were the Chinese porcelain pots in which it was brewed, and so the ships began to pack porcelain too, bringing it back to extremely fashionable homes in London and giving us the generic word 'china' for thin porcelain. A ton of tea came along with six tons of porcelain as ballast. As a result, London was inundated with cheap exotic porcelain: in 1712, a 216-piece tea and dinner service cost £5 10s; and in 1723, 5,000 teapots were imported costing only 1½d each.

Teapots and cups became desirable tableware for the rich and aspirational for the poor, who were seemingly determined to compete 'with their superiors, and imitating their luxuries, throw away their little earnings upon this fashionable herb'. The cachet of tea-drinking in London's most elegant drawing rooms was exploited by Josiah

Wedgwood with his tea services, which were at once a homage to the purest Chinese porcelain and yet a deliberate attempt to cultivate elite patronage.

Tea parties were not just for the rich. Women in almost all classes considered them social occasions, but many middle- and upper-class women used them to cultivate charity or encourage debate. One, Lady Mary Wortley Montagu (née Pierrepoint), would introduce London to inoculation against smallpox and used tea parties to spread the word. Mary had escaped an arranged marriage with the astonishingly named Clotworthy Skeffington by marrying Edward Wortley Montagu. Mary did not love Edward but she bore him a son, and her time in London was spent mixing in the highest circles. She cultivated literary friendships, and had a stormy love-hate relationship with Alexander Pope. In the winter of 1715, Lady Mary contracted smallpox. She survived, but she was 'very severely markt' in both appearance and temperament. Her looks, which had been remarkable, were gone, as were patches of her hair and her eyelashes, 'which gave a fierceness to her eyes that impaired their beauty'.

In August 1716, her husband was made Ambassador to Istanbul. The city was something of a shock for Mary, but she took to the climate and the people. Amongst her letters from Turkey is one dated 1 April 1717. It tells of the inoculation of her son against smallpox, using a Turkish method of 'ripping' four or five veins with a large needle, applying pus from the sores of a smallpox victim, then covering the site with a 'hollow bit of shell' and binding them up. She reported to her husband, 'The Boy was engrafted last Tuesday, and is at this time singing and playing and very impatient for his supper.' The success of this operation led her to 'take pains to bring this usefull invention into fashion in England'.

On her return to England, she found both smallpox and arguments about its treatment raging. During the epidemic of 1719, which saw many of her friends and acquaintances die of the disease, she was remarkably silent. In the early part of 1721, it was so warm that roses bloomed in January and smallpox went 'forth like a destroying Angel'. Lady Mary called upon Charles Maitland, an English doctor she had met in Turkey, to inoculate her daughter, Mary, but he hesitated. It was one thing to perform the operation in Turkey, but another to do it in London. He made sure he had two witnesses from the Royal College of Physicians before performing the operation. One was James Keith, who had lost two of his sons to smallpox, in 1717. After seeing the operation, he immediately inoculated his remaining son.

London's aristocracy began to visit Mary to see if they should engraft their own children. The visitors included Caroline, Princess of Wales, who sanctioned the testing of inoculation on condemned prisoners in Newgate. The experiment was a success, securing royal approval for smallpox inoculation, but the press did not take to it so kindly, or to Lady Mary. She was branded an 'unnatural mother who had risked the lives of her own children' and people began to 'hoot' at her in the street. Yet, the list of parents taking early action to protect their children is extensively drawn from Lady Mary's own friends and acquaintances. She exploited the tea party circuit and took her children all over London to show that they had been unharmed by the operation.

The fact that she was well known and held a high position in society contributed largely to the success of Maitland's subsequent career in inoculation. Their pioneering work laid the bedrock which would be built upon by Edward Jenner later in the century, when he introduced mass inoculation to England.

Local hospitals: Westminster and the Lock

In 1716, Henry Hoare (the banker), Robert Witham (a vintner), William Wogan (a writer) and the Reverend Patrick Coburn met in St Dunstan's Coffee House in Fleet Street and established the Charitable Society for the Sick, Poor and Needy. At first, they intended to visit and dispense charity to prisoners in 'the White Chapple, the Kings Bench, the Clink and the Marshalsea'. The men went themselves, money in hand, and took Mr Savile (an apothecary) and Mrs Sherman (a midwife) with them, when necessary. By that summer, they knew they couldn't keep up with the demand, and decided to limit themselves to providing a public infirmary for Westminster.

This was still an ambitious aim, as London's only public hospitals at the time were St Bartholomew's, in Smithfield, and St Thomas's, in Southwark. By 1720, they had taken a house in Petty France, south of St James's Park, and in May admitted their first patient, a man with inflammation of the joints and scurvy who was discharged almost a month later. The infirmary was soon oversubscribed and, in 1732, the governors acquired Lanesborough House on Hyde Park Corner and created St George's Hospital, known for its brilliant and sometimes eccentric surgeons. William Cheselden was highly skilled at extracting bladder stones, an operation known as 'lithotomy'. Samuel Pepys had survived this risky operation decades earlier; he gave thanks every year, and kept the stone as a memento. Many were not so lucky. Cheselden, however, had an excellent record, and could locate the stone, cut it out and start stitching in under one minute. His speed and assurance meant few of his patients died from shock on the table. Another St George's surgeon was Henry Watson, who carried on teaching there until his death, in 1793, aged ninety-one. He was known less for his surgical skill and more for his old-fashioned outfits of 'curled wig, a full-cuffed coat with a number of huge buttons, and a cocked hat', all complemented by a stylish cane. He referred to his medical students as 'cubs'.

The most famous of the students at St George's was Edward Jenner, who arrived as a 21-year-old, in 1770. He lived with John Hunter and his family and studied in Hunter's menagerie of exotic animals, some of which had come from the Tower. From Hunter he 'learnt the value of directness and simplicity of conduct and a passionate love of truth' that would serve him so well in his work against smallpox.

Nearby, work had already begun against a pox of a different kind: venereal disease. Slightly further out, behind Buckingham House, London's first Lock Hospital opened on 31 January 1747 exclusively to treat patients suffering from venereal disease. A 'lock hospital' was the old name for a lazar house, thought to come from the French word for rags: *loques*. It was the brainchild of William Bromfield, a Holborn Doctor and Demonstrator of Anatomy at Barber-Surgeons' Hall and later surgeon to Frederick, Prince of Wales. Bromfield had witnessed the difficulties of housing those infected by the pox: hospital boards had started putting these patients of 'low character' in yellow outfits, giving rise to the name 'canaries' for street prostitutes. Traditional remedies were poisons – arsenic and mercury – either applied directly to the affected parts, or administered in a number of unappealing ways. Often, it was only the natural remission of the disease between stages that led physicians to declare one third of their patients cured. Bromfield was convinced he could do better; from the beginning, the Lock Hospital sought to make the wealthier classes aware of the realities of venereal diseases through public meetings. On 17 November 1755, *The Public Advertiser* reported that a 'Lady of Quality', after attending one of these meetings, had endowed a new ward for the reception of afflicted married women 'injured by the Cruelty of bad Husbands'. It also reported that 'near two Hundred [children] from two to ten years old have been Cured in that Hospital that had fallen Victims to Villains Misguided by a Vulgar Notion that by a Criminal Communication with a healthy Child a certain Cure might be obtained for themselves'. The Lock Hospital also bore the expense of prosecuting at least one man who had tried to cure himself of venereal disease in this fashion. In 1764, the governors paid to prosecute Edmund Thirkell for the rape of five-year-old Mary Amelia Halfpenny, who had been admitted to the hospital suffering with venereal disease. He was tried before Lord Mansfield and convicted, but his fate is unknown.

Bromfield appointed the Wesleyan Martin Madan as chaplain of the Lock Hospital, and a chapel was constructed at Madan's expense so that patrons and patients could both attend the service without seeing each other. Madan began to adapt old hymns and create new ones with the chapel's blind organist, Charles Lockhart. These hymns became hugely popular with the smart congregation, and Madan put them on sale: *A Collection of Psalm and Hymn Tunes . . . To Be Had at the Lock Hospital near Hyde Park Corner*. In the 1760s and 1770s, the annual oratorio was a sell-out, and the musical events were consistently popular. Men and women were encouraged to sing together, with gusto, and the sermons sought to raise awareness about the social problems of venereal disease. Then Lockhart left, after an argument, and a rapid decline began. In 1780, the concerts were replaced by evangelical sermons, and Martin Madan published his book *Thelyphthora* in which he proposed that the problems of prostitution could be solved by polygamy. The matter was debated by the Christian Society and the magazine *La Belle Assemblée* that winter, but a priest preaching in favour of multiple wives was too much to be borne, and the fashionable patrons melted away.

The Lock Hospital would continue on, but never with the same level of success. Madan died a shamed recluse, in 1790, by which time a separate hostel for women who did not want to return to prostitution had been established in Knightsbridge. The hospital stayed put until the middle of the nineteenth century, when it was moved to Harrow. Finally, a century later, it was absorbed into the NHS.

The icemen of Hyde Park

Like St James's Park, Hyde Park had long been famous as the promenade of the smart set, particularly at weekends. The *Journal of Agriculture* noted, in 1831, that during the 'gay season', someone had been seen driving their curricle around the park, drawn by a pair of quaggas. Quaggas (the Khoikhoi word for the now extinct variant species of zebra) were popular with fashionable Londoners, as they were more biddable than their wild cousins. Like all London's parks, it was a public space and provided recreation for all. Charles I had opened the park to the public in 1637, and William III built Rotten Row as his private road to Kensington Palace. But it was Queen Caroline, George II's wife, who created the park we are familiar with today. In 1730, she ordered the Westbourne River dammed to form the Serpentine Lake, which had previously been eleven ponds, popular with swimmers and skaters. Such sports were not without their dangers, and fatalities were common when swimmers 'ventured out of their depth' or when skaters fell through the ice.

Drowning was a preoccupation among the medical pioneers of London. They knew there was a relationship between the cessation of breathing and the stopping of the heart. John Hunter had conducted gory experiments on a dog by removing the sternum of a living animal to observe what happened to the heart when breathing was severely restricted by use of a bellows mechanism. This prompted him to design a machine, again based on a bellows, which would restart the breathing in apparently drowned individuals. His paper, presented to the Royal Society in 1776, was full of good sense: he had observed that cold water often kept people alive for longer than if they were 'drowned' in warmer water, and that they should only be warmed up slowly. He did, however, think that blowing air up the anus might also be beneficial for the drowned. A mixed bag.

Nevertheless, Hunter's paper coincided with popular interest in resuscitation: ideas of 'artificial breathing' aided by bellows, or mouth to mouth, were gaining ground and the rudiments of cardiac massage were emerging.

For five years before Hunter's influential paper, an Islington-born doctor, William Hawes, had been agitating for funding and action to be taken for 'the resuscitation of people apparently dead'. In 1773, in his 'incessant zeal' to prove that it was possible to bring back the drowned from the edge of death, he organized and paid for 'reception houses' between Westminster and London Bridges where people could be brought 'within a certain time after the accident' and attempts would be made to resuscitate them. By summer 1774, he and the other doctors staffing the reception houses had been so successful that they met with a group of philanthropists including playwright Oliver Goldsmith in the Chapter Coffee House in St Paul's Churchyard and formed the Society for the Recovery of Persons Apparently Drowned.

The Society provided training in the new rescue techniques. In July of the same year, Thomas Vincent, a waterman, rescued a fourteen-month-old boy from an aqueduct and revived him using the massage techniques. In 1776, the Society changed its name to the Humane Society. Levels of public approval for reanimating those who had previously been thought lost were already high, as reported in the *Morning Chronicle* in January that year: 'As proof that the Society for the Recovery of Drowned Persons is well received by the publick, the Debating Society at the Crown Tavern in Bow lane where every subject is fully discussed, have given 5 guineas as a token of their approbation.'

Hawes and his colleagues continued to refine their methods of reviving the drowned by expelling water from the lungs and beating rhythmically upon the victims' chests. In the same year, William Henly, a Fellow of the Royal Society, wrote to the Humane Society with a suggestion that electricity be used to shock the heart and brain in 'cases of Apparent Death from Drowning'. After all, he reasoned, why not use 'the most potent resource in nature, which can instantly pervade the innermost recesses of the animal frame'? In 1794, the first clear success in using electricity to restart the heart was recorded by what had become the Royal Humane Society. Sophia Greenhill, a young girl, had fallen from a window in Soho and was pronounced dead by a doctor at Middlesex Hospital. Mr Squires, a local member of the Society, made it to the girl in around twenty minutes. Using a friction-type electricity machine, he applied shocks to her body. It seemed 'in vain', until he began to shock her thorax. Then he felt a pulse, and the child began to breathe again. She was concussed but went on to make a full recovery, and the Royal Humane Society was finally sure of the importance of electricity in reanimating those in 'suspended animation'.

In the same year, George III – who was already a patron of the Society – gave land on the north bank of the Serpentine for a head-quarters and principal receiving house to be erected. Lifeguards were stationed there, who were trained in the latest techniques of resuscitation and in using equipment for restoring respiration and pulse. By the early Victorian period, there were eighteen receiving houses in London, and the *Illustrated London News* estimated some 200,000 people were bathing in the Serpentine each year. In winter, the lifeguards donned greatcoats emblazoned with 'Iceman' on the back and patrolled the banks for any skater who might fall through the ice. Icemen operated throughout London at all regular skating grounds.

The success rate of the Royal Humane Society's operatives was undeniable. They were required never to drink on the job, and were made aware of the complications in rescuing suicides and working in icy conditions with hypothermic subjects. They couldn't always win, of course. In 1816, Percy Bysshe Shelley's wife, Harriet, drowned her-self in the Serpentine after he had abandoned her for Mary Godwin.

At the end of the Georgian period, in 1834, the Serpentine receiving house was given a grand makeover, with the Duke of Wellington laying the foundation stone. The Royal Humane Society had taught resuscitation techniques to many Londoners, and the Society's receiving houses formed the earliest model for what became Accident and Emergency departments. Lifeguards and icemen had become familiar sights, patrolling the Serpentine. Whereas at the beginning of the century chances of survival for those thought drowned were almost non-existent, by the end of the Georgian period the Society's operatives had learned to do everything they could because, in the words of their motto, 'a small spark may perhaps lie hid'.

For all their grandeur and undoubted importance, Westminster and St James's retained a variety and humanity which seem removed from them now. Boozing politicians, campaigning ladies, weight-conscious poets and Herculean chairmen mixed in with art, philanthropy and science. These areas also fuelled the luxury goods and entertainment industries which were growing rapidly in nearby Covent Garden and Soho. Next, we will visit some of the less polite attractions of Georgian London.

4. Bloomsbury, Covent Garden and the Strand

For a long time, Bloomsbury was part of the parish of St Giles-in-the-Fields. In 1624, Bloomsbury had 136 houses; by 1710, a return was made to Parliament which indicated that St Giles alone contained almost 35,000 inhabitants catered for by one church, three chapels and a Presbyterian Meeting House. The government decided to create a new parish to the north. In 1724, it came into being as St George's, Bloomsbury. The parish church was designed by Nicholas Hawksmoor, who came in with an estimate of £9,790 and exceeded it by just £3. It was orientated north–south, to fit the plot, and has an oddly stepped steeple with a statue of George I on the top. By the end of the eighteenth century, the parish contained 3,000 houses.

The changes in Bloomsbury were remarkable and some of the most dramatic in Georgian London: 'The fields where robberies and murders had been committed, the scene of depravity and wickedness the most hideous for centuries, became . . . rapidly metamorphosed into splendid squares and spacious streets; receptacles of civil life and polished society.' Previously, north of Holborn, there had been little other than marshy fields (where gentlemen held ill-advised duels), a few farms and some taverns, such as the Vine Tavern which sat at the bottom of Kingsgate Street on the site of London's ancient and only vineyard. The nearby Maidenhead Inn, which was probably named sarcastically, flourished as 'a liquor-shop and public house of the vilest description, and the haunt of beggars and desperate characters'. These were the places that the citizens of Bloomsbury wanted to see fade away.

In Bloomsbury Place, the seeds of a British institution were sown when Hans Sloane opened his medical practice after a trip to Jamaica. Jamaica had cemented his love of natural history and the exotic, and he began to establish his reputation as a naturalist. His ferocious love of collecting, and the large income from his practice, meant that he soon had the basis for a museum, and he bought a neighbouring house to accommodate his objects. As he aged, he became more dis-organized – though he still collected greedily. The young botanist Carl Linnaeus visited and was shocked by Sloane's lack of order. Upon Sloane's death, in 1753, his trustees offered the collection to George II, to no avail. Instead, the trustees petitioned Parliament, and the collection was secured for the nation. The nation had also acquired Edward Harley's library and the Cotton Library, and they too needed a new home. The aging Montagu House, a short distance from Sloane's old home on Bloomsbury Place, was acquired for the purpose. Renamed the 'British Museum', it opened on 15 January 1759. Tickets were by application, and they stated that 'No Money is to be Given to the Servants', who had no doubt hoped to make hand-some tips showing visitors around.

Three years after the British Museum was given the royal seal of approval, another temple to education emerged in Bloomsbury: Uni-versity College. It had long been observed that London had no true university to rival those of Oxford and Cambridge. Jeremy Bentham, the philosopher and legislator, along with Lord Brougham and the poet Thomas Campbell, wanted to create an institution which would deliver a 'literary and scientific education at a moderate expense'.

The land for the 'godless college' was found in the north of Bloomsbury, previously 'occupied as a farm by two old maiden sis-ters named Capper. They wore riding-habits and men's hats; one rode an old grey mare, and it was her spiteful delight to ride with a pair of shears after the boys who were flying their kites, in order to cut their strings. The other sister's business was to seize the clothes of the lads who trespassed on their premises to bathe.'

It was not only boys with kites who ran over the Capper sisters' dairy farm: some of the New River Company's conduits came into London over those fields. They were 'propped up in several parts to the height of six and eight feet, so that persons walked under them to gather watercresses, which grew in great abundance and perfection'.

All this was within a stone's throw of Southampton Row, one of Bloomsbury's oldest streets, and the long-time residence of another Bloomsbury character, Mrs Griggs. Upon her death, in 1792, the *Annual Register* remembered her as

... [that] eccentrical lady ... at her house, Southampton Row, Bloomsbury, Mrs. Griggs. Her executors found in her house eighty-six living and twenty-eight dead cats. A black servant has been left £150 per annum, for the maintenance of herself and the surviving grimalkins. The lady was single, and died worth £30,000. Mrs. Griggs, on the death of her sister, a short time ago, had an addition to her fortune; she set up her coach, and went out almost every day airing, but suffered no male servant to sleep in her house. Her maids being tired frequently of their attendance on such a numerous household, she was induced at last to take a black woman to attend and feed them. This black woman had lived servant to Mrs. Griggs many years, and had a handsome annuity given her to take care of the cats.

The Capper farm had disappeared beneath University College. The sisters' farmhouse still stood on the east side of Tottenham Court Road, but the land around it was becoming rapidly built up. In 1808, on a small patch of some open ground nearby, Richard Trevithick installed London's first passenger railway as an advertisement for his locomotive. The 'Catch Me Who Can' was situated close to where Euston Station is today, and ran on a circular track, with journeys costing a shilling a ride. It was meant to prove that trains were faster than horses but Trevithick hadn't laid his tracks well enough, and no one really saw how railways could take off. Ten years later, in 1818, John Harris Heal, a mattress-maker from the West Country, moved into what would become 196 Tottenham Court Road. He took over the old Capper farmhouse as a store and it survived until 1917, when it was demolished. Heal's still sits on the same site.

In only a few decades, Bloomsbury went from farmland to a fashionable neighbourhood, exemplified by the elegant Bloomsbury Square. Large-scale developments by James Burton and Thomas Cubitt make up vast swathes of Bloomsbury, and on Great Russell Street, just opposite the British Museum, is the small terrace which represents John Nash's first foray into domestic architecture. Burton and Nash would go on to be hugely influential in the West End of London with the Regent Street development, whilst Cubitt would develop Pimlico and Belgravia in a very different style. The most

'In Bloomsbury Square', engraving by R. Pollard and F. Jukes, 1787

important Georgian survival in Bloomsbury is Bedford Square, which was built upon the Cappers' cow yard, and for which no architect is known.

Relatively close by, to the west of Holborn, was the theatre neighbourhood of Covent Garden, with all its rackety allure. Francis Russell, the 4th Earl of Bedford, had begun developing the estate in 1631, and building progressed remarkably quickly, finishing in 1637. Covent Garden was unusual in that it was self-contained as a community, with the focus on the piazza designed by Inigo Jones. Here sat St Paul's Church with a small local prison and whipping post. In front of the church the first Punch and Judy show appeared in England, in 1662, when Pietro Gimonde brought his toy theatre to the square.

Bedford House sat on the north side of the Strand. The gardens stretched all the way up to the piazza, where they were hidden behind a high wall. Against this wall Covent Garden market started, in 1677, when Bedford granted a lease on a market, six days a week, to two local residents for the trading of 'all manner of Fruites, Flowers, roots, and herbs whatsoever'. The piazza was undeniably beautiful,

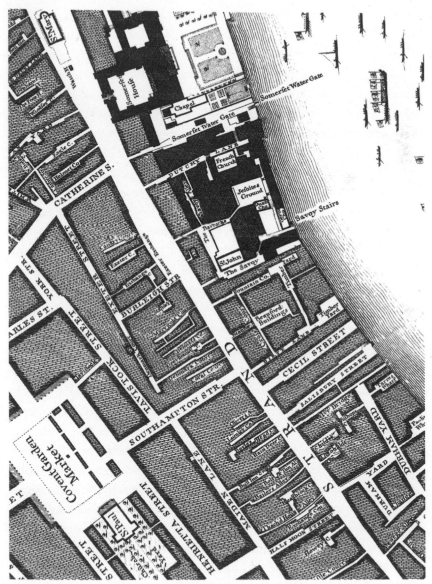

Covent Garden and the Strand, showing the Exeter Exchange and the area of the Savoy Palace, detail from John Roque's map, 1745

and retained the feel of the older pre-Restoration age. The sewerage provisions were good, at least until the end of the eighteenth century, so whilst the accommodations might be old-fashioned, they were well ventilated and not uncivilized. Only the noise and the press of people afflicted the piazza of Covent Garden – but to theatre people, what did that matter?

To the south was the Strand, the street connecting Westminster and the City. Roman in origin, its name originated during the Anglo-Saxon period and referred to the Old English word meaning 'shore', the road being close to the shallow banks of the Thames. In the Georgian period, the focal point of the Strand was the Exeter Exchange. It stood among taverns, eating houses and milk cellars where cows were led underground and milked for a fortnight before being sent back to local pastures. Between the Strand and the river were a maze of sub-divided medieval palaces with slum-like infilling. Numerous steps and narrow sets of stairs led down to the river, where the water slopped and slapped loudly at high tide. Even when William Chambers and the Adam brothers built their fine developments – Somerset House and the Adelphi – the tunnels beneath the Adelphi complex, which were meant to serve the river, almost immediately became the haunt of London's hookers and homeless. In amongst these narrow infested streets and courts were the most prominent areas of London's second-hand book trade, together with the sale of pornography. Holywell Street, in particular, became famous for it, with over fifty pornography shops there in 1837.

It was a bustling, vibrant area of London. But from respectable Bloomsbury, in the north, to the rough thoroughfare of the Strand, there was an underlying theme. Bloomsbury housed the illegitimate offspring of prostitutes and indiscreet girls. Covent Garden was filled with actresses trading on their looks and charm, as did the area's high proportion of female businesswomen in their shops and market stalls. The Strand was the home of London's street prostitutes plying their wares, and just to the south were the pornographers operating from shops and stalls manned and frequented by both men and women. The theme, of course, was that sex sells.

The Foundling Hospital: 'Be not ashamed that you were bred in this Hospital. Own it'

In 1722, Thomas Coram was fifty-four and had led a hard life at sea. On his return to London, he went to work in the City but chose to live in Rotherhithe, 'the common Residence of Seafaring People'. Naturally inclined to hard work, he walked to and from the City at dawn and dusk, and was shocked to see so many 'young Children exposed, sometimes alive, sometimes dead, and sometimes dying'.

Many of these children were the offspring of street prostitutes who had died, become too sick or too drunk to care for them, or who had simply abandoned them in the street. Coram, a foundling him-self, was not a wealthy man and decided to start a charity based on the joint-stock company model: the institution would operate as a legal

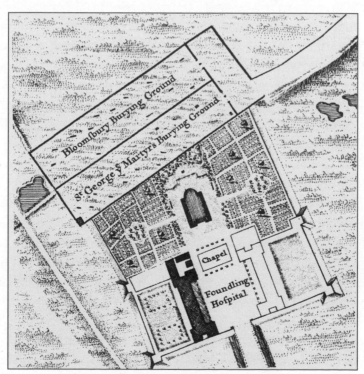

The Foundling Hospital complex, detail from
John Roque's map, 1745

business, taking care of the children by bringing in donations which would then be overseen by a proper board. But people were still smarting from huge losses after the South Sea Bubble fiasco, and donations were hard to come by. Coram was undeterred and scored his first coup by signing up the Duchess of Somerset as a patron, in 1729. Over the following six years, he managed to convince seven more duchesses, eight countesses and five baronesses to pledge their support. The 'Ladies Petition' was key to the success of the project, linking charity with fashion in the way which would do so much good during this century.

This application of pressure paid off: on 14 August 1739, George II signed the charter establishing the Hospital for the Maintenance and Education of Exposed and Deserted Young Children. In 1740, thirty-four acres of pasture near Southampton Row were purchased from the Earl of Salisbury, and 'The Foundling', as it became known, moved there from its cramped Hatton Garden premises.

Meanwhile, the governors had drawn up rules for admission. The children were to be less than two months old, free from venereal disease and otherwise healthy. The adult who gave up the child would have to wait while they were examined and take them away if they proved unsuitable. Once admission had been agreed upon, any possessions, birthmarks and scars were logged, with any items placed in a numbered leather bag. The corresponding lead 'tag' would be placed on a chain around the child's neck, and its removal forbidden, thus enabling the child to be reclaimed should the parents wish to take them back at a later stage. The children were then given to wet nurses on the borders of London. When they returned, they would be taught how to read and how to knit, spin and sew. The boys would be destined for manual labour or the sea, and the girls for domestic service.

The first children were admitted on 25 March 1741. There to supervise their admission were the Duke of Richmond and William Hogarth. A crowd had gathered outside, and the porter struggled to close the door on those wanting to get in. Thirty children were admitted, made up of eighteen boys and twelve girls, and 'the Expressions of Grief of the Women whose Children could not be admitted were Scarcely more observable than those of some of the Women who parted with their Children, so that a more moving Scene can't well be imagined'.

Like Bedlam, The Foundling was not mean accommodation: the children had space and light, and the buildings were handsome. Cows were kept on the estate to supply milk, and the children had their own spring, Powis Wells. Soon, they were to have their own art gallery, with pictures by 'four eminent painters - by Hayman, Hogarth, Hymore & Wills', and charity concerts, including benefit performances by Handel. Handel also donated a new organ, on which he would give many benefit performances of the *Messiah* in years to come. At the rehearsal for the annual performance of the *Messiah* in 1759, he suffered a fit and died a week later.

When the hospital was built, Great Ormond Street marked the northern limit of London, and the hospital sat out in the fields in the fresh air. The governors planned a spartan regime for their charges: they rose at five in the spring and summer, six in September, seven in autumn and winter. They had an hour to wash and put on their brown uniforms, made of a coarse wool called 'drugget'. These were designed by Hogarth, and the wool was brightened up with a jaunty scarlet trim. His sisters were dressmakers, so perhaps he had called on them for inspiration. Each child had jobs which they went about until eight, when they sat down at long tables for a breakfast consisting of broth, gruel or porridge. After breakfast, the younger children worked at their reading and the older children worked at their jobs. At noon, they had a half-hour break for a lunch made of boiled mutton, beef or pork as well as rice and dumplings. Supper was bread on its own three times a week, bread and milk twice a week, and bread and cheese twice a week.

The reaction to The Foundling was not altogether favourable. Newspapers speculated that courting couples would be tempted to 'sin' by the charity. The association of the area with illicit sex and bastardy was compounded by the opening of The London Lying-In Hospital, in Aldersgate Street, from 1751. One scathing broadside addressed 'Batchelors and Maids', and explained how a girl might go to the country 'to take the Air' at Aldersgate, give birth and return to London 'a Maid again' after the child had been given over as a foundling. In February

1760, Parliament effectively withdrew its financial support after granting The Foundling a large amount of money to be self-supporting. They set a deadline of 25 March for the final admission via their traditional reception method. The last child to be taken in before the deadline was a girl, and the governors named her Kitty Finis.

Withdrawal of government funding was a setback, but The Foundling became a giant with more than 6,000 children under its care. To bring in more much-needed funds, it began to hire out the older children as cheap day labour. This was one of The Foundling's least popular actions amongst supporters and the press. Often those who were willing to take on the parish apprentices were 'so inhuman, as to regard only the pecuniary Consideration; and having once received that, they, by ill Usage and undue Severity, often drive the poor Creatures from them'. Many children ran away, often turning up on the doorstep of their old wet nurse. One boy made it as far as Luton to get back to his foster family. The hospital's policies were strict, and wet nurses had to take the foundling in as one of their family, rather than on a puppy-farming model. Some wet nurses and their husbands, having seen first steps and heard first words, persuaded The Foundling to allow them to adopt. Others kept in touch with their former charges and visited them whenever possible, which often involved at least a day's travel each way from the countryside, by foot and wagon.

Back in London, most of the boys were apprenticed at sea, as gardeners, or to the master sweeps. Master sweeps patrolled the streets of London with their climbing boys, and sometimes climbing girls, waiting to be accosted by housekeepers and footmen. Only small children were agile enough to scramble up and brush the soot down inside the cramped, kinking chimneys. Suffocation, burns and falls were a constant threat.

In 1817, the story of the death of eight-year-old Thomas Pitts was recounted before a Parliamentary Committee. Thomas's boss was 'a chimney sweeper of the name of Griggs [who] attended to sweep a small chimney in the brewhouse of Messrs Calvert and Co.' The fire was still lit, so Griggs extinguished it and sent the boy down from the top. Inside the chimney was an iron pipe, perhaps carrying hot water. Thomas became lodged against it, and shouted, 'I cannot come up, master, I must die here.' The alarm was raised. A bricklayer working nearby came and smashed into the chimney with a sledgehammer, he and Griggs clawing at the bricks. They pulled Thomas from the chimney, but he was dead. The report of the surgeon attending was that most of Thomas's lower body was badly burned – as were his elbows, down to the bone – where 'the unhappy sufferer made some attempts to return as soon as the horrors of his situation became apparent'.

Griggs had not been an inhuman boss. He may have put Thomas in the situation which killed him, but he had done his best to get him out, even forcing himself up the hot, broken chimney to recover the boy. Thomas's death was just the luck of the draw for chimney sweeps, though luck of any kind had little to do with the lot of the sweep: should these boys survive to adolescence, they were prone to a testicular cancer known as 'sooty-warts' – 'a most noisome, painful, and fatal disease' brought on by carcinogens in soot. For decades, it was believed to be a venereal disease resulting from sooty love-making, because it arrived with the onset of puberty.

There were a few incidences of climbing girls, but mostly they were put out to do women's work. This included helping midwives such as Elizabeth Brownrigg, a respected midwife in Fetter Lane. She took girls from The Foundling to help her during births, but all was not what it seemed.

In 1767, a girl named Mary Clifford turned fifteen. Upon the death of her mother, her father had married another woman, also named Mary. Four years later, he left her. Unable to support a young girl, Mary had left her stepdaughter with The Foundling Hospital and 'gone into Cambridgeshire'. Young Mary Clifford was put into service with Elizabeth Brownrigg. Clifford had the misfortune to be a bed-wetter, which gave Elizabeth Brownrigg and her teenage son, John, an excuse to shave her head, strip her, make her work naked and beat her while she hung from a hook in this state. They locked her up for whole weekends, without food or water, while they went to their cottage in Hertfordshire.

After only a few months, Mrs Clifford returned to London in better circumstances and sought out her stepdaughter in Fetter Lane. She was turned from the door, John Brownrigg telling her that Mary did not want to see her. The real reason was that he and his mother had beaten Mary into insensibility.

William Clipson was an apprentice baker to Mr Deacon next door. He was upstairs in his master's house and happened to look into the Brownriggs' yard. There he saw Mary Clifford, lying in the filth with their pig. He crawled out of a skylight and 'spoke to her two or three times, but could get no answer . . . I saw her eyes black, and her face very much swelled . . . I went down and told my mistress what I had seen, and what a shocking condition the girl was in.' Parish overseers and a constable were called to the house. Mrs Clifford and the neighbours forced their way inside. When they found Mary

> . . . her face was swelled as big as two, her mouth was so swelled she could not shut it, and she was cut all under her throat, as if it had been with a cane, she could not speak; all her shoulders had sores all in one . . . cut by whips or sticks . . . her head was cut, she had a great many wounds upon it, and cuts all about her back and her legs.

Mary died later that day. Brownrigg was despised by the press as an unnatural mother and a monster. She was found guilty and hanged at Tyburn on the Monday following her trial. James and John Brownrigg spent six months in Newgate and were bound over for seven years. Such was the public hatred for John Brownrigg that when he was released, he shortened his name to Brown and moved further west, near Oxford Circus.

Despite such shocking cases, the governors of The Foundling did their best for the thousands of children in their care. They did not turn away children of mixed race. They took in children of insane mothers, and they became increasingly aware that The Foundling served a dual purpose: by relieving parents of a child they could no longer care for, the governors noted that there was a chance they could be restored 'to a course of Industry and Virtue so that almost every Act of the Charity is attended with a Double Benefit, the preservation of the Child and of the Parent'. One disabled boy, George Grafton, had been admitted aged ten with such severe club feet that he had learned to walk on the outside of his ankles. He underwent a successful surgical repair for the condition, paid for by The Foundling.

The hospital also paid for him to be apprenticed to a shoemaker. He returned to the hospital's employ to 'furnish shoes for the children'. Blind children were educated for a career in music. One of these, Tom Grenville, became the organist at The Foundling as a grown man, living locally with his wife and family. Some children were too profoundly disabled ever to leave, and were cared for all their lives.

What became of the children who left? Many returned at some point. Some came for help, some for advice, some for information about their parents. One such child was Sarah Billington who, aged twenty-eight, wrote, 'desiring to be informed who are her parents; she having laboured for many years under the greatest anxiety of mind, wishing to know them'. The governors could do no more than send her a copy of her admission notes.

The Foundling continued on the same spot until the 1920s, when the land was sold for development. All that remains of the hospital today are the colonnades, although in recent years The Foundling Hospital Charity has provided a playground for Great Ormond Street Hospital. Thus Thomas Coram's legacy still attends to the needs of children at a difficult time in their lives. The pride those involved felt in the institution was reflected in the instructions drawn up by the governors, in 1754, for those about to leave: 'Be not ashamed that you were bred in this Hospital. Own it.'

The London Irish of St Giles's and Hogarth's 'Gin Lane'

'The parish of St. Giles, with its nests of close and narrow alleys and courts inhabited by the lowest class of Irish costermongers, has passed into a byword as the synonym of filth and squalor.' The Irish presence in London ran through all social classes and occupations, but nowhere was it more visible than in St Giles.

Since at least the reign of Elizabeth I, Irish workers had travelled to London in May after they had planted their potato crops. They then worked through the summer, mainly on the hay harvest in the fields surrounding London, and returned home in time for their own harvest. They worked in the booming construction industry and monopolized the sedan chair business. Their wives and many children began to accompany them, and this tipped a precarious balance. Single men lodged in boarding houses or slept in barns and bunkhouses, but families needed somewhere to be together.

St Giles-in-the-Fields had been the haunt of the poor Irish since the sixteenth century. It represented cheaper, older housing with access to open ground north of Oxford Street for the pigs, and also for the bare-knuckle and dog fighting which were so staunchly pursued. The presence of such a persistent poor population meant that St Giles, in 1662, was one of the first places in London to ask for a general workhouse. In the 1690s, Thomas Neale laid out the plans for what became Seven Dials, a 'great haunt of bird and bird-cage sellers, also of the sellers of rabbits, cats, dogs, &c'. The medieval buildings with their deep window ledges held miniature gardens, adding cheer to a grim and declining area where ancient rural customs were clashing with the increasing restrictions of urban living.

Keeping a hog to provide meat for the family was an Irish habit, but in Tudor courts and alleys the space available for livestock was limited, making backyards noisome. To keep down costs, a family would inhabit a single room. The filthy broken-timbered buildings, like a group of scruffy nests, led the centre of St Giles's to be christened 'The Rookery', and the word would be used for any poor dwelling well into the late Victorian period. The last was cleared in the great 'improvements' of 1904–5.

As Irish men moved into year-round employment, their presence in London began to grate. In 1736, ever quick to point out the foreign and unwelcome element of competition, workers reacted violently. An explanatory pamphlet was published afterwards, entitled 'Spittlefields and Shoreditch in an Uproar or the Devil to pay with the English and Irish'.

The butcher-boy gangs of Clare Market were quick to join in. In 1740, gang violence between rival factions exploded when they burned a 'Paddy' effigy on St Patrick's Day, and Irish youths rampaged through the neighbouring streets. John Fielding wrote to the Secretary of State about what he saw to be an increasingly intolerable situation, pleading: 'If some restraint could be laid on the importation of the abandoned

Irish . . . it would be another means of preventing many robberies in this country.' Three things in particular rankled: the Irish habit of sharing their living space with pigs; the habitual overcrowding in their lodgings, because of their innumerable offspring; and the prolonged and unhygienic laying out of corpses.

Drink caused many of the problems in the Irish community of St Giles's. The extent of the problem can be seen in a report submitted by a local constable, in 1750, showing that one in every five buildings in St Giles's sold or made gin. When Hogarth's print 'Gin Lane' appeared, in 1751, it was at the end of a 31-year period in London known as the 'Gin Craze'. It had been a time of huge social and economic change, as well as altered attitudes towards alcohol. People viewed weak ale as a nourishing form of water; beer was seen as health-giving, as well as mildly intoxicating, but it was strictly controlled by licensing laws, and the price was relatively high. Wine was used as medicine by almost everyone, although not drunk by the very poor. Spirits, such as brandy, were the preserve of the rich. But then, the expansion of trade in the first part of the eighteenth century meant that spirits were being imported in larger quantities. This included gin, which was cheap and popular on the Continent. The government welcomed the increase in tax it brought, and encouraged trade. Strong drink was suddenly available, even to London's large working-class population.

Gin was soon being made in London. It was cheap, and could be made from the poor-quality grain that was not wanted by brewers. It was relatively easy to make, and the taste could be varied by the addition of ingredients such as juniper. Gin shops didn't need a licence, and so they rapidly proliferated in the poorer parishes. Adulteration was common, with dangerously raw batches causing fatalities. The poorest of London's workers often had time on their hands: dockworkers, laundresses, tailors and all manner of casual labourers were either run off their feet or waiting for work to come in. This, coupled with the sudden availability of cheap drink sold in chandlers' shops and ordinary houses, meant that men and women could drink together without stigma in places where they felt comfortable. The corresponding rise in casual sex, violence and visible drunkenness shocked London's emerging middle class.

By the end of the 1720s, the city was experiencing serious social problems because of gin consumption. There were thought to be at least 1,500 small-scale distilleries operating in London. Many saw the main problem as one of price, for 'Gin is sold very cheap, so that People may get muddled with it for three half pence and for three pence made quite Drunk even to Madness'. Gin was seen as incapacitating the workforce, raising the rates of illegitimacy, making men unfit for military service, disabling unborn children, as well as making the streets unsafe and unpleasant. It was also destroying the petty credit systems which had kept the urban poor going. Soon consumers were pawning even their clothes and furniture for drink. But the government was in a quandary: by 1730, one quarter of revenue came from taxation of alcohol, and in no small measure this was due to gin.

Hogarth produced 'Gin Lane' and 'Beer Street', as well as his 'Four Stages of Cruelty', as a response to the destruction of both the economy and the morals of the poor wrought by gin. Popular literature on the Gin Craze introduced the idea of addiction. For a woman it was deemed more dangerous, as addiction would lead not only to the neglect of her marital duties, but also put her family and her sexual health in danger. London was used to drunken men in the streets, but it feared gin-sodden women. Women were also more prominent in the gin trade: almost a quarter of distillers were female, as opposed to around a tenth of wine dealers. This was a frightening new departure.

The 1751 Gin Act set the licence for traders at £2, and introduced strict controls. Soon, most of those who held the licences were respectable traders under the control of local magistrates. Brewers began to respond to the competition and tied houses appeared, providing slightly cheaper beer. The 1751 Act was given a boost by poor harvests and grain shortages. This led to periodic bans on distilling, which disrupted gin production. Fashion turned against gin, and even the hardened drinkers of St Giles's chose brandy or punch instead. The Act had caught a lucky break, and the mania for gin petered out – although too late for St Giles's. The damage to working patterns, social structures and sexual restraint had been done, and drink continued to kill in the parish.

In 1814, a huge vat of beer at the Meux and Company Brewery broke and crashed into its neighbour, which then toppled others. More than 300,000 gallons of beer flooded through the streets, drowning six women and girls and one three-year-old boy, Thomas Mulvey.

St Giles's was a centre of prostitution, poor housing, drink and unemployment well into the late Victorian period. One ex-resident, James Dawson Burn, would recall living there. Burn was a Scottish boy who walked to London with his alcoholic father, a man who would later try to stab him and who subjected both of them to desperate squalor and dangerous situations. Yet it was St Giles's which stuck in Burn's mind as a place of 'huge sufferings, savage lives, and innumerable crimes'.

Enterprising heads and jovial hearts: David Garrick's Theatre Royal, Drury Lane

Only a stone's throw from the hovels of St Giles's were Drury Lane and the Theatre Royal. Covent Garden was the perfect place for a theatre, situated on the way home for City workers, and close to the shopping area of the Strand. Restoration theatre had been a cheerful and boisterous thing, but during the early Georgian period more high-brow offerings were made, reflected in the Licensing Act of 1737 which meant theatres performing 'costume plays' were regulated more leniently than those producing music and comedy. Theatres were also regarded as a place where women of 'loose morals' either performed as actresses or attended as prostitutes to pick up clients. As the eighteenth century progressed, the theatre became a legitimate career for women. But it would take time for the stigma to fade.

Initially, the emphasis of serious theatre was upon the playwright. The actors delivered in a way called 'declamation' with little show of emotion or personality. In the late 1730s, Aaron Hill, an influential theatre impresario, began a movement for more expression in theatre. Charles Macklin was in the vanguard with his moving and realistic portrayal of Shylock in *The Merchant of Venice*. Born Cathal McLaughlin to a Roman Catholic family in Ireland, Macklin came to London determined to succeed. He changed his name and acquired polish, adopting an English accent as well as smoothing over the subject of his religion. Shylock was usually portrayed as a 'comedy' Jew with red clothes and a large prosthetic nose, but Macklin made him pitiful, sinister and dangerous. The 1741 performance was a turning point in theatre history.

Macklin lived a dramatic life in more ways than one: in 1735, he killed another actor when he stabbed him through the eye with his cane during an argument about a wig. He escaped with a verdict of manslaughter, and there is no evidence that the sentence – the branding of 'M' on to his hand – was ever carried out. At the Theatre Royal Macklin found a protégé, David Garrick, who had come to London with his tutor, Samuel Johnson.

Macklin and Garrick shared a love of Shakespeare. In 1742, they visited Stratford and sat beneath Shakespeare's mulberry tree. Garrick was living just off the Strand, in Durham Yard, 'with three quarts of vinegar in the cellar, calling himself a wine merchant', according to playwright Samuel Foote, indicating a need to combine acting with another career. That was soon to change. Garrick played many parts over his career, but it was for Shakespeare that he was primarily lauded and remembered. He was sensitive to both his roles and the audience, as well as personally attractive and passionate – despite being only 5ft 4in, and not possessed of a particularly powerful voice.

In 1749, David Garrick took a lease in Southampton Street, at Number 27, paying five hundred guineas for it, 'Dirt and all'. He married a dancer and, despite his success, remained down to earth. Samuel Johnson said Garrick was unable to play 'an easy, and fine-bred gentleman', and in person was always his Lichfield self. By then he was a partner in the Theatre Royal, Drury Lane. The theatre of Georgian London entered a golden era, and Garrick could do little wrong. He was assisted by his brother George, who lived happily in his shadow, appearing in dressing rooms and in the wings with the constant question, 'Did David want me?' When he died soon after Garrick, one wag quipped it was because David had wanted him.

The architecture of purpose-built theatres had developed rapidly during the eighteenth century and soon consisted of a pit, boxes and galleries. This structure allowed for segregation of the crowds and made it much easier for couples to sit in the relatively private boxes together. Yet, theatres weren't always civilized: on one occasion, the persistent London antipathy towards foreign workers was seen in a riot at the Theatre Royal during Garrick's tenure, which was provoked when foreign dancers were featured rather than English ones. A Colonel Hardy was backstage and Garrick, in a nervous state, asked him to go on stage and calm the crowd. The Colonel went, saying that he had come to negotiate a treaty.

> A pause ensued for some time : — at last, two or three gentlemen in the pit, who had been attentive some time, asked the Colonel as to the nature of the treaty, and requested to know between whom it was to be established. The Colonel, turning his back to them, took up the skirts of his coat, and clapping his hand . . . 'just there,' replied, in a loud tone of voice, 'Between you and my ——.'

Garrick watched his friend's efforts:

> . . . with the utmost anxiety . . . [He] no sooner heard the coarse reply, than he ran out of the theatre to his house in Southampton Street . . . The mob, after doing very considerable damage to the theatre, proceeded to his dwelling-house, where they demolished his windows . . . however, after this, the extraordinary business subsided, and the theatre went on as usual.

The esteem in which actors and actresses were held by the public rose rapidly, as evidenced in Garrick's farewell to his audience. When he played his final role at the Theatre Royal, in 1776, he suddenly began to cry, falling out of character and telling them, 'Whatever may be the changes of my future life, the deepest impression of your kindness will always remain here, in my heart, fixed and unalterable.'

The departure of Garrick left a hole at the Theatre Royal and on the London theatre scene that remained unfilled until John Kemble and his sister, Sarah Siddons, took to the stage. The 'Garrick period' was when actresses cemented their position on the London stage, making the transition from charming and theoretically sexually available young women to commanding and talented performers. Sarah Siddons is a prime example. David Garrick had discovered her early in her career, but had dropped her after bad reviews. She did not give up, though, and honed her acting skills in provincial theatres.

By the time she returned to the Theatre Royal, in 1782, at the invitation of Richard Brinsley Sheridan, Siddons' powers of performance were such that her audiences were in thrall to her. William Hazlitt recalled how 'she was regarded less with admiration than with wonder, as if a being of superior order had dropped from another sphere . . . She was not less than a goddess.'

Although famed for being rather boring, greedy and ungracious in person, Sarah Siddons brought real life to the stage, where before it had often been stilted and contrived. She was a wife and mother, and often performed throughout her pregnancies. In her first dealings with Garrick, in 1775, she was spotted playing Rosalind in breeches in *As You Like It* whilst more than six months pregnant. A talent scout reported back that she must have a 'remarkably fine' figure when not pregnant. Garrick, eager to employ her but with some misgivings wrote back, 'Your account of the big belly alarms me! - when shall we be in shape again?' He and the scout continued to refer to Siddons as 'The Big Belly' and to discuss her forthcoming employment at Drury Lane until her husband reported to Garrick that Siddons 'was unexpectedly taken ill when performing on the stage and early the next morning produced me a fine girl'. Her son William performed with her on stage, in 1785. When her children died, it was common knowledge, and audiences empathized with her personal tragedies.

One of Sarah Siddons' greatest achievements was to legitimize women on stage. Recognition had already started to come, in the 1760s and 1770s, for popular female playwrights such as Hannah Cowley, Elizabeth Inchbald and Elizabeth Griffith. At the same time, actresses such as Frances Abington and Mary Robinson were enjoying great success. But their private lives were complicated, and the inference that they exchanged sex for money was a constant in the press. Sarah Siddons' life as a woman of great moral character allowed her to play murderesses and women of dubious morality whilst preserving her own identity, in a curious juxtaposition of celebrity and reality. Her career also saw the ushering in of the 'new theatre', where productions, scenery and costumes all formed part of the performance. The theatres grew in size; the rebuilt Theatre Royal would seat 3,600, staging innovative productions. Tickets, ranging from a couple of shillings to over ten shillings for a seat in a box, could be purchased from the box office in the lobby or from various outlets through the city.

The theatre of late-eighteenth-century London was at its high point as an art form, filled with men and women who were household names and popular idols. The cult of celebrity had begun. In 1777, the Robin Hood Society posed the question: 'Whether the love of fame may be truly said to be a universal passion?' It was carried unanimously 'in the affirmative'.

The Bow Street Beaks: Henry and John Fielding

The Covent Garden magistrate Henry Fielding is now remembered mainly for his novel *Tom Jones*, but in 1747 he was London's Chief Magistrate. Fielding, a colossal drinker and seditious playwright, was an odd character to make a magistrate. His assistant was his blind brother, John, who had lost his sight five years before and wore a black band across his eyes. They lived at 4 Bow Court, in the house of Thomas de Veil, the first Bow Street magistrate, and a man who believed in vigorous examination of the accused and the accuser before he committed a case to trial. The Fielding brothers learned much from him.

The Fieldings came to Bow Court at a time when London's problems with gin were at their height. Covent Garden was riven with petty theft and prostitution. The city's underworld was becoming more sophisticated as the trade in luxury goods grew. Fence-shops had been established since at least the 1630s, when Moll Cutpurse operated her thieves' warehouse from Fleet Street. Cohesive social networks formed in local communities, from the professional beggars at the bottom of the heap to the highwaymen and fences at the top. Thief-takers, who had traditionally brought in criminals in return for a reward, trod a thin line regarding the law. It was a system of pardons, rewards and informers, all of which encouraged dishonesty. Henry

Fielding couldn't stop this, but he knew its evils. He also knew that the deterrent of hanging at Tyburn wasn't working, writing in the *Covent Garden Journal* 'we sacrifice the lives of men, not for their reformation but for the diversion of the population'.

Fielding was sure that if he could get a group of men who had wages 'to apply themselves entirely to the Apprehending of Robbers' then he could really make a difference. The Bow Street Runners were formed in 1749–50, when Henry gathered a group of Westminster constables and had them track down suspected offenders. They were then brought to Bow Street to be examined before him. If the case warranted it, the offender was committed to the criminal courts. In 1754, he was granted £200 from the Secret Service funds to run a permanent team of between six and eight officers. But by this time he was sick, most likely due to long-term alcohol abuse, and departed for Lisbon to rest. He died there two months later, and John rose to the challenge of Bow Street.

John's blindness does not seem to have been an obstacle to his career. He carried on Henry's theories that effective 'policing' had to comprise rapid reporting by victims, a quick response by the Bow Street 'Runners' and effective judicial action within Bow Street itself. Encouraging the public to come forward to the authorities and report crime was the thing he deemed fundamental. For this, victims needed to feel that they had someone to come to, and to that end John opened up 4 Bow Street, creating a theatre-like arrangement where members of the public, 'whether brought there by business or curiosity', could see how the process worked. His method of working inspired other magistrates, and soon crimes could be reported to courts in Clerkenwell, Shoreditch, Whitechapel, Shadwell and St Margaret's Hill, in Southwark.

John Fielding was a skilled magistrate, and the 'Blind Beak of Bow Street' was famous for extracting the tiniest details about a crime. He was also diligent and hardworking: John tried half the cases at Bow Street. Between 1756 and 1780, Bow Street submitted anywhere between 35 per cent and 49 per cent of the Old Bailey's cases. It dropped to 20 per cent after his death. By the late 1750s, John had established a strong infrastructure at Bow Street, using such new methods as identity parades, and training the men who continued to act as his runners. The runners had to be men 'of tried courage'. Any 'act of cruelty or injustice' got them kicked out, which is probably why the band remained very small. They didn't even have their own office initially and were stationed at the Brown Bear pub opposite number 4. Much of the Fieldings' work in their court-theatre was petty crime to do with either alcohol, or Covent Garden's perennial problem: prostitution.

Certain motifs or items of clothing signified a prostitute: a red hood or scarf, a skirt hitched on the left side, or a nosegay of flowers pinned on to her breast. Johann Wilhelm von Archenholz, the German diarist, was agog at the numbers of streetwalkers in Covent Garden and the Strand, and taken aback by how the lower class of prostitutes would 'accost the passengers, and offer to accompany them: they even surround them in crowds, stop and overwhelm them with caresses and entreaties'. He was even more shocked by what happened after midnight, when 'the old wretches, of fifty or sixty years of age, descend from their garrets, and attack the intoxicated passengers, who are often prevailed upon to satisfy their passions in the open street'.

The girls interviewed by John Fielding suggest that street prostitutes were usually aged between eighteen and twenty, although some were younger. They were predominantly from London, the eastern counties and Ireland. Many eighteenth-century men and women believed that sex with a virgin, even a child, would cure venereal disease. Both Fieldings were well aware of the problems of child abuse, and John Fielding in particular made moves towards getting children off the streets who might otherwise be in danger; he was instrumental in assisting the philanthropist Jonas Hanway to found The Marine Society which took young boys off the streets. After all, it wasn't only the girls who fell prey. Link boys, who offered to light the way at night, would also sometimes prostitute themselves. Archenholz, after watching such children attempting to sell their bodies upon the street, wrote 'such is the corruption of the human heart, that even they have their lovers'.

Attitudes varied, and not everyone in London was outraged by the presence, practice and permanence of the exchange of money for sex. Men married, on average, at around the age of twenty-five, and it was accepted that young men, 'strangers to wedded love and domestic comforts, range at large on the common of prostitution'. The well-to-do James Boswell engaged many street prostitutes during his career in London, including his favourite kind, 'the civil nymph with white-thread stockings who tramps along the Strand and will resign her engaging person to your honour for a pint of wine and a shilling'. Not all Boswell's engagements left him feeling quite so pleased with himself. On Thursday 13 March, in 1763, he engaged the first whore he met on an evening stroll. 'She was ugly and lean and her breath smelled of spirits.' He did not ask her name, they exchanged few words, and he used a condom. Afterwards, she 'slunk off' and Boswell was left with the lingering impression of having engaged in a 'gross practice', although he was back for more exactly a fortnight later when he engaged with, ultimately unsuccessfully, 'a monstrous big whore in the Strand'. The casual, opportunistic nature of these encounters made sure that on the Strand, Piccadilly, Pall Mall, Oxford Street and Coventry Street, no woman would loiter making wilful eye contact if she did not want to be picked up.

Those who preferred to complete their business inside had various options, one of which was to retire to a free-thinking public house where rooms were set aside for women to entertain clients. These were ordinary pub rooms, rather than bedchambers, although some were decorated with pornographic tiles or hangings. Otherwise, the girls might rent a room or a building for the purpose. Covent Garden, much of which had started to be built at the same time as the creation of the piazza, was starting to fall into disrepair, particularly the area between the market and the Strand. Here, landlords did not bother to repair the housing; girls rented rooms simply to do business from, which enraged John Fielding. These were the women who featured in *Harris's List of Covent-Garden Ladies*.

Harris's List was written by a man named Samuel Derrick, a failed actor and poet. Lodging in Covent Garden, Derrick was familiar with Jack Harris/Harrison who was the chief waiter at the Shakespear's Head and kept a list of women inside his jacket from which he could choose the appropriate woman for a client's requirements. The list was famous, and Harris was known as 'The Pimp-General of All England'. In 1757, fresh from debtors' prison, Derrick began to pen the guide to London's ladies of the night and where they might be found, with graphic descriptions of their prices, bodies and talents. It was an instant success and ran for the next thirty-eight years. For the man who liked the larger lady, there was Miss Jordan at Number 20, Little Wild Street, who was 'an absolute curiosity, weighing at least seventeen or eighteen stone, and considering that this is no light weight to carry, she is very nimble - we must confess we should be very loath to trust ourselves with her in bed lest we should be over-laid'. Eliza was a 'downright mulatto' and a 'd——d fine hairy piece'. Redheads, whose 'carroty locks create lewdness', had their own section, as did busty girls including, in 1773, Betsy Miles, 'Known in this quarter for her immense-sized breasts . . . Very fit for a foreign Maca-roni - entrance at the front door tolerably reasonable, but nothing less than two pound for the back way'.

Derrick died in 1769, and with him the earlier distinctive humour. *The List* also contains some more comforting entries about sex workers, such as Mrs Dodd, from the 1788 edition, who 'is, indeed, turned of forty, rather fat and short, yet she looks well, dresses neat . . . keeps the house, and after giving you a whole night's entertainment, is perfectly satisfyed, and will give you a comfortable cup of tea in the morning, for one pound one'.

All these women kept their own house, or had a permanent lodging or place of business, but those who did not care to do so would work from a brothel or one of Covent Garden's many 'bagnios'. Bagnios had arrived in London at about the same time as Mary Wortley Montagu was writing her Turkish Embassy letters, in 1717, sparking a craze for all things Eastern. She wrote of a Turkish ham-mam: 'I am now got into a whole new World.' Many were respectable, offering steam baths, massage and cupping. Husband and wife teams catered for both sexes with propriety. But most of the Covent Garden bagnios were a cross between a tavern, a massage parlour or sauna, and a college hot-tub party. Bathing was available, as were drinks and girls. One such bagnio in the piazza went under the unfortunate name of Haddock's. Richard Haddock ran it with his wife, Elizabeth. He predeceased her and she then ran it alone for three years, until 1752, when it was taken over by a Sophia Lemoy. Haddock's was more sophisticated than some of its neighbours, which included the rough Piazza Coffee House, the notorious Shakespear's Head Tavern, Mother Douglas's brothel and the booth on the corner of Russell Street selling pornography. It was fitted out with good mahogany furniture, fine mirrors and good beds, and it was clearly a place of high, if rakish style.

In August 1760, Ann Bell had turned to make her living from prostitution. She and another girl picked up two men and went to Haddock's, where they stayed for two nights. On the second night, Ann was attacked by one of the men. She died painfully over the next few weeks, after such 'shocking usage' from 'some Libertine'. The incident and her subsequent death were the talk of the papers all that autumn.

The story was that Ann had been engaged to entertain a gentleman by another agent, an 'actor'. He and Ann were to meet at the bagnio. It seems clear from the peripheral material that the man had wanted a particular sexual service for which he felt he had to pay, and he believed that, in Ann, he had found someone who would comply. When he attempted to play out his desire, Ann proved 'quite averse to his inhuman proceedings'. When she resisted, he took a knife from his pocket and 'cut her in the most shocking manner'.

Ann was removed from the bagnio and taken to Marylebone, where she spent some weeks before dying, probably as the result of an infection. The coroner pronounced her death due to a fever. Someone, probably Ann's attacker, appeared to have paid off the surgeons and coroner, as they also paid to have the report put into the press. But two newspapers wouldn't let it lie. *The Gazetteer* reported that 'this rape was attended with circumstances of pitiless barbarity'. *The Ledger* repeatedly inferred corruption. Public opinion was also that someone rich and well connected had mutilated a poor girl, resulting in her death, and was now paying everyone to cover it up. In the end, the coroner had to put out a justification of his actions. This included a description of the wounds Ann had received, and only made things worse. She had sustained deep stab wounds near her anus, adding fuel to the barbarity claims. The authorities took the line that Ann had died of venereal disease due to her 'putrid' lifestyle, but the public were not content.

In 1761, the Old Bailey, swayed by public opinion, held a trial. It opened with the accusation that Ann had died of the wounds to her private areas 'whereof she did languish from the 30th of August, till the fourth of October, and then died'. The man in the dock was Willy Sutton, a merchant. He had been present at Haddock's, but had he killed Ann? The trial was full of contradictory evidence and, in the end, there was no conviction. Ann joined the ranks of the estimated 5,000 prostitutes to perish from assorted causes in London every year, as estimated by *The Times* in 1785.

Sex, food and garden supplies: Covent Garden shopping

Richard Steele the journalist went on a night run to Covent Garden Market, in 1712. He took a boat up from Putney with the traders in the early hours of a summer morning, where he

> . . . soon fell in with a fleet of gardeners . . . I landed with ten sail of apricot boats at Strand-bridge, after having put in at Nine Elms, and taken in melons. We arrived at Strand-bridge at six of the clock, and were unloading, when the hackney-coachmen of the foregoing night took their leave of each other . . . I could not believe any place more entertaining than Covent Garden, where I strolled from one fruit-shop to another, with crowds of agreeable young women around me who were purchasing fruit for their respective families.

Women dominated the market, and Steele tells of their cheerful, sometimes bawdy exchanges with porters and boatmen. Many labour under the misapprehension that Londoners of the past ate either nothing but meat, with no fresh vegetables or fruit, or they ate no meat at all and lived upon bread and cheese. The fruit mentioned in Steele's article are apricots and melons, which were grown in specialist 'pits' in Vauxhall. Pineapples and purple sprouting broccoli were also grown there. Salads and tomatoes seem to have been universal. In the cooler seasons Londoners resorted to cooked vegetables, and Frenchman Henri Misson de Valberg remembered his roast beef 'besiege[d] with five or six Heaps of Cabbage, Carrots, Turnips, or some other Herbs or Roots, well pepper'd and salted and swimming in Butter'.

The market fostered a healthy tavern and alehouse trade, with every level of toper catered for. Ned Ward required only an alehouse selling quality pints that would 'not fill my guts with thunder', but François de La Rochefoucauld praised the local taverns as 'fine inns where it is accepted that men go for prolonged bouts of wine drinking'. Nearby was Teresia Constantia Phillips' sex shop, the Green Canister, which she opened around 1732 after breaking up with her long-term keeper. During her time as a courtesan, Con had learned a thing or two, and so she set up shop in Half Moon Street, which is now Bedford Street. Printed handbills advertising her wares were given out in the street by link boys earning a few extra pence.

Con's 'preservatives', or condoms, were so famous they featured in Plate Three of Hogarth's 'Harlot's Progress'. They were made from the caecum of a sheep's intestine, and the standard length was between seven and eight inches, secured with a coloured ribbon about the base. The treatment process to make them thin and flexible was extensive, and they were tested by blowing them up to check for leaks. They were soaked in water then squeezed out before use, to keep them elastic and comfortable. They certainly had some degree of efficacy, and they were popular. Casanova swore by them, and bought them by the box whenever he found a reliable source.

Sex shopping of all kinds aside, the Strand was the main food shopping centre for the West End. Covent Garden Market provided fresh produce, almost all of which could be delivered by messenger boys or porters. Home delivery provided employment for thousands across the city. Coal was delivered to the house by men who rented storage space in cellars and then carried individual sacks or small barrowloads to each house. This was the same with water, which was usually clean water from a local well but also came from as far away as Epsom or even Buxton, for the discerning palate. Milkmaids carried their milk about the streets using a yoke and shouting their wares. Their hours were long, and their pay low. Independent self-employed milkmaids were often Welsh. Those who offered a premium service led their cow on their rounds and milked it at the door. Babies and those with a cow's milk intolerance could have milk from the asses who were also led around the streets. Pretty girls were deployed from the market gardens of Fulham and Chelsea to sell perishable foods and herbs – such as cherries, asparagus and lavender – from baskets carried on their heads.

Although most food was sold by roving basket carriers, or from market stalls, some foods with a longer shelf life, such as cheeses and preserved meats, were sold in large warehouses around the Strand. Many of these warehouses specialized according to nationality, including Mrs Holt's Italian warehouse, the trade card for which was designed by William Hogarth.

Italian diplomat Lorenzo Magalotti remarked in his diary that

Italian Warehouse
at ye two Olive Posts in ye Broad part of the Strand almost
opposite to Exeter Change are Sold all Sorts of Italian Silks as
Lustrings, Sattins, Padesois, Velvets, Damasks
Fans, Legorne Hats, Flowers, Lute & Violin Strings
Books of Essences, Venice Treacle, Balfornes,
&c.
And in a Back Warehouse all Sorts of Italian
Wines, Florence Cordials, Oyl, Olives, Anchovies
Capers, Vermicelli, Bolognia Sausidges, Par-
mesan Cheeses, Naple Soap

these shops were 'mostly under the care of well-dressed women' who were aided by their young apprentices. This seems to have been an excellent system, appealing to almost all buyers.

Later in the century, fixed shop windows became popular, with a permanent and often elaborate display of books, wallpapers, paintings, carving, silks and fabrics, gloves and lace. Many tailors' and dressmakers' shops doubled as places to meet and drink tea and coffee. Most sold clothes off the peg, which could then be altered by seamstresses who hung out large wooden needles from their windows when they were available to work. Pet shops on the north side of Covent Garden sold everything from song thrushes caught on Hampstead Heath to marmoset monkeys in little outfits. There were opticians who tested the eyes and sold spectacles, both made to measure and off the peg, with the 'focus' engraved on the arm. Plain green and blue lenses were also used as sunglasses. This was an idea imported from Venice, where reflections from the lagoon caused light sensitivity.

Shops were dependent upon the rhythm of daylight hours. Food shops opened at dawn and stayed open until they had sold out for the day, or until dark. Most other shops opened at 8 a.m. and stayed open until nightfall, or 9 p.m. in the summer. There were few chain stores, and each shop traded as they saw fit – much more interesting than the modern high street. I particularly like the sound of Arabella Morris's garden centre, also on the Strand.

ARABELLA MORRIS
At the Naked-Boy and Three Crowns, against the New Church in the Strand, LONDON

SELLETH all Sorts of Garden Seeds, Flower Seeds, and Flower Roots; Fruit Trees, Flowering Shrubs, Ever-Greens, and Forest Trees

ALSO Shears, Rakes, Reels, Hoes, Spades, Scythes, Budding and Pruning Knives, Watering Potts, Matts, Sieves, and all Sorts of Materials proper for Gardening. Also Riga, Dantzink and Dutch Flax Seed, and all Sorts of Grass Seed.
N.B. The True Durham, and the common Flower of Mustard Seed

All along the Strand were small outlets selling clothes and accessories, as well as books. The Exeter Exchange was built at the end of the seventeenth century, opposite the old Savoy Palace and close to what became Exeter Street. It was largely occupied by women selling hats, dresses and lace. This was all to change in 1773, when the upper rooms were let to the Pidcock family. The Pidcocks were entrepreneurs, specializing in exotic animals. Soon they had established a menagerie on the first floor of the Exchange. Like the Tower menagerie, the big cats were popular, but the biggest attraction was the elephant.

Elephants were alien creatures to most people in Britain, and to imagine the sound of cats roaring and an elephant trumpeting over the noise of the horses and people on the Strand is rather exotic. But caged on an upper floor, observers soon noted that the animals were not happy and developed a 'peculiar movement' whilst in captivity.

In 1810, the *Lady Astell* arrived in the East India Docks, in Blackwall. She belonged to the East India Company, and on board was a young male elephant. He was called Chuneelah, or Chuny for short. Chuny completed a short but successful stint in the Covent Garden Theatre. There, he would arrive on stage and then deviate from the planned scene by interfering with his fellow actors' clothing, or departing altogether. Edward Cross, the then proprietor of the Exeter Exchange, acquired him immediately. He was a huge hit, but Chuny's life was far from perfect. Without any exercise at all, he was growing. And growing. He was soon 'such a size that it was with difficulty he could lay down in his den, which so worried him that he became more mischievous and required additional care'.

On the morning of 1 March 1826, Chuny could stand no more, and started smashing himself against the bars. His musth had arrived, and his patience was at an end. Edward Cross knew he had to do something. He ran across the road to Somerset House, to ask the soldiers stationed there to come and shoot Chuny. The soldiers came. They shot at Chuny behind the half-demolished grill of his cage. He became enraged by the bullets and had almost broken through his cage, threatening to get out on to the unreinforced portion of the floor. One of the riflemen recalled how, now that their course had been set upon, they had to stop Chuny getting out of his cage at all costs, or 'through the whole flooring we should have gone together, lions, men, tigers and birds'. The soldiers panicked until an officer ordered them to shoot all at once. After a second wave of bullets, Chuny finally died, collapsing heavily on to the strengthened floor.

On that Saturday morning, *The Times* reported how a pulley had been set up on the first floor of the Exeter Exchange. Chuny was suspended and flayed, and his skin was sent to Greenwich for tanning. On Saturday afternoon, during the dissection, a steak was butchered from his rump and cooked on the spot, with several people (including the dissecting surgeon) sampling it. As darkness fell, Chuny's guts were carried down to the river and thrown off Westminster Bridge.

Edward Cross did not know what to do next. He had Chuny's skeleton reassembled and placed back in the cage. Awareness of cruelty to animals was gaining ground rapidly. The papers were full of arguments both for and against captive animals, including one in *The Times* on Friday 10 March, which was signed from Chuny himself, and told the readers:

> To place an elephant, or any beast, without a mate, in a box bearing no greater proportion to his bulk than a coffin does to a corpse, is inhuman; and there can be no doubt that confinement and the want of a mate caused the frenzy which rendered it necessary to destroy the late stupendous and interesting animal at Exeter Change.

Chuny's fate gave many Londoners pause: an animal that had been so amazing to them, that had picked up their coins and handed them back, and held on to their fingers with his trunk, had been reduced to a lump of running gore in an attic room. It furthered the cause for more 'natural' habitats. In 1857, one of the shooters involved that day wrote to Francis Trevelyan Buckland, a leading zoologist, to set the record straight about what had really happened. The rifleman remembered how Chuny 'folded his forelegs under him, adjusted his trunk, and ceased to live, the only peaceful one among us cruel wretches'. Chuny was eventually taken to the Hunterian Museum and stayed there for over a century, until he was blasted to pieces once more during the Blitz.

South of the Strand and 'a multitude of obscene prints'

To the south of the Strand was a labyrinth of medieval streets. Francis Place remembered how many of the area's children were 'infested with vermin' and 'used to be combed once a week with a small toothed comb onto the bellows or into a sheet of paper in the lap of the mother'. It was a poor and shabby place, which suited itself well to the sale of second-hand books and prints. In particular, Wych Street and Holywell Street were both full of booksellers specializing in cheap printed works and erotica.

Continental erotica had been around in England since at least the late sixteenth century, but designed for a small, wealthy market whose pleasures were largely literary. After the Restoration, Charles's relaxed court brought sexuality into the public sphere, and popular works of both literary and literal pornography began to appear. French pornography was deemed particularly saucy, and many titles included faux French words or phrases. Most English pornography from the same period is dominated by gross obscenity and defilement. Continental versions were more sophisticated and varied. The market for them flourished. Samuel Pepys probably represents the average consumer: he had a copperplate print of a naked Nell Gwynn above his desk at the Admiralty; and in the early part of 1688, he purchased a copy of *L'École des Filles* from John Martin, his bookseller. On a February Sunday, 'the Lord's Day', as he noted in his diary, he went to the office to do some work and have a little read of his new purchase, 'which is a mighty lewd book, but yet not amiss for a sober man once to read over to inform himself in the villainy of the world'.

In 1748, English erotic literature really got going with the publication of John Cleland's *Memoirs of a Woman of Pleasure*, or *Fanny Hill*. This marked a departure into that growing literary form, the novel. *Fanny Hill* is markedly different to its predecessors. It is narrated by a young woman and tells of her arrival in London and subsequent 'seduction' into becoming a prostitute. As she then climbs through the ranks to become a courtesan, Fanny relates the stories of what she sees and gets up to. It contains all the usual themes of English pornography but also features lesbianism, and first editions contained an episode in which Fanny related a male homosexual encounter in detail. This was later cut. *Fanny Hill* is remarkable in two ways: firstly for its form as a novel, and secondly because of the happy ending Fanny is given, marrying the boy she falls in love with at the beginning of the story.

Women were not only the stars but also the producers of pornography. Mary Cooper printed and sold *Lucina Sine Concubita*, in 1750. *Lucina* featured in *The Lady's Magazine* in the first year of its publication, and so could be bought quite legitimately by respectable women. In 1805, Baptisa Bertazzi was sentenced to six months in prison for selling obscene prints in a London girls' school. George Cannon was a pornographic bookseller who employed hawkers to throw pornography over the walls of girls' boarding schools.

Lewd, rackety, bursting with humanity, the Covent Garden and Strand districts were unique. There, women held a special, if earthy, power and managed independent lives in businesses of every kind. Next, we move west to Soho, where the artisans rule – making fortunes with their hands, and art out of death.

5. Soho and Charing Cross

In 1600, Soho was little more than fields. Less than a century later, it had become a combination of elegant little squares and a writhing mass of twisting infill. Unlike most of London, the area of Soho – quite literally 'south of Holborn' – has no parish boundaries and no defined limits. It encompasses the parish of St Anne's and the northern part of the parish of St James's, but its true boundaries are Oxford Street to the north, St Martin's Lane to the east and Regent Street to the west. The southern boundary is more fluid, and Soho proper traditionally peters out one street south of Leicester Square.

In 1650, the only significant clusters of buildings were along what was known as Colman Hedge Lane, which became Wardour Street. When the Great Fire displaced tens of thousands of citizens westward, they began to build rapidly on these empty fields. Then, in 1685, Louis XIV evicted Protestants from France, and many thousands of Huguenots arrived in London. Those who dealt in luxury goods, of which there were many, preferred to be near the court. And Soho was also close to their chapel in the abandoned and dilapidated palace of the Savoy.

Near where Charing Cross Station now stands were the Golden Cross and the Greyhound, the main coaching inns for those travelling to and from the coast and from the West of England. Local lodgings were filled with visiting dignitaries and foreign tourists whose diaries and letters provide detailed observations on the routine and the oddities of this varied area.

The inhabitants of Soho and Charing Cross, whether permanent or temporary, relied upon the court and its dependents. Artists and artisans predominated; they created works of art, collections, attractions and interiors. They also crossed paths and tempers, rubbed shoulders and frequented the same coffee shops. Above all, they vied for recognition and financial reward.

Golden and Soho Squares

Building work in Soho got under way in the 1680s, with Golden and Soho Squares. From the beginning, Soho Square was the more successful, probably because, as Charles Dickens wrote, Golden Square 'is not exactly in anybody's way to or from anywhere'. William Blake was born near Golden Square; in 1809, there was an exhibition of his work in the upstairs room of his brother's hosiery shop, on the square itself. It was entitled 'Poetical and Historical Visions'. *The Examiner* sent someone along, but their review was less than favourable, saying of Blake 'the poor man fancies himself a great master, and has painted a few wretched pictures, some of which are unintelligible allegory'.

Soho Square was the second of the area's squares and its most successful. It is a pleasant place, and Dickens describes it at the end of the Georgian period.

> There were few buildings then north of the Oxford Road, and forest trees flourished, and wild flowers grew, and the hawthorn blossomed in the now vanished fields. As a consequence, country airs circulated in Soho with a vigorous freedom instead of languishing into the parish like stray paupers without a settlement; and there was many a good south wall not far off on which the peaches ripened in their season.

Perhaps this country air, as well as access to open space, was one of the things which made the Soho Academy so successful. Founded in 1718 by Martin Clare, it was one of the premier London boarding and day schools of the eighteenth century. The pupils were from families of a more commercial bent than the academics who were at home at Westminster School. The boys were there to be 'fitted for business' and 'taught mathematics, geography, French, drawing, dancing and fencing, and there were weekly lectures on morality, religion and natural and experimental philosophy'. In 1736, the school passed to Cuthbert Barwis, who added 'theatricals' to the school's repertoire, for which it became famous. James Boswell sent his second son to the Soho Academy, noting:

. . . he is quite my companion though only eleven in September. He goes in the day to the Academy in Soho Square kept by the Rev. Dr. Barrow, formerly of Queen's College, Oxford, a coarse north-countryman, but a very good scholar; and there my boy is very well taught.

The theme of scientific learning in the square continued when Joseph Banks moved there and held the first meeting of the Royal Institution in his drawing room, on 7 March 1799.

Soho Square may have been perfumed by a countryside breeze, but from the middle of the century more exotic winds were blowing in residents such as Mrs Teresa Cornelys. She had been born Anna Maria Teresa Imer in Venice two years before Giacomo Casanova, and they knew each other as children – both the offspring of theatrical families. By the time she arrived in Soho Square, around 1760, she had her seven-year-old daughter, Sophie, in tow. Casanova was Sophie's father. Teresa moved into Carlisle House, on the east side of Soho Square, and began to give parties, having determined 'that the most extensive, most opulent, and most important City in Europe was the only one of note that had not a settled Entertainment for the select reception and amusement of the Nobility and Gentry'. These parties were lavish, and entry was by ticket only. She created an immediate vogue amongst the fashionable set. Often, the parties were masques, adding an air of Venetian glamour. The rooms of Carlisle House were decorated opulently on different themes, and she employed the best musicians available – from Johann Christian Bach to Marylebone's Stephen Storace.

Teresa Cornelys was very good at persuading people to pay to attend her parties; to this end, she gave parties for footmen and ladies' maids, in the hope that they would recommend the establishment to their employers.

On Saturday last, [18 February 1763] Mrs. Cornelys gave a ball at Carlisle House, to the upper servants of persons of fashion, as a token of the sense she had of her obligations to the nobility and gentry, for their generous subscription to her assembly. The company consisted of 220 persons who made up fourscore couples in country dances and as scarcely anybody was idle on this occasion, the rest sat down to cards.

The entertainments at the house continued for over a decade, but Teresa was spending more than she was bringing in; spells in debtors' prison loomed. And by now there were many who disapproved of her parties. Horace Walpole, prolific letter writer and arbiter of taste, was not taken in by Teresa's crafty ways. When she held an unlicensed opera and tried to pretend that the box office would buy coals for the poor, Walpole remarked, 'I concluded she would open a bawdy house next for the interests of the Foundling Hospital.' But he said it wouldn't happen, as he knew she wouldn't want the hard work of making so many beds.

In 1772, Carlisle House closed and the furnishings were sold to help pay Teresa's debts. She was imprisoned for an outstanding amount and was in and out of custody over the coming years. She even escaped from the King's Bench Prison during the Gordon Riots but was recaptured in the August, dying in The Fleet of breast cancer, aged seventy-four.

At the height of Teresa's success, in 1760, one of Soho and London's most flamboyant characters was a child in Soho Square. William Beckford was born at Number 22, now known as 1 Greek Street. His father had twice been Lord Mayor of London, and was a good citizen. Wishing to secure the best education for his son, he engaged the nine-year-old Wolfgang Amadeus Mozart to tutor the five-year-old William during Mozart's visit to London. Mozart stayed nearby, at 21 Dean Street.

Mr Beckford died when William was only ten years old, and the boy inherited a fortune of one million pounds in cash, land at

> . One Wolfgang Mozart, a German Boy, of about eight Years old, is arrived here, who can play upon various Sorts of Instruments of Music, in Concert, or Solo, and can compose Music surprizingly; so that he may be reckoned a Wonder at his Age.

Mozart's appearance in London as advertised in the *Oxford Journal*, 23 February 1765

Fonthill in Wiltshire, and four plantations in Jamaica. This was un-imaginable wealth, comparable with the greatest oil fortunes of modern times. Beckford married at twenty-two; though fond of his wife, he was a frequenter of the Lincoln's Inn bog-house and the parade grounds, where he looked for sexual diversion. On 18 February 1813, he recorded a memorable daydream in which he was carried off by 'some great Jock' of a soldier. His acceptance of his own sexuality, coupled with the insulation provided by his vast wealth, made him complacent. He fell in love with the young William Courtenay but his love letters fell into the hands of Courtenay's uncle, who chose to publish them in the newspapers from October to December 1784. William had no choice but to take his wife and daughter to the Continent. His wife died in childbirth in Switzerland, in 1786, aged twenty-four. That year he wrote *Vathek*, one of the great Gothic novels. It was an instant bestseller.

On the Continent, Beckford honed the collecting prowess that has won him fame with every generation of antiquarians since. He returned home, a lonely man, and was living like a recluse at Fonthill, which he rebuilt as a vast Gothic pile. The critic William Hazlitt condemned it as 'a desert of magnificence, a glittering waste of laborious idleness'.

Yet Beckford's art collection at Fonthill contained works by Raphael, Lippi, Bellini and Velasquez. He commissioned work by the finest silversmiths of the day, such as Benjamin Smith and Paul Storr, and bought early works from Turner and Blake. Unbelievably, he began to run short of money. In 1822, he put Fonthill and the contents up for sale. Christies printed over 70,000 copies of the catalogue and sold them for a guinea apiece. It was the sale of the century. London went mad for it, and there was not a room at an inn for miles around Fonthill during the sale. Beckford died in Bath, in 1844, still daydreaming and writing. Fonthill, his ambitious folly, collapsed and his collection is now dispersed amongst many of the great museums and collections of the world. His presence in London was not physical, but his influence upon it through his sexuality, his literature and his taste was remarkable.

As Beckford left Soho Square, another memorable resident arrived.

Thomas De Quincey fled his school in Manchester and came to
London, aged seventeen. Homeless, he gained access to an empty
house on Greek Street and there found a frightened girl. He thought
she might be 'ten years old; but she seemed hunger-bitten, and sufferings of that sort often make children look older than they are'. The
child was elated to have someone to share the dark hours with her,
and De Quincey paints a stark picture of what it was like: 'from the
want of furniture, the noise of the rats made a prodigious echoing on
the spacious staircase and hall; and amidst the real fleshly ills of cold
and, I fear, hunger, the forsaken child had found leisure to suffer still
more (it appeared) from the self-created one of ghosts'. At night they
slept together, she 'tolerably warm' and he in what he called his 'dog-
sleep', constantly waking up from fear. The girl was a servant for the
tenant of the house. He did not live there, but attended in the day to
get her to clean his shoes or run errands. His business had failed and
he did not dare live at the house full time, yet did not want to take the
girl with him to his own lodgings. Perhaps there was not enough
room, perhaps he didn't want to pay her.

De Quincey left the house shortly afterwards, but the memory of
the little girl remained with him: 'she was neither pretty, nor quick
in understanding, nor remarkably pleasing in manners . . . I loved the
child because she was my partner in wretchedness.' Soon, to quell
the pains of his hunger, the seventeen-year-old De Quincey turned
to opium, bought from the chemist at 173 Oxford Street. His only
companion during this time was Ann, a fifteen-year-old prostitute.
They wandered the streets together as she plied her business, or
sometimes he 'rested with her on steps and under the shelter of por-
ticoes'. One day, he collapsed in a doorway in Soho Square. He
realized he had to leave London and return to his family. Ann walked
with him towards the coach, but in Golden Square they sat 'not wishing to part in the tumult and blaze of Piccadilly'. He remembered
how she

> . . . put her arms about my neck and wept without speaking a word. I
> hoped to return in a week at farthest, and I agreed with her that on
> the fifth night from that, and every night afterwards, she would wait
> for me at six o'clock near the bottom of Great Titchfield Street, which

had been our customary haven, as it were, of rendezvous, to prevent our missing each other in the great Mediterranean of Oxford Street.

And yet, Thomas had forgotten to ask Ann her last name. On his return to London, he searched but never found her.

Leicester Square

Leicester Square smells bad. This may be a drains issue, or just something in the air. It is dedicated to ephemeral entertainments, continuing a theme established in the eighteenth century, and it is named for Robert Sidney, the 2nd Earl of Leicester, who built Leicester House at the top of St Martin's Field, in 1635.

The open ground of what is now Leicester Square was known as Leicester Fields until the second half of the Georgian period. Leicester House became the hub of the set surrounding Frederick, Prince of Wales, when he fell out with his father, George II. He was a dedicated supporter of the arts – in particular, the rococo style. Many of the best of Soho's artists and artisans worked hard to gain his patronage. Both Hogarth and Reynolds lived in the square for a time and are commemorated by statues there today. The Prince of Wales loved cricket; he was an avid supporter, and sometimes player. His death, in 1751 – apparently from a lung abscess sustained from being smacked in the chest by a cricket ball – was a great loss to London's artistic community, and to those in Soho in particular.

After the premature departure of the Prince of Wales, Leicester Square became a place for public entertainments. Leicester House, by now getting somewhat dilapidated, was occupied from 1775 by the Holophusikon, a natural history collection, containing items from around the world. Its owner, Ashton Lever, had accumulated pieces fiercely but with care, and the collection even contained objects from Captain Cook's voyages. Soon, the rent on Leicester House became too much and the Leverian Museum, as it was now called, moved south of the river.

In 1783, surgeon John Hunter's collection of human abnormalities moved to the square, and he began to display his teaching collection.

In Panton Street, just off the square, James Graham, sexologist, provided rooms for ladies to take nude mud baths under his close personal supervision. These were supposed to promote sexual health. Portrait painter Robert Barker arrived in the square soon afterwards, displaying his 'Panorama' of London. It was a huge success, and for the first time gave Londoners an opportunity to see how large their city had become.

Then, in 'the Large House, fronting Leicester Street, Leicester Square', Philip James de Loutherberg opened his Eidophusikon, in 1781, showing a moving panorama of various cityscapes and ships at sea, created using painted scenery, mirrors and special effects, such as smoke. The scenes included 'the Port of Tangier in Africa', the sunset in Naples, moonlight on the Mediterranean, as well as the action scenes of 'a Conversation of Sailors of different Nations', 'a Wood-cutter attacked by Wolves' and a 'Summer Evening, with Cattle and Figures'. The finale was 'a STORM and SHIPWRECK'. It ran for several seasons, with changing scenes, until Loutherberg sold it, whereupon it toured the provinces. The Eidophusikon is recognized as the first attempt at early 'cinema', and it is very fitting that Leicester Square is now synonymous with film.

Les réfugiés: the French quarter of St Anne's

The diversity of Soho was not only religious and social but also ethnic. In 1685, just as the foundations for the first Soho squares were being laid, something momentous happened in Europe: Louis XIV revoked the Edict of Nantes. The Protestant Huguenots of France were no longer able to worship in peace. Louis ordered them to convert, or to leave France. If they did leave, they were not allowed to remove any of their money or possessions. They fled in huge numbers: up to 700,000 left France in the years between 1685 and 1688, of whom 40,000 arrived in London. They called their flight *Le Refuge*, and themselves *réfugiés*.

They arrived in motley groups: a fourteen-year-old boy in charge of three siblings, including a baby too young to walk; a seventeen-year-old girl who had stayed behind to ensure her family had escaped without detection, then disguised herself as a man and walked half the length of France to board a ship for England's South Coast. They walked through the mountains into Germany, entrusting their lives to Huguenot guides, some of whom were later executed. Two teen-age boys made it out of France using scrawled safe routes pressed into their hands by fellow Huguenots and Catholic sympathizers. Babies, children and pregnant wives were entrusted to other members of the Huguenot faith, often complete strangers who had managed to get passage on a ship.

The French Church on Threadneedle Street, around which most of London's Protestant French lived, set up a relief fund for those fleeing the persecution. The Threadneedle Street Church was also the hub of a social network. Notices were posted seeking information about family members, jobs and accommodation. Detailed ledgers on the distribution of aid were kept, and these offer a fascinating insight into the situations and attitudes of the people, recording their desperate situations, such as 'big with child' and 'without shoes'. The Thread-needle Church was a powerful organization, but it had made mistakes. Its congregation had split down the middle when some declared for Cromwell during the Civil War. The Royalist half of the church left, forced to find somewhere else to worship. Some Huguenot booksell-ers had already set up in the Strand, selling bibles and religious texts. Someone with sharp eyes spied the disused chapel in the old Savoy Palace and there, amongst scaffolding, broken buckets and detritus, they began to meet. The palace itself had been made over for a hospi-tal by Henry VII, but was largely abandoned by 1702 – apart from a makeshift prison, and a few 'small dwelling houses' and gardens. Soon, the Huguenots were joined by the Lutherans; by 1736, the French Church was occupying its own building in the eastern part of the Savoy precinct. The Savoy Chapel is all that remains of the old palace today and still holds Sunday services, using the 1662 Book of Com-mon Prayer, and the King James Bible. The Savoy Hotel and the Savoy Theatre now occupy some of the old palace grounds.

The Huguenots had pitched up in the heart of a chaotic and changing London. Soho was becoming rapidly built up. In 1686, the

The Huguenot Pezé Pilleau's trade card, promoting his gold and silver ware and
his denture-fitting service, 1720

new parish church of St Anne's, between Dean Street and Wardour
Street, was consecrated by Bishop Compton in order to accommodate a growing population. Many Huguenots assimilated readily into
their new communities, and St Anne's was a focus for those keen to
fit in. Soon, William Maitland said of St Anne's: 'Many parts of this

parish so greatly abound with French that it is an easy matter for a stranger to imagine himself in France.' By 1700, there were 23 Huguenot churches in London, with 14 in the West End and 9 around the eastern edge of the City. In 1711, the vestry of St Anne's in Soho reckoned the population of 8,133 to be 40 per cent French. The Huguenots are defined by their religion, but their faith is only the smallest part of what made them a force to be reckoned with: they were soldiers, artists, thinkers, writers, artisans and craftsmen, and women. Britain owes a great, but barely acknowledged, debt to the Huguenots, particularly in the fields of art, science and industry, optometry and dentistry: John Dollond of the high-street chain of opticians Dollond & Aitchison was a Huguenot who was the first to patent the achromatic lens, in 1759; and the Pilleau family made London's finest dentures.

Teeth were a problem in Georgian England. There would have been more crooked teeth, as there were no braces to straighten them, but the image of Georgian Londoners with black, gappy mouths is incorrect. People knew sugar caused tooth decay, and they were also very conscious of plaque build-up, hence the many toothpicks and home-scaling sets in shagreen cases. To have 'scales' or 'scurf' on the teeth was frowned upon, and to pick one's teeth at the table was deemed vulgar. Good or particularly white teeth are mentioned regularly in personal correspondence, and people did take time and care over their dental hygiene. Toothbrushes were imported from France and Turkey. Toothpaste was available and usually contained a ground abrasive, such as cuttlefish bone, coral or alabaster, as well as sweetening agents, such as rose or orange-flower water. It could be bought as a powder and mixed to a paste, as required, or bought as little rolls known as 'dentifrice', which were chewed and used with the brush.

The biggest problem with teeth in Georgian England was what happened when they fell out. Barber-surgeons and dentists were known to transplant teeth, but with what measure of success is unknown. French dentists were usually considered the best. In February 1696, *The Postman* reported: 'Mr Pilleau as French Goldsmith does give Notice that by Experience of 18 Years he has found out a way to make and set Artificial Teeth in so firm a manner that one may chew with them.' This was the Holy Grail of denture manufacture. False teeth had been made for a long time, from bone, precious metals and ivory. Hippo tusk was preferred because it remained white, whereas elephant tusk was known to yellow in the mouth. Until now, false teeth were useless for eating, rather limiting one's ability to dine out.

In January 1719, *The Postman* reported: 'Mr Pilleau continueth to make and set Artificial Teeth and whole Jaws or Rows with the utmost nicety.' The Pilleau here is Pezé Junior. It was usual for a son to issue a new trade card when he inherited the business, and the younger Pilleau's speciality was clearly advertised as 'ye Art of Making and Setting Artificial Teeth No ways discernable from Natural ones'.

At the sign of the golden ball: Huguenot silversmith Paul de Lamerie

Paul de Lamerie was born on 9 April 1688 in 's-Hertogenbosch, in the Netherlands. His father, Paul Souchay de la Merie, was a minor French nobleman, a soldier and a Huguenot, and had taken service with William III after the Revocation in 1685. They came to London and took up residence in Berwick Street, Soho. How they survived is a mystery, as Paul Souchay had no profession, nor any money. In Pall Mall 'over by the Duke of Schomberg', lived a Huguenot goldsmith named Pierre Platel. Silversmiths were, at the time, routinely called goldsmiths, as they would often work in both materials and the word goldsmith was more appropriate for the profession's position at the top of London's artisan hierarchy. Platel was a shrewd and cautious man, active within the Huguenot community. He apprenticed only four boys during his working life. Somehow, in 1703, he agreed to take on fifteen-year-old Paul.

In July 1703, Souchay applied to the Huguenot charity for the £6 premium Platel demanded for taking Paul on (which is about £1,000 now). By 1711, the young man had served his time. He disappeared for almost two years, selling large and expensive silver items to the nobility. He had, after all, served in Platel's shop, establishing his reputation and making excellent contacts in Pall Mall and St James's. In Goldsmiths' Hall, in 1713, Paul enters his first maker's mark in the official ledger there, giving his address as 'in Windmill Street near the Haymarket'.

By 1714, what was plain was that Paul had an utter disregard for authority. He was up before the private court at Goldsmiths' Hall for failing to have his work hallmarked. Many pieces by him are not marked, other than with his own maker's mark, proving he was dodging the duty levied on finished silver, and selling to people who trusted him to provide them with objects of superior quality. The court fined him £20 (equivalent to over £3,000 now). It was a sharp and rather spiteful rap, considering the court failed to prove the extent of his crime. Lamerie pushed back almost immediately by presenting large quantities of basic domestic silver for testing at the hall – a procedure known as 'assay'. He didn't make the silver himself; he took in work from anonymous French smiths working in the back streets of London and had it hallmarked as his own. He was soon back up before the court, accused of having bought 'Foreigners work and got ye same toucht at ye Hall'.

By 1717, in what was becoming an annual event, Lamerie was charged with 'making and selling Great quantities of Large Plate which he doth not bring to Goldsmiths' Hall to be mark't according to Law'. However, the hall realized they had to admit defeat: Lamerie was simply becoming too big a player to be ignored. Shortly after the court appearance, he was summoned to Goldsmiths' Hall and 'discoursed with by ye Wardens about his admission into the Livery and he accepted thereof'. The livery is the first stage of the upper hierarchy of the company. He probably thought he'd been summoned to explain why he'd changed his maker's mark illegally the year before.

In 1722, the silver and jewellery shop in Windmill Street was doing well, and the insurance policies were becoming much larger. In the same year, a unique case appears in the King's Bench Court Reports: Lamerie vs Armory. Armory, the plaintiff, was

> . . . a chimney sweeper's boy [who] found a jewel and carried it to the defendant's shop (who was a goldsmith) to know what it was, and delivered it into the hands of the apprentice, who under pretence of

weighing it, took out the stones, and calling to the master to let him know it came to three halfpence, the master offered the boy the money, who refused to take it, and insisted to have the thing again; whereupon the apprentice delivered him back the socket without the stones.

Lamerie was found guilty of trying to cheat the boy and was ordered to pay the sweep compensation to the order of a 'diamond of the finest and first water' of a size to fit into the setting. It is the first known pro bono work in Britain, and gives us the law we now refer to as 'Finders, Keepers'.

Not content with building a serious London-based business, Lamerie expanded into the export trade. Robert Dingley was a goldsmith on Cornhill who had connections to the Russian court. He took orders for certain items and had them made by Huguenot craftsmen, but he wasn't in the habit of paying the tax on them before they were exported. In August 1726, officials tried to seize the cargo as it lay aboard ship near Customs House. Dingley, who had been tipped off, was waiting for the officials and took them to the Vine Tavern in Thames Street, just around the corner from the ship's mooring, to discuss the matter. As soon as they were inside the inn, the ship slipped its mooring and sailed for Russia. Dingley was brought before Guildhall Court, where he testified that the 18,000 ounces of the Tsarina's purchases had all been properly hallmarked. The vast majority of the Tsarina's collection, now in the Hermitage, is not hallmarked. More than half of it bears only the maker's mark of Paul de Lamerie.

However, in December 1737, the poacher turned gamekeeper when Paul de Lamerie was appointed to a Parliamentary Committee to prevent fraud in gold and silver work. The committee intended to restore the Goldsmiths' Company's medieval right to search the premises of goldsmiths. This was the year Paul de Lamerie sold a large duty-dodging ewer to Lord Hardwicke. Unsurprisingly, he insisted the clause be 'entirely left out of the new intended bill' and then failed to turn up for the subsequent meetings.

He died in 1751, from a 'long and tedious illness', and was interred in St Anne's Church, Soho. *The General Advertiser* reported that: 'His corpse was followed to the grave by real Mourners, for he was a good man, and his Behaviour in and out of Business gain'd him Friends.' His tomb was destroyed in 1939, when the church suffered significant damage during an air raid.

It would be easy to cast Paul de Lamerie in the mould of villain: cheating the system, swindling a chimney sweep and lying to anyone in authority. Yet a document pertaining to the French Hospital for Huguenots ties Paul de Lamerie to an act of decency, and one typical of the close-knit French community in Georgian London. James Ray was a gilder. The heated mercury used in the gilding process often sent workers mad and, in 1734, Ray began 'running about the streets like a madman, forsaking his business and crying "oranges and lem-ons"'. Before admitting a violently 'distracted soul' to any hospital, it was customary to find a member of the community who would pay for damage caused by the patient. The signature on James Ray's bond is that of Paul de Lamerie.

'All Englishmen are great newsmongers': St Martin's Lane and Old Slaughter's Coffee House

Close to the French parish of St Anne's was St Martin's Lane, full of creative types and pioneers. Here, treatises on fireworks and the first English pamphlet on figure-skating were written by Robert Jones, who would later be condemned to death for abusing a twelve-year-old boy in his lodgings. Many engravers, painters and intellectuals lived on or close to the street, and they all congregated in Old Slaugh-ter's Coffee House.

Over the years, Old Slaughter's played host to William Hogarth, William Kent, the engraver Hubert Gravelot, the sculptors Henry Cheere and François Roubiliac, the writer Henry Fielding, the artists Francis Hayman, Thomas Gainsborough and George Moser, and the Huguenot mathematician Abraham de Moivre. When money was tight, de Moivre gave maths lessons here. Isaac Newton lived nearby, and the two were friendly. Theirs was far from a serious society, yet the coffee house was not a frivolous place of entertainment. The inhabitants of these quasi-public spaces were not only thinkers, writers and artists but also ordinary men. 'All Englishmen are great newsmongers,' the visitor César de Saussure was to remark. In 1730, he wrote that they 'habitually begin the day by going to the coffee rooms to read the latest news'. Just as City coffee houses catered for remarkable and specialist cabals in stocks, banking and insurance, Old Slaughter's catered for a band of artists known as the St Martin's Lane Group.

The art group was organized by William Hogarth, who set up a life-drawing class in Peter's Court, just off the lane. Hogarth's sign was Anthony van Dyck's head: from 'a mass of cork made up of several thicknesses compacted together, [he] carved a bust of Vandyck, which he gilt, and placed over his door'. It harked back to a golden age of British 'courtly' art, when van Dyck was court painter to Charles I, the greatest royal patron.

The following year, a young Yorkshireman rented three houses in St Martin's Lane. The move was a departure from everything he knew, a monumental risk for a man of thirty-six with a rapidly expanding family. The young man was Thomas Chippendale.

His St Martin's Lane premises were not so much a workshop as an expression of his desire to change the way the English occupied their drawing rooms. In 1753, Hogarth published his ideas on art in *An Analysis of Beauty*. In 1754, Chippendale published his *Gentleman and Cabinet Maker's Director* and changed the way English furniture was bought and made.

What Chippendale did was not particularly new; others, such as Batty Langley, had been producing books of designs for gardens and buildings since the early eighteenth century. What Chippendale did was to imagine a harmonious interior, much in the way that Hogarth thought about the composition of a picture. His designs were fashionable, and available. Soon, he had a large group of men and apprentices working from what became 61 St Martin's Lane while he and his wife lived next door.

Chippendale changed the way his contemporaries thought about design and furniture, and he continues to define a style and type. He did not sign his furniture, so only pieces accompanied by an invoice from Thomas Chippendale can be connected to him. Chippendale's success was to do with the coherent, distinctive themes of his manual. Anyone with reasonable skill could buy the book and create 'Chippendale' furniture in the latest fashion, in whatever wood was available. Examples are seen in oak, elm, walnut and mahogany. The *Director* was so successful that there is nothing to tell between pieces made by Chippendale and his more talented imitators.

'The Art of Dissecting': the Great Windmill Street Anatomy School

The artistic environment in Soho was pervasive. In 1746, William Hunter the anatomist arrived in Paul de Lamerie's Windmill Street and set up his Anatomy School so that 'Gentlemen may have an opportunity of learning the Art of Dissecting during the whole winter season, in the same manners as at Paris'.

Hunter was already making large strides into the science of obstetrics. This included making casts of women and their reproductive organs when they had died in various stages of pregnancy. These casts in plaster were then painted to resemble the living form and used for teaching purposes.

Knowledge of the human body was essential for artists, and had been a vital part of artistic education since Michelangelo and Leonardo da Vinci. In the early 1750s, the artists of the St Martin's Lane Academy engaged William Hunter to help them develop their understanding of the human body, how it worked and moved. This combination created one of the most important artistic experiments in the eighteenth century.

'Écorché' means flayed, and by removing the skin and fat of a corpse William Hunter was able to explain the underlying musculature to his pupils, who by now had their own corpse to practise upon. Realizing this musculature would be equally valuable to art students, Hunter set about creating a series of écorché casts. The first, a man with his right arm raised and his left slightly out from his body, was chosen by Hunter and the St Martin's Lane group from criminals executed at Tyburn. The body of a murderer was chosen because of the beauty of his physique. He was transported to St Martin's Lane before rigor mortis had set in, then Hunter and the artists placed him into 'an attitude'. When 'he became stif we all set to work and by the next morning we had the external muscles all well exposed ready for making a mold from him'.

The resulting écorché figure is now part of the collection of the Royal Academy, who appreciate life models who can keep very still. In his opening address as President of the Royal Academy on 2 January 1769, Joshua Reynolds posited his theory that life drawing was essential to the skills of an artist, stating: 'He who endeavours to copy nicely the figure before him, not only acquires a habit of exactness and precision, but is continually advancing in his knowledge of the human figure.' In the same year, William Hunter was appointed Professor of Anatomy at the Royal Academy. In the late 1760s, as Hunter became more closely allied to the artists who would become the Royal Academicians, he associated art with medicine ever more closely, resulting in the work for which he is still remembered: *The Anatomy of the Human Gravid Uterus Exhibited in Figures* (published in 1774). This beautifully illustrated book, with its engravings by Jan van Rymsdyk, did much to advance the understanding of the mechanics of pregnancy.

In 1775, the most famous of the Royal Academy's écorché figures arrived. William Hunter arranged with the sculptor Augustino Carlini that they would obtain a corpse from Tyburn. The identity of the dead man remains controversial, as Hunter chose the best physical specimen on the day. It could be one of two men: Thomas Henman or Benjamin Harley. The body was taken back to Windmill Street and flayed, which took most of the night. When the work was done, he was placed in the position of the Dying Gaul, allowing the head to fall forwards on its broken neck. The original bronze used in the Royal Academy rooms has now been lost but another cast survives in the Edinburgh College of Art. He became known as 'Smugglerius', supposedly after the crime for which he was executed.

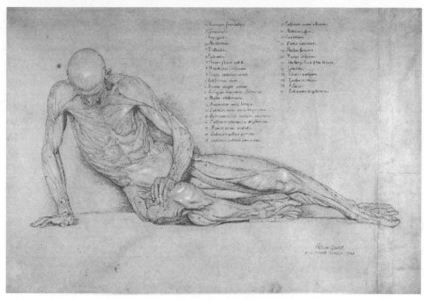

'The Dying Gaul, or Smugglerius', the flayed body of a Tyburn corpse, drawing
by William Linnell, 1840

In 1801, Richard Cosway, by then President of the Royal Academy, was keen to do another anatomical figure, that of Christ Crucified. The body of murderer James Legg was taken back to Windmill Street and flayed whilst still malleable. He was crucified, and they watched as he 'fell into the position a dead body must naturally fall into'. He was then cast.

The Royal Academy also used skeletons and life models, and these became increasingly important as public taste turned against using the écorché criminals. 'These kind of figures,' a critic stated, in 1785, 'do very well for the Academy in private, but they are by no means calculated for the Academy in public.' Increasingly, models were chosen from the streets, often being men of extraordinary natural musculature or cases where the body had become superannuated through physical labour, such as coal-heaving.

One life model, Wilson, arrived in London in the summer of 1810. He was 'a black, a native of Boston, a perfect antique figure alive'. On the journey, or soon after disembarking from the ship, he was injured and visited Dr Anthony Carlisle. Carlisle was one of

William Hunter's successors as Professor of Anatomy at the Royal Academy. He immediately saw his patient's potential, and hauled him into life classes. Thomas Lawrence was particularly impressed, and declared Wilson 'the finest figure . . . [he had] ever seen, combining the character & perfection of many of the Antique statues'.

Benjamin Robert Haydon, Wilson's regular employer, soon took him on for extended periods of time to make the detailed sketches which would inform an entire career. Haydon's admiration bordered on the fervent. Years later, he would wistfully remember how, 'pushed to enthusiasm by the beauty of this man's form, I cast him, drew him and painted him till I had mastered every part.' He cast Wilson's whole body, up to his neck in seven bushels of plaster, but noted: 'In moulding from nature great care is required . . . by the time you come to his chest he labours to breathe greatly.' Wilson passed out inside the casing of hot plaster, and Haydon and his workmen broke him out 'almost gone'. At first, they were busy attending to Wilson, who 'lay on the ground senseless and streaming with perspiration', but when he began to recover Haydon looked at the mould of Wilson's buttocks 'which had not been injured'. He described them as 'the most beautiful sight on earth' before remarking, 'the Negro, it may be said, was very nearly killed in the process, but in a day or two recovered.' Indeed, Wilson came back to Haydon after 'having been up all night, quite tipsy' and wanted to make another cast.

Wilson's fleeting cameo in London is too short, and much of what it reveals does not reflect favourably upon the attitudes of artists or critics; he was at once beautiful, yet parts of his face and body corresponded to 'the animal'. In every modern sense, Wilson was an American man who came to London and made a small fortune in a short time. For him, London's streets really were paved with gold. The image his body created – that of the noble savage – would endure to become an icon for abolitionists. For most of the nineteenth century, his body-type dominated the image of the black male in British and American art. The details of Wilson's life may be sparse, but we are left with the image of an 'extraordinary fine figure'.

The 'porridge island' of Charing Cross

Samuel Johnson once said the 'full tide of human existence is at Charing Cross'. Here were the large coaching inns, including the famous
Golden Cross, sending and receiving travellers from the West. Some
idea of the size and concomitant racket is given by the fact that the
ground floor of the Golden Cross held stabling for seventy-eight
horses, as well as a bar and tap room for the coachmen, a farrier's shed
and a booking office. The entrance to the old inn was too low for the
modern coaches, proving fatal at least once. In 1800, the coach leaving
for Chatham bore, 'a young woman, sitting on the top, (she) threw her
head back, to prevent her striking against the beam; but there being so
much luggage on the roof of the coach as to hinder her laying herself
sufficiently back, it caught her face, and tore the flesh'. She died soon
afterwards. The Golden Cross sat roughly where South Africa House
is now, on the east side of Trafalgar Square. Travellers arriving here and
at other coaching inns, such as the Greyhound, then took local lodgings. The wealthier ones lodged close to the court, in St James's and
Pall Mall; the less well off disappeared into Soho, or south of the Strand
for the cheapest accommodation.

Where Charing Cross Station is today sat Northumberland House,
a massive early-seventeenth-century house, commemorated by
Northumberland Avenue leading down to the Embankment. Facing
down Whitehall were the statue of Charles I and the pillory. On the
north side of what is now Trafalgar Square, where the National
Gallery now stands, was the Royal Mews, providing stabling for the
King's horses. The quality of housing available was fairly low and
much of it was old and shabby, so socially the area was very mixed.
The area south of Charing Cross was full of grand but rotting buildings, street and river traffic, and more of the Huguenot French
immigrants.

One of the larger properties between the Thames and the Strand
was Durham House, now commemorated in Durham House Yard.
In 1632, Sir Edward Hungerford was born in Wiltshire. He inherited
a fortune and, with it, Durham House. Heavy debts sustained at the

gambling tables left him unable to repair the mansion, and it fell into disrepair. However, the house had one huge advantage: the Hungerford Stairs, leading up from the Thames. It was a convenient place for traders to land their commodities to sell at the nearby Covent Garden market, to the north.

Small street markets were everywhere, but it soon became apparent that the densely populated area of Charing Cross and the Strand needed its own market. Edward Hungerford applied to the King for permission to establish a market on the site of Hungerford House. It opened in 1682, a thriving shopping-mall-type affair with a covered piazza. Unlike most London markets, Hungerford had no particular speciality. It sold fish, meat and all types of fruit and vegetables. After 1685, the area became very popular with the Huguenots, and the market was known for selling foreign foods.

There was a large meeting hall upstairs which, in 1688, the refugees established as Hungerford Market Church. It remained a church until 1754, when the market itself was already in decline. However, demand for a market in the area remained high, and so many people came and went via Hungerford Stairs that it limped on for another century, when Peter Cunningham, in his *Hand-book of London*, declared that it failed because it was 'of too general a character and attempts too much in trying to unite Leadenhall, Billingsgate, and Covent-garden Markets'. Despite attempts to revive it, Hungerford Market failed and was eventually pulled down to make way for the development of Charing Cross Station, completed in 1864.

Very close to the Hungerford Market was the dwelling Benjamin Franklin occupied for sixteen years whilst working in the London print trade. He was fond of London, although he thought that his colleagues drank too much beer. He taught two of his colleagues to swim, and once swam from Chelsea to Blackfriars as a demonstration. On his first visit to London as a young man, he made a pass at his best friend's girlfriend, a 'genteelly bred . . . sensible, lively' milliner with her own shop. She repulsed him, and he noted the incident in his autobiography as 'another *erratum*'. The Benjamin Franklin House survives as a museum at 36 Craven Street.

By the 1740s, the problem with Strand streetwalkers had become so pronounced that one night the constables of the watch, having drunk too much on duty, rounded up twenty-five women and stuck them into the St Martin's Lane Watch House. Six of them suffocated to death overnight, including a laundress who had been caught up in the fray on her way home from work. St Martin's and the surrounding area continued to be a rough area, largely dependent upon prostitution. In one court there 'were 13 houses . . . all in a state of great dilapidation, in every room in every house excepting one only lives one or more common prostitutes of the most wretched description - such as now cannot be seen in any place'.

The walls of Scotland Yard, then filled with old wooden buildings, were

> . . . covered with ballads and pictures . . . miserable daubs but subjects of the grossest nature. At night there were a set of prostitutes along this wall, so horridly ragged, dirty and disgusting that I doubt much there are now any such in any part of London. These miserable wretches used to take any customer who would pay them twopence, behind the wall.

Scotland Yard served as the way in and out of 4 Whitehall Place, which was the police headquarters after the formation of the force, in 1829. By the late Victorian period, the headquarters had spread into almost all the buildings surrounding the yard and so, in 1890, when they moved to Victoria, the new building was named New Scotland Yard.

Near the original Scotland Yard, Charles Dickens worked as a boy in Warren's Blacking Factory on the Hungerford Stairs and describes the factory as a

> . . . crazy, tumbledown old house, abutting of course on the river, and literally overrun with rats. Its wainscotted rooms and its rotten floors and staircase, and the old grey rats swarming down in the cellars, and the sound of their squeaking and scuffling coming up the stairs at all times, and the dirt and decay of the place, rise visibly up before me, as if I were there again.

By the time Dickens was working at Warren's, the Charing Cross district was an eyesore in the heart of fashionable London. Lord Berkeley still kept his staghounds in kennels there. The Royal Mews, where the National Gallery now stands, stabled the King's horses. Apart from the grand church of St Martin-in-the-Fields, the buildings and their tenants were poor, including small pockets such as 'the Bermudas', 'the Caribbee Islands' and, notably, 'Porridge Island' which Hester Thrale described as a 'mean street, filled with cookshops for the convenience of the poorer inhabitants; the real name of it I know not'.

The makeshift nature of the area before the Trafalgar Square and Charing Cross developments is further encapsulated in the mystery of Bow Wow Pie.

> Immediately in front of the Horse Guards, were a range of apple stalls, and at twelve noon every day two very large stalls were set up for the sale of 'Bow Wow pie'. This pie was made of meat very highly seasoned. It had a thick crust around the inside and over the very large deep brown pans which held it. A small plate of this pie was sold for three-halfpence, and was usually eaten on the spot, by what sort of people and amidst what sort of language they who have known what low life is may comprehend, but of which they who do not must remain ignorant.

Quite what the highly seasoned meat in Bow Wow Pie was, is sadly – or perhaps thankfully – lost to us now.

At the beginning of the nineteenth century, the area had become hopelessly run-down. The Prince Regent desired something better, along the continental model. John Nash set about devising a recklessly imprudent plan. He imagined a straight Regent Street, smashing through the existing, blurred borders of Mayfair and Soho and designed to 'cross the eastern entrance to all the streets occupied by the higher classes and leave out the bad streets'. It would create a continental-style boulevard in the heart of the West End, leading from Carlton House up northwards to Regent's Park, giving the rich of St James's, Mayfair and the newly emerging Marylebone somewhere pleasant to stroll, sup and be seen.

The reality was a compromised street which was built piecemeal. It is most successful at its northern end. The clearance of Charing Cross began in 1820, but the Trafalgar Square development was to stall for years. The National Gallery, finished in 1838, is the square's finest feature, yet even that is a compromise, built on the plot of the old Royal Stables and recycling some of the columns and decorative features from the demolished Carlton House. Trafalgar Square is a London landmark, but it is a stagnant place, robbed of its diversity and vivacity by a bad attempt at a Parisian street. Caught between a spendthrift prince and an architect of overweening ambition, one of the liveliest, if roughest, parts of London was cleared and left derelict. With the arrival of Charing Cross Station, one of the last remnants of old London was railroaded out of existence. Although Nash's Regent Street development was ultimately compromised, his idea of corralling the 'bad streets' of Soho was successful, securing the area's decline in the late nineteenth and twentieth centuries.

We now leave behind the artists, artisans, soldiers, the English whores and French goldsmiths, the shoppers and travellers and head across Regent Street into Mayfair, London's ghetto of the 'higher classes'.

6. Mayfair

Mayfair takes its name from The May Fair which moved here from Haymarket in 1686–8, occupying the space now covered by Shepherd Market and Curzon Street. The Haymarket was exactly that, dealing in tons of hay and straw for London's many thousands of horses. Shepherd Market was named for the owner of the land, rather than any idyllic meeting of shepherds and their flocks, but the area remained rural. In the reign of George I, the May Fair was banned as a public scandal, and soon after that it was history. Instead, Mayfair was becoming dominated by the mansions on the north side of Piccadilly. Behind them, it was still mostly empty fields up to Oxford Street. This was the scene of some of the fastest growth in Georgian London; by the mid-eighteenth century, it was almost entirely built up, with grand townhouses and leafy private squares for the aristocracy and the fashionable set.

What had started in St James's Fields quickly moved north of Piccadilly, the dividing line between Mayfair and St James's. Mayfair residents were in town to play and to shop. Renting houses and apartments suited them well. Leases ranged from part of a single season to decades, depending upon the inclinations and pockets of both parties. Mayfair comprises seven major estates named mainly after the owners who developed them: Burlington, Millfield, Conduit Mead, Albemarle, Berkeley, Curzon and, of course, Grosvenor. The Grosvenor estate is the only one which remains in family hands today without having undergone major dissipation.

The building of these estates was sporadic and relied upon periods of boom, but the trade cycle of the century was frequently interrupted by war. The Treaty of Utrecht, in 1713, coupled with the arrival of George I on the throne created a sense of stability. This, in turn, encouraged a wave of building which would establish the West End. The rapid bricking over of Mayfair's greenery caused consternation

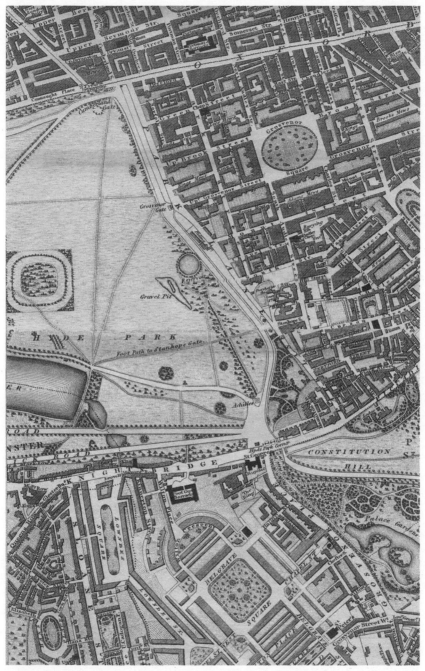

Mayfair, showing the main squares, detail from John Greenwood's map, 1827

amongst her more vocal intellectuals: 'All the Way through this new Scene I saw the World full of Bricklayers and Labourers; who seem to have little else to do, but like Gardeners, to dig a Hole, put in a few Bricks, and presently there goes up a House.'

Mayfair was where a new breed of aristocrats emerged, buoyed by increasing wealth, obsessed by taste and reputation. They built some of London's most spectacular houses and most beautiful garden squares. They cultivated art and refinement in a new way, creating eighteenth-century English style as we know it.

Burlington House, Piccadilly: a 'Man of Taste'

From 1660, mansions such as Clarendon House and Burlington House began to spring up on the north side of Piccadilly, but they were red-brick country houses and soon fell out of fashion. The next generation rebuilt them, but few men would so prominently yet unobtrusively influence London's architecture as Richard Boyle, 3rd Earl of Burlington. Like William Beckford, he inherited his father's title at the age of ten. That was in 1704. When he reached his teens, Richard began to travel to the Continent on a series of grand tours. The 'grand tour' had evolved from a drunken tour of the Low Countries, to take in the cultural seat of Europe: Italy. Burlington adored Italy. He began to collect on a grand scale – and not just things, but also people. On a trip during his twenty-first year, he returned with a sculptor, a violinist, a cellist and some domestic artisans, as well as 878 crates of works of art, and two Parisian harpsichords.

Burlington loved, in particular, the works of Venetian architect Andrea Palladio and his Classical and severe style of building. In 1715, Scottish architect Colen Campbell published the first volume of his *Vitruvius Britannicus*. It was a catalogue of designs, including works by Jones and Wren. In the same year, Richard Boyle turned twenty-one and appointed Campbell as the architect of Burlington House, which was to be rebuilt and modernized. Burlington was by now a cultured and intelligent young man with a love for all things Italian,

Burlington House gate, engraving from William Hogarth's *The Man of Taste*, 1731.
Alexander Pope stands on the scaffolding splashing paint on to the coach of the
Duke of Chandos as Lord Burlington carries a plasterer's float up the ladder

including music. In 1719, he was one of the original contributors to the Royal Academy of Music; that summer, he conducted a lively correspondence, in French, with Handel on the subject of baroque opera. Burlington had found his feet as a patron of the arts.

When complete, Burlington House was a triumph. Horace Walpole described it as 'one of those edifices in fairy-tales that are raised by genii in a night's time'. The house was an inspiration for the aristocrats who visited it, and many sought to emulate it. Burlington continued as a gentleman-architect, designing assembly rooms, houses for his friends, and even a dormitory at Westminster School. Palladian motifs – such as the Classical pediments above the porches, and the rusticated quoins on the corners of buildings – were soon seen all over London. They featured in books for gentleman-architects, and then in trade manuals for builders and carpenters. The ubiquity of the Palladian style in British architecture is clearly seen in the doorways and windows of most of the Edwardian office buildings along Piccadilly still standing today, testifying silently to Pope's back-handed swipe at Burlington, whose simple but elegant building formulae had filled 'half the land with imitating fools'.

'The heiress of a scrivener': the Grosvenor estate

The fields between Park Lane and Oxford Street came to the Grosvenor family in 1677, through the marriage of 21-year-old Cheshire baronet Sir Thomas Grosvenor to twelve-year-old Mary Davies. Mary was the 'heiress of a scrivener in the City of London' and holder of the Manor of Ebury, upon which most of Mayfair, Belgravia and Pimlico now sit. She, her mother and a not-quite-rich-enough-step-father were encumbered by the estate, which was deeply in debt. A fortuitous marriage was the only way out. The Grosvenors had money and a name but were small beer in terms of nobility. Mary had property but neither money nor breeding. The marriage produced two daughters and five sons before her husband's death, aged forty-four.

The day before her husband was buried, Mary introduced her

family to Father Lodowick Fenwick, a Catholic chaplain. By September, Mary was planning a trip to Paris with various members of the Fenwick faction, including Edward, Father Fenwick's brother. What took place there became known within the family as 'The Tragedy'. On returning to London, Mary drew up a petition to Queen Anne alleging that Edward Fenwick and his brother, the chaplain, had lured her to a Paris hotel and drugged her 'with a great quantity of opium and other intoxicating things'. Then, whilst drugged, she had been married to Edward. For the Grosvenor family, their children and myriad dependents, this was a disastrous turn of events. They sent agents to France, scouring for witnesses. Mary was declared a lunatic, probably to strengthen the case, and the marriage was finally annulled. She died in 1730; by 1733, her youngest surviving son, Robert, was the only heir. Two of his brothers had died in infancy, and the other two had inherited the title before dying.

Robert's plans for the estate were grand. Grosvenor Square is the largest of all the Mayfair squares, and Colen Campbell was brought in to create a design for the east side. All the plots were taken by the builder John Simmons, who had a respectable stab at creating London's first palace-front, a grand terrace of houses which looks like one enormous building. However, in 1734, the architecture critic James Ralph slammed it, even going so far as to call Number 19 'a wretched attempt at something extraordinary'.

Still, there was no shortage of takers. The wretched Number 19 was soon inhabited by the 7th Earl of Thanet, who parted with £7,500 for it (the equivalent of about £11 million now). Like most of the finest houses in the square, it was demolished in the twentieth century. The nine-year-old Mozart performed there, in 1764. And in the same year, the Adam brothers began to make improvements to the house. They were busy all over the square for years, providing work for a veritable army of builders and craftsmen. Most of the houses were built with mews behind, containing smaller houses for servants, as well as stabling and storage.

By the middle of the eighteenth century, Grosvenor, nearby Berkeley Square and the surrounding streets were fully inhabited. Of the first 277 houses built on the estate, 117 (or just over 42 per cent) were occupied by titled families. There was also a large 'support staff' taking up residence. In Brook Street there was an apothecary and a shoemaker, as well as a grocer, a cheesemonger and a tailor. In 1749, almost 76 per cent of the Mayfair voters in the Westminster election were tradesmen; they included builders, caterers, dressmakers, two peruke-makers and a stay-maker. At the same time, there were 75 public houses, inns and places to eat. By the last decade of the century, almost two-thirds of the 1,526 residents were involved in 'trade' – ranging from muffin-makers to dressmakers to a gentleman-architect – and all were dependent upon the voracious consumers amongst the aristocracy who, by the 1790s, dominated the area.

Boyle's court guide was first published in 1792, a hybrid of an A–Z and *Hello!* magazine, showing the London visitor which were the fashionable streets and where the serious players lived. Upper Brook Street was almost entirely dominated by the elite of the court circle, with 49 out of a possible 55 houses listed in the guide. The listings followed a strict sense of hierarchy, almost an aristocratic caste system.

The magnates, or grandees, were at the very top, roughly 400 peers and peeresses who owned on average 14,000 acres each; below them were the great landowners at about 3,000 acres, and at the bottom were the country squires with at least 1,000 acres each. During the eighteenth century, many men rose to tremendous wealth through business. They tended to buy houses and country estates, yet often disposed of them during their own lifetimes when a better investment came along. For the aristocracy, holding on to a family seat for three generations or more conferred gentility, and a country seat gave a sense of permanence reflecting family standing. London, in contrast, was a hubbub of unknown potential and danger, artistry and fakery. The things the aristocracy stood for – culture, politics, gambling, scandalous sex lives and flashy wealth – were best suited to the urban landscape. The London Season, revolving partly around the sessions of Parliament, which ran from November until the summer recess, was also a whirl of shopping, visits, parties, exhibitions and recitals. For the two-thirds of Mayfair residents involved in servicing this four-month party, September must have been bittersweet.

As Mayfair became an increasingly covetable address during the eighteenth century, the success of the original speculation, and speculators, was assured. Yet all was not well within the Grosvenor family. Upon Robert's death, his son Richard inherited. He was not a stupid man, but he had inherited little of his father's good sense, and it wasn't long before he began to gamble seriously. Gambling, however, was not to be the sum of his problems. In 1765, he found his wife, Henrietta, in flagrante delicto with Henry, Duke of Cumberland. Richard was thirty-eight, whilst the lovers were both twenty-four. He sued the Duke for 'criminal conversation', or adultery. It must have been pride which made the wealthy and handsome Grosvenor sue; he could not obtain a divorce, as Henrietta could prove him guilty of cheating too. Richard won and was awarded damages of £10,000. He and Henrietta separated in the high-profile case, leaving him free to continue as one of the 'most profligate men, of his age, in what relates to women' and a 'dupe to the turf'.

In 1785, Richard was forced to hand over the estate to trustees, who administered it in order to pay his oceanic debts. He died, in 1802, from complications of surgery, with debts of £150,000 (about £120 million now). It was a sum only achievable by a man with an overweening love of horse racing and the gaming tables. Fortunately, the vast holdings of the Grosvenor estate had remained untouched, although cash was seriously depleted. By the 1820s, all the 99-year leases granted by Robert had begun to expire and his grandson, also Robert, began to consolidate an empire.

Lord Chesterfield: Mayfair's man of letters

Philip Stanhope, 4th Earl of Chesterfield (1694–1773), laid out a set of rules for aristocratic men to live by. Chesterfield House sat on the corner of Curzon Street, south of the sprawling Grosvenor Square development. There the Earl wrote Georgian London's most celebrated series of letters. They were aimed at one target: his illegitimate son, also Philip, born in March 1732 to Elizabeth de Bouchet, a French governess. In 1733, Chesterfield had married the illegitimate daughter of George I and the Duchess of Kendal, Petronilla Melusine von der Schulenberg. She was his next-door neighbour and, at forty-one, a year older than him. He maintained mistresses of varying social standing, and Petronilla contented herself with taking an active interest in her stepson's welfare. Chesterfield could not afford to be too fussy: his stock may have been noble but he was very short, with a large head and bad teeth. 'I have wished myself taller a thousand times, but to no purpose, for all the Stanhopes are but a size above dwarfs.' He was painfully aware of the importance of appearance and tried to impress this upon his son in his 448 letters, which were often harsh and insensitive. There was hardly an aspect of Philip's life he did not seek to either dominate or invade.

Philip was a straightforward and gentle boy. Chesterfield sent him on a grand tour, and his instructions by letter become increasingly precise as the distance between them increased. He saw the grand tour as Philip's 'apprenticeship', which must be served diligently in order to become a gentleman. Philip should get to grips with language and the fundamentals of a 'proper' education.

Poor, good-natured Philip tried to please and wrote chatty letters back, including observations upon the English abroad in eighteenth-century Turin, to which his father replied: 'Who they are, I do not know; but I well know the general ill conduct, the indecent behavior, and the illiberal views of my young countrymen abroad; especially wherever they are in numbers together.'

Chesterfield's preoccupation with appearance continued, and he fretted:

> Mr. Tollot says, that you are inclined to be fat, but I hope you will decline it as much as you can; not by taking anything corrosive to make you lean, but by taking as little as you can of those things that would make you fat. Drink no chocolate; take your coffee without cream . . . It is a real inconvenience to anybody to be fat, and besides it is ungraceful for a young fellow.

All such advice is accompanied with the balm of 'dear boy' and 'dear friend' but quite how far that removed the sting is hard to tell. Yet

Chesterfield wasn't a humourless man. He was often funny and expressive in his correspondence, but his ideas of life and conduct were fixed and finely detailed.

It seems unlikely that Philip was dedicated enough to spend his time at the bottom of the garden reading the great poets. He was no star, but he pottered along with a career facilitated largely by his father's influence. In 1768, he died at the age of thirty-six, at which point Chesterfield was shocked to discover that his only son, himself illegitimate, had been married to the natural daughter of an Irish gentleman for a decade and had two sons of his own. Perhaps he had simply been too frightened of his father to tell him about his wife. Philip's death caused a decline in his father, and Chesterfield wrote, 'I feel a gradual decay . . . and I think that I shall not tumble, but slide gently to the bottom of the hill of life.' He was right; it took eight years for him to reach the bottom of the hill, at Chesterfield House, on 24 March 1773. He left money to his servants, whom he described in his will as 'equals by Nature, and my inferiors only by the difference of our fortunes'. Chesterfield's letters to his son reveal the tiny incidences, pressures and expectations of upper-class life in Georgian London, and really do seem to have been written from the heart.

Berkeley: square of empires

Around the edges of the Grosvenor estate, other aristocrats were building. The buildings are less regular, and so were their occupants. In 1696, the 3rd Lord Berkeley sold Berkeley House to the 1st Duke of Devonshire. Devonshire didn't want the house's view to the north compromised, and the open space left for this purpose in the end became Berkeley Square.

The east side's most famous resident was Horace Walpole, who occupied Number 11 for the last fifteen years of his life. There he wrote many of his famous letters, full of 'lively descriptions of those public events whose nicer details, without such a chronicler, would be altogether hid under the varnish of what we call history'. The site of his home is now covered with car showrooms and offices.

Commercial buildings also cover Domenico Negri's ice cream parlour, which would go on to become the legendary Regency cake shop Gunter's. In 1757, Negri established himself as a confectioner at the Pineapple, in Numbers 7 and 8 Berkeley Square. His elaborate trade card proclaims him as making

> . . . all Sorts of English, French and Italian wet and dry Sweet Meats, Cedrati and Bergamot Chips, Naples Diavolini and Diavoloni. All sorts of Biskets and Cakes, fine and Common, Sugar Plums, Syrup of Capilaire, Orgeate and Marsh Mallow, Ghimauve or Lozenges for Colds & Cough, all Sorts of Ice, Fruits and Creams in the best Italian manner, Likewise furnishes Entertainments in Fashions, Sells All sorts of Deserts & Glass work at the Lowest Price.

Two of Negri's apprentices went on to publish successful recipe books of their own. Frederick Nutt's *The Complete Confectioner* contains recipes for ice creams which are now served up as modern and innovative, such as almond and parmesan. Ice cream was made in a pewter sabotiere, or 'freezing pot', which was packed into a wooden tub of ice. A wooden paddle or spade was then used to pull the freezing crystals away from the sides, churning the mixture to keep it smooth. Negri's also served brown bread, elderflower and pistachio ice creams. All flavours we assume to be 'modern'.

In 1777, Negri took James Gunter as a partner and, by the end of the century, Negri's became Gunter's, a fixture in many a Regency romance. Far from being a run-of-the-mill pastry shop, Gunter's was a place full of ambition. James Gunter wanted to source his own produce and so began to buy small market gardens in the area to the west, known as Old Brompton. He would buy enough land to build Earl's Court Lodge, cheekily christened 'Currant-Jelly Hall' by the press. Over time, he acquired the land on which The Boltons is now built, ensuring wealth for the future generations of his family. His name carries on in the form of Gunter Grove, Fulham.

The west side of Berkeley Square was home to another type of empire builder. Robert Clive was a badly behaved schoolboy, but he grew into the man who secured India for the British Empire. Part soldier, part civil servant, part stockbroker and all self-publicist, he was born in Shropshire to an old family engaged in the law. He was still a teenager when he was sent out to work as a scribe for the East India Company in Madras.

Less than one lonely year into his time in India, Clive twice attempted suicide. His pistol misfired both times. His failure encouraged him to commit himself to his work instead. In September 1746, Madras fell to the French and Clive was called to help with the English defence of their compounds. By the time of the Treaty of Aix-la-Chapelle, in 1748, Clive was a quartermaster and had begun to lay the foundations of his private fortune. He began to turn to opium to help him with his nerves. He was twenty-five.

Edmund Maskelyne was Clive's closest friend in India and read to him the letters he received from England.

> 'Who is the writer?' inquired Clive. 'My sister,' was the reply; 'my sister whose miniature hangs there.' 'Is it a faithful representation?' Clive asked. 'It is,' rejoined Maskelyne, 'of her face and form; but it is unequal to represent the excellence of her mind and character.' 'Well, Maskelyne,' said Clive, taking him by the hand, 'you know me well, and can speak of me as I really am. Do you think that girl would be induced to come to India and marry me?'

Remarkably, Edmund persuaded his seventeen-year-old sister Margaret to come to India and marry his charming and wealthy young friend, who was by now a depressive drug addict. Just over one month later, they set sail for London, but not before Clive had put his Indian investments into diamonds. In England, he tried to break into politics. But two years later, still not yet thirty, he was persuaded by the East India Company to return to India. In August of the following year, 1756, the Nawab of Bengal seized Calcutta, and forty English soldiers died in the 'Black Hole' incident. The Battle of Plassey, in 1757, saw Clive victorious and in receipt of huge gifts of cash and land from Mir Jafar, the grateful nawab who was placed in power.

It was in Calcutta that Clive was given four giant tortoises by British seamen who had brought the animals from the Seychelles. Three died almost immediately and the sole survivor was known as Adwaitya, or 'The Only One'. Clive kept Adwaitya as a pet, and the tortoise patrolled the garden in Calcutta long after his owner had left India for the last time. (In 1875, with no one left to look after him, he ended up in Calcutta Zoo, where he died in 2006, aged 256, having enjoyed the longest recorded lifespan of a giant tortoise.)

In 1760, Clive returned to London and arrived at 45 Berkeley Square a stupendously rich man. He was relying heavily upon opium to manage his nervous 'pain', and public outrage at his personal fortune was growing. He entered politics by buying parliamentary seats, but *The Public Advertiser* together with *The Gazetteer* and *New Daily Advertiser* featured pages of letters, accounts and debate over his wrongdoings in India. Londoners knew too much about his ruthless climb to the top.

By summer 1769, things were becoming unsettled in India and the East India Company itself was in chaos. A select committee looked into the company's affairs and subjected all the upper officers to interviews, Clive included. He would not admit to any wrongdoing, and his arrogance at times bordered upon delusion: when questioned about his actions in accepting the huge payment from Mir Jafar, he exclaimed angrily, 'Mr Chairman, at this moment I stand astonished at my own moderation!'

In 1773, it was put before the House of Commons that Clive had acted illegally in taking the money from Mir Jafar. Clive was cleared of wrongdoing – his actions had, ultimately, helped secure India for the British Empire – and later that year, Parliament passed an Act which pulled the East India Company into governmental control. The Act was also the beginning of the end for Clive. Increasingly alienated from the East India Company and from his former allies, he went off to Italy to buy pictures. He returned to London in November of 1774, and arrived in Berkeley Square suffering from a heavy cold. On 20 November, he excused himself while playing cards with friends; a short time later, he was found dead on the floor of the next room. Clive died by his own hand, but quite how is still unclear. Some say he stabbed himself in the throat with a penknife, others that it was a fatal dose of opium.

The newspapers reported his death quietly, with none of their usual vitriol. The outpouring of public scorn and criticism which had been a constant during his final decade ceased. His monument bears the simple and truthful line: 'Primus in India'.

The emporium of William and John Linnell: curious carvers in wood

Many of Berkeley Square's occupants refused to conform to the uniformity of the rest of Mayfair. Most of the north side of the square belonged to the Grosvenors, and here, one of Georgian London's most remarkable furniture workshops set up in business.

William Linnell trained as a carver and established himself in business as a carver of frames and furniture in Long Acre. The firm prospered – diversifying from carving and going into all types of fine furniture and mirrors – and so, in 1754, they had to find bigger premises. William had a new house built on land he had acquired from a farrier who was living and working on what had been farmland on the north side of Berkeley Square, four years before Clive arrived. The house had a 65ft frontage. It covered three floors, four in some parts at the back, of which workshops filled almost every part. On the ground floor at the front was the showroom or 'Fore Ware Room', with a 'glass-room' or mirror showroom, and a joinery shop as well as an office and lumber room. The lumber room didn't contain virgin wood but picture frames and pieces of furniture customers had traded in. In the hall were marble slabs, stacked up waiting to be made into tabletops. Through the hall into the wood yard there was a saw pit (for the joiners), equipment for sharpening tools and also a ladder. The yard was used to pack the furniture for transport to its new home. Some of these homes were hundreds of miles away, and each piece was carefully packed for its journey along bumpy unfinished roads. Mats woven from plaited rushes at a shilling each were used to cushion the furniture which was then suspended in a frame inside a crate. Smaller items, such as mirrors, were delivered to London buyers by sedan chair.

On the first floor was a cabinet-making and chair-making room, housing thirteen workbenches, and an upholstery room. Also on the first floor was the studio of William's son John, educated at the St Martin's Lane Academy and 'an excellent carver of wood'. The room was hung with pictures and also held 'a box with colours, a painting box for travelling, a mahogany eazel, a porphiry stone and muller (for grinding paint pigment) and a hat box of drawings'. The top floor held the carving, gilding and 'feather' garrets, where the cushions were stuffed. The gilding room would have been one of the cleanest rooms in a house full of sawdust. In jars on the benches were over 50lbs of gold 'size', the gilt paste used for getting the gold on to the furniture, giving some idea of the amount of gilded furniture the Linnells were producing and how much money they must have put into it. Also key to the mixture were linseed oil, parchment, white lead, turpentine, spirits of wine and whiting – all kept indoors, rendering the garrets highly flammable.

After his father's death, in 1763, John Linnell took the business into the upper realms of furniture manufacture. He often worked with Robert Adam, designing furniture to suit the architect's interiors or executing Adam's own designs. John's private life was unconventional. He had a great love of actresses and the theatre. He finally married, aged sixty-five, but made no mention of his wife in his will, which was made in favour of a series of other women and an illegitimate daughter.

John was determined that the Linnell furniture-making empire should die with him. On his death, his house became one of London's first 'hotels' owned by Tycho Thomas. Venture into Berkeley Square today and there is little of merit to see, but the London plane trees in the central garden have been shading the square since John Linnell was carving furniture in a garret on the north side.

Hill Street and the birth of the bluestockings

In nearby Hill Street, 26-year-old Elizabeth Montagu set up home, in 1744. She determined that it was to be 'the central point of union' for 'all the fashion and intellect of the metropolis'. She once wrote to David Garrick, 'I never invite idiots to my house.' Montagu would earn the nickname 'Queen of the Bluestockings', but in her child-hood was called Fidget for her inability to be still. It was a mental as well as physical characteristic.

Just like Lady Mary Pierrepoint, Elizabeth married, somewhat reluctantly, a man named Edward Montagu. Montagu was not a dip-lomat but a fifty-year-old bachelor with extensive coal mines in the north-east. He too would live in the shadow of a brilliant wife. Their son, John, nicknamed Punch, was born nine months and six days after the wedding. Punch died in September of the following year, during the building of the Hill Street house. Elizabeth was devas-tated, doubly so when she lost her mother to cancer almost immediately afterwards. There is no record of how Edward felt. They remained good friends for the rest of his life, but there would be no more pregnancies, and they spent more and more time apart.

In 1746, Elizabeth's father moved to London and set up home with his housekeeper. A general lack of convention in the family's married state was also seen in Elizabeth's sister, Sarah. After a short marriage she was removed from her husband by her family, and they divorced on grounds of non-consummation. In 1762, Sarah published anony-mously *A Description of Millennium Hall and the Country Adjacent*. This utopian novel features a group of smart women from the higher reaches of society who manage to avoid courtship and marriage and thus avoid a wedding night, which probably played a prominent part in Sarah's idea of utopia. It went through four editions, becoming something of a bluestocking bible.

After giving her sister much support and working hard to suppress the scandals of her family, Elizabeth threw herself into becoming a London hostess, bringing together the kernel of an intellectual group which would form the 'bluestockings'. They met to talk in consider-able depth about the theatre and literature, Elizabeth's two great loves. They gained their nickname from the botanist Benjamin Still-ingfleet, who used to attend the smart parties in his rough blue worsted stockings.

By the 1760s, her parties were becoming famous. Cards and heavy boozing were banned. Samuel Johnson, Horace Walpole, David Garrick and Joshua Reynolds were all friends, and her gatherings

were the London equivalent of a Parisian literary salon. Getting to
and from Hill Street, though, was not always a sedate and civilized
affair. Mayfair – and the areas of Hay Hill and Hill Street, in particular – were the focus for a rising wave of street robbery during the
middle of the century and were described as 'infested with highwaymen and footpads'.

The footmen of Mayfair

When carriages became common in the late sixteenth century, footmen went before them and cleared a route, carrying a stout stick for
the purpose. They were called 'running footmen' because as carriage
speeds increased, grander owners continued to employ footmen to
run alongside. In summer 1663, Samuel Pepys recorded in his diary
for 3rd July that the 'town talk' was

> . . . of nothing but the great foot-race run this day on Banstead
> Downs, between Lee, the Duke of Richmond's footman, and a tyler,
> a famous runner. And Lee hath beat him; though the King and Duke
> of York and all men almost did bet three or four to one upon the
> tyler's head.

Pepys records two other races in his diary, both featuring a footman
as one of the contestants.

Life as a footman was good: 'they swarmed in anterooms: they
sprawled in halls and on landings . . . guzzled, devoured, debauched,
cheated, played cards, bullied visitors for vails'. The average wage in
1750 was about £7, but 'vails', or perquisites, were worth about £40,
which means it paid very well (somewhere in the region of £60,000
in modern money). You had the best uniform in the house, including
a good supply of white stockings and shirts, and your job was to be
at least six feet tall, look fit, nonchalant and handsome. Public houses
for Mayfair workers included The Three Chairmen (a taproom in
Bruton Mews), and The Only Running Footman (in Berkeley Street).

Footmen were notorious for being sources of the best gossip, and
traditionally trusted with clandestine errands. They were also famed

for being cocky and 'above their station'. In 1725, César de Saussure complained: 'If you take a meal with a person of rank you must give every one of the five or six footmen a coin on leaving. They will be ranged in a file in the hall, and the least you can give them is a shilling each, and should you fail to do this you will be treated insolently the next time.'

John Parry, a footman turned Mayfair street criminal, was twenty-seven when he was executed for theft, in 1754. 'He was a genteel well-made young Fellow, not a little fond of his own Person.' He came to London after being brought up in Monmouthshire, taking employment as a footman in Hanover Square. He was an accomplished fives player and often played at Higgins's Court, near Leicester Square. After a brief spell at sea, he came back to London to work as a footman again, life on the waves being 'too boisterous' for him. He returned to his first employer, by that time living in Berkeley Square. Whilst living there, he 'contracted an Acquaintance with a Publican's Wife' and the two absconded, having stolen about £60 from her husband. She came back after seven weeks, and her husband took her back. Parry crept off to Oxfordshire to continue working as a footman, 'but he remained not long there, the Town being his chief Enjoyment and Delight'.

In 1750, he was taken on by another noblewoman in Berkeley Square, where he was

> . . . looked upon as a good handy Fellow, and of good Appearance, he was frequently borrowed to wait at Table by Nobles of the Lady's Acquaintance, when they had any extraordinary Entertainment. He was very active, and would do the Work, and be as useful, as any other two or three People.

In July 1753, Parry was 'sent to his Lady's Banker's to receive a considerable Sum of Money, in order to pay off some Bills'. He pocketed the money and forged receipts from the tradesman. In one week, he had been entrusted with £1,100, showing the amount of good faith footmen were often given. He absconded to Charing Cross, where he took the midnight Dover coach. Soon he was in Paris, living the life of a gentleman, cutting a 'great Figure at the Tennis-Court there, and beat the best Players in Paris; and 'tis thought he was the best Player at Fives and Tennis in Europe'.

His ex-employer was determined to track him down and wrote letters to her contacts in Paris. Parry was arrested. He confessed and returned £400, but France would not deport him. Then, after nineteen weeks, they relented and kicked him out of France. He went to Genoa, but soon fled after being involved in a murder. He returned to England in March 1754.

Parry's arrival in London saw him embark on a life of further criminality. He arrived at Woolwich and took lodgings at the Vine Pub, in Vauxhall. For one day, he slept. The next day, at ten in the evening, he rode into Mayfair on a hired horse and 'just against Lord Chesterfield's Garden-Wall, he stopped a young Lady, and robbed her of some Money and a Gold Watch'. The watch must have been very fine: he got fourteen guineas for it the following morning. 'Then he went to a Gunsmith in the Strand, and gave four Guineas for a Brace of Pistols, and went back again, by Water, to his Quarters at the Vine.'

That evening, after dark, he stopped a Mr Nisbet in Berkeley Square and took his watch and nine guineas in cash. Then he held up a coach in the square and robbed Lord Carisforth and Captain Proby of around £9. He pawned the watch that night, in one of the shady shops near the Strand. Then he paid a chairman to take his horse back to the Vine and walked to the Leicester Square bagnio where he engaged a whore.

On 30 March, four unnamed men of Mayfair set out to see if they could apprehend the man who 'had put such a Terror upon all the Quality at the upper Part of the Town'. They met Parry almost at the same spot where he had robbed the young lady the previous evening. When they questioned him, he said he was from Oxford and on his way to Bloomsbury Square. The men were not convinced and found a cocked and loaded pistol tucked between his leg and the saddle. They asked him to dismount, but he spurred his horse and attempted to get away. One man hung on to the horse's bridle, and the others set their dog on the horse. It had been bred for fighting and leapt for the horse's muzzle, rendering it immobile. Parry was placed under citizen's arrest and brought before Henry Fielding to whom he confessed everything. He was committed to Newgate, found guilty at trial and hanged at Tyburn.

Parry's downfall came at the beginning of the end of the glory days of the footman. By the end of the eighteenth century, the streets were too crowded or carriages too fast to be accompanied. Running footmen were 'passing out of the world where they once walked in glory'. The Duke of Queensberry, known as 'Old Q', is said to have kept the last ones as a mark of his own virility. The Duke was in the habit of trying the pace of candidates for his service by seeing how they could run up and down Piccadilly, watching and timing them from his balcony. They put on a livery before the trial. On one occasion, a candidate presented himself, dressed and ran. At the conclusion of his performance he stood before the balcony. 'You will do very well for me,' said the Duke. 'And your livery will do very well for me,' replied the man, as he gave the Duke a last proof of his ability by running away in it.

'Such abundance of choice as almost to make one greedy': Bond Street and Oxford Street

Initially, the leisured classes were drawn east to spend their money in the warehouses of the City, but shops soon spread along the smarter streets of Mayfair. Old Bond Street was established as early as 1696, and building began on the second section twenty years later. The *Weekly Journal* of 1 June 1717 recorded: 'The new buildings between Bond Street and Mary-le-bone go on with all possible diligence, and the houses even let and sell before they are built.' As Old Bond Street met New Bond Street across the open field known as Conduit Mead, the newer part became a haven for shopping and other activities of the fashionable rich.

The shops and establishments along Bond Street and Oxford Street reflected the sudden variety of pastimes and material goods available to those with money. Along the latter, hackney carriages waited for shoppers. At night the street was brightly lit with lamps, and shops stayed open until midnight. On Bond Street, art galleries, hairdressers, tailors, jewellers, a veterinary surgeon, music shops, an opera ticket shop, hatters, print- and booksellers, as well as a lending library and a bathhouse called Culverwell's, were all ready to take your money. In addition there were ordinary shops selling clothes, boots, gloves and ribbons. Hotels and eating houses sprang up to cater for those who were weary.

The rooms above the shops provided cheap lodgings and the perfect place for writers and other artists to be close to their patrons. In 1768, Laurence Sterne – the cheeky Irish priest, author of *Tristram Shandy* and friend to David Garrick and Elizabeth Montagu – died, aged fifty-four, in his lodgings on the west side above the 'silk-bag shop'. He was suffering from consumption and had just returned from a tiring journey. 'In vain did the female attendant, a lodging-house servant, chafe his cold feet, in order to restore his circulation. He complained that the cold came up higher, and he died without a groan.'

Other lodgers on Bond Street included the extraordinary Thomas Pitt, 2nd Baron Camelford (1775–1804). Born in Boconnoc, Cornwall, to wealthy parents, at six years old he was listed on the books of HMS *Tobago* as the captain's servant. Whether HMS *Tobago* was a threat, a promise, or even whether Thomas truly went to sea at six is unclear. He was certainly at sea in 1790 when, aged fourteen, he helped his commander guide the *Guardian* into Table Bay, Cape Town, after the ship hit an iceberg and the crew deserted.

In 1791, Thomas joined HMS *Discovery* as an able seaman rather than an officer. They were destined for the exploratory Vancouver Expedition to Canada, headed up by Captain George Vancouver. On the journey Thomas was flogged repeatedly for insubordination and general high jinks, but particularly for trying, aged sixteen, to win the favours of a local girl in Tahiti using a piece of broken iron from a barrel. Vancouver had him punished and, in the end, clapped Thomas in irons to try to control the boy. Aboard ship, he was regarded as one of the men. So it came as something of a surprise when, in 1793, his father died and he was called home to take over the helm of the estate. He didn't rush back, serving instead on a series of ships before finally getting back to London in 1796.

He had been home only a few days when he caught sight of George Vancouver on Conduit Street. Incensed by old slights dating from their journey, the twenty-year-old Camelford ran across the street and set about the forty-one-year-old Vancouver with a stick. The beating made front-page news, and James Gillray caricatured the row, with Camelford shouting 'Rascal . . . Coward!' at Vancouver as the latter squealed for help. Camelford was bound over to keep the peace and cleared off back to sea. In 1798, he was court-martialled in Martinique for shooting dead an officer who had threatened to mutiny. Later that year, he decided to travel to France, which was illegal at the time as Britain and France were at war. He was arrested and tried by the Privy Council, possibly as a spy, though the Council agreed that he hadn't done anything wrong – but he could no longer serve in the navy. The newspapers decided that he was crackers but quite liked him anyway. He sounds rather dashing at almost 'six feet two inches in height, with curly brown hair, bold blue eyes, and a lithe muscular figure'.

He took lodgings in Bond Street above a grocer's shop rather than live with his mother in the grand but gloomy mansion, Camelford House, on Park Lane. He had an interesting style of interior decoration: 'over the fire place in the drawing-room a bludgeon lay horizontally supported by two brass hooks. Above this was placed parallel one of lesser dimensions, until a pyramid of weapons gradually arose, tapering to a horsewhip.'

Camelford's anger management issues didn't lessen with age, and he quarrelled publicly over anything, even including whether to wear a hat or not. In 1801, London staged an illumination to celebrate George III's return to health. Every house was supposed to have candles in the window, but 'when all London was lit up with a general illumination on account of "the peace," [in Europe] no persuasion of friends, or of his landlord, could induce him to suffer a candle to be put in his windows'. The mob attacked the shop and Camelford's flat above. He ran out with a 'good stout cudgel, which he laid about him right and left, till at length, overpowered by numbers, he was rolled over and over in the gutter, and glad to beat a retreat indoors, for once in his life crest-fallen'.

In the winter of the same year, he was caught in Paris, having crept over the Channel with a specially designed pistol, apparently on some cracked mission to assassinate Napoleon. He came home and devoted his time to pugilism and furthering his education, living above the grocer's in Bond Street with his best friend from his naval days, Robert Barrie. In March 1804, Camelford quarrelled over a woman with his old friend and known marksman Thomas Best. On 7 March, they met at dawn in the wet spring grass of the meadows surrounding Holland House in Kensington. Camelford fired first, and missed. Best aimed, then fired. He didn't miss. Camelford's short, riotous life ended at twenty-nine. Too young to die; too diehard to last much longer. He had left a will instructing that he would like to be buried upon an island in the middle of a Swiss lake, 'where the surrounding scenery may smile upon my remains', a sentiment Lord Nelson thought admirable. He was instead interred at dawn in the crypt of St Anne's Church, in Soho, near the de Lamerie family.

Camelford's love of pugilism reflected, although in an extreme fashion, the way upper-class men embraced lower-class pursuits. One establishment to make the most of this included Gentleman John Jackson's boxing school, at 13 New Bond Street. Bond Street and Oxford Street had been, for over fifty years, popular boxing venues. Giants of men, such as James Figg, gave boxing, cudgel and short-sword lessons. Boxing consisted of standing still and exchanging blows until one of the opponents gave in. As boxing developed, showmen like Jackson sold the sport to bored and glamorous young men of the upper classes. Like Henry Angelo's fencing school next door, boxing offered a gladiatorial form of exercise, previously associated with the cockpit crowd and the Irish. Jackson's perfectly located school, established in his mid-twenties after he retired from boxing as a champion, meant that upper-class men could legitimately combine rigorous exercise with violence, although many questioned the sport's propriety. It was even the subject of public debate during 1788, when speakers 'equally replete with severe irony and strong reasoning . . . decided against the brutality of the practice'.

Soon, boxing was so popular amongst the 'bloods' that it was an accepted part of the education and physical regimes of well-bred youths. As Lord Byron wrote to a friend in April 1814, 'I have been boxing, for exercise, with Jackson for this last month daily. I have also been drinking.'

'Not paid': Beau Brummell

For those who could afford it, Bond Street was a shrine to the new luxury lifestyle of the eighteenth century. It was both a place to be seen and a place to satisfy every consumer urge. This decadent consumption reached its height in the 1790s, during the first part of the Regency, when George, the Prince of Wales, affectionately-ish known as 'Prinny', attracted a coterie of chattering hangers-on. Part of this set, embodying the height of Regency style and fashion in his dress and person, was Beau Brummell.

He was born George Bryan Brummell, in 1778. His grandmother was a washerwoman who is buried in St James's Churchyard, Piccadilly. Her son, George's father, is also buried there. He became an aide to an MP and rose to the position of High Sherriff of Berkshire, whilst living at 10 Bury Street, St James's. This tremendous success involved a kind of social mobility seen both in the eighteenth century and now, but little in the intervening years. The washerwoman's grandson, George Bryan, was educated at Eton, where 'his gaiety and good nature to lower boys were felt and acknowledged'. On his father's death, George inherited £20,000 (a fortune in the region of £2 million today). By this time, he was a soldier in the 10th Light Dragoons with the nickname Beau. He had made a friend of Prinny, who was drawn to his wit and charisma. Brummell's army career was cut short when he refused to relocate to provincial Manchester, and resigned his commission.

Fastidious from an early age, Beau worked on a particular personal fashion. His clothes were severely tailored and, in the main, white, buff and blue-black. He changed his linen frequently, and shaved and bathed daily. Many men washed every day, and many changed their linen at the same time, but most shaved only once a week before church on a Sunday, or before a big occasion or date. And Brummell kept his linen immaculately white, disposing of it before it greyed. Most of the claims about him, such as polishing his boots with champagne, are apocryphal. And he never did refer to Prinny as Lord Alvanley's 'fat friend'. (Rather, this appears to be a mid-Victorian urban legend, appearing famously in a print of 1861 called 'The Wits and Beaux of Society'.) He pioneered 'dandyism', although the term is now more derogatory than its original meaning. A favourite with society men and women alike, his affectation was 'principally assumed for the amusement of those around him' and was delivered in a tone of mischief rather than scorn. It appears a great deal of Beau's success depended upon his comic timing. Upon riding out one morning, he came across a curly-headed friend driving his curricle, with a pet poodle on the seat beside him. 'Ah,' Beau called out, greeting them, 'a family vehicle, I see!' After which the poor boy was known as 'Poodle'.

Before long, Beau began to live beyond his means. His tailoring costs, his home and general lifestyle, contrary to modern popular opinion, were not extravagant, but his gambling was. As a member of the specialized high-stakes gaming and dining club Watier's, he played deep and could not control his losses. He fell out of favour with the Prince Regent sometime in 1811, but it took until January of 1816 for his final debt in the 'book' of gentlemen's club White's to be marked 'not paid'.

> [At] five o'clock on a fine summer's morning, in 1813, he was walking . . . through Berkeley Square . . . bitterly lamenting his misfortunes at cards, when he suddenly stopped, seeing something glittering in the kennel. He stooped down and picked up a crooked sixpence, saying, 'Here is an harbinger of good luck.' He took it home, and before going to bed drilled a hole in it, and fastened it to his watch chain. The spell was good: during more than two years he was a constant winner at play and on the turf, and, I believe, realised nearly £30,000.

Beau died of syphilis whilst exiled in France, but he assessed his legacy neatly when he summed up his fame – putting men into a clean shirt, trousers and a dark jacket. His home was in Chesterfield Street. Berkeley Square was his route home at dawn after nights at the tables. Bond Street was his haunt, and on his doorstep was the vastly changed Piccadilly. Far from the country road it had been in Burlington's time, it had become a busy street of mixed fortunes and a place for viewing the stranger side of London life.

A 'Parliament of Monsters': Piccadilly's entertainments

In Georgian London there were many 'freaks' whose main source of income came from displaying themselves as tall or strong women, tiny people, progeria sufferers and 'mer-people'. Sexual freaks such as bearded ladies or hermaphrodites were particularly popular. Anything exotic caused queues to form in the street outside the chosen venue of display. All of these factors combined to make the exhibition of Saartjie Baartman, the 'Hottentot Venus', one of the sideshows of the age.

Sara, 'little Sara' in Dutch, was of the Khoikhoi people of South Africa. They proved of particular interest to missionaries and early travelling scientists for numerous reasons, not least their distinctive features and their clicking language. However, the greatest attraction for the 'collectors' of natural phenomena of the day was the physical appearance of Khoikhoi females, with their large breasts and high, round buttocks. The women of the tribe wore little or no clothing when in their natural environment, making their super-developed genitalia the focus of great curiosity for the white male visitors.

Sara was 'acquired' by Alexander Dunlop, a ship's surgeon who sourced 'specimens' of all kinds for museums from the African Cape. In 1810, he brought Sara to England through Liverpool. There, Dunlop sold Sara to showman Henrik Cezar who brought her to 225 Piccadilly. A flyer was produced advertising her presence, with the invitation to view, at two shillings a go. 'One gentleman poked her with his cane; one lady employed her parasol to ascertain that all was, as she called it, "nattral".' Sara wore an English dress, but her small waist was bounded with African beads and ornaments.

The exhibition caused an uproar amongst those rushing to see it and amongst the abolitionists, who saw her condition as slavery. A liberal newspaper, the *Morning Chronicle*, featured a letter on 12 October 1810, declaring, 'It was contrary to every principle of morality and good order.' But Cezar soon responded, arguing that it was Sara's right to exhibit herself and earn her living. The situation prompted a court case, with her would-be protectors stating that she was held against her will and pressing for her repatriation to Africa. The case failed, with the court finding for Cezar. The case soured the exhibition in London. Sara and Cezar moved on to Paris, where she died, in 1815.

Piccadilly was a place for all sorts of curiosities to be displayed. Almost opposite Burlington House, at 170–173 Piccadilly, a Starbucks coffee shop now sits where William Bullock's Egyptian Hall once stood. From 1798, when Nelson triumphed at the Battle of the Nile, English interest in the 'East' began to soar. While obelisks and other monumental pieces had been leaking out of Egypt for a century, Napoleon's heavy thieving from Luxor and Karnak made Egyptian objects desirable amongst the European elite. The victory of the Battle of the Nile also coincided with a period in which an extended grand tour took in Turkey or Egypt. The romance of the East rapidly took hold of the English upper-class imagination, with books, prints and Eastern costume all the rage.

Thomas Hope, a merchant banker resident in Marylebone, was part of the Hope dynasty (later of Hope Diamond fame). With no pressing need to commit to an occupation, he spent much of his young life on a succession of grand tours, taking in much of the known world. He decorated his home in a manner reflecting his travels, and was much taken with Classical and Egyptian themes. His Egyptian Room was open to the public, and this may have been the forerunner to the Egyptian Hall.

In 1809, Bullock's Museum arrived in London from Liverpool; in 1812, the Egyptian Hall was ready for occupation. It must have appeared quite surreal to the man on the street. The grand hall of the interior was an extraordinary replica of the avenue at the Karnak Temple complex, near Luxor. By 1819, Bullock was ready to sell his collection of real and spurious objects, and did so in an auction lasting twenty-six days. It was dispersed all over the world. Emptied of its original tenant, the Egyptian Hall received a new and rather more suitable guest: Giovanni Battista Belzoni, known to his English friends as 'John'.

John Belzoni was born in 1778, in Padua. He was an actor and a strongman who moved around Europe before arriving in London, in 1803. That year, he married and performed as the 'Patagonian Samson' at Sadler's Wells. But Belzoni had trouble staying in one place; Europe had no sooner quietened down after the Napoleonic Wars than he was off again, taking his wife, Sarah, with him. In 1815, he reached Egypt where the British Consul, Henry Salt, engaged him to journey to Luxor to retrieve the 'Younger Memnon' from the Memnonium. This was the head of Ramesses II in what is now called the Ramesseum near the Valley of the Kings. It was the perfect job for an adventurer like Belzoni. He even went so far as to say the statue of Ramesses II, famously beatific in expression, was 'apparently smiling on me, at the thought of being taken to England'.

In 1817, he travelled to the Valley of the Kings and broke into the tomb of Seti I. From Seti's tomb, Belzoni took a sarcophagus of white alabaster inlaid with blue copper sulphate of great beauty. The retrieval of the sarcophagus, however, was not without peril: the tomb was located in the catacombs, a maze of traps and dead ends, dug to confuse grave robbers. The French interpreter panicked and an Arab assistant broke his hip in a booby trap. Undeterred, Belzoni retrieved the sarcophagus and brought it to England along with the head of the 'Younger Memnon'. Belzoni suffered constant vomiting and nosebleeds in Egypt, whilst Sarah was unaffected by so much as a case of sunburn – much to his chagrin.

London eagerly anticipated the imminent arrival of these treasures. Shelley's famous poem of 1818, 'Ozymandias', was written for a newspaper competition held by *The Examiner* in advance of the arrival of Belzoni's treasures. The exhibition opened at the Egyptian Hall in May 1821, but a year later the collection was put up for auction. The sale drew two of the greatest collectors of the day: the British Museum and Sir John Soane. The Museum acquired the colossus and Soane the sarcophagus. John Belzoni, financially if not spiritually satisfied, handed in the manuscript of his travels to his publisher, John Murray, and set off for Benin. He died of dysentery one week after arriving there.

Before long, the Egyptian Hall moved on to displaying real-life Laplanders, who gave sleigh rides up and down the central space. It continued on as an exhibition space until redevelopment in 1904, when this extraordinary Georgian flight of fancy was replaced with offices bearing miniature versions of Andrea Palladio's Venetian windows.

By the end of the Georgian era, the old fields of the May Fair and Shepherd Market had been filled in. The Hay Market had relocated close to the new Regent's Park, though open fields were still lying to the north. Piccadilly was no longer just a road to the Knight's Bridge and the outlying village of Chelsea, but was now a busy thoroughfare. At dawn, as the first coaches rattled out towards Bath and Bristol, a constant stream of girls and women could be seen passing Burlington House. They walked in from the distant market gardens of Fulham, heading for Covent Garden, baskets of produce on their heads. As the century went on and Mayfair grew, many looked north towards London's wetlands and ancient hunting grounds, full of natural pools and ponds, and where the parishes still offered sixpenny rewards for dead polecats: Marylebone.

7.   Marylebone

Like Mayfair, the infilling of the fields of St Mary-le-Bourne began after the Treaty of Utrecht, in 1713. Unlike Mayfair, Marylebone engulfed the small villages of St Mary's and Paddington, which had been in existence for centuries. Though rural infrastructure was already in place, the patterns and nature of development were markedly different to that of the 'great estates' to the south.

During the first half of the eighteenth century, Marylebone retained a village atmosphere, despite the large amounts of development. It had a high street, pleasure gardens and was surrounded by open fields. This changed in 1756, when the New Road running from Paddington to Islington was built to prevent cattle and heavy goods traffic moving up and down Oxford Street, and it formed the northern limit of the original development. (This road is now the A501, the northern limit of the Congestion Charge zone. Beneath the road runs the Metropolitan Line. It is still one of London's defining borders.)

Marylebone was more bohemian and creative than Mayfair. It was also diverse, housing painters, builders, musicians and aristocrats, as well as London's largest black population. In this area of London, the core of the collections of the British Library and Kew Gardens were formed. Here, Handel listened to bad renditions of his own music. Gentlemanly pursuits were a theme in Marylebone, and the area played host to hundreds, if not thousands, of the better kind of prostitute, who 'live decently and without being disturbed. They are mistresses in their own house, and if any of the magistrates should think of troubling them, they might shew him the door.'

In the later part of the eighteenth century, Marylebone was transformed, becoming a huge settlement bordered on one side by John Nash's Regent's Park. The park contains London's finest surviving Regency architecture, with ten stuccoed terraces, seven smaller terraces, a crescent, a barracks, a church and two small residential estates, as well as a serpentine lake and a canal. Nash did not neglect the middle classes, creating for them the unique ranks of individually styled semi-detached villas in St John's Wood. Built in the second decade of the nineteenth century, they are believed to be the first of their type and were copied on estates all over England in the century that followed. In 1828, the Zoological Society of London opened on the north side of the park, taking in many of the animals from the Tower of London menagerie. The animals were all kept inside, in heated environments, and included the now extinct quaggas and the strange thylacine, or Tasmanian wolf.

Meanwhile, the area which had been the village of Paddington was being swamped by Irish labourers building the new Regent's Canal. The coming of the canals meant the birth of the Irish 'navigator', or 'navvies', and their connection to the waterways. They spilled out of St Giles's to the open space of Tyburnia, bounded on the east by Tottenham Court Road and on the west only by the encroaching, genteel streets of the 'great city north of Oxford Street'. They kept pigs and held dog fights and bare-knuckle competitions, much to the chagrin of their smarter neighbours. Nearby, the Tyburn scaffold stood (near what is now the Marble Arch roundabout), a constant reminder that the consequences of a life of crime were never far away.

Tyburn: 'The public was gratified by a procession; the criminal was supported by it'

The first hangings at Tyburn date from the late twelfth century. In 1560, the gallows feature on a map of the area; in 1571, the 'Triple Tree' was erected, consisting of a triangle of beams from which eight offenders could be hanged.

London's eight hanging days a year were public holidays, and huge numbers of people attended the executions. The condemned were driven through the streets from Newgate in a wagon, taking pause for alcoholic refreshment along the way. Many arrived at Tyburn mercifully drunk, but for even the most hardened of criminals the clamour and crush would have been overwhelming.

The hanging was not the final moment in the day's programme. Bernard Mandeville observed that 'the next Entertainment is a scuffle between the surgeons and the mob'. The hangman received the clothes as a perk, and the bodies were destined to further human understanding through undergoing dissection by surgeons, and sometimes by artists. It was not unusual for the crowd to distract the surgeons whilst the family removed a corpse. The accounts of the Company of Barber-Surgeons record that, in 1720, they 'paid the hangman for the dead mans clothes which were lost in the scuffle and for his Christmas Box £0.15.0'.

Hangmen themselves were not above the law. In 1718, John Price was executed for murdering Elizabeth White, who sold 'Cakes and Gingerbread about the Streets'. Price was a petty criminal from the 'fog-end of the suburbs of London, and, like Mercury, became a thief as soon as ever he peeped out of the shell'. He was appointed hangman after a spell in Newgate and excelled at it, having 'cruelty at his finger-ends'.

In March 1718, Alexander Dufey was on his way home in the dark when he heard a woman groan, and he 'heard the Man say, D—mn you for a Bitch . . . if you won't put it in I'll rip you up.' Torn by fear and indecision, Dufey saw another man ahead of him, who also realized what was happening. They went in search of the source, finding Elizabeth White in an appalling state with Price on top of her. She was 'very Bloody in the Face, and one of her Eyes beat out of her Head'. The two men set upon Price and dragged him to the watch house. Price tried to use his station as hangman to wriggle out of it, but the watchman 'knew him to be a Thief and a Rogue, and if he did not sit down he would knock him down, or throw him into the Fire'. Price secured, Dufey took the constable out to try to find Elizabeth White, but in the darkness of the fields they couldn't see her. In the end, only a dog 'barking about the Body, gave them notice where to find her'.

The picture painted in the courtroom is one of extreme violence on Price's part:

That when they came they found her lying in a sad Condition, as had been before described; and besides some of her Teeth knock'd out . . . and one of her Arms broke; that then he got her carried to the Watch-house, and sent for some Women to hold her forwards, for she was choak'd with Clots of Blood in her Mouth and Throat, and could not speak.

The surgeon said he had never seen head injuries like it. Elizabeth was assigned a nurse but died four days later. Price was found guilty, sentenced to death and went to the gallows drunk on gin.

The Price case was clear-cut, but throughout the eighteenth century there were many other Tyburn hangings which left the mob divided. Accounts of hanging days include tales of parents who walked many miles to watch a child hang for petty theft, anxious to protect their body in death as they could not protect them in life. For many of the assembled mob, the highwaymen who were hanged at Tyburn were heroes in the tradition of Robin Hood.

In 1763, James Boswell watched Paul Lewis hang, convicted as a highwayman, aged twenty-three. Lewis was the son of a gentleman and, although a 'genteel, and spirited young fellow', had struggled to live up to family expectations as he had never learned to 'spell, or write even his own language grammatically' and had been held back at school for years. On the morning of the execution, Lewis suffered a nervous attack in chapel, mentioning for the first time that he had a wife and children. He recovered 'and again acted the hero before the spectators', standing up in the cart, and appearing 'unconcerned and hardy'.

Boswell watched from one of the 'Tyburn pews', wooden grandstands rented out at two shillings a seat. They were privately owned and one key-holder was the memorably named Mammy Douglas. Boswell was haunted by the spectacle, remembering how Lewis had walked 'firmly, with a good air'. He decided never to return to Tyburn. But Samuel Johnson, Boswell's great friend, reasoned that if the executions did 'not draw spectators, they do not answer their purpose . . . the public was gratified by a procession; the criminal was supported by it'. Yet public opinion was changing, and the Sheriffs of London and Middlesex decided that 'the final scene' had 'lost its terrors' for the mob. In 1783, the public executions at Tyburn were stopped and moved to a site at Newgate Prison.

Oxford, Cavendish and Brydges: the 'knick-knack' collectors of Marylebone

One year after hangman Price presided over Tyburn for the last time, John Prince, self-styled 'Prince of Builders' finished designing Cavendish Square for Edward Harley, 2nd Earl of Oxford. He inherited his father's love of the written word, and bought old and foreign papers and manuscripts with 'incessant Assiduity and at an immense expense'. He even maintained a private book-binding workshop, pouring thousands of pounds into the binding of beautiful books with the Oxford coat of arms on the front. His librarian browsed London's shops and auctions, spending anything from hundreds of pounds to the two shillings he paid for an Ethiopic manuscript from a bargain bin in a bookshop.

Such abandon in collecting landed Edward in financial trouble. In 1728, he was forced to admit to his wife, Henrietta, that their finances were failing 'in very great measure due to my own Folly and my neglect in looking into them as I ought to have done'.

The Harleys' financial situation deteriorated and Edward died a melancholy, alcohol-related death, in 1741, swamped by massive debt and an equally colossal library. Many of the manuscripts were housed in a purpose-built warehouse in 35 Marylebone High Street, though it was soon realized that the house was far too small for the purpose. Henrietta sold the printed books to bookseller Thomas Osborne for £13,000 – just less than it had cost Harley to bind them. Only the manuscripts were left behind.

With the future of the library in such disarray, a meeting was called by the trustees at the house in the High Street. Present were the President of the Royal Society, as well as book dealers and a journalist, Samuel Johnson. Johnson had arrived in Marylebone in March 1737, with his pupil and friend David Garrick. They lodged at Mrs Crow's, 6 Castle Street, near Cavendish Square. After the meeting,

Samuel Johnson and Harley's literary secretary were charged with cataloguing the manuscripts they thought of particular interest.

Samuel Johnson's time spent with Edward Harley's library would be of great significance to his later work in producing his *Dictionary*. Here he was exposed to many Anglo-Saxon manuscripts, and the *Dictionary* is notable for its 'Saxonic element'. It was also here that he studied Greek and Latin dictionaries, finding in them much to admire. In the early 1750s, Henrietta and her daughter, Margaret, entered into negotiations to sell the library to the nation. It was eventually purchased for £10,000 by the government, in 1753, and housed in the British Museum along with the collections of Hans Sloane and Robert Bruce Cotton. These three now form the British Library's core collection of early manuscripts, vindicating in some small way Harley's ruinous bibliomania.

Margaret Harley, Edward's daughter, was an avid gardener. Letters from her father to her grandfather describe her as a cheerful little girl with a love of flowers and animals. She married 'the handsomest man in England', William Bentinck, 2nd Duke of Portland (1709–1762) in June 1734. In her married life, this love of flowers became a career. She sponsored many botanists to travel the world, and was one of the first people to successfully cultivate the American import *Magnolia grandiflora*. Margaret contributed significantly to the core botanic collection of Kew after it was founded, in 1759. William Curtis, the compiler of an early Kew catalogue, makes note of her generosity regarding the 'many scarce and valuable plants, both British and foreign, received by Mr Aiton at Kew'. Thus, in two generations, the Harley family gifted London with the nuclei of two of its great institutions: the British Library and Kew Gardens.

In 1784, Margaret bought a Roman cameo-glass vase, later known as the 'Portland Vase'. It dates from between 27 BC and AD 14, during the reign of the Emperor Augustus, and has been called 'the finest piece of Roman cameo-glass in existence'. First mention of it comes in 1582, when it was discovered in a burial mound near Rome. The vase passed through the hands of various cardinals who displayed it in their palaces, where it was essential viewing for any young man who made it to Italy on his grand tour.

The vase is made from layers of cobalt-blue glass. The exact technique is a mystery, and without light the vase appears black. On top of the blue glass is a layer of opaque white, cut back by gem engravers to form a continuous frieze around the body. This frieze contains two scenes, one on each side. The first is the parents of Achilles, and the second is identified as Paris choosing between Hera, Aphrodite and Athena. Some believe it was made to celebrate a wedding. Others believe it to have been made to celebrate the birth of Rome from the 'ashes of Troy' and the success of Augustus.

In 1778, collector William Hamilton acquired it for £1,000. A catalogue of the Hamilton collection reached Josiah Wedgwood, who had just begun to make his 'Etruscan' vases. Wedgwood at first overlooked the Portland Vase, and made copies of others. Three years later, the sculptor John Flaxman sent him a letter: 'I wish you may soon come to town to see Wm Hamilton's Vase, it is the finest production of Art that has been brought to England and seems to be the very apex of perfection to which you are endeavouring to bring your bisque and jasper.'

Margaret paid Hamilton eighteen hundred guineas for the vase, in 1785. She died in the same year, and was remembered by Horace Walpole as 'a simple woman, but perfectly sober, and intoxicated only by empty vases'. Her collection was auctioned to pay her debts, and her son bought the vase back in the sale. He then loaned it to Wedgwood for one year, during which the now famous copy in jasperware was made.

When Margaret's son died, in 1810, the vase was placed on loan with the British Museum. On 7 February 1845, a youth of Irish origin entered the Museum and smashed the vase to pieces, blaming his actions on a week of intemperance. He was fined £3. Meanwhile, the vase lay in 139 pieces. The museum staff managed to put it back together and return it to the display. The 4th Duke of Portland declined to prosecute the man, on the grounds that he had mental health problems. Despite its battered history – buried, smashed, reassembled – the Portland Vase is still on show in the British Museum, a truly remarkable object and part of Margaret Cavendish's little-known legacy to London.

If the Harleys gifted London rare books and objects, another Marylebone collector was equally influential in contemporary music. James Brydges, Duke of Chandos, who was one of the earliest to buy a plot in Cavendish Square, was also was one of Georgian London's most important music patrons.

Brydges' finances took a tumble in the South Sea Bubble. He originally acquired the whole of the north side of the Cavendish Square project, but scaled himself back to building two large mansions on the north-east and north-west corners. He lived in the north-western one, although he would never complete it, and eventually sold both mansions to buy Ormonde House, in St James's Square. This impetuosity and lack of commitment characterized Brydges' business dealings. In the fields just north lay the Marylebone Basin Reservoir, supplying water for the square and other parts of the village. He planned to make a fortune from a water company for the new development, but that too would fail; during 1769, the Basin was filled in to build Mansfield Street. Marylebone parish had many lakes and ponds which proved fatal on more than one occasion. *The St James's Chronicle* for 8 August 1769 relates a tragedy in the small and dangerous pond nearby, known as The Cockney Ladle. There, 'two young chairmen were drowned. They had been beating a carpet in the Square and being warm and dirty had decided to have a bathe, not being aware of how deep the pond was.'

Brydges, though a poor businessman, was a fine patron of art and music. He was a lover of Italian opera and a member of the Society of Gentleman Performers of Music. He was determined that his household should be dedicated to furthering his love of music. With Burlington, he was involved in the early Royal Academy of Music, and an orchestra played to Brydges even as he ate. Like Burlington, Brydges collected antiques and European objects.

He was generous with his houses and his collections. Servants were allowed to earn extra money by admitting guests to the house and taking them around for tours. Anyone was admitted, provided they were smartly dressed. They were led on a tour of the collection and given a cup of tea or some other refreshment. If they were of sufficient interest, the Duke was alerted and came down to meet them.

Brydges was remembered as a good-humoured man. In the only duel he ever fought, he disarmed his opponent, apologized and invited the man for dinner that evening. His own words on his collecting habit are summed up by 'we knick-knack men when once a fine thing is bought for us like other children are wonderfully impatient till we have it'.

High and low life: the aristocrats of Cavendish Square

Cavendish Square still retains a cheerful country air. In the 1770s, Billy Ponsonby, Earl of Bessborough, leaned on the railings here and watched the world go by. He lived at 3 Cavendish Square with his wife, Caroline. They had two daughters and a son together, but Caroline died when the children were in their teens. Her devoted widower took to wearing her diamond buckles on his shoes on his lonely perambulations around the growing village north of Oxford Street. A familiar sight on the streets, he

> . . . was once standing to see the workmen pull down the wooden railing and brick-work which surround the centre of Cavendish-square, when a sailor walked up to him and asked for a quid of tobacco: his Lordship answered, 'My friend, I don't take tobacco.' . . . As [the sailor] was turning away, his Lordship turned to him and said, 'Here my friend, here is something that will enable you to buy tobacco,' and gave him half a crown.

In another instance of kindness, the Earl once noticed a woman in widow's weeds curtsey to him in the street. She looked poor, 'but remarkably clean' and had two small children with her. He stopped, turned back and gave her money. But in the transaction, the coins fell into the dirty kennel, or channel, in the middle of the road. Billy picked them up, cleaned them on his handkerchief, then handed them over to her.

His kindness did not stop at people. The Earl was a great fan of the work of renowned miser Joseph Nollekens, and often used to visit the sculptor's Marylebone studio. The Nollekens kept a thin,

Looking north from Cavendish Square, with the rear view of the statue of the
Duke of Cumberland, 1771. The sheep were removed later that year

badly treated dog but 'whenever the animal saw his Lordship's leg
within the gate, he ceased barking, and immediately welcomed the
visitor; who always brought a French-roll in his blue great-coat-
pocket purposely for him'.

In the late 1780s, Billy's charwoman at Number 3 was 'took sudden' and had her baby in the house. He was named Billy. Billy grew
up in the house until Billy Ponsonby's death, in 1793, 'for whilst he
lived [his mother] wouldn't leave him, not for nothing'.

Aged nineteen, Billy took to selling watercress about the streets
but he had to stop as the market wouldn't support him, his mother
and his aged father. He struck upon the idea of working as a crossing-
sweeper in Cavendish Square: 'I'm known there; it's where I was
born and there I set to work.'

Crossing-sweeping was one of the humblest professions, but Billy
was known as the 'aristocratic' crossing-sweeper. In wet weather he
could be seen sheltering 'under the Duke of Portland's stone gate-

way'. Billy's unique position as street furniture gives an insight into the charitable inclinations of the Marylebone rich. Some gave him clothes, some money, one 'a shilling and a religious tract'. Billy remembered his religious benefactor as 'a particular nice man'.

Billy was such a familiar sight around the square that he was given odd jobs, such as scouring the mild-steel knives, taking cash to the bank for the Duke of Portland, and even cashing cheques for other gentlemen. He attended houses early in the mornings to clean shoes, knives or put letters in the post: 'It's only for the servants I does it, not for the quality.' In a twist of social hierarchy, although he was entrusted with £80 in cash by one gentleman, the servants didn't allow Billy to intrude into the domestic setting beyond the kitchen, where he received 'broken foods'. Like anyone in a job for a long time, Billy remembered 'the good old days'. In particular, he wasn't fond of the new invention of tarmacadam – or 'muckydam', as he liked to call it reducing the life of a broom from three months (on cobbles) to a fortnight.

The story of the two Billys of Cavendish Square highlights the area's slightly more relaxed social structure. After all, many of the local residents, no matter how wealthy, were outsiders. Marylebone was popular with officers of the East India Company, who often returned to England with their racially mixed households. However, these mixed households were not only East Indian; many white West Indian families had returned to London to spend their sugar money.

Portman Square: Montagu vs Home

On 31 January 1765, *The Public Advertiser* declared: 'Portman Square now building between Portman Chapel and Marylebone will be much larger than Grosvenor Square; and that handsome walks, planted with Elm Trees, will be made to it, with a grand reservoir, in the middle.' Construction on the north side did not start until 1773, when Robert Adam undertook to build a house for Elizabeth, the Countess of Home. At the same time, Elizabeth Montagu, whose star was firmly fixed in London's social firmament, left Hill Street in Mayfair and took the lease of the large plot which ran, unusually,

across the south-west corner. She employed James 'Athenian' Stuart
to raise a huge mansion in competition with her neighbour. The
Countess of Home was proud of her colonial heritage. Elizabeth
Montagu and her bluestockings were violently opposed to slavery.
As the question of slavery became increasingly uncomfortable, the
battle lines were drawn in Portman Square.

The Countess of Home had been born Elizabeth Gibbons, in
Jamaica. She married young, to the son of the Governor; his death,
in London in 1734, had left her a very wealthy eighteen-year-old.
Social mobility was high in the West Indies, and the rougher, hardier
European men and women often flourished. A commonly held view
was that the islands were 'the Dunghill wharone England does cast
forth its rubbish'. Jamaica started out as a trading island but when it
gave itself over to sugar plantations there were opportunities to make
huge fortunes. European mortality rates were staggering at around
27 per cent a year, owing to 'bad fruit', hurricanes and yellow fever.
With the rate of attrition so high, marriages did not last long and
relatively few islanders succeeded in bringing up families. Native-
born white islanders surviving to adulthood were scarce. The
successful few were opportunists and adventurers. Added to this
potent mixture, as well as the ever-present spectre of violent uprising
and death, was the massive wealth attainable through sugar. The
average white plantation owner on Jamaica was ten times richer than
those in mainland America.

Sugar was an increasing presence in London. In 1700, national consumption was 4lbs per head per annum; by 1800, this had grown to
18lbs. Jamaica and its cash crop was the jewel of the British Caribbean.
White Jamaicans were starting to exert an influence on British politics
and the City. The planters and merchants who represented them
formed an influential lobbying group which successfully opposed the
attempt to introduce large quantities of East Indian sugar to Britain.

Elizabeth arrived in London as a rich planter's wife. But after her
husband's early death, she disappears and doesn't reappear until 1742,
when she married the Earl of Home. She was thirty-eight, he was
some years younger. He deserted her in the first year of their marriage. Upon his death, in 1761, his possessions were auctioned and

Elizabeth bought back the silver dinner service he had taken with him. William Beckford, himself an heir to sugar money, described Elizabeth as a 'flamboyant eccentric, given to swearing like a trooper'. In 1772, aged seventy, she decided to build a new house on the north side of the square, where she was 'known among all the Irish Chairmen and riff-raff of the metropolis by the name and style of the Queen of Hell'. Money was no object when Elizabeth engaged James Wyatt to design her new house, in June 1772. Wyatt was only twenty-six, and unable to keep up with the amount of commissions he was receiving. The two fell out. Elizabeth sacked him and brought in Wyatt's great rival, Robert Adam, to finish the job.

Adam's taste coupled with Elizabeth's money produced one of London's finest interiors. Adam blended formal with informal, blurring the line invisibly between family and servants whilst keeping the two entirely separate. In Home House he was triumphant, and the house was used as an entertaining space of the highest order.

Elizabeth's heyday in Home House coincided with the consolidation of virulent abolitionist feeling amongst London intellectuals. Public sentiment was turning against the 'sugar rich', their unbelievable wealth and the methods on which it was founded. William Cowper wrote a pamphlet addressed 'To Everyone Who Uses Sugar', reproving those who used it with: 'Think how many backs have smarted, for the sweets your cane affords.' It was no hole-in-the-corner publication, and was exactly the sort of thing the West Indian planters were hoping to avoid. East Indian tea accompanied by West Indian sugar had become an English staple, but now the ordinary man and woman were exhorted to think, to consider the reality behind this daily treat, and: 'As he sweetens his tea, let him consider the bitterness at the bottom of the cup.'

On the other side of the square were the tea parties of Elizabeth Montagu and her intellectual circle.

Montagu House was vast: the housewarming party was a breakfast for a modest 700 guests. Elizabeth later held a May Day breakfast for London chimney sweeps, where they had only to present themselves on the front lawn to receive a celebratory meal of beef and a pudding. Her literary salons continued, as they had in Hill Street, but the topics of the conversation were evolving with the times, and abolition became a constant feature.

The bluestockings put great store by intellectual equality between the sexes and by 'conversation'. Their debates reflected popular feeling at the time. On 20 March 1783, *The Gazetteer* ran an advertisement asking, 'Are there any grounds for supposing that the understandings of the female sex are in any respect inferior to those of the men?' There were even debates asking 'Ought not the Word Obey to be struck out of the Marriage Ceremony?' Elizabeth's salons were held in the beautiful drawing rooms of Montagu House, where chairs were ranged around her in a semicircle and she literally acted in the role of 'chairwoman'. Samuel Johnson said of her: 'She diffuses more knowledge than any woman I know, or indeed, almost any man.' Hester Thrale described her, kindly, as 'brilliant in diamonds, solid in judgement'. Her friends included Elizabeth Vesey, Sir Joshua Reynolds, David Garrick, Samuel Johnson, Fanny Burney, Hester Thrale, Margaret Bentinck and the abolitionist William Wilberforce.

Quite what the Countess of Home thought of her neighbour's abolitionist tea parties is unknown. Her steely identity as a white Jamaican is unlikely to have allowed her to feel regret for the vast wealth she inherited through the sweat and sometimes the blood of others. The true movement towards abolition was played out in Westminster Hall and other quarters less glamorous than the rival Home and Montagu Houses. Yet Marylebone would continue to hold a curious attraction for both those who profited by slavery and those who had suffered from it.

In 1833, when West Indian plantation families lodged compensation claims for the financial damage caused by abolition, a large proportion of those families gave Marylebone addresses. Black Londoners also made Marylebone their own. In the earlier part of the eighteenth century, numbers were relatively low, and most found employment in the grander houses. Thus London's black population during the eighteenth century is largely hidden and hard to assess. Guesses range from 4,000 to 10,000. They comprised freed and unfree slaves, soldiers who had fought for Britain in the unsuccessful Revolutionary War, and domestic servants. Marked out as 'alien' by the colour of their skin, many found it hard to integrate. By the 1780s, the 'black poor' had become a distinct problem but also a fashionable one. The abolition movement was gaining ground quickly, and in liberated circles it was the done thing to be seen to support the 'indigent blacks'.

Soon, the Committee for the Relief of the Black Poor was established, and prominent abolitionist members of society were signing up, encouraged by Elizabeth Montagu and others. When the Duchess of Devonshire became involved, many others of her position followed, including the Countess of Salisbury, the Countess of Essex and the Marchioness of Buckingham. The committee set up a scheme for a new 'colony' in Sierra Leone. It remains unclear whether the ultimate motive was to get rid of the poor blacks from London's streets, or whether it represented a naive attempt to return them to their 'native Africa'. Either way, the scheme and the colony failed soon after 1791.

In January 1786, *The Public Advertiser* ran with a notice that Mr Brown, the baker in Wigmore Street, was to 'give a Quartern Loaf to every Black in Distress, who will apply on Saturday next between the Hours of Twelve and Two'. Two pubs were used to distribute alms to the needy: the Yorkshire Stingo, in Marylebone, and the White Raven, in Mile End.

The Yorkshire Stingo became something of a legend. It had been named after the brand of particularly strong beer, and it hosted Thomas Paine's large-scale cast-iron bridge model, in 1790 – the second ever to be built. It was also the departure point for the first commuter omnibus service running into the City, in 1829. As well as acting as the focus for the poor members of the black community in west London, it long remained a stopping point for those heading in and out of the city. (It was demolished in the 1960s to make room for the Westway.)

The Hindostanee, London's first known Indian restaurant

It wasn't only West Indians who were attracted to Portman Square and Marylebone. Those arriving or returning from the East Indies brought with them the tastes of India, and a small infrastructure grew up around them, providing ethnic food and experiences. One such character was Deen Mahomet. Born to a Muslim family in Bihar, in 1759, he was raised as a servant in the Bengal branch of the British East India Army.

In 1784, Deen was in Cork, after following an officer who had taken him under his wing. There he met Jane Daly and, in 1786, they eloped. Deen began to write the story of his travels. In 1794, he published the first book by an Indian written in English, *The Travels of Deen Mahomet*. He and Jane came to London, where he found employment with the Hon. Basil Cochrane, who had made a fortune in India and liked the people and way of life. Basil opened a bath house at 12 Portman Square and employed Deen to offer Indian head and body massage, or 'champissage', with perfumed oils. It became a huge success, and we derive the word shampoo from the Indian 'champi'.

HINDOSTANEE COFFEE-HOUSE, No. 34, George-street, Portman-square.—MAHOMED, East-Indian, informs the Nobility and Gentry he has fitted up the above House, neatly and elegantly, for the entertainment of Indian Gentlemen; where they may enjoy the Hoakha, with real Chilm Tobacco, and Indian Dishes, in the highest perfection; and allowed by the greatest epicures to be unequalled to any Curries ever made in England; with choice Wines, and every accommodation; and now looks up to them for their future patronage and support, and gratefully acknowledges himself indebted for their former favours, and trusts it will merit the highest satisfaction when made known to the public.

Advertisement for the Hindostanee Coffee House, 1811

Late in 1809, Deen opened the Hindostanee Coffee House, and *The Times* announced its arrival. Although the Hindostanee was reviewed favourably in the publications of the time, Deen expanded too quickly after early successes. By 1813, he was bankrupt. However, the coffee house continued until 1833, under different management.

Deen and his wife moved to Brighton, where the building of the Pavilion was lending an exotic flavour to local life. He became 'Shampooing Surgeon' to George IV and, later, to William IV. His son, Frederick, became a surgeon at Guy's Hospital and completed pioneering research into hypertension before his early death, at the age of thirty-five. Deen Mahomet and his family's integration into British society is a heady mixture of affection, family, money, skill and intellect, as well as financial mismanagement and disaster.

Manchester Square: a prophetess and a pig-faced woman

Manchester Square is dominated by Manchester House, now Hertford House, situated on the north side, home of the Wallace Collection. The house was built originally by the Duke of Manchester, but became Hertford House in 1797, when the 2nd Marquess of Hertford acquired it. Francis Seymour-Conway, the 3rd Marquess of Hertford (1777–1842), was remarkable not only for his spectacular romantic career, but also the lineage of his wife. Maria Fagnani was a half-Italian beauty, possibly the daughter of the Marquess of Queensberry (the lecher known as 'Old Q') or possibly the daughter of the Tory George Selwyn. Both men left her huge legacies, but it is most likely Maria's father was Selwyn's butler. Contemporary gossips sniped that her mother had never learned the English words for constancy and fidelity, and William Makepeace Thackeray parodied Maria and her husband in *Vanity Fair*.

Manchester Square later made the papers when prophetess Joanna Southcott moved in. Born in Ottery St Mary, Devon, in 1750, she realized she had the gift of 'prophecy', though not until 1792. She thought the French Revolution heralded an apocalypse. Napoleon became her Antichrist. She made special 'seals' which would protect the wearer 'even at the cannon's mouth' and called herself 'the woman clothed with the sun'. In 1814, she declared herself to be pregnant with the 'Prince of Peace'. She was sixty-four.

Joanna called the bump 'Shiloh'. The medical profession was unsure whether it was a phantom pregnancy, or a colossal tumour. She died in a house in Manchester Square during December 1814, undelivered of the Saviour.

Joanna's followers were widely reported in the press as delusional. At exactly the same time, London was under a different delusion regarding another resident of Manchester Square: the 'pig-faced lady'. In February 1814, *The Times* reported: 'There is at present a report in London, of a woman, with a strangely deformed face, resembling that of a pig, who is possessed of a large fortune, and we suppose wants all the comforts and conveniences incident to her sex and station [as in, marriage].'

This was followed by what was essentially a denunciation of the existence of the pig-faced lady, comparing it to Joanna Southcott's folly. Yet many hundreds tried to find the house in Manchester Square where she was supposed to live, including the hunchbacked and dwarfish Sholto, Lord Kirkcudbright, who wanted to pay his addresses to one equally unfortunate in looks. *The Times* continued its scathing denouncement: 'The pig's face is as firmly believed in by many, as Joanna Southcot's pregnancy, to which folly it has succeeded . . . there is hardly a company in which this swinish female is not talked of; and thousands believe in her existence.'

The pig-faced lady hoax was cruel and misogynistic, but it was inspired by an undertow in current affairs. Just as women were asking if they had to keep 'obey' in their marriage vows, others were taking the initiative in getting a man to the altar. They were even going so far as to advertise. The City Debates club asked in the *Daily Advertiser*, on 11 November 1790: 'Is it consistent either with female prudence or delicacy to advertise for a husband?' Even more intriguing, it appears that women were seeking companionship abroad. A London society asked: 'Do Ladies by going to India, for the purpose of obtaining Husbands, deviate from their characteristic delicacy?' The question was 'almost unanimously decided in the affirmative'.

That women were advertising for husbands, or actively seeking them in another country, was a reflection of the growing desire for marriage in the late eighteenth century. Fashion, a rise in the standards of living and health, plus the growth in media and art meant that there was an ever-greater emphasis on beauty and desirability. In the late seventeenth century, up to 20 per cent of women didn't marry but remained within extended family groups as quasi-servants. By the late eighteenth century, this number had dropped below 10 per cent, as women became wealthier and increasingly unwilling to live out their lives in spinsterish limbo. The more affluent women of the

Georgian period, and particularly the Regency, are often imagined as a simpering, corseted bunch. Yet many were questioning their position in marriage and society, and some of them were actively seeking happiness on their own terms.

John Elwes: 'an enemy to himself'

One man who was definitely not seeking happiness was John Elwes, 'London's meanest man', and possibly the inspiration for Charles Dickens' Ebeneezer Scrooge. As Marylebone grew, there was money to be made from speculative building. Portman Square, with its elegant and varied residents, was rapidly followed by Portland Place, which isn't a square, but a street. By the 1770s, it was filled with huge and elegant terraced houses.

The land was developed using the money of the 'vastly eccentric' John Elwes. He was inducted into the ways of the miser at a young age by his mother, who left him £100,000 after starving herself to death through meanness. Elwes thus came under the influence of his uncle, Sir Harvey Elwes, 'the most perfect example of human penury perhaps that ever existed'.

After inheriting his uncle's fortune as well, he was by the age of forty an extremely rich man and increasingly eccentric; he ate 'Game in the last state of putrefaction and meat that *walked about his plate*', though he soon gave up luxuries such as meat. He travelled between his country houses, maintaining them as little as possible, avoiding paying the turnpike tolls and once fishing an abandoned wig out of a hedge and wearing it in London for a fortnight.

Only on building, gambling and horseflesh would he spend a penny. It was said that Portman Place 'rose out of his pocket' after he began building there. Elwes found this very handy, as the half-built houses meant that he didn't have to rent anywhere to live when in London. He hauled an old maidservant around with him, as well as a few sticks of furniture. The two of them were sometimes reduced to burning the carpenter's leftover wood shavings for warmth. His monumental meanness reached its peak when a nephew tracked him down in a building site in Great Marlborough Street, in a state of near starvation. The maidservant was in another room, apparently dead for some days.

Upon his recovery, Elwes took an even greater interest in his building projects and became a nuisance to the workmen, often sitting on the doorsteps at dawn and waiting for them to arrive. He died, in 1786, having succumbed to dementia. Despite his wealth, he was increasingly paranoid about loss and theft and took to hiding guineas about the place and then getting up to check they were there, as well as sleeping in all his clothes in case they were stolen in the night. His legacy lived on: John Nash would call Portland Place 'the finest street in London', and incorporated it into his plans for Regent Street and Regent's Park.

Thomas Lord and the Gentlemen Players

Early cricket in London tended to be based more in the east and south. It was played by a combination of schoolboys, apprentices, parish labourers and the aristocracy, and was their choice of sport in the summer. In July 1739, a match between London and Kent had an estimated 10,000 spectators, all paying 2d each.

In 1744, The Laws of Cricket were laid down by the London Cricket Club, which played at the Artillery Ground on the eastern end of the City. They set the length of the pitch at 22 yards and limited an over to four balls. The batsman was also restricted to one attempt at the ball: previously, he'd been allowed two. This had resulted in serious head injuries and even some fatalities amongst enthusiastic fielders, who would crowd the batsman on the second ball. The death of a female fielder had caused widespread criticism of the two-ball rule. As the century went on, cricket became more formal. By the later 1700s, clubs began to emerge, including the Marylebone Cricket Club and the Hambledon Club.

The Hambledon Club was formed in Hampshire and marked a turning point in English cricket employing professional players. It was also a social club, and members liked a good dinner with plenty of toasts, which included 'cricket', 'the King' and 'the immortal memory of madge'. The madge of immortal memory is a jocular reference to female genitalia. Hambledon must have had a joker in the pack: Thomas Paine is down as one of the attendees at a meeting, just after he had been exiled for sedition after the publication of *Rights of Man*. By the late 1790s, the Hambledon was finished. But by then the Marylebone Cricket Club had taken up the slack.

The MCC was formerly the White Conduit Club (which played at White Conduit Fields in Islington). The WCC was a club for gentlemen, including 'J. Wyatt', who was very likely the busy young architect. The gentlemen, however, did not like to lose. By 1785, the club was employing professional players, including Edward 'Lumpy' Stevens, John 'Little Joey' Ring, as well as a bowler, one Thomas Lord. Lord was an enterprising man; when they grew out of White Conduit Fields, he was asked to find a new ground. In 1787, Lord took a lease on a piece of ground in Dorset Fields, and the MCC was born. There is no evidence the ground was ever called anything but Lord's. In 1806, it hosted the first Gentlemen vs Players match. In 1810, a row over the lease caused them to move again. Three years later, in 1813, the development of the Regent's Canal threatened Lord's once more, and the wily bowler shifted the ground to its current site. By this time, cricket was part of the London summer scene. Surrey and Hampshire Ladies played at Ball's Pond in 1811, and 1827 saw the first Oxford vs Cambridge match at Lord's.

'Poor Tiny Cosmetic!': Marylebone's artistic community

The mixture of artisans, gentlemen and aristocrats in the early lists of players at Lord's is typical of Marylebone. Successful artisans and artists, in particular, were quick to move into the comfortable and elegant, yet not too grand, housing offered by the area.

The area's artistic community would fill a book, so numerous are the names. They include Edward Gibbon, the historian, whose epic work *The Decline and Fall of the Roman Empire* was published in 1787 to great acclaim, and was unsurpassed until the twentieth century.

Others included the artist Henry Fuseli, who lived in Berners Street, and also the Rose family of plasterers, who lived in Queen Anne Street East. The workshop of Robert Adam's 'ingenious' Mr Rose was responsible for most of the fine plasterwork within the homes Adam built. The Ward family of builders was busy in Berkeley Square for generations. They were so well regarded that their odd-job man and plumber were dispatched by carriage to customers at country houses in the home counties.

Marylebone artists included J. M. W. Turner, John Opie, George Stubbs (whose house is now buried beneath the north-west corner of Selfridges), John Constable and Sir Edwin Landseer. One of the most prominent names of the time was Richard Cosway. After a fairly meagre start, in Tiverton, Devon, he arrived in London, aged twelve, where he became the pupil of William Shipley, drawing master on the Strand. Shipley had founded the Society for the Encouragement of Arts, Manufactures and Commerce (now the Royal Society of Arts), which offered prizes on the presentation of 'the Best Drawings, by Boys and Girls, under the age of 14 years, and Proof of their abilities, on or before the 15th day of January, 1755'.

The young Cosway went on to win all the drawing prizes there, and came second only to Joseph Nollekens for the sculpture prize. Key to establishing Cosway's popularity was his ability to paint beautiful portrait miniatures with a trademark 'blue sky' background. They functioned as photographs, painted on ivory so that the skin tone was always perfect, no matter what ravages smallpox, acne and age had left behind. Shipley's Society of Arts organized a landmark exhibition of living British artists. Previously, the fashion had been for dead continental artists, but the exhibition – comprising 130 works by 69 artists – was seen by 20,000 visitors in a fortnight. It turned the tide for London's artistic community. People started buying modern art.

Cosway prospered. He moved from Marylebone to Pall Mall before returning to Stratford Place, where he established a beautiful household of great taste and style. This grace was not matched by his person, for 'Cosway, though a well-made little man, was certainly very much like a monkey in his face'. He suffered many 'monkey' pranks in his time, but played up to it, even owning a baboon as a pet until it bit him, wounding him quite seriously. His friend John Townley reported that:

> . . . the last time I called I found him laid on a sofa in his night gown and the calf of one of his legs bundled up; on my enquiring the cause he acquainted me, that his monkey or Baboon had tore a great Piece out of his leg and that he was under Dr Hunter's hand of a cure; the Poor animal has been put out of its pain, by the same hand, and the Dr had the pleasure of Dissecting him, and put him in spirits, in terrors to all Monkeys.

Cosway wasn't only an artist but also a dealer and broker often 'at the Elder Christie's Picture-Sales, full-dressed in his sword and bag; with a small three-cornered hat on the top of his powdered toupee, and a mulberry silk coat, profusely embroidered with scarlet straw-berries'. The cartoonists mocked him in his vanity – 'Poor Tiny Cosmetic!' – though they did allow him to be far better than the 'indifferent daubers' of the day.

In his late thirties, he decided to marry. Maria Hadfield was born in Italy, the daughter of a gentleman who had 'kept [a Florence hotel] these twenty and eight years and where most of the English Nobility and Gentry have lodg'd . . . It is and always has been a house in very great Esteem.' His convent-educated daughter Maria was the only survivor of a serial killer. Her parents had sent out four or five of her elder siblings to a wet nurse, but all died. Suspicious, they decided to keep Maria at home. A short time later, a nanny found the wet nurse in Maria's bedroom, inside the Had-fields' home, and alerted the household, whereupon the wet nurse said she was only 'sending them to Heaven'. This extraordinary and tragic event caused the family to convert to Roman Catholicism, a faith Maria clung to and used as an increasingly large crutch during the rest of her life.

Maria was an artist of some note in her own right. Richard did not allow his talented wife to paint for money, and so her career was limited, though she did exhibit occasionally. Along with Anne Damer and Mary Moser, Maria Cosway was one of the foremost women exhibiting in London in the 1780s. She and Richard held artistic salons for London artists and intellectuals. They 'kept a house in style, in a sort of co-partnership of so novel a character, as to surprise their new neighbours, astonish their old friends, and furnish wonderment for the table-talk of the town'. William Hazlitt said, 'they were not fashionable – they were fashion itself'. They employed a black servant, Quobna Ottobah Cugano, known to them as 'John Stewart'. He was part of the Sons of Africa group and campaigned against slavery, using his and the Cosways' address when he wrote to those he hoped to win over to the cause.

Richard and Maria had one child, Louisa. Maria loved to travel to the Continent, and probably had an affair with a smitten Thomas Jefferson in Paris, during 1786. She returned there, ostensibly to make drawn catalogues of the pictures in the Louvre, just after Louisa was born. In reality, the Cosway marriage was in crisis and Maria was probably suffering from post-natal depression. By the time she returned to London, almost six years later, Louisa was dead and Richard heartbroken.

Richard struggled with his mental health after Louisa died. The extant sketch of her, dead and peaceful, is deeply affecting. He had her body embalmed and kept it in the hall of their house in a marble sarcophagus. His collection of drawings, particularly his important old masters, became less and less important to him. Thomas Lawrence, himself responsible for the greatest collection of drawings by old masters ever to have existed in Britain, thought Cosway's collection more important. The 1820 catalogue of the Cosways' Stratford Place home included: 27 Correggios, 67 Michelangelos, 44 Raphaels (school of), 39 Titians, 92 Rubens, 46 van Dycks and 30 Rembrandts. They were dispersed in 1822, after Cosway's death; of the 2,500 sold, less than 10 per cent have been traced.

Richard Cosway died suddenly in a carriage on the way to a friend's house at the same moment as, unbeknownst to him, Maria had the body of their daughter interred and the sarcophagus sent to Joseph Nollekens for safekeeping.

Marylebone Pleasure Gardens

Regent's Park is now Marylebone's premier green space, but during the eighteenth century the park had yet to be created and was a wild, open space. Instead, Londoners preferred the safe and enclosed space of Marylebone Pleasure Gardens. The gardens were on a smaller, more intimate scale than Vauxhall and Ranelagh, but their contribution to London's contemporary entertainment scene was significant.

The first prominent mention of the Marylebone Pleasure Gardens is by Samuel Pepys on 7 May 1668, when he went 'to Marrowbone, and there walked in the garden, the first time I ever was there, and a pretty place it is'. The gardens Samuel visited were on the east side of what is now 35–37 Marylebone High Street. They extended from the back of the Rose of Normandy Tavern, and at the beginning comprised little more than a bowling green and a gaming house with a beautiful, unobstructed view of Highgate and Hampstead.

As the Cavendish Square development grew, the gardens began to provide more high-quality entertainment, such as music, illuminations and fireworks, for which it became famous. It wasn't all about formal entertainment, and the gardens were open for breakfast between ten and one o'clock. Daniel Gough, the proprietor, set the entrance fee at a shilling for every gentleman, allowing his lady in for free. The gardens had a no smoking rule and a refined atmosphere. Fidget, the young Elizabeth Montagu, and her teenage friends used to swim in the nearby ponds before rolling in for a late breakfast, where they chatted with the other guests.

Swords and pistols were checked at the gate to prevent quarrels getting out of hand, but outside the premises they were necessary. Owing to demobbing and the economic uncertainty of the 1740s, London suffered waves of street crime. The journey to and from the gardens was dangerous, and muggings were common. It even became necessary to have a company of armed guards to escort groups to and from the gardens, and torches burned along the field path down to Marylebone Lane.

In the 1750s, Handel's favourite tenor, Thomas Lowe, took over

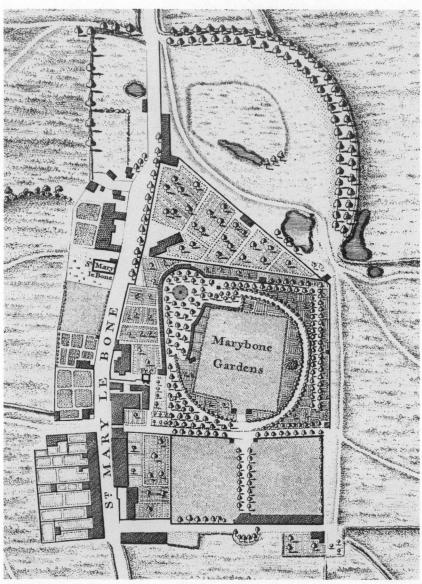

Marylebone Pleasure Gardens, detail from John Roque's map, 1745. The buildings on the lower left housed the Harleian Collection, which formed the core of the British Library

the gardens. He spent a fortune on them, which almost ruined him, but this was probably the high point in the gardens' history. The quality of the music reached a peak. Thomas Arne, composer of 'Rule, Britannia!', had a talented ten-year-old son, Master Michael Arne, who sang through the summer season of 1750, drawing large crowds.

By this time, the local school – originally run by Huguenot Denis de la Place – had been taken over by Dr Fountain and his wife. Dickensian ideas of harsh schooling are rather displaced by the images conjured up by one boy who remembered the pupils calling Dr Fountain 'Bushwig', owing to his preference for an old-fashioned full-bottomed wig. They also called his wife 'Rainbow', because of the frequency with which she dyed her hair varying colours. Rainbow, in particular, was remembered for cajoling the homesick boys to do their homework with sweets and rewards.

Both Rainbow and Bushwig were regulars at the Marylebone Gardens. Dr Fountain was a friend of Handel, and one day the two men were walking in the garden, as they often did. The band was playing.

Handel paused at the back, saying, 'Let us sit down, and listen to this piece, I want your opinion on it.'

They sat, and after a short while, the robust, bushwigged Dr Fountain declared, 'It's not worth listening to – it is very poor stuff.'

Handel got to his feet and sighed, 'You are right. I thought so myself when I had finished it.'

The gardens continued to flourish, specializing in *burletta*, a type of short, comic opera. But by 1757, the end was in sight – although the Truslers, who bought the gardens that year, could not have known. The increasing number of wealthy residents both south and north of Oxford Street were protesting about the filth and noise from the many cattle driven along it to Smithfield. The Turnpike Trusts, local authorities with permission to manage the roads, were gathering clout. A new road was seen as a lucrative speculation, given the weight of traffic. The New Road was London's first large bypass, running from the end of the Edgware Road to Tottenham Court Road, past St Pancras to St John Street, in Islington. It was created quickly and bounded by fence posts. Initially, the traffic didn't bother the pleasure gardens, and things carried on as usual.

The Truslers had three great strengths: the Neapolitan musician Stephen Storace, who married their eldest daughter; their interest in good fireworks; and their second daughter, Miss Trusler, who did the catering. The Truslers' son-in-law was an able composer and musician. He was often employed by Teresa Cornelys, in Soho Square, and was one of London's busiest and most admired popular musicians. His own compositions were sold exclusively at the gardens, and the print runs were large. He and his wife, Elizabeth, had two children. Their son, also Stephen, studied music in Vienna and befriended Mozart, but died young at thirty-two. Their daughter, Anna Selina, known to everyone as 'Nancy', would be Mozart's first Susanna in *The Marriage of Figaro*, in 1786.

The fireworks were presided over by some of the most skilled technicians of the day, and included 'turbillons, mortars, Air balloons, Porcupine quills, pyramids and Sun & Stars'. There were rockets too. Rainbow, who was by this time the headmistress of the next-door school for girls, complained about them falling into their garden.

Miss Trusler's cooking was taken very seriously. A print still exists of her sitting at a table wearing a mob cap, sleeves rolled up, a cup of brandy in one hand and a cake in front of her. She is young and jolly and round at the edges, the perfect cook for a pleasure garden. It seems she took her trade very seriously. Breakfast was revived as a big event, and she kept her own cows for 'the finest Butter, Cream and new Milk'. Her fruit was her own, 'having great Quantities in the Garden' and her 'rich seed and Plum Cakes [could be] sent to any part of the Town at 2s 6d each'. Later, she would go off on her own to take over the Gold Lamp in Boyle Street, near Savile Row, where she specialized in sweet stuff, including, as her advertisement proclaimed 'a Dish called Trifle which is exceeding good'.

In 1762, the Iroquois Indians who had come to London to complain to George III that their land had been 'taken by some Persons from New York', were brought to the gardens for dinner. The young Oliver Goldsmith came up to them to say hello and handed over a gift he had brought with him, an unrecorded 'trifle'. The men were so pleased with this gift that they embraced him suddenly, transferring much of their coppery face-paint on to a surprised Goldsmith.

By now, the New Road had become a highway traversed not only by cattle but also by coaches and wagons. Marylebone was becoming built up, obscuring the views of the distant villages and compromising the gardens' rural qualities. Pressure on land began to make the eight acres and ramshackle old tavern look ripe for development. Perhaps this was why they were refused a Public Musick Licence in 1773. In the same year, a City surveyor searching for wells found a natural spring in the gardens, and they were marketed as a 'spa'. Sadly, they just weren't 'country' enough any more. On 2 April 1777, *The Public Advertiser* carried the advertisement for the sale of the gardens and their assets. Marylebone Pleasure Gardens stumbled on for a short while, but were soon consumed by Marylebone High Street.

The 'extensive waste' of Tyburnia and the Regent's Canal

The consumption of Marylebone's open space by building didn't happen overnight, or by magic. For many years, construction workers dominated the area. As the century went on, these workers were increasingly of Irish extraction. Their sedan chair business was dying and construction was the obvious trade, as the Irishmen liked to work together in groups. One of the most interesting contrasts provided by Marylebone is the area where the poor Irish lived in the east, in the elbow of Tottenham Court Road and Oxford Street. They earned their living in Marylebone but were still close to the employment opportunities of the sedan chair business in Mayfair and St James's, and also the hay business in the meadows to the north. Geographically, it was perfect.

The Irish population was tolerated as a necessary, if grating, evil. One commentator noted that 'the turbulent and barbarous habits of the lower orders of the people of Ireland, their abject poverty, and their sufferings have long been a subject of unavoiding complaint'. The Irish rapidly spread out from St Giles's to occupy temporary dwellings closer to their work: 'The extensive waste which Tyburnia now covers was occupied with the most wretched huts, filled with squatters of the lowest of the community, whose habitual amusement on a Sunday morning was that of dog fights.'

As the Georgian period came to a close, the parish of Marylebone and its workhouse had become as burdened as St Giles's was with the 'lower Irish'. The Calmel Buildings, near Portman Square, were little more than a shanty town; the Marylebone Vestry Minutes reported that it was 'such a scene of filth and wretchedness as cannot be conceived'. Soon after this, the Calmel Society was founded to help alleviate the suffering there. Montagu Burgoyne, the Secretary, surveyed 24 houses in the Calmel Buildings and found 700 people living in them. In his report to the Mendicity Committee, published in 1816, he commented, 'neither in town nor in the country have I ever met with so many poor among whom there is so much distress, so much profligacy, and so much ignorance'.

Burgoyne was reporting at the height of the building of the Regent's Canal, upon which many of the men worked. The canal was designed to run 'over the top' of London from the end of the Grand Junction Canal, at Paddington, to Limehouse Basin. That way, freight could be transported around the city by water. The building of the canal was a grim time for Paddington. It 'had then an evil reputation. To walk in the fields there through which the canal flowed was not very pleasant and certainly not safe.' The Paddington Basin area has been redeveloped in recent years, with new flats overlooking the canal, but it has taken a long time to shake off the earlier associations with industry and poverty.

New roads and waterways were detrimental to Marylebone, but commerce and the transport of goods has been an essential part of London since the beginning. The River Thames is the defining feature of the city. We will go there now, to find the lightermen and sailors who lived their lives on the water, as well as the thieves and widows of London's 'nautical hamlets'.

8.   The River Thames

In 1717, George I requested a pageant be arranged on the Thames, for his entertainment. He 'took Water at Whitehall in an open Barge' which rode the tide to Chelsea in great splendour. It was eight o'clock in the evening. Other barges and boats accompanied them, including a barge full of musicians, who played Handel's specially written *Water Music* for the first time. The King enjoyed it so much that he requested it to be played three times, exhausting the musicians. He and his company dined at Chelsea around midnight, and returned to the water at two, when they were rowed back to Westminster, once again to the sound of 'the finest Symphonies'.

The Thames has always played a large role in London's ceremonies, but its real value to the city was economic. London has no clearly defined harbour. In the Pool of London, bounded roughly by Wapping and London Bridge, goods from all over the world were unloaded for sale or re-export. In theory, all had to be declared between sunrise and sunset at the legal quays, which were twenty wharves between London Bridge and the Tower. These had been appointed by Elizabeth I, in 1558, for the collection of the appropriate duties and taxes. By the eighteenth century, these wharves were severely congested, leading to the creation of 'sufferance wharves' on the south bank, which were allowed to take in goods on 'sufferance'. By the 1760s, the system was totally overwhelmed. The Pool had official capacity for no more than 545 ships but it regularly held around almost 2,000, with goods spoiling aboard because they couldn't be unloaded. 'In fact, the whole river, from the bridge, for a vast way, is covered with a double forest of masts, with a narrow avenue in mid-channel.' At times, even this channel closed, presenting young boys aboard with the challenge of getting from one bank of the Thames to the other by clambering across unbroken decking.

Many associate Britain's Age of Sail with the heyday of the navy,

Old Westminster Bridge, showing Westminster Hall and Westminster Abbey in
the background, 1754

but Britain's naval might was nothing compared to her greed for the new and luxurious. War interrupted these supplies but Port of London Authority statistics still show that, between 1700 and 1770, commerce doubled. From 1770 to 1790, it doubled again. In 1792, London logged imports at £17,898,000 and exports, many of which were the same goods, re-exported westward, at £23,674,000. London consumed a massive 65 per cent of the incoming goods.

These days, the river traffic is relatively dull, with only the odd police speedboat to liven things up. In the eighteenth century, the huge 1,000-ton ships of the East India Company drew into the Thames, tired, wormy and barnacled, with crews of Englishmen, tanned like leather, and exotic, agile Indians, known as Lascars. London had very few docks which could hold a ship of this size, so they were usually unloaded into smaller vessels downriver. Queenhithe, in the City, could hold something small, Puddle Dock something even smaller, and Small Profit Dock only the tiniest of seagoing craft. They were docks in the loosest sense, little more than inlets allowing vessels to get out of the river traffic. In Rotherhithe, the deep old

Howland Wet (later Greenland) Dock was kitted out to deal with blubber and other whale products.

Processing whale carcasses was a filthy business. The first stages were often done at sea, but also in processing facilities at the edges of the Greenland Dock. First, the whalebone cutters removed the baleen. Then, the head was opened carefully to extract the sperma-ceti, or fine wax, which sits in a reservoir at the front of the skull. It was a valuable product for cosmetics such as lip balm and moisturiz-ers. To obtain it, a man with a bucket scooped it out of the hole carefully. As the level dropped, he would climb inside the whale's head. When the wax had been safely extracted, the blubber was stripped away with huge, scythe-like knives and then rendered down to produce the lamp oil which lit most London homes. The innards were dumped into the water after the ambergris was removed from the lower intestine. Ambergris is a waxy secretion which initially smells faecal, but over time this fades. It was used as a fixative for perfumes and fetched a high price. With the move from whalebone to steel for corsetry, and whale oil to gas for lighting, Greenland Dock was given over to timber in the nineteenth century, which no doubt pleased the neighbours.

With deep, convenient docks scarce, ships queued near the wharves. Here they were unloaded by lightermen, whose nimble craft drew up alongside the behemoths. The lighters, laden with goods, then negotiated the trip to the wharf. Porters, with their lethal billhooks, brought the cargo ashore and carried the goods up the nearest set of stairs. London's river stairs have particularly evoca-tive names, which always refer to a visible landmark nearby – so that sailors could navigate by them. Often, this was a riverside pub, as in the case of the Cricketers' Stairs, Popham's Parlour Stairs and Golden Anchor Stairs.

Edging the river were hundreds of warehouses into which the goods were taken and accounted for. Eager buyers strained for a first glimpse of the tea bundles, sacks of coffee or bales of whalebone from which they made their living. Opportunistic children lounged nearby, waiting for the sighting of a particular vessel, before bolting back to one of the City coffee houses where they were paid for news of the new arrival. The customs officials clambered over shipments to make sure they didn't miss anything, trying to keep hold of their documents and a handy writing instrument: Ned Ward remembered one customs official with a pen twisted into his ponytail for safekeeping. They didn't only check the exteriors of the boxes; shipments were liable to be thoroughly searched for smuggled goods. Sailors' wives gathered to welcome their husbands home and extract wages from their hands as the 'garblers' began to sort the goods. These were then inspected by the all-important warehousemen. Warehousemen were respected by everyone: they saved time, and therefore money, with their speedy identification of commodities and their no-nonsense allocation of grades. These jobs were often hereditary, leading to London's rough-and-tumble East End warehousemen becoming connoisseurs of such goods as rum, cinnamon (which came tied in bales consisting of bundles of sticks up to twelve inches long), ginger and pimento. Apprentices in tea warehouses carried small books called 'chop-books' with the Chinese characters for the different types of tea written against their English translation, helping them to decipher the marks chalked or burned on to the sides of the crates. Skirting the edges were the river thieves: the 'Pirates', the 'Night-Plunderers', the 'Light and the Heavy Horsemen' (small jobs and big jobs), and the 'Scuffle-Hunters', who were gangs of children who crept aboard, created a diversion and then tipped goods overboard to be retrieved at low tide. In 1796, the levels of such theft were thought to be around half a million pounds a year, and a Parliamentary Commission looked into 'the best mode of providing sufficient accommodation for the increased trade and shipping of the Port'. It led to the formation of the Thames River Police, based in Wapping High Street, in 1798: 'A RIVER POLICE, for securing Commercial Property against the unexampled Depredations to which it has been Subject, and for improving the Morals of the Maritime Labourers.' Reformer Patrick Colquhoun was in charge, and the force was initially composed of fifty officers funded by the West India Committee. They policed around 33,000 river workers, of whom a third Colquhoun guessed to be 'on the game'.

The Thames River Police succeeded mainly because their officers were well salaried and prohibited from other work. In the first year it was estimated they had prevented the theft of goods worth around £122,000. They were an unqualified success, although deeply unpopular amongst the river workers.

In addition, new and more easily regulated docks were built to the east. First, in 1802, the West India Docks opened on the site of what is now Canary Wharf. The West India Docks covered thirty acres and was guarded by a wall twenty feet high. Their official capacity of 600 vessels equalled that of the Pool. Loading and unloading was more orderly, and the losses from theft immediately reduced.

The eighteenth century marks the high point for the river in the commercial life of London. And it wasn't only the ships coming in and out of the Pool which created revenue. Industrial mills were built alongside the river, and one of the main focuses along the south bank was engineering, with over 300 businesses by 1820. Both trade and industry were reliant on London's great waterway, as were all those who earned their living upon it. These people were some of London's most resilient and roughest characters. Yet they were not poor, and rarely without hope, for who knew what the next tide might bring?

'They were hospitable and hearty . . . but often saucy, abusive and even sarcastic': the Thames watermen

London's watermen were a special breed: mainly Londoners, and mainly resident on the South Bank or Wapping. They were rough and hardy, working in all weathers in their small, exposed craft. The Thames is a turbulent river with a fast current. Their black boats criss-crossed on the water, ferrying people to and from work and social engagements. Like hackney carriages and sedan chairs, they were regulated; watermen were required to wear badges and numbers. Proud of their Englishness and their long heritage, the watermen formed a little guild near Garlickhythe. They worked largely to the west of London Bridge, where they plied the river stairs and shores for trade.

The pleasantest way of moving from one end of the town to the other in summer time, is by water, on that spacious gentle stream, the Thames, on which you travel two miles for six-pence, if you have two watermen, and for three-pence if you have but one: and to any village up or down the river, you go with company for a trifle.

Henry Mayhew described the Thames watermen as 'slightly-informed, or uninformed, and not unprosperous men'. Becoming a waterman was a decent option for someone with limited academic potential but substantial physical strength; it was a strenuous job requiring relatively little capital to start out with. It was also dangerous, the rapids at London Bridge being a particular hazard. One poor waterman froze to death, in 1771, after his taxi became caught in the Thames ice. He cried out 'piteously' to large passing craft but no one could reach him. The papers reported 'a waterman . . . had his boat jammed in between the ice and could not get on shore, and no waterman dare venture to his assistance. He was almost speechless last night and it is thought he cannot survive long.' A week later, the papers reported, 'the Body of Jacob Urwin the Waterman who was unfortunately drowned last week at London Bridge was drove up with the Tide on a shoal of Ice, and brought ashore at Monsoon Dock'.

The watermen waited at the various river stairs for custom, where they queued (much as black taxis do now on a taxi rank). Pitched and violent battles with unlicensed boatmen often made the news, and concerns over safety made them the minicabs of their day. Thames watermen were known for being cheeky and rowdy: 'On the river a curious habit was to assail all passing boats with a torrent of abuse. This was called river wit.' They were also renowned for their rather smelly diet of 'broil'd red herring' and 'bread and cheese and onions'.

Working in potentially dangerous conditions every day made the watermen highly aware of the river's 'moods'. They were also superstitious, and nothing brought that out more than 'strange tides'. The Port of London has two high tides a day, and a history of odd behaviour. On 22 March 1662, the Thames reached high water three times in four hours, and this was recorded three further times during the eighteenth century. But repeated high tides were not as alarming as the phenomenon of long 'dead waters' which were experienced in the 1760s and 1770s. During this period, the few minutes of dead water, when the tide turns, became extended for up to an hour and a half. The watermen placed objects such as buckets in the water and made them spin to illustrate the stillness of the current. For men so familiar with the water, such things were a bad omen. Dead waters still occur occasionally and remain an eerie time on the river.

If life was not easy as a waterman, some light relief was provided by rowing races. Gentlemen sponsored teams of professional watermen to row in races, sometimes against apprentices, who regularly hired cutters on a Sunday to row up to Richmond and Kew with their girlfriends. These land-based apprentices were a constant niggle for the watermen – who were banned from working on Sunday – so races between the two factions were always fraught with tension.

On 1 August 1716, a notice was posted upon London Bridge, announcing that:

> This being the day of his Majesty's happy accession to the throne, there will be given by Mr Doggett an Orange Colour Livery with a Badge representing Liberty to be rowed for by six watermen that are out of their time within the year past. It will be continued annually on the same day forever.

'Out of their time' means that they had obtained their freedom after apprenticeship. Thomas Doggett was an actor sprung from a family of watermen. It marked the beginning of popular rowing races on the Thames. Towards the end of the century, it was particularly desirable as a prize because it gave the winner immunity from being press-ganged. Watermen were a target for pressing because they were already so familiar with water. Today's competitors are not so much in need of immunity from the press gang, but Thomas Doggett's race is still held, and he gives his name to the pub on the South Bank by Blackfriars Bridge: Doggett's.

River sports included sailing and swimming, although the latter was only for the very strong. Benjamin Franklin swam in the Thames, much to the surprise and admiration of his colleagues. By the end of the century, sailing was becoming a popular sport for the young bloods, but it was mainly carried on to the west, closer to Chelsea and Putney, where there was much less traffic.

London on ice: the frost fairs

The English obsession with weather means we have one of the oldest sets of climate records in the world. They reveal a very different London than the one we know now. London froze regularly between December and March, and the 1690s had six winters when the temperature was consistently below 3°C for more than three months; this was definitely the sort of weather when a man like Samuel Pepys would have worn two shirts, a waistcoat and a jacket.

Before Sir Joseph William Bazalgette's Embankment of 1862, the Thames was a wider, slower river with gently sloping muddy banks covered in duckboards, which must have been very slippy in wet and icy conditions. The bridges were shored up with wide wooden 'starlings' which trapped debris and slowed the current. London Bridge, in particular, blocked the flow of the river, making it easier for ice to form. The couple of days it took for the Thames to freeze completely was a dangerous time. The watermen wanted to keep trading as long as possible, and some traded their lives for the opportunity of one last fare.

However, once the river had frozen, it was time to celebrate. Frost fairs have been recorded since Elizabethan times, when it was customary to push a printing press out on to the ice as a test. If it held, souvenir cards were printed off and sold as a memento of the occasion. Booths and cook-stalls were set up, selling skates (made from whalebone), puppets, gloves, hats and scarves as well as hot chestnuts and pork sandwiches from spits, along with sticky gingerbread and baked apples eaten from newspaper with a spoon. There were street performers, puppet shows and other entertainments, such as singing. Sometimes, as in the winter of 1683, the freeze was so solid that the Thames became a miniature shopping village and the booths were arranged into 'streets'. The Reverend Derham wrote up London's

unusually cold winters for the Royal Society, recalling the Long
Frost of the 1680s:

> . . . the Waters were so frozen, that above the Bridge, 'tis well known,
> many Booths were erected, Fries made, and Meat dress'd; and on Jan-
> uary 10th I my self saw a Coach and two Horses drive over the River
> into Southwark, and back again, a great number of People accompa-
> nying it.

Even the earliest frost fairs had merry-go-rounds for children, boat-
swings and pony-drawn rides, but life off the river probably wasn't
quite so much fun. One of the greatest problems during freezes
such as this was that the ground froze to depths of two or three
feet, making the drawing of water from the wells in the streets difficult, if not impossible. Ice was gathered and melted, then boiled
for domestic use. One group of people who didn't complain were
the ice merchants who used this weather to fill their underground
stores and cellars with the cold stuff, packed in straw so that it could
be sold in warmer weather. By the 1720s, the demand for ice had
become great enough for dealers in 'ice and snow' to be making a
living all year round. From then on, they were importing ice from
the frozen north.

The thaws, when they came, were sudden and terrifying. The *Universal Spectator* of 26 January 1740 recorded how

> . . . the inhabitants of the west prospect of the Bridge were presented
> with a very odd scene, for on the opening of their windows there
> appeared underneath on the river a parcel of booths, shops and huts
> of different forms [on a broken-off piece of ice], but without any
> inhabitants.

Booths rarely fell *through* the ice, so the stallholders knew when to get
out. But in 1789, a ship moored to the quay of a public house pulled
down both structures when it fell back into the thawed river. There
is also the sad tale in *The Gentleman's Magazine*, in 1763, of a wretch,
'with skaits on . . . found frozen to death upon some floating ice over
against the Isle of Dogs'.

The Thames froze for the last time in 1814, and the ice was solid for four days – solid enough to lead an elephant across the ice near Black-friars Bridge and erect fairground rides. The innovations of the Victorian period, such as the new London Bridge and the Embankment, made the river narrower, deeper and faster, ending London's life on ice.

London Bridge: 'bridge of wonders'

I remember well the street on London Bridge, narrow, darksome, and dangerous to passengers from the multitude of carriages: frequent arches of strong timber crossed the streets, from the tops of the houses, to keep them together, and from falling into the river. Nothing but use could preserve the rest of the inmates, who soon grew deaf to the noise of the falling waters, the clamours of the watermen, or the frequent shrieks of drowning wretches.

The bridge that now joins the north to the south bank, one hundred feet west of its predecessor, is little more than an ugly though useful advertisement for the properties of concrete. Three centuries ago, London Bridge was a busy village in its own right with a church, houses, shops, gardens, roof terraces and plenty of traffic. The history of London Bridge stretches from the tenth century, at least, right up to the present day. Early in its life, it was the southern defence of the City. For hundreds of years, it bore the heads of traitors as a warning: William Wallace was the first and Oliver Cromwell one of the last. Houses stood three storeys high above their cellars, which were within and between the piers. Over the houses at the north end were stately platforms surrounded with railings; there were walks and gardens over the street, which was twenty feet wide. In contrast, the south end appeared a mass of awkward structures and narrow passages above a street fourteen feet and, in some places, twelve feet wide.

The street was lined with shops and 'piazzas', with a row of colon-naded shops at the north end. For centuries, many of the shops had been famous for selling needleworking tools and other small easy-to-transport items, whilst other shops included Edward Butling, a wallpaper maker in the 1690s, John Allan at the *Locks of Hair*, selling 'all sorts of Hair Curled or Uncurled' and Robert Vincent, 'Scale Maker, at the *Hand & Scales* . . . the Second Door from the Bear Tavern, Southwark-side. Makes Curious Sets of Scales & Weights for Diamonds.'

By 1722, traffic on the bridge was so great that the wagons and carts were fined if they didn't have their pennies ready to pay the toll. Traffic ran on the west side coming into the City, and on the east side out of the City. Legend has it that this is one of the precedents for why we now drive on the left.

The opening of Westminster Bridge, in 1740, meant that London Bridge had competition. For the City aldermen, it was a clear signal from the west that their monopoly on London traffic from the south was over. Plans were soon drawn up to improve London Bridge and to increase the traffic it could bear: the houses had to go. During this period, the old bridge was captured in all its ramshackle glory by a young Italian painter living in London at the time: Giovanni Antonio Canal, better known as Canaletto. He had come to the city to find patrons, as the flow of 'grand tourists' to Italy had been stopped by the War of the Austrian Succession. His drawing of 'Old London Bridge', now in the British Museum, gives perhaps the truest picture of what was a bridge, a shopping mall and a residential neighbourhood.

No matter how beautiful Canaletto rendered it, the 'bridge of wonders' was finished. Much of the stone was recycled, with the stone columns from the piazzas going to David Garrick, who recycled them in his villa at Hampton. In 1756, a wooden bridge was built alongside the stone one to bear the traffic for a short while as the houses, some of them five centuries old, were taken down. In 1758, the wooden bridge burned down, possibly the work of an arsonist. If it was meant to sabotage the work on London Bridge, it failed and instead speeded it up: the houses were cleared in the same year. London's antiquaries began to document the history of the bridge, recording both the memories of those who knew it and the artefacts and relics found as the bridge was repaired and later destroyed. Many were genuinely sorry to see it go.

They especially regretted the demolition of the bridge's Chapel of Thomas of Canterbury. It was in the ninth pier from the north end and had an entrance from the river, as well as the street, via a winding staircase. It was also said to be beautifully paved, with black and white marble. On the chapel pier was a square hollow, covered by wire netting with a hole in it. This netting created a pool in which to catch fish, and at low tide the young men used to climb down to fish in it. From July to September, the whole bridge was covered with self-seeded *Sisymbrium irio*, or London Rocket, painting it with bright yellow flowers.

Despite this sense of romance, London Bridge was lethal. Beneath the bridge, tales of boats 'upset' or 'overturned' were common. Usually, 'all perished'. Of the 27 people reported who fell in between 1758 and 1770, 11 died. The crowded street, full of vehicles with their grinding wheels, coupled with the roar of the water, meant that broken legs were commonplace. In 1752, a young man, unknown, was crushed between the wheels of two carts going in opposite directions, as was a young woman and her child, in 1758. Fatalities reached a peak during the demolition of the houses, when two workers fell from ladders into the river, and one man was killed by falling masonry which was being pulled down by the labourers.

The bridge was not only a site of accidental death: it also drew those looking for a permanent exit from their troubles. John Temple, the only son of a diplomat, hired a small boat with one waterman, on 14 April 1689. He told the waterman to shoot the bridge rapids, and threw himself into the water. The waterman said Temple sank so quickly he had probably filled his pockets with stones. He left a note on the seat of the boat: 'My folly in undertaking what I could not perform, whereby some misfortunes have befallen the king's service, is the cause of my putting myself to this sudden end: I wish him success in all his undertakings, and a better servant.' He left a wife and two small daughters. Later, the waterman was distressed to find out from a colleague that Temple had hired his boat earlier that day, and had stared fixedly out at the water as they shot the bridge. But he had then alighted, having lost his courage. On a Sunday evening in 1752, a man who outwardly had every reason to live carried out his purpose.

He was 'a middle-sized man, clean dress'd with ruffles, and a fine drab great coat, black stockings and clean shoes' and was seen on the bridge, looking over the rails. A fisherman called up to him, but he didn't take any notice. When the fisherman looked away, he threw himself into the river. 'The fisherman threw a rope to him but he took no notice and was soon afterwards carried under one of the water wheels and drowned.'

At the end of the eighteenth century, the cleared London Bridge was six centuries old and still struggling on. In 1811, building began on Waterloo Bridge, and it appeared that traffic on London Bridge would lessen again. In the hard winter of 1814, frost set in on 27 December along with a freezing fog which didn't shift for the following eight days, when two days of heavy snow fell. The bridge was damaged but struggled on until, in 1824, work began on a replacement bridge to designs by Scottish engineer John Rennie.

Rennie's bridge was remarkable. Weight of traffic meant that it was widened between 1902 and 1904. More granite corbels were quarried on Dartmoor for the work and some still lie there, unused. Eventually, the bridge began to sink under its own weight. By the 1920s, engineers realized they had made a mistake: it would not stand the test of time, although there was little reason to replace it. A historian noted, in 1927, 'One day Rennie's bridge, whose granite stones were quarried from grey and rain-swept Dartmoor, will go, and some great structure of strange design will be built in its place.'

Forty years later, Rennie's bridge was put up for sale. It was eventually sold to an American entrepreneur who had it shipped to Arizona, where it was reassembled. The 'structure of strange design' which replaced it was designed by Lord Holford and engineers Mott, Hay and Anderson, and opened in 1973.

Wapping: 'that nautical hamlet of Stepney'

Wapping was a hive of taverns, full of dock workers and day labourers. Rough and unpredictable, it was home to London's early trade in opium, and to the Chinamen who provided it. Blewgate Fields hosted one of the first of London's 'dens'. That, and other infractions, led to rough justice being meted out by the merchant navy at Execution Dock. The bleak and lonely dock is still there, not far from The Prospect of Whitby pub. It was 'in use as often as a melancholy occasion requires. The criminals are to this day executed on a temporary gallows placed at low-water mark; but the custom of leaving the body to be overflowed by three tides, has long since been omitted'.

Going to sea was a hard decision, but for young men of decent families it could lead, like the army, to social improvement. It could also be a miserable and perilous life, and some never got that far: 'Fishermen off Poplar caught a shark on New Year's Day, 1787, and inside it found a watch and chain and a cornelian seal. Apparently the watch had been bought by a man in Whitechapel for his son's first sea voyage. The boy fell overboard almost immediately and was never seen again.'

Samuel Johnson said most men would rather go to prison than to sea, as the food and company were both better in prison, and 'being in a ship is being in a jail with the chance of being drowned'. Press gangs operated throughout London, particularly in the river areas and on the bridges, snapping up 'persons who had not any visible method of livelihood'. They were looking for the aimless and friendless.

Apart from the shipwrights and male workers on the docks, the area contained the largest population of women living alone in London. Wives, widows, girlfriends and whores lived in tenements, no doubt feeling pestered, harassed and lonely by turns. Mixed-race children, fathered by foreign sailors, roamed the streets along with their white siblings. Women didn't always stay ashore; a letter to Samuel Pepys detailed how the navy ships were 'pestered with women'.

It wasn't only the navy ships but also the merchant boats that allowed women aboard. Henry Teonge was, in 1675, the chaplain on *Assistance* when he wrote, 'You would have wondered to see here a man and a woman creep into a hammock, the woman's legs to the hams hanging over the sides or out at the end of it.' Complaints continued regularly throughout the eighteenth and nineteenth centuries, and opinion was deeply divided. Admiral Thomas Hardy, of Nelson-kissing fame, stated, 'I consider it right that women should be admitted into ships; when I was at sea, I always admitted them.' Others, though, considered it gross indecency.

Admiral Edward Hawker, an overzealous reformer, wrote in 1821 that the sailors and their women go below decks and

> . . . in sight and hearing of each other, shamelessly and unblushingly couple like dogs . . . In a case that has lately occurred, the captain and his wife were actually on the quarterdeck on a Sunday morning while seventy-eight prostitutes were undergoing an inspection of the first lieutenant to ascertain that their dress was clean.

The first lieutenant wasn't checking out the girls' latest fashions; 'clean dress' was Admiral Hawker's euphemism for inspecting the women for venereal disease. William Robinson, who served in the Royal Navy, wrote about their condition in the early nineteenth century, coming to the conclusion that: 'Of all the human race, these poor creatures are the most pitiable; the ill-usage and the degradation they are driven to submit to are indescribable.' These women lived mainly in small dwellings strung out between the river and Ratcliff Highway, now known just as The Highway. Those who worked as prostitutes kept an eye out for ships arriving. They didn't have to look far, as 'between the houses and the water, in all this long tract of street, are frequent docks, and small building yards. The passenger is often surprised with the sight of the prow of a ship rising over the street, and the hulls of new ones appearing at a number of openings.'

The 'best remembered atrocities of the century': the Ratcliff Highway murders

As Ratcliff became rapidly more built up, it became associated with the vagaries of seamen and their variable fortunes. 'The Wapping Landlady', looking to make a quick turn on the 'tars just come ashore', either through girls or drink, was a London icon famous enough for Francis Hayman to feature her in his canvasses for Vauxhall Gardens. Ratcliff Highway was

> A long narrow street, well-paved, and handsomely flagged on both sides, winding along the banks of the Thames, as far as the end of Limehouse, an extent of near two miles; and inhabited by multitudes of sea-faring men, alternate occupants of sea and land: their floating tenements lie before them.

The area was rough and the general quality of the inhabitants poor. But poverty cannot explain everything. Mention a famous East End killer and no doubt Jack the Ripper's name will come up, but he wasn't the first. The Ratcliff Highway murders, committed within a fortnight in 1811, terrified London.

On 7 December, just before midnight, 24-year-old draper Timothy Marr was shutting up his shop at 29 Ratcliff Highway. He had been a sailor with the East India Company for four years during his teens, but had returned to London and was making his way running his own business.

Living above the shop with him were his wife, Celia, their three-and-a-half-month-old baby, the apprentice James Gowan and their serving girl, Margaret Jewell. Timothy Marr sent Margaret off to get them some oysters for a midnight snack, and to pay their bill at the baker's around the corner. Margaret found both shops closed. Nipping back to the shop, she saw her boss still inside, working. She decided to try another shop for the oysters. That decision saved her life.

She returned, again empty-handed, at twenty past midnight. The shop and house were in darkness so she pulled the bell. No answer. She tried again; inside, there was a scuffle and the baby cried. Suddenly anxious, Margaret attempted to kick the door in, only desisting when she was heckled by a passing drunk. She stopped and sat on the step, frightened and cold. When the watch arrived at around one, she told parish watchman George Olney what had happened. George had already passed by while Margaret was on her second oyster run. By this time, the shutters were closed, so he tried them and found they weren't locked. Someone was in the shop, and he shouted through that they hadn't locked their shutters. A voice he hadn't recognized called back that they knew, and it was fine.

John Murray was a pawnbroker and the Marrs' neighbour. He

17. 'The Frost Fair of the Winter of 1683–4 on the Thames, with Old London Bridge in the Distance', c. 1685

18. 'Mr. Lunardi's New Balloon, 29 June 1785', by J. C. Ibbetson

19. 'Christie's Auction Room', by Thomas Rowlandson and Augustus Pugin, *Microcosm of London*, 1809

20. 'Watch House', by Thomas Rowlandson and Augustus Pugin, *Microcosm of London*, 1809: a view of the interior of St James's Watch House

21. 'The Hall and Stair Case of the British Museum', by Thomas Rowlandson and Augustus Pugin, *Microcosm of London*, 1809

22. The Portland Vase, currently dated *c.* AD 25, purchased by Margaret, the Dowager Duchess of Portland, in 1785

23. 'Workhouse', by Thomas Rowlandson and Augustus Pugin, *Microcosm of London*, 1809: a view of the interior of St James's Workhouse

24. Tokens given by mothers to their children on leaving them at the Foundling Hospital, eighteenth century

25. 'View of St James's from Green Park, London', by Benjamin Read, *c.* 1838

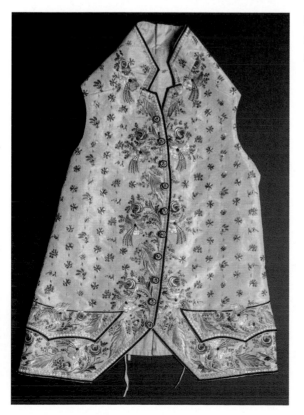

26. A Spitalfields silk waistcoat made for a wedding, early nineteenth century

27. 'The Rhinebeck Panorama', depicting the Thames in the early nineteenth century

28. 'A View of the London Docks, 1808', by William Daniell

29. 'Entrance to the Thames Tunnel, 1836', engraved by B. Dixie

30. 'A View of the Highgate Archway, 1821', engraved by John Hill, after Augustus Pugin

had heard the same noise inside the house as Margaret, but hadn't acted upon it. He came out to speak with the watchman. Worried, he then went to the back of the house and let himself in through the back door, which wasn't locked. He carried a candle and called out as he went.

Inside, John found the body of James Gowan the apprentice. His skull had been smashed in with a heavy object, his face was destroyed. Near him lay Celia Marr. She was face down on the floor and blood was still pouring from the bloody mess where her face had been. John Murray cried murder, bringing in other neighbours. The body of Timothy Marr was found in another room, his head smashed to pieces. Someone then remembered the baby: it was found in its cot, skull broken on the left side. Worse than that, the baby's throat had been cut so deeply the head was almost severed.

The shout went up, and brought Charles Horton from the Thames Police Office. He searched the scene himself, going through the victims' pockets and finding more than five pounds on Timothy Marr. In the Marrs' bedroom he found, leaning against a chair, a ship-wright's maul, or heavy hammer, with the letters 'JP' stamped into the head. They later discovered that this belonged to an 'Old Swede', John Peterson, who lodged at the nearby Pear Tree. There was also over £150 in the chest of drawers: either Margaret's attempted break-in had alerted the murderer, or money had not been the motive.

John Harriott, the magistrate in charge, had bills printed looking for information. For the next fortnight, the authorities investigated every avenue, with no results. Then, on 19 December, at the King's Arms (in what is now Garnet Street) the publican John Williamson, Elizabeth his wife and the barmaid, Bridget Harrington, were found dead. A watchman had found their lodger, John Turner, shinning down knotted sheets from an upper floor and shouting murder after having disturbed a large man rooting through the dead Williamson's things. They forced the cellar trapdoor and found the bodies. John Williamson's body was hanging from the cellar stairs, his skull shattered and his throat cut. Their fourteen-year-old granddaughter, Kitty Stillwell, alone survived out of the Williamson family. She had been sleeping in an obscure back bedroom and escaped notice.

The following morning, the Home Secretary appointed a Bow Street magistrate to come and sort things out. Several arrests were made, but they had little idea who they were chasing. One of the arrestees was James Williams, a sailor who had been drinking at the King's Arms and was acquainted in a roundabout way with Timothy Marr through the East India Company. It was never clear whether the two had sailed together. He also lodged at the Pear Tree, and so could have taken John Peterson's maul. Williams did not fit the lodger's description, but circumstantial evidence was against him. Williams was never tried, or even questioned for a second time after his arrest; he hanged himself in his cell on the morning of Christmas Eve.

On New Year's Eve, Williams' body was drawn through the streets on a wagon. The driver of a hackney coach leaned over and struck the corpse about the head three times with his whip, but there was no other disorder from the 10,000-strong crowd. The fury of the people was directed not only at a murderer – for murder was not uncommon in Wapping and Ratcliff – but at someone who would enter a private home. At St George's East burial ground, where the Marrs had recently been interred, the body had a stake driven through the heart and was buried kneeling in the grave. James Williams remained there until he was dug up during the laying of the gas mains, decades later, and reburied elsewhere.

Decline: 'nobody cares enough'

By the end of the Georgian period, the glory of London's water trade was over. Wapping, Rotherhithe and Deptford, which had been a lively, if rough, riverside sprawl began to decline into urban slums. The river was becoming increasingly polluted, and the last salmon was caught in this stretch of the Thames in 1833. The wooden ships which had been built in Deptford and Greenwich had run their course and were returned to London to be broken up. By 1815, steamships were on the Thames; and by 1830, iron ships were dominating the waterways. Henry Castle, born to a ship-building family in 1808, was living in Rotherhithe in the 1830s when he realized more wooden ships were being decommissioned than built. He set up a ship-breaking business in Rotherhithe and also on Baltic Wharf, Millbank.

The yards were littered with the hulks of wooden ships being stripped down and recycled, often into garden furniture. A catalogue of their furniture later featured at the Great Exhibition of 1851, available for same-day delivery. Some ships were burned on the foreshore and the metal remnants scavenged for scrap afterwards. Legend has it that Turner's *Fighting Temeraire* was being towed to Castle's yard in his famous picture, mastless and damaged. Castle was keen to collect figureheads from old ships. In perhaps one of the most telling stories of the move from sail to steam, from Georgian to Victorian, the navy found that figureheads, absent from iron ships, had been a source of morale and inspiration for sailors, who wanted them preserved. The naval authorities found themselves in an awkward position, forced to deal with a new breed of 'salvage' dealers who knew the value of a 15-foot-high wooden woman. Castle's yard perhaps best represents the sweeping away of an age: Georgian London's sea-going stock might become Victorian London's deckchairs.

This area was particularly affected in the years leading up to Queen Victoria's reign. In 1832, London's first cholera epidemic hit Wapping. In 1831, cholera was spreading across Europe, and was particularly prevalent in the Baltic. Ships arriving in London were made to wait out a ten-day quarantine at Standgate Creek, in Deptford, but the precautions were not enough. Cholera arrived in Newcastle in the winter, and soon the Tyne colliers, whose vessels went up and down the east coast free of quarantine restrictions, brought it to London. One man, John Potts, arrived on a vessel named *Mould*, and was waiting to take another vessel, *Dirt*, back. He died quickly in Shadwell workhouse with cholera-like symptoms. A twenty-inch section of his bowels was removed for inspection, and the Central Board of Health pronounced that he had died, not from cholera, but 'spontaneous gangrene of the bowels'. In February, three women who picked coals on the shore in Limehouse died of the disease. Their desiccated bodies had turned blue just before death, a sure sign of Asiatic cholera, or *Cholera morbus*. The whole of London was thrown into a panic.

A cholera hospital was set up on HMS *Dover*, at Hermitage Pier, Wapping. Bodies from the ship were buried deep in the Woolwich scrubland, but the disease could not be contained. Cholera is spread through contact with contaminated faecal matter. Given the sheer scale on which sufferers evacuated water from their bodies, maintaining clean conditions was almost impossible. There is no accurate figure for the total number of deaths, but it was estimated between 2,000 and 3,000, of which almost half were in the nautical hamlets of east London. Cholera would revisit the city in the Broad Street epidemic of 1854, when a leaking cesspit contaminated with cholera polluted the water supply. A doctor, John Snow, began to understand how it was spreading, and progress was finally made on tackling the disease.

As cholera swept Limehouse and Wapping, the old industries faded from the river, and new ones took over. The Thames Tunnel, running between Rotherhithe and Wapping, was bored beneath the river. It took a long time to complete, and work went on in fits and starts from 1825. Marc Brunel and his son, Isambard Kingdom, finally succeeded in getting the tunnel open in 1834, following an earlier failed attempt by Richard Trevithick. It took years and lives to build, eventually opening in the Victorian era, when it was a huge attraction and proved that underwater tunnels could be built. (It is now part of the London overground system, after lying empty for years.) Further rapid innovations in engineering were evident in the area, and Deptford hosted London's first railway station, opening in February 1836. The line was soon extended to London Bridge, linking the ancient with the modern along the arterial heart of London.

The river, docks and surrounding areas continued to become increasingly busy and crowded during the nineteenth century. But slowly, slowly the advent of improved rail and subsequently road travel meant that goods could come into other more convenient and deeper ports, such as Southampton, and still make it to London in reasonable time. Then, during the Blitz, bombs rained down upon the neglected Georgian squares of Stepney and the ancient, shabby tenements of Wapping. Some of the buildings were already empty, and many of the older residents did not return after the war. Soon, vast sullen estates would cover what had been London's nautical hamlets. As historian and journalist Ian Nairn recalled, visiting in 1966, 'Nobody cares enough.'

9.   Southwark and Lambeth

South of the Thames was a marshy scrubland and a 'hideous' fore-shore overladen 'with dank tenements, rotten wharves, and dirty boat-houses'. Southwark encompasses Bankside, the Borough and Bermondsey, and away to the west lies Lambeth. It was a landscape punctuated by industrial buildings and windmills.

These vast areas were too wet for building, and the expense of draining the land coupled with the lower returns meant people were not in a hurry to live there. Worse, the nearby tanneries filled the air with a pungent reek, relying as they did on human urine and dog excrement for the curing. Collectors of the excrement trolled the streets of the city, performing an entrepreneurial social service and filling buckets with what was ironically known as 'pure', which they then sold to the factories. Soon, these factories were exiled away from the city to belch their stink further afield.

Here and there, small bonfires burned rubbish, and old women pegged out their washing on lines and bushes dotting the open spaces. To the east of London Bridge was St Saviour's Dock, 'or, as it is called, Savory . . . It is at present solely appropriated to barges, which discharge coals, copperas from Writtlesea in Essex, pipe-clay, corn and various other articles of commerce.' Behind it lie the Borough and Bermondsey – an ancient, patchy settlement with a busy fruit and vegetable market and a medieval hospital, St Thomas's. By the end of the eighteenth century, Savory marked the swampy boundary of London's most terrifying slum, Jacob's Island. The area was rid-dled with prisons: the King's Bench and the Marshalsea, the County Gaol, the House of Correction, as well as Borough Compter and the Clink.

Away to the west is Lambeth, home then to a rambling bishop's palace and the Baltic timber yards. There was also the School for the Indigent Blind where, from 1779, blind children were taught to

Southwark, showing Guy's and St Thomas's Hospitals due south of
London Bridge, detail of John Greenwood's map, 1827

weave baskets and to play musical instruments so that they might be
able, wholly, or in part, to provide for their own subsistence. By the
end of the Georgian period, the children were taught to read from
books with raised letters. Small groups of blind musicians were
employed throughout London, most famously in Covent Garden as
depicted by Hogarth, to play at orgies.

Lambeth was rapidly becoming a pretty Surrey suburb housing

nurseries, 'pineries' and melon pits for growing exotic fruits and forced vegetables. On the edge of the river was the huge Guy's Hospital, founded in 1721 as a hospice for the 'incurables' from St Thomas's. Close to the southern end of London Bridge were the lanes leading into Southwark, the medieval entertainment centre on the south bank, the back streets and rotting theatres of Bankside, and the already ancient Borough Market. Old and new was the theme of Southwark: medieval remnants, the new industries and pioneering medicine.

Bankside: where butchers do a bear

Bankside had traditionally been the site of London's bear-baiting. The Elizabethan court was particularly keen on this cruel sport. Bankside was a popular destination on Sundays where crowds of both rich and poor gathered to place wagers on the unfortunate contestants, though not everyone agreed it was an acceptable pastime.

> What folly is this, to keep with danger
> A great mastive dog, and fowle ouglie bear;
> And to this and end, to see them two fight,
> With terrible tearings, a full ouglie sight.

Bear-baiting was prohibited under the Puritans, and only hare coursing remained as a dog-based sport. Upon the Restoration, the Bankside Bear Garden cranked back into life, but Charles did not encourage the sport. Cock-throwing (aiming stones or bottles at a cockerel tied to a stake), dog-fighting and dog-versus-rats matches abounded throughout. Bandogs, the frightening relative of the pit bull, were bred in Clerkenwell and used specifically for baiting larger animals. But when tastes turned towards seeing bears perform rather than die, these animals needed new targets. In February 1675, an elderly lion was baited to death on Bankside. In the same year, the Earl of Rochester's 'savage' horse was 'baited to death, of a most vast strength and greatness'.

Approximately 19 hands high, the horse stood 6ft 3in at the shoulders. It had destroyed 'several horses and other cattel' and was responsible for human fatalities. Rochester sold him to the Marquess of Dorchester, but the horse then hurt his keeper and was sold to a brewer, who put him to a dray. Soon, he was breaking his halter and carting the fully laden wagon off behind him in order to attack people in the street, 'monstrously tearing at their flesh, and eating it, the like whereof hath hardly been seen'. Realistically there was no option but to destroy this particular animal. Baiting was not the humane way of doing it, but nevertheless, the horse was put to the dogs for 'the divertisement of his Excellency the Embassadour from the Emperour of Fez and Morocco; many of the nobility and gentry that knew the horse, and several mischiefs done by him, designing to be present'.

The horse was put to the dogs in the ramshackle Hope Theatre (a Jacobean playhouse which had been taken over exclusively for blood sports). It killed or maimed them, all. The owner decided to stop the contest, but the crowd became a mob, demanding to see the horse baited to death, and started to pull the tiles from the roof of the theatre. Dogs were 'once more set upon him; but they not being able to overcome him, he was run through with a sword, and dyed'. The ambassador failed to attend, owing to inclement weather.

By the turn of the eighteenth century, baiting had moved north of the river – to Hockley-in-the-Hole, in Clerkenwell. In 1710, there was

> . . . a match to be fought by two dogs, one from Newgate-market, against one from Honey-lane market, at a bull . . . which goes fairest and fastest in, wins all. Likewise, a green bull to be baited, which was never baited before; and a bull to be turned loose with fireworks all over him. Also a mad ass to be baited. With a variety of bull-baiting and bear-baiting, and a dog to be drawn up with fireworks. To begin exactly at three of the clock.

Hockley was the centre of bull terrier breeding in London, and so perhaps it is natural that the sport would move there. In 1756, Hockley disappeared with the continuing Fleet development, and bull-baiting moved to Spitalfields. Increasingly unpopular, it was soon confined almost exclusively to market towns.

At the same time, Hogarth was campaigning against the 'barbarous treatment of animals, the very sight of which renders the streets of our metropolis so distressing to every feeling mind'. His 'Four Stages of Cruelty' connected the cruel treatment of animals with the degenerate mind. The first plate of the 'Four Stages' features Tom Nero attempting to force an arrow into a dog's anus, and another youth pleading with him not to.

Attitudes were changing in London. In 1785, it was reported that

> . . . a fine horse, brought at great expense from Arabia, would be delightfully worried to death by dogs, in an inclosure near the Adam and Eve, in Tottenham-court-road; and to exclude low company, every admission-ticket was to cost half-a-guinea. But the interposition of the magistrates, who doubted of the innocence, or of the wisdom of training dogs and horses to mutual enmity, put a stop for once to that superfine exhibition.

In 1822, the Act to Prevent the Cruel and Improper Treatment of Cattle was passed. It was known as Martin's Act. Richard Martin was a politician and campaigner for animal rights who brought Bill Burns, a costermonger, to trial for abusing his donkey. Deploying shock tactics, Martin brought the donkey into the courtroom so that its injuries could be seen. Burns was the first man to be convicted for animal cruelty. In 1824, in Old Slaughter's Coffee House on St Martin's Lane, a group of men met with the idea of forming a new society concerned with enforcing Martin's Act and heightening awareness of animal welfare. They were headed by the Reverend Arthur Broome and included Richard Martin and William Wilberforce. This society would soon have a new name: the RSPCA.

Cuper's and Vauxhall: 'the great resort of the profligate of both sexes'

From the early seventeenth century, Londoners busied themselves finding spas, or 'spaws' as they were often known. Mineral springs abounded, and the waters were sold throughout the city. Streatham water was a natural emetic sold in coffee houses as a rather drastic hangover cure. It was also said to have the alarming ability to expel worms from the body. Hoxton's 'balsamic' water was a purgative, causing 'much bustle and ferment in nature'. The water of St Pancras Wells made the boldest claims of all: it could, apparently, cure scurvy, scrofula, leprosy, piles, running sores, ulcers and cancer.

After the Restoration, these spas became larger and more formal. More sophisticated food and drink were served, and events were held to bring in the customers. Usually, gardens were built around these spas, some with innovative designs and water features.

Cuper's was an old formal garden dating from at least 1589, on what is now the approach to Waterloo Bridge. In 1624, the Earl of Arundel acquired it and then leased it to Abraham Boydell Cuper, his gardener. The Cupers opened it as a pleasure garden, 'with Bowling greens . . . whither many of the Westerly part of the Town resort for Diversion in the Summer Season'. The gardens were also famous for 'their retired arbours, their shady walks ornamented with statues and ancient marbles, and especially the fireworks'.

The marbles were smaller pieces of the Arundel Marbles:

> . . . which had for that purpose been begged from his lordship . . . On the pulling down of *Arundel*-house, to make way for the street for that name, these, and several others of the damaged part of the collection, were removed to this place. Numbers were left on the ground, near the river-side, and overwhelmed with the rubbish brought from the foundation of the new church of *St Paul's*.

The main collection is now in the Ashmolean Museum, and it is extraordinary to think of such antiquities lying amongst the rubble of the ancient cathedral.

Despite such highbrow entertainments and surroundings, Cuper's was gaining a reputation: it was seedy, though, and old-fashioned. Nearby, Vauxhall Gardens were on the rise. Cuper's would close in 1760, when the competition simply became too much. From then on, Vauxhall was the dominant London pleasure garden.

Vauxhall was originally known as New Spring Gardens. Samuel Pepys visited, in 1662, and during the following century the gardens grew larger and more popular. In 1729, the gardens were taken over by Jonathan Tyers, a cultured man with big ideas. He paid for a twenty-year lease and introduced art, architecture and music. There were works by William Hogarth and Francis Hayman, and music by Handel. The Soho-based Huguenot sculptor Louis Roubiliac created the statue of Handel which stood in the gardens for years and is now in the Victoria and Albert Museum. Frederick, Prince of Wales, was an enthusiastic patron of the gardens and had his own pavilion built there amongst the fake ruins, arches and temples, which were added as the years went on.

In 1785, the Tyers' children were managing their father's gardens. The gardens had become an impressive enterprise:

> ... that substantial Brick Dwelling Houses called Spring Garden House, the Tap House and 36 other Dwelling Houses, Coach Houses, Stables, Out houses, Workshops, Sheds, Icehouse, Great Room, Orchestra, Covered Walks, open Walks, Ways, Passages, Pavilions, Boxes and Spring Gardens Yards, Pond and an Aquiduct to supply the said Pond from Vauxhall Creek.

Much of the food served was grown locally. Borough Market sold both local fruit and vegetables, as well as produce brought in from Kent and Surrey. Southwark was famous for its melon pits and nurseries, where exotic fruit such as pineapples were grown. An article in the *London World* during 1755 mentions that, 'Through the use of hothouses ... every gardiner that used to pride himself in an early cucumber, can now raise a pineapple.' Andrew Moffett's 'Pinery' on Grange Road in Southwark, stocked 'Fruiting and Succession Plants' of the sweetest sort, guaranteed 'free of Insects'. By February 1798, any problems with the surrounding environment had clearly been overcome, as Mr William North, at his Nursery near the Asylum in Lambeth, Surrey, was advertising new forms of dwarf broccoli above his pineapple plants in the *Morning Chronicle*.

The gardens had been known as 'Vauxhall' for years; from 1785 onwards, they were officially renamed as such. The gardens entered an extended heyday which lasted into the Victorian period. They were often

... splendidly illuminated at night with about 15,000 glass lamps. These being tastefully hung among the trees, which line the walks, produce an impression similar to that which is called up on reading some of the stories in the Arabian Nights Entertainments. On some occasions there have been upwards of 19,000 persons in them, and this ... with the illuminated walks, add not a little to the brilliant and astonishing effect of the whole scene.

Vauxhall Gardens were London's biggest nightclub. Music and copious amounts of alcohol were served up in glittering surroundings, with just enough dark corners. The fun faded out around 1840, when music halls became popular. The last event was held in 1859, when the fireworks picked out 'Farewell For Ever' in the night sky. Only a few years later, the abandoned gardens were eaten up by the expansion of Waterloo Station.

Debtors' prisons and Jacob's Island

Southwark and Lambeth were rural, and the existing infrastructure was largely medieval. As late as the 1780s, the only built-up areas were around the south end of London Bridge and a short way east into Bermondsey. Jacob's Island was an old slum, sitting on the creek where trendy Shad Thames is now. The houses were, quite literally, rotting. Broken windows were patched with rags and paper, and the street in front was little more than a gutter. Many of the houses had communal lavatories which sat over the creek, making the whole area fetid and deeply unappealing at low tide. Multi-family occupation in each house was the standard, and children roamed barefoot.

The knife-edge existence of the Jacob's Island dwellers was compounded by the presence of four of London's prisons just a stone's throw away, near Borough High Street. The King's Bench, the Marshalsea, the County Gaol and the House of Correction all sat on the east side of the street, housing hundreds of prisoners between them. The King's Bench, connected to the court at Westminster, and the Marshalsea were debtors' prisons, where men and women were held for periods of time, largely decided by their creditors.

Before the Bankruptcy Act of 1869, imprisonment for even very small debts was common, and had been since the medieval period. The Marshalsea existed as early as 1294, and the King's Bench around a century later. In the seventeenth century, attempts were made to stop debtors being imprisoned for small sums. But the attitude to debt amongst the population was severe, and it took until the reign of George III for a minimum threshold of forty shillings to be set. However, as soon as lawyers were involved, the threshold was breached – and then, as soon as the debtor was imprisoned, they lost the ability to repay the debt by earning. For ordinary people, it was a vicious circle.

The prisons themselves were thriving private enterprises, and life for prisoners was expensive; food, clothing, laundry and even the cells themselves were all charged for at relatively high prices. Without friends, or some sort of charity, debtors could remain in these prisons for many years. Charles Dickens' father was sent to the Marshalsea for debt, in 1824. The boy had to leave school and enter Warren's Blacking Factory on the Hungerford Stairs. Dickens was lucky, though, as he was just old enough to work. Many children had to enter the prison with their parents. There, they became an additional burden, requiring food and clothing. Some inmates remained in the prisons all their lives, for owing small sums. Dickens recalled this part of his life through Amy 'Little' Dorrit.

The King's Bench and the Marshalsea were medieval buildings, ill equipped to deal with a growing number of prisoners. In the Marshalsea, in particular, if a prisoner was unable to afford the fee to dwell in one of the rooms on the Master's Side of the prison, they were locked up in one of nine rooms on the Common Side, with up to 300 others. Women, if they could afford it, were housed in The Oak, otherwise they were in the Common Side with everyone else.

In 1728, John Grano was a 34-year-old musician who had been working for Handel. He specialized mainly in music for the flute, but also played the trumpet. As a young man he lost his savings in the South Sea Bubble crash, and since then had struggled to make ends meet. In May 1728, he was imprisoned in the Marshalsea for owing £29 to an assortment of creditors. Inside the prison, he found a bar run by the governor's wife, and a shop selling everyday essentials. There was a tailor and a barber. Sarah Bradshaw, a prisoner, was running a coffee shop, and there was a chophouse called Titty Doll's, also run by a prisoner and his wife.

Doll's was named after the famous gingerbread seller Tiddy Doll, who patrolled Southwark Fair in the reign of George II. Doll was so well known that he appeared in Hogarth's 'Southwark Fair'. He could be found by his hat, with an enormous feather and gold lace banding, and his long sales chant, only two words of which could be made out: 'Tiddy Doll'. People even dressed up as Tiddy Doll for fancy-dress parties, and James Gillray immortalized him in the cartoon 'Tiddy-Doll the great French Gingerbread-Baker, drawing out a new Batch of Kings'. Tiddy Doll became a popular name for London eating houses. The last such one, in Shepherd Market, Mayfair, closed in the late 1990s.

Although Marshalsea created a social structure which the prisoners and staff understood, by the mid-eighteenth century – and probably long before – it was always an unhappy place. The practice of 'garnish', or paying off prison bullies and the warders, was rife and stripped people already in debt of what little money they had. 'Chummage' was the term used for the social and financial hierarchy amongst the prisoners. Through garnish and chummage those on the Master's Side could construct a tolerable existence for themselves. Life on the Common Side was desperate. In 1729, when John Grano left the Marshalsea, a Parliamentary Committee began to look into the situation in London's prisons. What they found at the Marshalsea shocked London. Prisoners on the Common Side were routinely starved to death when they couldn't pay for food. If they became rowdy or difficult, they were tortured with medieval instruments, such as thumbscrews. William Acton, prison governor, was tried for the murder of Thomas Bliss, an inmate, in addition to being suspected of the murder of three other prisoners. But the trial was weighted heavily in his favour, and he was found not guilty. The Parliamentary Committee had made people aware of what was happening, but it was powerless to introduce real change.

The prison had become so decrepit by the end of the eighteenth century that, in 1811, it had to be rebuilt. The new quarters were still cramped, and many people continued to be imprisoned for very small debts, usually under £20. The same traditions of garnish and chummage carried on, as before. The Marshalsea remained a strange community, removed from daily life by the stigma and reality of debt, yet essentially a London neighbourhood, full of all social classes. In 1842, it was closed by an Act of Parliament, and the prisoners were dispersed throughout London gaols. But it remained a legend in the London consciousness, what Dickens described as 'this right little, tight little island'.

St Thomas's and Guy's Hospitals

At the beginning of the eighteenth century, Southwark was largely medieval. And yet, close to the rural pleasure gardens and the crumbling medieval prisons, new technologies were being put into practice.

St Thomas's Hospital was founded in the twelfth century and soon fell into a gentle cycle of update and disrepair. Writing on 2 December 1664, the diarist John Evelyn noted that part of the building was reserved for 'such sick and wounded as should from time to time be sent from the [naval] Fleete'. A large-scale refurbishment was completed, in 1732, and from then on the numbers admitted each year rose from a few hundred into the thousands, housed in over 'twenty wards . . . each under the care of a sister or female superintendent, and two or three nurses'. These wards included two for the treatment of venereal disease with mercury, also known as 'salivation', and the 'cutting-ward', as it was called. 'Here also are the surgery, bathing-rooms, theatre, and dead-house, in which corpses are deposited until the time of interment.'

Rapid advances were being made in medicine, and the approach was usually holistic, focusing as much on diet and well-being as symptoms. But doctors were becoming more sceptical about 'alternative' medicine. When the craze for homeopathy reached London in the early eighteenth century, one doctor, John Hogg, scoffed that to cure a brain fever, one might as well make 'the patient drink out of the Thames, into which a glass of gin had been thrown an hour previous at London-bridge!' Homeopathy was, however, very popular with 'the softer sex'.

John Birch, a doctor at St Thomas's, began to experiment with electricity as a cure for various ailments, including nervous complaints. In 1803, he published his book on the subject, *An Essay on the Medical Application of Electricity*. In the introduction he acknowledged that it was, after all, 'a bold experiment', but he felt it was one that he, along with the instrument maker, Mr Banks of the Strand, had made safe enough. Under his guidance, electricity might be 'with discretion, passed through the tender fabric of the brain'. Using an insulated chair, a Leyden jar and instruments made of brass and wood (one a pointer, one a ball), Birch conducted electricity through the body, 'to the most exact nicety'. He treated a woman suffering from Bell's palsy with electricity, a method still used now. Her condition improved dramatically, although it is an affliction which resolves itself spontaneously in most cases. He noted that 'these cases are not uncommon'.

Birch recalled how

> In the month of November, 1787, a porter at the India warehouses was sent to me by a lady of great humanity for advice, being in a state of melancholy, induced by the death of one of his children . . . He was quiet, would suffer his wife to lead him about the house, but he never spoke to her; he sighed frequently, and was inattentive to everything that passed.

After three treatments with Birch, he became cheerful and returned to work. Encouraged by this apparent success with depression, Birch began to try large electric shocks on patients who were resident in asylums, including one 26-year-old man who was suffering from melancholy. He surprised himself, and the patient, by passing the strongest possible shock through the man's brain three times. There was no improvement in the condition, and Birch said he had carried the experiment 'as far as he wished'. He also experimented on reviving a working man who had tried to hang himself with a silk handkerchief, and was successful in reviving him. Birch felt his experiments at St Thomas's had fallen on deaf ears, and he ended his *Essay* with this prophetic passage: 'I own, I do still indulge the hope, that I shall live to see an electrical machine considered among the necessary instruments of every surgeon.' That day would come, though it didn't feature in the operating theatre installed in the herb garret of St Thomas's Church on the hospital grounds, which can still be viewed today.

Although Birch didn't believe St Thomas's took enough risks in adopting new methods, it was a successful and busy hospital. In the 1780s, the peak years of his experiments, St Thomas's 'admitted and discharged, of In-patients, 30,717 and Out-patients, 47,099'. The hospital was vast and would have been overburdened, had it not been for the vision of one of the early governors, Thomas Guy. In 1721, Guy decided to establish another hospital just behind St Thomas's to cater for those who would need continual medical care for the rest of their lives.

Thomas Guy was a Southwark-born bookseller who never married and lived simply: he 'dined on his counter, with no other tablecloth than a newspaper' and didn't spend money on clothes. 'At the age of seventy-six, he took a lease, of the governors of the former [Guy's], of a piece of ground . . . [and] began to build the hospital which bears his name.' Thomas Guy left over £200,000 to his new hospital, amassed by 'his great success in the buying and selling of South Sea Stock, in the memorable year 1720; and also a vast sum by the sale of bibles'. As a contemporary commentator said, 'He seems to have profited both of GOD and *Mammon*.'

As the Georgian period progressed, the hospital expanded dramatically. In 1829, one benefactor, William Hunt, gave enough money for the capacity to be almost doubled. By that stage there were six physicians, two obstetricians, seven surgeons, eye and ear specialists and a dentist. The hospital had new teaching departments, including anatomy, pathology and chemistry, as well as the 'electrifying-room'. Guy's hospital continues to be famous for its dentistry, treating over 100,000 patients every year.

Resurgam Hommo: the Lambeth bodysnatchers

London and Edinburgh were twin centres for medical teaching throughout the eighteenth century. Both cities struggled with the moral and practical issues of securing corpses for teaching purposes: 'Great respect for the body of the dead has characterised mankind in nearly all ages.' Italy's medical students had been using human corpses since the fourteenth century. Thus, by the beginning of the seventeenth century, Italy was viewed as the place to study human anatomy, particularly at Padua university. In England, in 1541, Henry VIII handed control of dissection to the Guild of Barber-Surgeons, allowing them four bodies a year from the Tyburn gallows. Charles II increased this to six, in 1663.

From around 1690, anatomy schools appeared in London, and began proliferating in the first half of the eighteenth century. As well as these private schools, the hospitals earned extra money by giving anatomy lessons, often using patients who had died friendless and 'unclaimed' on the wards. St Bartholomew's and St Thomas's both started early schools. The hospitals had a better chance of meeting their own demand for corpses to study, having wards full of poor people, but the private schools had to be more inventive. From the start of the eighteenth century, bodysnatching became a problem.

The corpse had no legal status in England; it could not be stolen. But a fresh human corpse had a significant material value to the medical profession. This peak condition was a matter of a few days in winter and much less in the warmer months. In 1752, the medieval stigma that dissection was a form of punishment was reinforced when the statutory law came into place decreeing that all murderers would be subject to dissection, with the words 'it is thereby become necessary that some further terror and peculiar infamy be added to the punishment of death'.

Intimate knowledge of the human body, its possible variations from patient to patient, and the courage to act swiftly with a steady hand did not come easily. Natural revulsion at cutting into human flesh was compounded by popular sentiments about the sanctity of the body, particularly in death. Yet the would-be surgeon had to overcome this. In 1811, Fanny Burney recounted in a letter the story of her mastectomy following a diagnosis of breast cancer:

> I began a scream that lasted unintermittingly during the whole time
> of the incision . . . when again I felt the instrument - describing a

curve - cutting against the grain . . . then felt the Knife tackling against the breast bone - scraping it!

The entire operation was done, including dressing, in twenty minutes and with no form of anaesthetic. It was understandable that surgeons were regarded, in Burney's words, as 'practically insensible' to the sufferings of their patients. They had to be. This insensibility was cultivated in the very early stages of their education by the handling of fresh corpses, and perhaps contributed to the moral ambivalence which surrounded the procurement of the necessary bodies. There is no doubt that the surgeons running these schools were treading a fine line.

Although bodysnatching was common in London as soon as, if not before, the private anatomy schools were established, the only available documentation dates from the 1790s onwards, when the practice of surgery and the number of medical students grew dramatically. In 1793, there were 200 medical students in London; by 1823, there were over 1,000. In theory, they were all competing for access to the 100 corpses legally available. Even by the early eighteenth century, anatomists had separated themselves from the act of obtaining corpses. Instead, they employed their medical students, or 'agents' – men and women who went into prisons and hospitals to persuade those approaching the end of their lives to turn over their corpse in exchange for a financial incentive. Other agents were the bodysnatchers, known as the Resurrection Men.

The Borough Gang of resurrectionists operated from the beginning of the nineteenth century until 1825. They were led by Ben Crouch, a former porter at Guy's Hospital. Sir Astley Cooper, the Professor of Anatomy at Guy's, employed Crouch and his gang to source bodies for the students. Cooper was so dependent upon the gang's efficient and constant service that when a member ended up in prison, usually for unrelated petty crime, Cooper continued to make payments to their family.

The Borough Gang were particularly good at what they did. They hung around graveyards and funeral processions to identify their targets. The night after burial, they dug down to one end of the coffin and smashed their way in, then hauled the body out. The dirt was then replaced and the grave put back as it was found. Londoners were increasingly aware that the graves of their friends and family might not be safe, and they placed markers in the fresh earth so that they could check for disturbance. Some even rigged booby traps. Still, the Borough Gang were successful. They didn't always wait to dig bodies up either, but broke into houses where the body was being prepared for burial.

The resurrection trade became increasingly sophisticated, with complicated pricing structures. Freakish or unusual bodies commanded high prices. Children under three feet in height were classed as 'large small', 'small' or 'foetus' and priced by the inch. There was a separate trade in teeth, which were sold to dentists to furnish dentures. Some may even have attempted to transplant the dead teeth into living mouths. In 1817, Ben Crouch left the Borough Gang to follow the British Army in France and Spain where he raided the bodies of the dead for teeth, making a prosperous living.

In Lambeth, in 1795, 'three men were discovered conveying away five human bodies in three sacks'. The authorities 'ascertained that the grave-digger was the chief robber; and that eight eminent surgeons were in the habit of buying these bodies . . . for each adult corpse, if not green or putrid, two guineas and a crown; and for persons under age, six shillings for the first foot, and ninepence per inch for all above it.' Apparently, one of the surgeons 'made a wanton use of these bodies, by using the skulls for nail-boxes, soap-trays, &c., and his child had an infant's skeleton to play with as a doll.' He became known as the Lambeth Articulator. The authorities also heard that 'much of the human flesh had been converted into an adipose substance resembling spermaceti, and burnt as candles, whilst some had been converted into soap'.

The public horror of the resurrectionists and dissection was growing as rapidly as the trade itself. Joseph Naples worked with the Borough Gang in 1811 and kept a diary of the gang's extensive work throughout London, often taking five bodies a night from assorted cemeteries, and sometimes many more small corpses. On Tuesday 10 December, he wrote: 'Intoxsicated all day: at night went out & got 5 Bunhill Row. Jack all most buried.' The diary also shows how profitable bodysnatching was: on the 9th and 10th of the following January, Naples took in over £20 from St Thomas's – and that was only his share of the profits. An average annual wage for a labourer was only around £40 at that point. Naples was caught, after being turned in by Ben Crouch, and was sentenced to two years in prison. He escaped, Sir Astley Cooper having intervened on his behalf.

At around the same time, many surgeons in London formed a loose club which served two purposes. The first was to share information on both bodies and pricing, and to prevent the snatchers charging outrageous prices. The second was to raise awareness of the need for bodies. In 1828, the Burke and Hare murders in Edinburgh, committed to supply corpses for dissection, shocked Britain. A Select Committee was appointed to look into the need for a better system. Before the committee, Sir Astley Cooper described his loyal gang as 'the lowest dregs of degradation'. This led to the passing of the 1832 Anatomy Act which allowed the corpses of paupers, and people who had died 'friendless', to be anatomized. The rising popularity of surgical procedures, as well as the Act, lessened the stigma about dissection, although bodysnatching remained one of London's marginal trades right into the twentieth century.

Southwark industry: the Albion Mills and Coade stone

Southwark was home to some of London's major industries. All along the river were the 'great timber-yards . . . One would fear that the forest of Norway and the Baltic would be exhausted, to supply the want of our overgrown capital.' There were also steelyards and 'the vast distilleries . . . There are seldom less than two thousand hogs constantly grunting at this place; which are kept entirely on the grains.'

Windmills throughout Southwark and Lambeth milled flour for much of London. In the early 1780s, Samuel Wyatt decided to employ new technology in the creation of a large flour mill. In March 1783, he negotiated the lease on land now covered by the railway into

Waterloo. He began to build quickly and, in 1786, the first engine was installed. It was the first of three steam engines designed by Boulton & Watt, and was one of the earliest to be used for such industrial purposes. The mills were opened in a flush of publicity, attended by prominent Londoners, including Josiah Wedgwood.

The first engine could grind ten bushels of wheat per hour between twenty pairs of millstones. It was a wonder of the new industrial age, and many visited to see it in action. The second engine was up and running by 1788. In 1791, before the third engine could be installed, the Lambeth mills burned down, destroying a massive stock of flour and grain.

Arson was suspected. The local mill owners had watched Albion Mills turning out far more flour in a day than they could hope to produce in a week. Steam power had divorced Albion Mills from the vagaries of the weather, and many suspected that the owners were speculating by stockpiling flour. William Blake, born in Lambeth, had seen the significance of Albion Mills: even the name conjured some idealized version of the nation. But for Blake, these were the 'dark, satanic mills' of Jerusalem.

The Albion Mills were never rebuilt. On the night of the fire, many of the poorer inhabitants of Southwark danced in the street for joy at the demise of the industrial monster. It was a symbol of the industrial revolution, heralding the arrival of a new, mechanized age – an age that could not be held back for long.

The south bank was already a centre for brewing, wire-making, glass-making and anchor-smithing. Then, in 1769, Widow Coade arrived in Lambeth from Lyme Regis, bringing with her one of Georgian London's forgotten wonders: Coade stone or, as she called it, *Lithodipyra*.

Eleanor Coade was born, in 1733, to a family of ceramicists, and to a father who couldn't stay solvent. He died in 1769, and in the same year she and her daughter, also Eleanor, arrived in Narrow Wall, Lambeth, taking over an artificial stone foundry from one David Picot, who retired or left the business two years later.

There had been a history of artificial stone being made in the area, but the Coades had a secret. Their stone was finer and more durable than anyone else's and could be cast into very fine relief. They made it to a secret formula, which they guarded during their lifetimes. The younger Eleanor Coade was a formidable artist and businesswoman, and she took on the title 'Mrs', although she never married. After her mother's death, in 1796, she took the business to a new level, and the improvements in the 'mix' are probably down to her.

Coade soon became the stone to have, due to the imaginative and lively modelling. In addition, it stays clean and isn't eroded by pollution. Sculptors were drawn not only from Britain but also included some of the talented foreigners working in London at the time, such as John de Vaere who later worked for Wedgwood. Customers could commission what they wanted, or choose from the Coade's catalogue. They could also visit the premises, where huge garden statuary and architectural ornaments were displayed everywhere. In 1799, Eleanor Junior appointed her cousin and chief modeller, John Sealy, as her partner. In the same year, they opened Coade's Gallery on the Pedlar's Acre at the south end of Westminster Bridge.

There was almost no style, or size, in which Coade's were not willing to work. Their designs range from Indian animal friezes to gates to Greek Revival statues. They had a team of in-house designers but also worked to designs by Joshua Reynolds, Benjamin West and James Wyatt. The stone was used throughout London, and was also shipped to South Africa, Ceylon, Gibraltar and the West Indies. A Gothic font was created for a church in Bombay. A bank in Montreal ordered much of its decoration from the Lambeth firm. The King of Portugal ordered a special set of architectural works for his complex in Rio de Janeiro (some of which now form the gates to Rio's zoo).

Eleanor Coade died in her house in Camberwell Grove, in 1821. She was a devout Baptist. The recipe for the stone still exists, and Coade stone can be made today. The special ingredient which made the mix so workable was not cement, but ceramic. Amongst London's extant Coade is the shopfront of Twining's at 216 Strand, and Captain Bligh's tomb in St Mary's Churchyard, Lambeth. On the south-east side of Westminster Bridge stands a large Coade stone lion on a pedestal, close to the site of his creation. Originally he had stood outside the Red Lion Brewery, close to County Hall, but was moved

Eleanor Coade's stone factory, Lambeth, 1784. The interior of the kiln shows the firing of the statues of the Thames river god and the Four Seasons

to Waterloo Station in 1949. He was brought to the current spot in 1966, and gazes towards the Houses of Parliament with a somewhat defiant expression. Little wonder, as his testicles were removed in case they caused offence to public decency.

From the industries of the south bank, large and small, we next turn back to north London proper, and the industries of the East End, which were born, flourished and died all within the eighteenth century.

10. Spitalfields, Whitechapel and Stepney

Daniel Defoe, born in 1660, recalled the Spitalfields of his youth: 'The Lanes were deep, dirty, and unfrequented; that Part now called Spitalfields-market was a Field of Grass, with Cows feeding on it, since the Year 1670.' This pastoral scene did not last long. By 1700, Spitalfields, and Whitechapel to the east, was a mass of open spaces given over to brewing, cloth workers' animals, and illegal housing. The area had held religious houses and early theatres, including Richard Burbage's predecessor to The Globe. These open spaces were used for recreation and the relatively low-level commerce of London's woollen industry. It was also a refuge for many dissenting religions, including the Huguenots and the Jews; immigration has been a constant theme, as well as a bone of contention, throughout the area.

London had been the centre of Britain's cloth trade for centuries; throughout the city there were areas which concentrated on buying, storing, weaving, dyeing and treating. Even during the late medieval period, the City's weavers and textile businesses were moving east to make the most of the ample water supply and the open ground. Open ground was very important to the cloth industry: when large bolts of fabric were treated, they needed to be dried on the 'tenter grounds' marked on many of the maps of the area. To prevent the dyes settling unevenly, they were pulled out tightly with tenterhooks, giving us the saying 'being on tenterhooks'.

The ample natural springs and lack of confinement were attractive to other light industries, such as brewing. In 1694, Joseph Truman established the Black Eagle Brewery in Brick Lane, and the 'brewhouse' came to dominate the area as one of the greatest single employers in Georgian London. The firm soon took up six acres on the east side of Brick Lane. Their output was tremendous. (The Truman Brewery building, although a later version, still exists today, now converted into trendy studios for media businesses.)

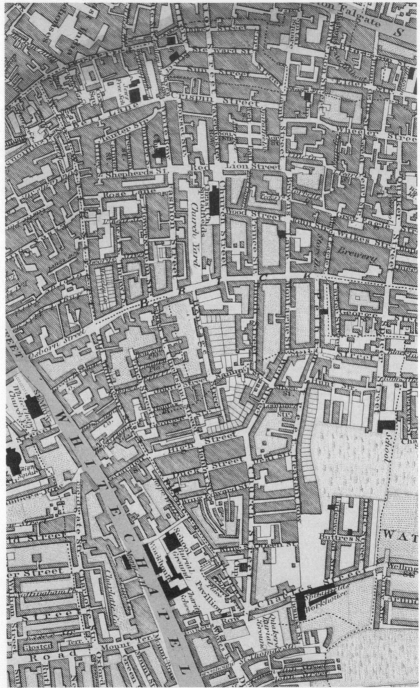

Spitalfields (top) and Whitechapel, detail of map by John Greenwood, 1827

But the area was, and would remain for two centuries, dominated by weaving and cloth-finishing. Wool, long the English staple, was being supplanted in popular taste by linen and, soon after the beginning of the Georgian period, silk. Wool was grown in the provinces, linen usually originated from Ireland, and silk was an exotic product which was imported ready-made. An early attempt at keeping silkworms in England had failed, when James I planted many thousands of trees inedible to silkworms near Hampton Court Palace. From then on, it was deemed easier to obtain silk as a finished product. It was not until the arrival of the Huguenots en masse, in 1685–6, that the weaving community began to dominate the area. Huguenots had brought new techniques, designs and organization with them from France. So devastating was the effect of the Huguenot silk weavers leaving France that, within a few years of their departure, the country went from being a bulk exporter of silks to a bulk importer.

Spitalfields is famous now for the weavers' houses in and surrounding Spital Square, Fournier Street and Elder Street, which were built in the early eighteenth century and survived both the demolition and 'improvements' of the subsequent decades. The area is now associated with London's artistic community. But as late as the 1970s, it was still relatively run-down, despite being right on the edge of the City. Now, the weavers' houses are some of the most sought after in London, yet they are not all they seem. Many of them appear large and imposing from the outside, with their basements, three or four upper storeys and light, airy roof garrets, but inside they are only one or one and a half rooms deep, and sometimes these are very small. Elder Street, with its varied architecture, is a fine example of this. The houses were built quickly, on small old plots, and sometimes the rooms did not come up quite square. So the internal fittings, where they survive, contain the odd trompe l'oeil here and there to fool you into thinking they are symmetrical. The weavers of Spitalfields, even at the peak of their success during the first half of the eighteenth century, did not live in such grand style as might at first be imagined; in their housing, as in their fashion, they put on a fine show. The rapid rise and fall of the English silk trade created these streets and then left them, almost as if frozen in time, waiting for another group of artists to move in.

Les réfugiés: the Huguenots

The arrival of the Huguenots revolutionized the English silk business. As they had come to dominate Soho, so they also came to dominate the Spitalfields and Shoreditch areas of London throughout the eighteenth century. Suzanne de Champagné sailed for England, in April 1687, with her siblings. Desperate to escape France, Suzanne's mother, Marie de Champagné, and her children set out for La Rochelle. Marie was heavily pregnant, and unable to make the sea voyage straight away, but nineteen-year-old Suzanne made a plan to get the children to safety. She negotiated with an English sea captain, Thomas Robinson, to get them to England. At two o'clock that night, she took her smallest sister into her arms, and four sailors carried the whole family on to the boat on their shoulders. They were stowed inside a secret compartment, on piles of salt.

> After we were put there and seated on the salt . . . the trap door was closed again and tarred like the rest of the vessel, so that no one could see anything there . . . we took care to hold our heads directly under the beams so that when the inspectors, as was their lovely custom, thrust their swords through, they would not pierce our skulls.

The family were let out of the small hold, where the salt was stored with ballast, after the ship had been successfully inspected by the French authorities. Suzanne said that by the time of their release, they had been 'suffocating in that hole and thought we were going to give up the ghost there, as well as everything we had in our bodies, which was coming out of them every which way'.

They made it to England, but not without some difficulty, as Captain Robinson decided that he wanted more money and would not take them to their chosen destination of Topsham. Suzanne said this was 'unjust and complained to the governor of the town', who told Robinson to fulfil his contract. Robinson, of course, dumped them as soon as he could – in Salcombe, where they were found by local children.

In the end, the Champagné family were successful in their various escapes and were reunited. Suzanne's experience is by no means unique amongst the Huguenot community; many of the most extraordinary escapes went unrecorded, apart from family legend. Once they had reached London, many of these people, whether noble or not, turned up at the French Church on Threadneedle Street.

The church offered a familiar form of worship. It seems that the Huguenot church was largely an informal one – not dissimilar, for the most part, to a Quaker meeting house. In a sixteenth-century picture of the temple in Lyons, there is even a dog sitting in the aisle, apparently listening to the sermon.

The 'court' of the French Church of Threadneedle Street, where members were summoned if they had committed a crime such as adultery, also recorded petty infractions – for example, leaving the church early during the service. 'This scandalizes the English, who hold pastoral blessing in high esteem, whereas we should neglect nothing that may persuade them we are Protestants truly Reformed according to the word of the Gospel.' English people, such as Samuel Pepys, attended services at the Huguenot churches (Pepys particularly enjoyed the singing).

Not all Huguenots were the serious, God-fearing people Hogarth depicted in 'Noon'. The court had to reprimand those 'members of the congregation spending their days and nights in taverns to abandon their excesses, debaucheries and licentiousness'. The court warned them this was 'ill befitting their condition as persecuted Protestants and refugees'. Whatever their expertise in beer, the Huguenots assisted the Trumans with brewing England's first hop beers, belying the sober reputation the French Church wanted for them.

The Threadneedle Street Church was not only a meeting place and a source of charity, it was also the hub of a knowledge network. Many of these people, particularly those dealing in luxury goods, found Soho to be the most congenial place to settle. Soho, however, would not do for the weavers or those associated with the silk industry, who needed abundant water supplies and large open spaces.

Weaving in England had been conducted largely as a cottage industry, or by piecework, and was therefore one of the industries most susceptible to changes in the market. Robert Campbell's words of advice to those thinking of the weaving industry for their children are edged with warning: 'They are employed Younger, but more for the advantage of the Master, than anything they can learn in their Trade in such Infant Years.' So, the weaving industry tended to make the masters – those at the top – wealthy, particularly if they had a good eye for silk design and fashion. Those at the bottom, who cleaned and fixed machinery or 'ran' for rooms full of weavers, remained poor and were liable to be laid off at any given moment, as soon as there was a lull in demand.

Still, there was far more demand for unskilled workers in the silk factories being built in east London than there was in the small, tightly knit households of Huguenot tradesmen establishing themselves in Soho. The poorest of the refugees arriving at the Threadneedle Street Church were sent to Spitalfields to labour for the weavers, and to take sustenance from 'La Soupe', the Huguenot charity kitchen.

Many English perceived all the Huguenots who arrived as penniless, and this suited the rich Threadneedle Street Church very well: it could administer charity from within, and strengthen the community. But, in fact, many Huguenots arrived with plenty of money. In 1691, the French Church scolded the parishioners for their large and noisily extravagant weddings 'undermining [the English people's] compassion for our poor refugee brethren. We should weep with those who weep, not undermine their cause by flaunting wealth and so discouraging charity.' So, within the Huguenot community itself, there was already a division between those who had arrived with means, and the 'poor refugee brethren'. The richer members soon established their own church, separate from Threadneedle Street, but allied to it.

At 19 Princelet Street lived the Ogiers. Peter was a silk weaver from Poitou, and his daughter, Louisa, married Soho silversmith Samuel Courtauld. After Samuel died, Louisa continued the business on her own. In their Cornhill shop she employed women such as Judith Touzeau, a Huguenot girl whose signature appears on receipts from the shop. In the interconnected fashion typical of the Huguenots, Samuel and Louisa's son, George, was apprenticed in the silk trade, and Courtauld textiles was born, soon employing many French hands.

The structure of employment and social life was very different in the East End to that of the West End, where silversmith Paul de Lamerie was his master's servant and social inferior only so long as he was an apprentice. The situation for female members of the family and workforce was also different in these larger East End establishments. In the small messuages of Clerkenwell and Soho, a cohesive family structure enabled widows to control the business after the death of a master. They had known many of the apprentices and journeymen for years, most of whom would be happy to pull together to perpetuate a successful enterprise. However, in the larger business model of the East End – where employee numbers were higher, and trade was often business to business – women struggled to continue after their husband died. Daniel Defoe commented on the situation for a widow in such a business, particularly if she had not taken the time to become well acquainted with her husband's dealings:

> . . . if her husband had e'er a servant, or apprentice, who was . . . acquainted with the customers, and with the books, then she is forced to be beholden to him to settle the accounts for her, and endeavour to get in the debts . . . and, it may be at last, with all her pride, lets the boy creep to bed to her.

By the time Christ Church, Spitalfields, was finished, in 1729, there was already a growing problem with indigent poor in the area. The Huguenots had, largely, got themselves together and were starting to make huge progress with the creation and sale of fashionable new silks. These were not only used for clothing, but also in furnishings and wall coverings. There was almost nothing fashionable that silk could not be applied to. Yet it could not be grown here. Every attempt to establish native British silkworms had failed. So the nature of the supply of raw material – coming in from wherever it could be obtained from overseas – plus the fickle nature of fashion itself meant that not everyone was employed all the time, and those who were out of work were finding things increasingly difficult. Violence was not uncommon, as was extreme poverty through lack of work. In 1729, the same year that Hawksmoor's glorious church was finished, the Spitalfields Soup Society was established to cater for those who had no other means of feeding themselves or their families.

The weavers and the Spitalfields Mathematical Society

Despite the charming streets around Christ Church, Spitalfields remained largely given over to warehouses and workshops, as well as the large Truman Brewery. London weaving was affected terribly by the introduction of the power loom. It also suffered through the wars with France, which affected the supply of raw silk, and re-export sales. As early as 1736, the Spitalfields weavers gathered in Moorfields to protest about standards of pay. In 1742, outsourcing to the provinces began. The Spitalfields weaving community was soon on a slippery slope into large-scale poverty.

A typical manufacturer would employ wage-earning weavers. During the early part of the century, there was an agreed list of piecework rates, which was kept in a 'book' and adhered to, more or less, by all manufacturers and master weavers. By 1767, the rates in the book were being undercut. Pressure from the provinces and the power looms was making London-manufactured goods increasingly unviable. Riots resulted, during which the weavers 'traversed the streets at midnight, broke into the houses, and destroyed the property of the manufacturers'.

The book was reinstated and new rates negotiated. In 1773, Parliament granted the first Spitalfields Act, designed to force the weavers to agree piecework rates. Sadly, they were up against an economic decline so marked that there was little to be done. The weavers of Spitalfields battled on. The Act was extended twice, once to bring in all types of silk-mix materials, and the second time to include the journeywomen often employed in the silk-ribbon trade and previously neglected. But almost all but the finest silk work had been driven out of London. One weaver, Stephen Wilson, kept 'a book of lost work' in which he lamented: 'They had driven away crape, gauze, bandanna handkerchiefs and bombazine in turn.' The crêpe and gauze were now manufactured largely in Essex, the bombazine in Kidderminster and the bandannas in Macclesfield. A short time later, Wilson noted London had lost 'all small fancy works'.

By the early nineteenth century, London couldn't compete with the far lower wages more provincial workers could subsist upon. This was particularly marked after the French Wars ended, when fashion became more fleeting, international and hungry for novelty. The Spitalfields model, as protected by the Acts, was even more outmoded. Other parts of the country struggled under fierce competition, yet the weavers of Spitalfields had their rates protected by law and the Justices. It was unsustainable; in 1824, an Act was passed which essentially left Spitalfields to the mercy of the free market. Poverty descended upon the area – a poverty it would not shake off for another century and a half.

London's weavers could be dismissed as largely foreign, uppity and violent. But their skill as craftsmen, as well as the social and intellectual vigour which permeated Spitalfields, was unique. The atmosphere of endeavour and creativity, and the eternal prospect of poverty, created in Spitalfields an atmosphere of self-improvement more often associated with the later Victorian period. Many Huguenots were educated to a good level and continued to place a high value upon education. It was seen as by no means impossible for an intelligent man to learn the basics of almost everything there was to know.

Most of those who wished to continue their education and discover more of the world could not hope to join the Royal Society, which was really open only to the upper echelons of society. So a group of Spitalfields men decided to create their own society to hold experiments and feature lectures for the improvement of their members. In the eighteenth century, there were sharp divides between what was 'scientific' and what was not, and many wanted to explore that divide. The Spitalfields Mathematical Society was born.

This interest in finding out more about scientific advances, as well as promoting self-improvement, was significant amongst the humbler Huguenot weavers of Spitalfields. In 1717, John Middleton was a teacher of mathematics and a navy marine surveyor. He began, with a group of Frenchmen numbering around sixty, to meet at the Monmouth Head Tavern in Monmouth Street, near the building site that was Christ Church, Spitalfields. 'The Society met on Saturday evenings and it is said that one of its rules was that any member who failed to answer a question in mathematics asked by another member was fined twopence.' Middleton's emphasis was on practical mathematics, and those who attended were relatively prosperous men – even if they were classed socially as artisan labourers.

A mathematical academy soon opened in Spital Square, and one of the masters, John Canton, went on to become a famous electrical experimentalist and Fellow of the Royal Society. Another member was the naturalist Joseph Dandridge, who began to design silk patterns based on scientific illustrations. Spitalfields became known as a place of educated trades and craftsmen.

From the late 1740s, the Mathematical Society invested heavily in scientific apparatus that was used for demonstrations. By the 1790s, this 'cabinet of instruments' had grown so large that it indicated the society was conducting demonstrations before considerable audiences. By 1804, it had a large library at the disposal of its members. To belong was a mark of both education and sensibility.

Towards the end of the century, the proportion of weavers in the society began to fall, and the number of gentlemen rose. What remained was the society's commitment to public education. From the middle of the century, weavers comprised about 40 per cent of the subscribers, but they were increasingly supplanted by chemists, druggists, apothecaries and seedsmen, as well as distillers, dyers, brewers, sugarmen, ironmongers, instrument makers and teachers.

The Mathematical Society was the first and most important of all the Spitalfields societies. A resident of Spital Square for over thirty years reminisced:

> . . . it may appear strange, but I believe the origin of many of our most flourishing societies may be traced to Spitalfields. The Spital-

fields Mathematical Society is second in point of time to the Royal Society, and still exists. There was an Historical Society which was merged into the Mathematical Society. There was a Floricultural Society, very numerously attended, but now extinct. The weavers were almost the only botanists of their day in the Metropolis.

He also remembered that many of the weavers were 'great bird-fanciers and breeders of canaries, many of whom now cheer their quiet hours when at the loom'.

The mixed fortunes of Whitechapel and Stepney

South of Spitalfields, in Whitechapel, there were many French-descended weavers, but another type of textile-dealing immigrant was more prominent on the local streets. Jewish dealers in second-hand clothes were traditionally situated in Whitechapel and dominated the local population. From there they could easily make it to Rag Fair, near the Tower of London, to ply their trade; and their accommodation remained cheap, yet was within striking distance of the City synagogues.

These dealers, often working in family groups, offered ready money for clothing that was worn out, or no longer wanted, which they then sold on to others who could use it, for industrial or recycling purposes. Samuel Taylor Coleridge had a curious story to relate about an Old Clo' Man he met in the street, showing how those who used street cries were adopting an accepted, yet indistinct 'patter'. Coleridge was so irritated by one Jewish man's cry of 'Old Clo' that he snapped at him. The man

> ... stopped, and looking very gravely at me, said in a clear and even fine accent, 'Sir, I can say "old clothes" as well as you can; but if you had to say so ten times a minute, for an hour together, you would say Ogh Clo as I do now;' and so he marched off . . . I followed and gave him a shilling, the only one I had.

The Jewish population of Whitechapel was distinctive in that, unlike Spitalfields, there wasn't a coherent band of workers, and very few masters. The vast majority of the Jewish population just 'got by', working as hawkers, pedlars and dealers. By the beginning of the Victorian period, they numbered over 15,000.

St Mary Matfellon Church, at the heart of the area, became known as the White Chapel during the medieval period due to its white-washed exterior, giving the district its name. In 1711, Brasenose College, Oxford, purchased the right to appoint a priest of their choosing there. After 1715, the Rector fell out with the Dean and painted his likeness over the character of Judas in the painting depicting the Last Supper, above the altar. He annotated it helpfully with 'Judas, the traytor'. The Dean pretended not to notice, and the Bishop of London ordered the picture removed and repainted. St Mary's was destroyed in the Blitz and never rebuilt, like much of Whitechapel.

When John Strype revised Stow's *Survey of London*, in 1720, he described Whitechapel as 'a spacious fair street, for entrance into the City eastward, and somewhat long'. The area housed many successful medium-sized businesses, such as the Whitechapel Bell Foundry, founded in 1570 (and Britain's oldest continual manufacturer). By the eighteenth century, the foundry was exporting bells to the Americas, including the Liberty Bell, in 1752. The Liberty Bell left England bearing a biblical inscription which would have been familiar to both the French Protestants who had sought refuge only a stone's throw away, and also the Jews who worshipped close by. It came from the book of Leviticus 25: 10: 'Proclaim LIBERTY throughout all the land unto all the inhabitants thereof.'

Further out again from the rapidly filling Whitechapel was Mile End. Mile End, named for being one mile from Aldgate, had long been a settlement on the road to Colchester. At the beginning of the Georgian period, plans were made for a newer settlement closer to Spitalfields. Mile End was divided into Old Town and New Town. Old Mile End is now covered by the modern Stepney Green conservation area. It was one of the earliest country retreats for Augustan and Georgian bankers and the more prosperous members of the maritime community, including the Scandinavian merchants who had profited so handsomely from the demand for timber created by the rebuilding.

In 1696, a Danish-Norwegian Church was constructed in Well-close Square, by which time the square was already neat and prosperous. Just to the east, in Princes Square, a Swedish Church was completed in 1729, as the area was popular with Scandinavian merchants trading in the City.

But by the 1760s, the area was losing its prestige. The arrival of the sickly-smelling sugar refineries pushed the more respectable residents out. The sheer volume of traffic using the Port of London meant that sailors were swarming through streets and squares which had previously been so genteel. The Scandinavian merchants moved out and, in 1816, handed their church over to trustees so that it could be used as a charity base to benefit seamen from their own countries.

In contrast, Mile End New Town, to the west, was on the rise. In 1717, John Cox and John Davies declared they were in possession of 'diverse Lands in the hamlet of Mile-End new towne' and they set about draining what had been known as the Hares Marsh, intending to create a smart new community. Early attempts to install public amenities weren't without hiccups: in February 1718, James Withy was caught with a bag containing '25 Fountains of Lamps of the Convex-Lights' from the Mile End New Town High Street. Mile End New Town, despite such setbacks, continued to flourish. In the 1780s, it was a model of civic planning, creating a workhouse and providing funds for lighting and patrolling of the streets. It was just close enough to Spitalfields to thrive, and it avoided the decay which was already setting into Stepney.

Stepney would continue to decline, and although much of the Georgian village survived the Blitz, it was swept away in the improvements of the 1950s as London's planners drove all before them in the prolonged fit of barbarity which buried so much of the eighteenth-century city under concrete.

11. Hackney and Bethnal Green

Hackney is one of the largest parishes in London. The marshes alone covered 335 acres at the end of the eighteenth century. The parish itself stretched from Stamford Hill in the north to Cambridge Heath in the south. It began in the west at Shoreditch workhouse, and terminated in the east at the boundary with the parish of St Matthew, in Bethnal Green. Within Hackney, the hamlets were Clapton, Dalston, Homerton, Shacklewell and Kingsland. Throughout the eighteenth century, most of the land was turned over to farming, with a small proportion of market gardening and horticulture, concentrating mainly on 'exotics'. It was a community where cattle were raised on the lush pastures, and where Samuel Pepys saw trees of oranges ripening in the sun. South of Homerton High Street were extensive watercress beds. The area was attractive, with small pleasure gardens, pubs, ponds for swimming and fishing, and pleasant open spaces within striking distance of the City.

For centuries, Hackney had been served by St Augustine's Church, built in 1253 – at the same time as the parish was mentioned in Henry III's state papers. From 1578, the Black and White House sat beside the church, serving first as a grand private home for a merchant of the Muscovy Company and then for many years as a boarding school for girls before being shut down and demolished at the end of the eighteenth century. By then, it was clear that St Augustine's would not do. In 1789, St John-at-Hackney was built to hold 2,000 parishioners. The nave of St Augustine's was demolished, leaving just the tower standing. The ancient settlement had given way to the modern, just as Hackney's pastures were giving way to the brickfields of Kingsland and the encroaching streets.

Hackney had long been famous for its quality of education. In the Elizabethan period, many intellectuals made it their home, and various highly regarded schools were established over the next centuries.

Sir John Cass, whose family moved from the City to South Hackney to escape the plague, left money for the education of ninety boys and girls. Forty years after his death in 1708, the Sir John Cass Foundation was formed to continue his work. Various John Cass institutions still remain in London, forming part of the London Metropolitan University, the John Cass School of Art in Whitechapel and the John Cass School of Education in Stratford.

Throughout Hackney there were also the 'dissenting academies', which arrived in the late seventeenth century to provide a grammar school-type education to boys from dissenting religions, such as Calvinism and Unitarianism, who would not be admitted to Oxford or Cambridge – or subsequently to the mainstream clergy or education system as teachers and tutors. Dissenting academies were particularly important in the encouragement of independent thought in London during the eighteenth century and eventually in the formation of the Victorian Nonconformist movement. Many of the boys educated in these schools became ministers and missionaries who would go on to represent their churches throughout the world.

The earliest of the academies were small, private establishments attached to the households of wealthy dissenters. Many were located around Newington Green, where 'Protestant nonconformity and London commerce ... featured strongly in local society'. Stoke Newington, a convenient three miles from London, had long been a favoured place for wealthy merchants to keep a country house. It had a small population, occupied locally in farming and market gardening. It was a pleasant and private place in which to found a small dissenting academy of ten or so pupils.

These academies were dependent upon the tutor, usually well known in his field, and the patron who made the space and funds available. One of the most prominent of these academies was run by Thomas Rowe from 1678. In his book called *The Nonconformist's Memorial*, Edmund Calamy wrote that Rowe had 'a peculiar talent of winning youth to the love of virtue and learning, both by his pleasant conversation and by a familiar way of making difficult subjects easily intelligible'. As was typical of these small colleges, it closed when Rowe left for America, in 1686, eventually becoming Vice-President of Yale. Amongst his pupils were Daniel Defoe, Samuel Wesley (father of John) and Isaac Watts, who would return to Hackney and help design Abney Park with Lady Mary Abney (which was transformed into a non-denominational cemetery, in 1840). At the end of the seventeenth century and the beginning of the eighteenth, dissent became more tolerated, and the academies could grow.

Hoxton College, another dissenting academy, had already existed in previous incarnations in Moorfields and Stepney before becoming established in Hoxton, in 1762. It adhered to Calvinist teachings and had a strong scientific curriculum. Several of the tutors were Fellows of the Royal Society, and the young William Godwin (1756–1836), later the radical writer and husband of feminist Mary Wollstonecraft, was a student there.

The Hackney academy, founded in 1786 and called New College, was also of particular note but did not last long. It occupied what had been Homerton Hall and provided a liberal and broad-ranging education regardless of religious belief. It had been founded in the London Coffee House on Cheapside one December evening, in 1785, when a group of thirty-seven Protestant City men decided to create a school which would focus on intellectual excellence. The college was an instant success, thriving in the atmosphere of religious tolerance which followed the Gordon Riots. It was, however, soon associated with radicalism and sedition. This was something the college seemed to encourage: they invited Thomas Paine as their after-dinner speaker only weeks after he was charged with seditious libel for *Rights of Man*. In 1794, William Stone, a governor of the college, was arrested on charges of high treason. He had allegedly been passing information to the French Republic. Although he was eventually acquitted, his trial sounded the death knell for the dissenters' college. By 1796, it was closed, after a decade of huge success. Joseph Priestley – the theologian and philosopher, and the man responsible for the discovery of oxygen – had been a popular tutor. The critic William Hazlitt had been a pupil, amongst many other young men who went on to play significant roles in early nineteenth-century life in Britain. Hazlitt wrote to his father in 1793, recording his weekly expenses at the school, which included 'a shilling for washing; two for fire; another shilling for tea and sugar; and now another for candles, letters etc.'. The closure of the school marked the beginning of Hackney's slow decline from its eighteenth-century heyday. Today, the Jack Dunning Estate stands on the eighteen-acre site of New College.

At the time of New College's short reign, industry began to move in, attracting large numbers of unskilled migrant workers in need of accommodation. The River Lea had always been navigable, and at Hackney Wick there were wharves where goods came and went. In 1780, the Berger family arrived and began to manufacture and refine paint pigments. (Two centuries later, their business was absorbed into Crown Paints, in 1988.) Hackney saw the manufacture of silk, printed calico, boots and shoes, and finally the very first plastics, before the local industries died altogether under the crush of population.

Nearby Bethnal Green remained rural for longer than Hackney. It was further out, around two and a half miles north-east of St Paul's Cathedral, and for a long time it was part of Stepney. Dairy farms flourished there. In 1743, the hamlet was created a parish in its own right. Like Hackney, most of the origins of the hamlet were Tudor and rather grand, with impressive manor houses dotting the open fields. The south end of the parish sat partly on Hares Marsh and Foulmere, with a causeway known as Dog Row. Along the edges of Bethnal Green, cattle and carriages flooded into London from Essex, resulting in broken pavements and 'heaps of filth . . . every 10 or 20 yards'. Old Bethnal Green Road had previously been known as Rogue Lane, and was still called Whore's Lane as late as 1717. In 1756, Bethnal Green Road, just to the south, replaced it as the main thoroughfare.

By the mid-eighteenth century, Bethnal Green was beginning to house a poorer sort of inhabitant. The large Tudor manor houses were being subdivided into tenements or let as private asylums. Then, from the 1760s, a building boom took hold and hundreds of small houses, with frontages anywhere between thirteen and nineteen feet, were thrown up using local bricks. They were to house the weavers of Spitalfields, who were gradually moving east and were

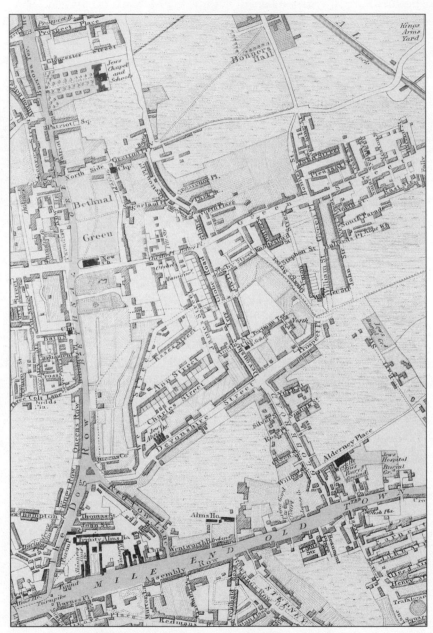

Bethnal Green, detail of map by John Greenwood, 1827

mainly concentrated in the south-west part of the parish. In 1751, Bethnal Green village had only contained around 150 dwellings. By the early 1790s, the parish of Bethnal Green had gained around 3,500 new houses.

In the 1790s, boxing became a popular sporting feature of the area. The Jewish boxer Daniel Mendoza lived there when he became the English heavyweight champion, between 1792 and 1795. He lost the title, in 1795, to Byron's boxing tutor, John Jackson. A charismatic and popular local figure, Mendoza ran a pub in Whitechapel, then turned to teaching boxing to supplement his income. York Hall, on Old Ford Road, is one of Britain's most well-known boxing venues, continuing the tradition of the sport in the area. Mendoza's thirty years in Bethnal Green represent its move from a solidly middle-class area, to a working-class one, populated by people of English, French and Jewish origin. The wealthier residents retreated from this torrent of incomers, and from the pockmarked landscape which brick-making and building had created in what had been open countryside.

From 1800, the construction of Globe Town to house weavers who worked from their own homes, rather than in the dying factory system, further changed the landscape of Bethnal Green. Thousands of poorer weavers came to occupy Globe Town in the last decades of the Georgian period, with up to 20,000 looms working in the area.

Hackney and Bethnal Green were altered dramatically during the Georgian period. Such turbulence also created the two recurring themes of these neighbouring areas: violence and madness.

'Beating her very barbarously': Hackney justice

Many roads from the east passed through the large parishes of Hackney and Bethnal Green. Traffic was a fact of life. Much of it was cattle heading to Smithfield, or traders coming and going from the City. The long gaps between the hamlets meant the roads were dangerous at night, and the long distances between neighbours saw an early rise in crimes against property.

Highway robbery rose dramatically after the Restoration. The reasons are straightforward: people were moving around more, carrying cash and wearing valuable accessories. The rise in business travel meant lone men were more likely to have money on them, not just for transactions, but for subsistence. In the early 1700s, banknotes were still relatively untrustworthy, and coins were king. The lonely roads of Hackney, where many came and went from East Anglia and the north, provided rich pickings for men who could arm themselves and had a taste for danger.

Quaker Francis Trumble turned to highway robbery, in 1739, when he accosted Thomas Brown on a footpath through a cornfield in Hackney. First, he asked Brown the way to Newington, but then, after Brown had directed him and turned away, he finally summoned the courage to begin the hold-up. Trumble had a pair of pistols and demanded money from Brown, who handed over about ninepence. He also took Brown's silver pocket watch. As Trumble took off towards Hackney village, Brown shouted for assistance. Villagers nearby began a chase that lasted over three-quarters of an hour. They included Edward Dixon, who was standing drinking outside a pub with a friend. He found Trumble hiding under a hedge at the edge of Hackney Downs. Trumble threatened to shoot, and took off again towards the Kingsland Road, 'through an Orchard, into a large Field of Beans and Peas'. Dixon finally ran him down, at the head of what had become a 'thick' crowd. Trumble, cornered, threatened them again with his pistols but finally agreed to give himself up to the man 'in his own hair', the wigless Dixon. Dixon took him to a nearby 'Publick house' where he noted Trumble 'behaved very well', and turned him over to Justice Henry Norris.

Norris was Henry Fielding's counterpart in Hackney, serving as Justice for a long period and overseeing a period of substantial change in both the local area and the nature of London crime itself. Norris used The Mermaid Tavern in Mare Street as his base, although this wasn't always to the liking of the landlord who, in 1738, refused to 'store' prisoners Norris wanted to commit for trial. The Mermaid still stands at 364 Mare Street, although it closed as a pub in 1944 and is now Mermaid Fabrics, a haberdashery.

Norris committed Trumble for trial at the Old Bailey, where Dixon testified that when he had confiscated Trumble's pistols, they had contained nothing but bullets and paper wadding, with no charge. His threats to shoot had been mere bluff. The Old Bailey heard how both Trumble's parents had killed themselves – his mother by hanging, and his father by drowning himself. His father's suicide, only weeks before Francis Trumble took to the road, appeared to have been the trigger for his crime. Witnesses testified that, in the weeks leading up to the robbery, Francis had been increasingly melancholy and distracted. He refused to answer the door when worried friends called at his house in Hackney, and he had a 'wildness' in his eyes. After his committal to Newgate, his fellow prisoners kept him on suicide watch, successfully defeating his attempts to cut his own throat and to hang himself. The court found him guilty, on the basis that he was conscious of the difference between right and wrong. On 18 July, he was sentenced to hang. Nine days later, he secured a royal pardon. What became of him after that is not known.

Another, and more famous, highwayman associated with Hackney is Dick Turpin. His ties with Hackney's Gregory Gang came as they were moving from deer poaching to housebreaking. As with highway robbery, housebreaking was a relatively unusual phenomenon outside central urban areas, but the rise of personal wealth and the appetite for new luxury goods meant that burglary had become highly profitable by the 1730s. The Gregory Gang operated all over London, staying away from Hackney, but eventually they were caught after one of their own members turned them in.

John Wheeler could have been as young as fifteen when he became involved with the gang. He came from a notorious Hackney family: his father, also John Wheeler, was a scourge of the area who came up before Norris numerous times during the 1730s. The first time was in 1731, when his wife, Thomasin, made a complaint to Norris against him for 'beating & abusing her being Sick & for denying to assist in the maintenance of her & her Children & threatning her Saying were no more pity to kill her than to kill a dog'. Norris granted a warrant for his arrest. Two years later, after being in and out of prison, Wheeler again threatened to murder his wife, and was again arrested.

In 1735, Norris committed him to Newgate for 'beating her very barbarously'. He was to be released 'at his wife's desire'.

Norris recorded many instances of domestic violence. They are not all instances of husbands beating their wives and girlfriends. William and Mary Kingsland were a constant nuisance in the area, in the late 1730s. He beat her, she beat him, and they both assaulted other people on different occasions. Fights between women were common, and violent family rows make regular appearances in Norris's notebook. His approach seems matter-of-fact, and though his entries are bald, they convey blame and painful details eloquently, such as 'pulled by ye hair', 'punching him in the face with a Cartwhip' and 'beating her with a broomstick'. Just as now, it is impossible to impose any sort of measurement on the incidence of domestic violence in Georgian London, but Norris's notes indicate that some justices took it seriously. From the scanty details surrounding the circumstances of those reporting the crimes, it appears they came predominantly from the lower social classes. However, Mary Wollstonecraft, who was born to a middle-class family in neighbouring Hoxton, took to lying outside her mother's room as a teenager to prevent her father entering in a drunken and violent rage. This, like so many incidences of domestic violence, was hidden from the authorities.

The 1730s and 1740s, when Henry Norris was active, saw a spike in London crime – a result of the demobilization of parts of the army and widespread unemployment. Highwaymen were often out-of-work or demobbed soldiers. Housebreaking was on the rise, and householders were taking desperate measures to protect their property. In October 1736, *The Gentleman's Magazine* reported that Mr Jones, a florist near the Hackney turnpike, having been 'several Times Robb'd of Valuable Flowers-Roots, had provided a Gun with Several Wires to the Trigger that when touch'd would go off, which unawares doing himself, it shatter'd his Shoulder to Pieces'.

Hackney made early efforts to maintain public order: its night watch was instigated in 1617; and by 1630, there was a cage, a whipping post and a ducking stool installed in St Augustine's churchyard. By the end of the seventeenth century, there was a watch house nearby and another at the end of the road to Cambridge Heath. In

1708, a fire station was also erected by the churchyard. In 1728, another watch house was opened in part of the Shoulder of Mutton at the end of Hackney Broadway, which is now the Cat and Mutton. Sixteen constables patrolled the streets at night. By 1740, the beats were well defined and the constables patrolled in pairs. Those watching the main roads to London were mounted. The watch was a serious business: each constable was equipped with a gun and bayonet, and keen to use them.

Hackney's watchmen were initially paid through parish funds. But later, private subscriptions supplied most of the money. In 1738, the Turnpike Trust was set up to maintain the road to London; soon afterwards, it became clear that it would be necessary to light the road at night to deter criminals. By 1756, the roads towards London were lit by oil lamps. Hackney continued an impressive and committed night watch for the rest of the century. As the streets became built up, more foot patrols and more comprehensive street lighting were introduced.

The parish was rightly proud of its efforts. Yet criminal corruption was flourishing only a stone's throw away, in Bethnal Green. Joseph Merceron was born to parents of Huguenot extraction in Brick Lane, around 1764. He began his career as a clerk in a lottery office but was soon appointed a churchwarden of St Matthew's, Bethnal Green. He then became, in rapid succession, a vestryman, a tax commissioner and a Justice of the Peace. Soon, he dominated the area through the taxation system, receiving backhanders for favourable assessments. He was a larger-than-life rough character, who encouraged dog fighting and bull-baiting. Merceron's success illustrated the power of the parish over local affairs, and the dominance that one man, if determined enough, could achieve. The Vicar of St Matthew's was his arch-enemy, but he disappeared in 1818, whilst Merceron was imprisoned for appropriating £1,000 of public funds. Another enemy of Merceron's was John Wilmot, whose father had been a labourer who raised enough money to start building houses in Bethnal Green. Merceron died, in 1839, with a fortune of £300,000, 'though he always appeared to be in poor circumstances'.

In Merceron's most successful period of corruption and extortion,

Hackney and Bethnal Green were celebrating their success at maintaining public order. Hackney even petitioned against the
Metropolitan Police Act of 1829, providing evidence of over a century of efforts to control their own crime. They also said they had
driven all the criminals into lawless Tottenham.

The 'Lunatic Trade': the east London mad-farms

From the early 1700s, the 'Lunatic Trade' flourished in east London.
Just north of the turnpike was Hackney Mad House, more correctly
known as Brooke House. Private madhouses were a feature of the
Hackney and Bethnal Green area. It was quiet, peaceful and close to
the City.

Until the 1845 Lunatics Act, there was little public provision for
those suffering with mental health issues. Bedlam and St Luke's in
central London had limited capacity. Nor were all patients eligible
for admission. Small private madhouses had been in existence all over
London for centuries. Usually, they had one or two patients; the
household was maintained by a minimal staff and supervised by a
doctor, who was unlikely to be resident. These establishments usually escaped the notice of the authorities for the first three-quarters
of the eighteenth century. Many were well respected and maintained
a high standard of sympathetic care for their patients. Brooke House
was a grand Tudor building, converted to use as an asylum, in 1758,
by a Hackney resident, William Clarke. It sat upon a fifty-acre estate,
which was let out as farmland. Clarke was a friend of the Monro
family of Bedlam asylum doctors, and John Monro recommended
patients to be sent to Brooke House after 1762. These patients were
mainly middle and upper class, and the standard of care they received
was good.

The better establishments, including Brooke House, used treatments such as bleeding, purging and cold baths, as well as early forms
of occupational therapy. But they were reserved for gentlemen and
women who could pay. One of the main problems with these smaller,
private madhouses was the confinement of those who were perhaps

difficult and troublesome, but not mentally ill. It was easier to incarcerate a wife for madness and appropriate her property than it was to obtain a divorce, after all. Awareness of mental health rose in the latter part of the eighteenth century: the periodic madness of King George III brought the matter into the public consciousness, where before it had been something to be hidden away. In 1774, an Act of Parliament was passed ensuring the regular inspection of London's private madhouses by commissioners from the Royal College of Physicians.

More problematic were the pauper lunatics, the responsibility for whose care fell upon the parish. Larger asylums were established in east London to care for these patients. The Bethnal Green Asylum, established in the early 1700s, was one of the largest, taking patients from all over London and the south-east.

Conditions in London's pauper madhouses, and particularly in Bethnal Green and Hoxton, were exposed by John Rogers in his 1815 pamphlet 'A Statement of the Cruelties, Abuses and Frauds which are practiced in Madhouses'. He told of patients chained on filthy straw, and force-feeding techniques using iron spouts which had resulted in smashed teeth. Some patients became gangrenous after being restrained and subsequently neglected. There was a public outcry, and a Select Committee was hastily set up to inquire into the matter.

Thomas Warburton had been the proprietor of the Bethnal Green Asylum since 1800, and was called before the Committee. He explained the difficulties of caring for violent patients, the need for restraints and assertive handling. The subsequent report of 1816 was damning. Yet it did not stop Warburton continuing in business in Bethnal Green – both at the main asylum, now housing many hundreds of patients, and at smaller establishments, including Whitmore House in Hoxton. Then, in 1827, a Select Committee was again established to investigate conditions at the Bethnal Green Asylum. The investigating officers found conditions beyond their worst fears: 'disgusting objects of humanity' lay chained to the walls and floor, covered in their own excrement. The smell was so offensive that one of the officers had to excuse himself to vomit outside.

Thomas Warburton was discredited, yet the asylum was not closed down. Where, after all, could the hundreds of inmates go? Warburton's son John took over the business, as the 1828 Act for the Regulation of Madhouses came into effect. One of the Act's key stipulations was that in the large asylums, such as Bethnal Green, there must be resident medical officers. John Warburton appointed Charles Beverly. Beverly was not the obvious choice for the post. A forty-year-old Scottish naval surgeon who had spent most of his career in Arctic exploration, he had married, and wanted to settle down in London. Beverly was, however, competent and unflappable.

Warburton and Beverly set about transforming the asylum. The buildings, known as the Red House and the White House, were old and in poor repair. They were tidied up, and better provision was made to separate men and women. More staff were employed to supervise the inmates; at the time of the 1827 inquiry, there had been as few as one member of staff to every fifty patients.

The lack of pastimes or occupation had been a worry for the Committee, and soon Beverly installed an extensive library of 500 books, to which he added constantly until it numbered over 2,000. Fresh air and exercise began to play a part in the lives of the inmates, who had before been confined. It took fifteen years to transform the Bethnal Green Asylum, and massive investment on Warburton's part. He had been made a wealthy man through his father's 'mad-farming', and he had married the eldest daughter of John Abernethy, the prominent surgeon at St Bartholomew's Hospital. The 1827 inquiry had almost destroyed his credibility, along with his father's, and the improvements to Bethnal Green were also part of a professional transformation. By the mid-Victorian period, Bethnal Green Asylum was held up as a model of mental healthcare.

'The Italian Boy': Carlo Ferrari

The cheapness of life in the emerging East End can be seen in the story of Carlo Ferrari, who became known by the press as 'The Italian Boy' after he was murdered for the value of his corpse. Carlo earned his living exhibiting white mice as a little sideshow on the streets of London. He lived mainly on the streets, moving around so as to exploit new audiences. In the winter of 1831, Carlo was murdered to order for dissection, because it was presumed, as a friendless immigrant, his disappearance would go unnoticed.

On 5 November

> . . . two men, named Bishop and May, called at the dissecting-room at King's College, and asked Hill, the porter, if he 'wanted anything'. On being interrogated as to what they had to dispose of, May replied, 'A boy of fourteen.' For this body they asked 12 guineas, but ultimately agreed to bring it in for 9 guineas . . . The appearance of the subject excited Hill's suspicion of foul play, and he at once communicated with Mr. Partridge, the Demonstrator of Anatomy . . . To delay the men, so that the police might be communicated with, Mr. Partridge produced a £50 note, and said that he could not pay until he had changed it. Soon after, the police officers appeared upon the scene, and the men were given into custody.

The gang were found guilty and sentenced to death. Their evidence revealed

> . . . that they had enticed the boy to their dwelling in Nova Scotia Gardens, a small slum now underneath Columbia Road Flower Market; there they drugged him with opium, and then let his body into a well, where they kept it until he was suffocated.

They had hawked the body around most of the London hospitals before trying King's College in desperation. Throughout the trial, they swore that the boy they had murdered was an unknown from Lincolnshire, not Carlo Ferrari.

Quite why they insisted on a different identity for Carlo is a mystery. It seemed that he was a known figure on the streets, and perhaps they feared public backlash against their crime. They had removed his teeth to sell 'to Mr. Mills, a dentist, for twelve shillings' and they hadn't treated his body well in transit, all of which was reported in the papers and pamphlets to a huge public outcry. One paper reported a record circulation of 50,000 on the day of the confessions, which was massive by the standards of the time. Carlo's sad story highlights the vulnerability of London's street children, and the cheapness of life in the poorer areas of the city.

The dramatic social changes in London's East End followed a distinct downward trend as the pressure of population increased. To the north, the villages survived longer and maintained their rural qualities well into the nineteenth century. They are visible in the distance from Hackney Marshes, and we set our course there now. Here we will find meadows, fruit farms, stabling and grazing for many of London's thousands of coach horses, as well as springs, spas and theatres before the geography rises and we head up to the hills to find a Romantic view of London.

12.   Islington, Hampstead and Highgate

To the north, the villages of Highgate and Hampstead escaped the urban creep for far longer, retaining their country status. On the way, we pass through the small settlements of Islington and Kentish Town.

Islington, bordered by the City in the south and Stoke Newington in the east, had long been a thoroughfare for traffic from and to the north of England. In the late seventeenth century, mineral waters had been discovered at what became known as Sadler's Wells, after the owner, Richard Sadler. He claimed the warm waters were most effective against 'distempers to which females are liable – ulcers, fits of the mother, virgin's fever and hypochondriacal distemper'. Sadler's Wells became infamous by the beginning of the eighteenth century as a notorious pleasure garden, probably not helped by the large pass-ing trade brought to Islington by its many thoroughfares to and from the City.

The Aquatic Theatre, Sadler's Wells, 1813, by an unknown artist

Roads were the village's main feature. In 1717, it had one of the earlier Turnpike Trusts, set up to maintain them. By 1735, the main roads all had houses along them, although infilling would not come until the nineteenth century. The Angel, Islington, was an inn near one of the tollhouses on the Great North Road. The courtyard of the Angel is thought to be depicted in Hogarth's 'Stagecoach', and here Thomas Paine wrote passages of his *Rights of Man* during one of his stays in London in 1790–91. The sheer amount of traffic passing through the village dictated its character, and it was always a busy place populated by those who made their living from travellers, or those who wanted to be just one mile from the City of London and didn't mind the clamour from the cattle and carriages.

Many of the buildings around Upper Street were medieval in origin, and there had been several fine manor houses in Barnsbury. The majority of the new buildings, though, were solid eighteenth-century stock, for the retired or those connected with commerce. By the 1790s, the village had two hairdressers, warehouses selling pottery, tea and fabric, as well as a wine merchant's and a toy shop. Yet it had an air of neglect, and the green with its associated pond became drab and dirty.

By the beginning of the nineteenth century, Islington's population had risen to over 10,000, and there were thriving, if slightly seedy, music halls and entertainment venues. Sadler's Wells was now a theatre. In the first decade of the new century, it styled itself an 'aquatic theatre', specializing in 'aquadrama', where the theatre was flooded for the purpose of re-enacting naval or mythological battles or scenes. The illusion of flooding was created by a tank ninety feet long, some twenty feet wide and three feet deep. The New River, which carried water into London, was used to fill the tank. Charles Dibdin the Younger, of the Dibdin theatre family, staged the Siege of Gibraltar there, in April 1802. Children were cast as the Spanish sailors and threw themselves about in the water, 'swimming and affecting to struggle with the waves'.

Islington's true building boom came in the Victorian period. Camden and Kentish Towns were consolidated in the Victorian years, but the process began in 1791, when Lord Camden sold building rights for 1,400 houses on his land. Horace Walpole said it heralded the spread of London to 'every village ten miles around'. Kentish Town had previously been used to pasture coach horses and animals on their way to Smithfield. It had rich grazing meadows with dugout ponds in the centre, collecting rainwater in the clay soil. There were also enclosures with high grass-studded mud walls. The walls were made from the insides of the horns of the thousands of cows slaughtered every week at Smithfield. The exteriors went to make cheap drinking cups, or horn handles, books and tablets, but the tapered interiors formed the 'bricks' for these walls, which were then mortared with mud into which grass seed was pushed. Cheap, sturdy and opaque, they were the safest place to keep expensive livestock and horseflesh close to London.

From the middle of the eighteenth century until well into the nineteenth, Kentish Town had a fashionable assembly room where tea and coffee were served 'morning and evening' and public and private dinners could be arranged, 'on the shortest notice'. They also served a 'good ordinary on Sundays at two o'clock', with 'ordinary' meaning a good roast lunch.

Islington and Kentish Town were both country villages for the majority of the Georgian period. In the minds of Londoners, as long as they could see Hampstead and Highgate from the city's northern limits, London was still contained. Both villages had long been the resort of fashionable London: Hampstead in the summer months, to enjoy the clean air and water, and Highgate for the smart professional set, to provide commutable housing. Hampstead was built up first with the 'charming old red-brick mansions which make Hampstead what it is'.

Defoe gave a heady image of the village, in 1727, when he noted in his tour of Great Britain that

> Hampstead indeed is risen from a little country village, to a city, not upon the credit only of the waters, tho' 'tis apparent, its growing greatness began there; but company increasing gradually, and the people liking both the place and the diversions together; it grew suddenly populous, and the concourse of people was incredible.

He did, however, consider it 'so near heaven, that I dare not say it can be a proper situation, for any but a race of mountaineers'.

Hampstead had a long association with quality schooling and intellectualism. This may have been a result of the cosmopolitan population: as far back as the sixteenth century, the names of land-owners indicate Jewish and European origins. Wildwood, a house first mentioned in Domesday, was one of the most significant within the parish boundary and is remembered today in Wildwood Road and Grove. There, William Pitt the Elder recovered from his nervous breakdown, in 1767, 'a miserable invalid . . . he refused to see anyone, even his own attendant, and his food was passed to him through a panel of the door'.

At the top of Hampstead Heath stood the vast house of Kenwood, known commonly during the Georgian period in speech and letters as Caenwood. Dating originally from the early seventeenth century, it was bought by Lord Mansfield, in 1754. He had it remodelled extensively, by Robert Adam, in the 1760s and 1770s. It was here that the Mansfields lived with Dido Elizabeth Belle, their illegitimate mixed-race grand-niece. Dido died in 1804, aged a little over forty. In 1975, Dido's last relative, Harold Davinier, died a free white South African in a land still struggling under apartheid.

Near the Hampstead reservoir, through which the Hampstead Water Company had been supplying the West End with water since 1692, there was the Upper Flask Tavern. Clarissa fled here from Lovelace in Samuel Richardson's novel after his 'wicked attempt' upon her, and the Whigs' Kit-Cat Club used to meet here during the summer, sitting under the shade of a splitting mulberry tree which was later preserved with iron bands in memory of the club. There, too, lived George Steevens, who was famous for his edition of twenty-one Shakespeare plays published in 1766, a year after Samuel Johnson's edition. Steevens walked into London before seven o'clock each morning to discuss Shakespeare with various eminent researchers, before making the rounds of all the bookshops, then walking back to Hampstead for the evening. Johnson was so impressed with Steevens' work that he suggested they produce a complete works of Shakespeare together, which appeared in 1773, in ten volumes. In order to get the work done, and with Johnson not fulfilling his part of the bargain, Steevens had, for twenty months, left Hampstead with the watch patrol at one in the morning, walked into London to his printer 'without any consideration of the weather or the season', taking with him as much work as he had ready. He would then collect the previous day's pages, go home and edit them, before writing the next batch. He would sleep briefly before setting off for London again.

On the west side of the Heath, in Well Walk, sprang the well producing Hampstead's renowned purgative chalybeate waters, drawing hundreds of Londoners on sunny days. The waters contain 'oxyde of iron, muriates of soda and magnesia, sulphate of lime, and a small portion of silex; and its mean temperature at the wells is from 46° to 47° of Fahrenheit'. In the reign of Charles II, a halfpenny token stamped with the words 'Dorothy Rippin at the well in Hampsted' on the back was issued, exchangeable for a pint of water. In 1698, Susanna Noel with her son Baptist, 3rd Earl of Gainsborough, gave the well along with six acres of ground to the poor of Hampstead. From here, the water was carried every day for sale to Holborn Bars, Charing Cross, and throughout the streets, for purchase by those who preferred Hampstead water.

A Pump Room was built on the south side of Well Walk, which was opened in August 1701 with a concert. On the northern side of Well Walk was built the Long Room for dances and assemblies. These parties were a fixture of Hampstead and London life. The addition of the Pump Room transformed Hampstead into a 'spa town' in its own right, and by the 1760s, it had 500 dwellings. The artist John Constable lived for a while in Well Walk, at Number 6, though he continued to go into work to his London studio. By the time he was living in Hampstead, many people commuted daily to the city, and by 1834, eight omnibuses were making twenty journeys each day. London merchants had favoured Hampstead as a retreat since the Civil War, but now it became possible to live there and still work in their counting houses. The atmosphere was wealthy, liberated and educated.

Like Hampstead, Highgate had become a wealthy village in the late sixteenth century. Highgate village straddles the border between Hampstead and Hornsey. It became built up in the seventeenth and eighteenth centuries, with good houses and a prosperous high street. Like Hampstead, and Hackney, it had originally been a place to enjoy fresh air and peace, whilst staying close to London. Highgate's church, St Michael's, is at the same height as the dome of St Paul's Cathedral: 365 feet. The soil and altitude made the area ideal for the growing of soft fruit, and from Islington to Highgate there were many fruit farms. There were also dairy farms, and the absence of smallpox in the milkmaids led Londoners to credit Highgate with having particularly healthy air, which kept the girls' skin fresh and clear. It was from this high point that Boswell 'went in' to the theatre of London on 19 November 1762, after the long journey from Scotland, recording in his journal: 'When we came upon Highgate Hill and had a view of London, I was all life and joy.'

Highgate could not rival Hampstead socially, but it acquired one coup with the arrival of Harriet (née Mellon), the widow of the banker Thomas Coutts, who took a lease on Holly Lodge, on the west side of Highgate Hill, after her first husband died. Her rise from actress to desirable mistress was not unlike that of Coutts's own ancestor and fellow Highgate resident, Nell Gwynne. Like Nelly, of 'the ten or twelve ladies who have been raised from the stage to wear coronets, few names stand forth more pleasantly than that of Harriet Mellon'. Her biographer noted, 'It is not known who was her father, though probably she had one,' and that she was born on 11 November 1777, behind Lambeth Palace. Her father was later said to be a chimney sweep from Sheffield, or perhaps a soldier in the Madras Infantry.

Harriet made her debut at the Drury Lane Theatre, in 1795, but it wasn't until 1805 that she met the seventy-year-old Thomas Coutts. She was his mistress until the death of his wife, in 1815, and they married soon after. They had to marry twice, after the first ceremony was mysteriously deemed invalid. Upon her marriage she became one of Britain's richest women, and she was desperate to become London's most popular hostess. Her desperation to be liked by the *haut ton* was often caricatured, but her kind-hearted, flamboyant style and her love for entertaining gradually won them over. Thomas died in 1822, leaving Harriet his fortune and his share in Coutts Bank, much to the annoyance of his daughters from his first marriage. Harriet, however, refused to be cowed and gave them all generous allowances. In 1827, she also brought their wrath and London's scorn upon herself again when, aged forty-nine, she married William Beauclerk, the 26-year-old Duke of St Albans. The caricatures were even more scathing, but just as her first marriage had been a happy one, it seemed that the new Duchess of St Albans' cheerfulness and her husband's easygoing nature meant they were content enough together.

Yet William's family were very rude to his new wife. Harriet had her fill of unpleasant in-laws, and when she died, in 1837, a clause in her will specified that were any of William's family to come and stay with him for more than a week at any of the properties she left him, all her bequests to him would cease. The Duchess of St Albans left most of her wealth, the vast sum of £1.8 million, to Thomas Coutts' granddaughter, Angela. Angela Burdett-Coutts would become Victorian London's greatest philanthropist until she forfeited the fortune, aged sixty-nine, by also marrying a 26-year-old. It wasn't the cradle-snatching her step-grandmother's will objected to, but that he was American: a clause specified that Angela must not marry an 'alien'. The American husband lived on at Holly Lodge after Angela's death. When he died, in 1922, the estate was developed as bedsit accommodation for young women who came to London to work after the First World War left the City in dire need of clerks and secretaries. For a long time, the housing remained for women only.

As Harriet Mellon's transformation began, Highgate was changing too. In 1813, John Nash's Archway was being built to bridge the hill between Highgate and Holloway and to provide a toll road for traffic which struggled with the steep Highgate Hill. Many images of the picturesque scene of Highgate Hill and the Archway Road were produced, depicting cattle and hay wagons rumbling in and out of London. But The Archway also became a magnet for the suicidal, and high railings were installed to try to prevent further deaths. Then, in the 1830s, Highgate was decided upon as the site of one of London's new, vast cemeteries. Space for the dead within the city was fast running out, and the Burial Act of 1835 meant that London's dead would now be laid to rest in one of the 'Magnificent Seven' on the edges of the city. Highgate Cemetery now holds approximately

Archway Turnpike, engraving by an unknown artist, 1825

170,000 bodies in 53,000 graves; it was observed upon its opening, in 1839, that Londoners, like the ancient Athenians, 'bury their dead in the fairest suburb of the City'.

Keats and Coleridge: the Romantics of Hampstead and Highgate

The most famous of Hampstead's residents is John Keats. He and his brothers lodged in Well Walk, next to the Wells Tavern, between 1817 and 1818, when John's brother Tom was dying of the consumption that had killed their mother. John's life would end only a few years later.

Keats was a familiar figure in Hampstead. He was not fond of London, finding that everyone there was 'always at Loggerheads', but the city was where he was born and raised. His short and painful life began at the Hoop and Swan by Moorgate, where he was the eldest of three boys and a girl. The pub is still there and known now as Keats and the Globe. When Keats was seven, he was sent to a school in Enfield, north London. Nine months after he started at the school, Keats' father came to visit him and on the way home was thrown from his horse. Thomas Keats' skull was fractured, and he died hours later. John's mother died in March 1810, leaving her fourteen-year-old son in the charge of Thomas Hammond, an apothecary.

John shared Hammond's lodgings, where he developed an interest in medicine that led him to become a student at Guy's Hospital when he was eighteen. He studied there for five years as a 'dresser', attending in theatre and dressing the patients' wounds after surgery. In 1816, he passed his apothecary exams, and had his first poem published. A collection followed, in 1817, to little acclaim.

During a Scottish summer holiday, in 1818, with his friend Charles Brown, Keats developed a cold so severe that he could not continue the vacation. When he came home, it was to the reality of his brother Tom's tuberculosis, termed 'consumption' at the time. Keats nursed Tom at Well Walk, but he was probably succumbing to the early stages of the disease himself. He had also started to take laudanum, to become 'drowsed with the fume of poppies', claiming it eased the tightness in his chest.

John wished to devote himself to poetry, and so had to make some money out of writing. These hopes were almost dashed, in 1818, with the publication of *Endymion*. It was savaged by the critics, and Keats was heartbroken. He lamented that he would 'ever be a weaver's boy to them'. Byron sniped at Keats as a 'Cockney' and a 'dirty little blackguard'.

Tom died in December of that year. Keats moved in with Charles Brown on Hampstead Heath. There they met the elusive Miss Fanny Brawne, who inspired so much of Keats' work. The Brawne family lived at West End, a hamlet nearby. She was an incorrigible flirt, and not just with John. He wrote her cruel and often spiteful notes, then others full of contrition, but they formed a close relationship which led to an engagement.

In 1820, towards the end of winter, Keats returned from the City to Brown's house, thoroughly chilled. He was sent to bed by Brown. Keats coughed once, but blood hit the sheet. His surgical training allowed him to recognize it as arterial blood, meaning his lungs were compromised. 'That drop of blood is my death warrant,' he told his friend. Brown later remembered the calm with which Keats wiped his chin and remarked, 'This is unfortunate.'

John consulted three doctors and was bled, starved, fattened and opiated. He fretted for Fanny's company and began to suffer palpitations. Finally, the doctors recommended a warm climate. Joseph Severn, a promising young artist with an award for travel from the Royal Academy, was singled out as a friend for John, and Rome was settled upon as the place for him to convalesce. Fanny gave John a large marble she used to cool her fingers when sewing. It would rarely leave his reach for the rest of his life.

John Keats and Joseph Severn left England on 17 September 1820. When Keats continued to decline, the doctor confirmed what John already knew: he was dying. Keats became frightened of the dark, so Severn rigged up a system whereby one faltering candle lit the wick of the next, an invention Keats named 'the fairy lamplighter'.

Keats encouraged Severn in his nursing: 'Now you must be firm for it will not last long.' He and Severn sat, hand in hand, for the next seven hours, until John Keats died. Severn wrote to Brown, telling him:

> I am broken down from four nights' watching, and no sleep since, and my poor Keats gone. Three days since, the body was opened; the lungs were completely gone. The Doctors could not conceive by what means he had lived these two months. I followed his poor body to the grave on Monday.

Keats was buried in the Protestant cemetery, as they had agreed. His tombstone bears no name:

> This grave
> contains all that was Mortal,
> of a
> YOUNG ENGLISH POET,
> Who on his Death Bed,
> in the Bitterness of his Heart,
> at the Malicious Power of his Enemies,
> Desired these Words to be engraven on his Tomb Stone:
> Here lies One
> Whose Name was writ in Water.

The news took a month to reach London, where it was published in *The Times* on 23 March 1821: 'At Rome on the 23rd of Feb., of a decline, John Keats, the poet, aged 25.' Fanny married Louis Lindo of Marylebone, in 1833. By this time, the 'weaver's boy' was already hailed as one of the greatest British poets. In 1829, Charles Brown began to write his own history of Keats' life. He wrote to Fanny and asked her if she had anything to add. Fanny feared she had nothing, for her relationship had been with a man, not a poet, and suggested that 'the kindest act would be to let him rest for ever in the obscurity to which unhappy circumstances have condemned him'.

If Hampstead belongs to John Keats, then Highgate must belong to Samuel Taylor Coleridge. In 1817, Coleridge arrived at Dr Gillman's house in The Grove, Highgate, to attempt to conquer his opium addiction. He had, over long use, become accustomed to '4 & 5 ounces in a day' – a tremendous dose – and he had been taking it since before he wrote 'Kubla Khan', in 1797, a poem inspired by an opiate haze.

He may well have come into contact with opium first through his benefactor, Tom Wedgwood, Josiah's son. Tom, who was instrumental in the early development of photography, was also an opium addict. He had come to depend upon the drug to alleviate the symptoms of his depression and delicate health, the one probably feeding off the other. Tom was uninterested in the family business, although he had previously been involved in the decoration of the Greek Street premises, and wrote: 'I mean to exert myself for the good of my fellow creatures.' At twenty-three, he inherited from his father a sum of money which would allow him to do just that. After having met Coleridge through friends, he heard of the poet's financial difficulties and wrote to him, enclosing a cheque for £100.

Coleridge was overcome with gratitude, but returned the cheque. The Wedgwoods were moved to then set up an annuity of £150 a year for the poet. Tom died of complications arising from heavy use of opium, in 1805. Coleridge was already on the slippery slope of drug addiction. He would remember the time he first began to take opium: 'I was seduced into the use of narcotics not secretly, but (such was my ignorance) openly and exultingly, as one who had discovered, and was never weary of recommending, a grand panacea, and saw not the truth till my body had contracted a habit and a necessity.'

Like all drug addicts, Coleridge became ever more divorced from the truth, which – while it may have been necessary for his poetry – was fatal to his marriage and his friendships, knowing that: 'I have in this one dirty business of Laudanum an hundred times deceived, tricked, nay, actually & consciously LIED.'

Eight days after his arrival in Highgate, Coleridge wrote to John Murray, for whom he was supposed to be translating Goethe's *Faust*, with a 'note for a Porter' who was to run the errand and then put what he obtained 'carefully with the Books'. This, of course, was laudanum wrapped up in the *Quarterly Review*. He believed it kept him 'tranquil and capable of literary labour'.

The Gillmans built a wing on their house for Coleridge, unaware that their long-term guest was still feeding his habit not only through John Murray's porter but also through the local apothecary in the High Street, Mr Dunn. A young apprentice called Seymour Teulon Porter worked there. Seymour saw Coleridge as a shifty drug addict; he remembered how, in addition to the Murray supply, Coleridge would come for a pint of laudanum a week, paying once every three months or so, and how he did not speak until the bottle was filled, coming and going by a side door.

It was in these early years that Coleridge, walking with Leigh Hunt in a lane near Hampstead, recalled how a 'loose, slack, not well-dressed youth met Mr. Green and myself in a lane near Highgate. Green knew him, and spoke. It was Keats.'

In July of 1824, Lord Byron's remains passed through Highgate and most of the village turned out to watch the funeral procession. Seymour Porter recalled how he was 'a white-aproned youth of fifteen years of age' when Coleridge came over to join him and watch the procession, recalling the dead poet's 'unhappy youth' and predicting that 'Byron's literary merits would continually rise, while his personal errors, if not denied, or altogether forgotten, would be little noticed'. Coleridge might well have hoped the same for himself.

Yet, on paper, Coleridge managed to maintain some truth; in 1832, he would describe opium as a 'Poison, which for more than 30 years has been the guilt, debasement, and misery of my Existence', indicating that he had never conquered his addiction. By the time he was writing this, the Georgian period was over. William IV, the last Hanoverian king, occupied the throne. The political landscape was in the grip of reform. The London that Coleridge saw from Highgate was a modern metropolis. He died in his 'peculiar room' at the Gillmans' two years later, where the view from the window was of the 'ocean of London, with its domes and steeples definite in the sun, big Paul's and the many memories attached to it hanging high over all. Nowhere, of its kind, could you see a grander prospect on a bright summer day.'

Afterword

We end where we began, high above the City in the Golden Gallery of St Paul's Cathedral. The London below us has changed immeasurably. It spreads far into the distance in all directions, although maps are still commonly divided into the City, Westminster and Southwark. The villages, such as Marylebone, Hackney, Bethnal Green, which were outlying satellites are now mere suburbs.

In 1825, Thomas Cubitt's plans for Pimlico and Belgravia began to cover the ancient gardens and willow beds of the Ebury estate. Greenwich was, and remains, a self-contained river settlement. Chelsea was a pretty village, full of nurseries and gardens towards World's End. Kensington had the palace and grand retreats, but Notting Hill was known for its unglamorous gravel pits. Fulham was taken up with prosperous market gardens, which relied on the night soil carted down from London's cesspits to fertilize its beds. When it was developed during the early Victorian period, many of the gardens were sold off to different builders. Small estates went up, with as many dwellings crushed in as possible, and resulting in a mass of ordinary housing with bad transport links.

Clapham came to prominence late in the eighteenth century – not for the place itself, but for its association with the religious group based there, the Clapham Saints, and their abolitionist campaigning. William Wilberforce was their central member. Another William, Cobbett, denounced Herne Hill as nothing but 'two entire miles of stockjobbers'. Camberwell Grove was built deliberately at the end of a road to nowhere – the key to its survival as one of London's most beautiful streets.

We are on the threshold of a new era. Victoria will take the throne, and the city will change again, spreading ever outwards, this time in uniform ranks. Within forty years, London will be a vast suburbia of metropolitan works and template housing. It will have an underground railway and the most advanced sewerage system in the world. Solid, wealthy, philanthropic and worthy, it will be a splendid and civilized place. There will be urban poverty and disease on a terrifying scale.

But that is not our remit. Here, our story finishes. London has made an incredible journey in little over a century. It has left behind the medieval and become a modern city: polluted, populous, vibrant and bursting at the seams. Grinding penury and vast wealth remain close neighbours, but science, medicine and industry are innovating at an unparalleled speed. The city is on an artistic and cultural high. Londoners are wealthier, more educated and healthier than ever before. They are setting standards of taste and refinement which are still emulated today. Look around you at their many legacies in our streets, hospitals, museums and institutions. Listen. Their voices can still be heard.

Acknowledgements

I wish I could put this book into my father's hand and see his face. I hope my mother and sister know what it means to me that they will hold it.

But that this is a book at all is due to Kirsty McLachlan at David Godwin Associates. Kirsty, Heather, David, Anna, Caitlin and everyone there have served Georgian London above and beyond the call of duty.

That this is the book it is, is due to the vision and commitment of my editor, Eleo Gordon. Thanks also to Jillian Taylor, Ben Brusey and the team at Viking who reined in, tactfully, my desire to explore every last detail of the hernia corset, dockside prostitution and fireworks. And to Shân Morley Jones for making copy-editing a charm rather than a chore.

The original manuscript for this book was so unwieldy it would have made most people put their aprons over their faces and weep (and probably did). Thanks to historians Patrick Baty and Adrian Tinniswood for endless encouragement and wise words. You have been stars by which I have navigated.

Thanks to Alex Werner of the Museum of London, who took the time to read the final manuscript and tell me so much I didn't know. Many thanks also to everyone at the Museum of London for all their help, enthusiasm and good cheer.

But if there are errors in these pages, they are mine.

For being a haven of peace, assistance and tiny tokens of comradeship with strangers, the London Library is without parallel. May we continue to not talk and bless each other's sneezes. And to all the librarians and archivists whose doorsteps I have darkened by phone, email or in person, thank you.

To Brand Inglis, Richard Courtney and Kaye Michie, because family is not biology. To Anne, Hank and Carly Martin, because family is not geography.

Love and thanks to Katie, Sam and Michael Sedler for our history. To Sue and Paddy Linaker, and Brian and Biffy Rolleston, for always asking how the book was going and being willing to listen to the answer. To Fiona Kirkpatrick, Rory Maxwell and David Child for keeping me sane on a daily basis, and for those nights in that Soho. To Lyn Prendergast for organizing and feeding me, and telling me what it really takes to get into the French Foreign Legion. To Simon Surtees for fifteen years of sarcasm and everything internet. To Bridie for silent support and shared biscuits.

And again, to my husband. If, as Lord Chesterfield said, 'Frequent and loud laughter is the characteristic and folly of ill manners,' long may we remain so badly behaved.

Notes

Introduction

p. 1 'Bow Bells': *The Diurnal of Thomas Rugg, 1659–1660* (London, 1961), 80.

p. 1 'Impudent Harlot': Daniel Baker, 'One Warning More' (London, 1660).

p. 1 'above 20000 horse . . . and blessed God': diary entry dated 29 May 1660.

p. 2 'a great impression of fear': Gideon Harvey, *The City Remembrancer* (London, 1722), 2.

p. 3 'charms, philtres . . . as near as they can': Daniel Defoe, *A Journal of the Plague Year* (London, 1722), 44–7.

p. 3 'they talked of': ibid., 140.

p. 3 'stiffnesse under his eare . . . tolling of bells': John Allin in W. G. Bell, *Unknown London* (London, 1920), 43.

p. 3 'people that were infected': *A Journal of the Plague Year*, 73.

p. 4 'Faggots, faggots': quoted in *The Gentleman's Magazine Miscellany*, vol. 192, 51.

p. 4 'sweated kindly': *A Journal of the Plague Year*, 284.

p. 4 'an innocent Frenchman . . . dismembered': 'Autobiography and Anecdotes of William Taswell (1652–82)', reprinted by *The Camden Miscellany* (London, 1853), vol. 2, 11.

p. 6 'whole as to skin': ibid., 13.

p. 6 'a poor distracted wretch': *The Life of Edward, Earl of Clarendon (1609–74), as written by himself* (London, 1827), vol. 3, 96.

p. 7 'in the four years after the Fire': *The City Remembrancer*, 23.

p. 9 'the Church of England': Edward Gregg, *Queen Anne* (London, 1984), 16.

p. 9 It was recovered: Sir James Mackintosh, *History of the Revolution in England in 1688* (London, 1835), 572.

p. 10 This figure remained relatively steady: L. D. Schwarz, *London in the Age of Industrialisation: Entrepreneurs, Labour Force and Living Conditions, 1700–1850* (Cambridge, 1992), 128.

p. 10 in a 'mad' attempt . . . with tiles': Johann Wilhelm von Archenholz, *A Picture of England* (1789), 121.

p. 10 'royalty, legislation, nobility': *The London Magazine*, vol. 6 (August 1822), 137.

1: The City

p. 14 'several expert workmen . . . of wonderful grace': Henry Milman, *Annals of St Paul's Cathedral* (London, 1868), 367.

p. 16 'without hovels': T. F. Reddaway, 'The Rebuilding of London after the Fire', *The Town Planning Review*, vol. 17, no. 4 (December 1937), 276–7.

p. 17 Bricklayer Thomas Warren: James Chambers, *Building St Paul's* (London, 2007), 36.

p. 18 The idea of resurrection: ibid., 56.

p. 18 'natural philosophy . . . universal science': Paul Elliott and Stephen Daniels, 'The "School of True, Useful and Universal Science"? Freemasonry, Natural Philosophy and Scientific Culture in Eighteenth-Century England', *The British Journal for the History of Science*, vol. 39, no. 2 (June 2006), 207–29.

p. 18 Fraternity was one: livery companies are ancient trade guilds which had been granted the right to their own 'livery', or uniform. The 'Great Twelve' are the Mercers, Grocers, Drapers, Fishmongers, Goldsmiths, Merchant Taylors, Skinners, Haberdashers, Salters, Ironmongers, Vintners and Clothworkers.

p. 20 'Sarah Freeman . . . Smith': quoted in Leo Hollis, *The Phoenix: The Men Who Made Modern London* (London, 2009), 173.

p. 20 'A Youth designed': Robert Campbell, *The London Tradesman* (London, 1747), 120–21.

p. 21 'for dispersing scandalous': Paula McDowell, *The Women of Grub Street: Press, Politics, and Gender in the London Literary Marketplace 1678–1730* (Oxford, 1998), 33.

p. 22 Ephraim Chambers was born: the account of Chambers' life is taken from *Gentleman's Magazine, and Historical Chronicle*, vol. 44, part 2 (London, 1785), 673.

p. 22 Chambers laid out his considerable aspirations: the full title was 'Cyclopaedia, or, An Universal Dictionary of Arts and Sciences: Containing the Definitions of the Terms, and Accounts of the Things Signify'd Thereby, in the Several Arts, both Liberal and Mechanical, and the Several Sciences, Human and Divine: the Figures, Kinds, Properties, Productions, Preparations, and Uses, of Things Natural and Artificial: the Rise, Progress, and State of Things Ecclesiastical, Civil, Military, and Commercial: with the Several Systems, Sects, Opinions, etc; among Philosophers, Divines, Mathematicians, Physicians, Antiquaries, Critics, etc.: The Whole Intended as a Course of Ancient and Modern Learning'.

p. 23 'if ye ship be gone': Susan Whyman, *The Pen and the People: English Letter Writers 1660–1800* (Oxford, 2009), 61.

p. 24 'who keep coffeehouses': Milton Percival, *Robert Walpole, Earl of Orford, 1676–1745* (Oxford, 1916), xiii.

p. 24 Thirty years later: A. M. Ogilvie, 'The Rise of the English Post Office', *The Economic Journal*, vol. 3, no. 11 (September 1893), 453.

p. 24 'without question': Daniel Defoe, *A Tour Through the Whole Island of Great Britain: Volume II*, first published 1724–6 (London, 1971 edition), 313.

p. 25 'no sooner had we entered': Ned Ward, *The London Spy*, first published 1706 (London, 1955 edition), 187.

p. 25 'oysters, fruit': William Hone, *The Every-day Book* (London, 1826), 591.

p. 26 'no more than three feet': *London Chronicle*, 17 November 1764.

p. 27 In the middle of the eighteenth century: George Dodd, *The Food of London: A Sketch of the Chief Varieties, Sources of Supply, Probable Quantities, Modes of Arrival, Processes of Manufacture, Suspected Adulteration, and Machinery of Distribution, of the Food for a Community of Two Millions and a Half* (London, 1856), 228.

p. 28 'The cubicles were neat': Claire Williams, *Sophie in London, 1786* (London, 1933), 71.

p. 28 'crying, wandering, travelling': *Supplement to the Harleian Miscellany* (London, 1812), 325.

p. 29 'a mere sluggish': Walter Thornbury, 'The Fleet River and Fleet Ditch', *Old and New London: Volume 2* (London, 1878), 416.

p. 30 'rear of the houses': letter dated 22 August 1838.

p. 31 'the frequent sign': Thomas Pennant, *An Account of London* (London, 1790), 309.

p. 31 'near a hundred pair': John Southerden Burn, *History of the Fleet Marriages* (London, 1846), 5.

p. 31 'large tribute': Alexander Pope, *The Dunciad* (London, 1723), ll. 267–8.

p. 32 'mighty mass': Lord Byron, *Don Juan* (London, 1823), canto X.

p. 32 The baleen to oil ratio: Lynn Sorge-English, '"29 Doz and 11 Best Cutt Bone": The Trade in Whalebone and Stays in Eighteenth-Century London', *Textile History*, vol. 36/I (May 2005), 22.

p. 32 'The women use no paint': quoted in Valerie Steele, *The Corset: A Cultural History* (New Haven, Connecticut, 2003), 26.

p. 32 'very nearly purgatory': Elizabeth Ham, quoted in Kristin Olsen, *Daily Life in 18th-Century England* (Westport, Connecticut, 1999), 96.

p. 32 'my poor arms': Georgiana, Duchess of Devonshire, *The Sylph* (London, 1738), 34.

p. 33 'three bales of Aniseeds' . . . a mere half-load: Henry Kent, *The Shopkeeper's and Tradesman's Assistant* (London, 1768), 144.

p. 33 'the Green-Yard . . . or Horses': ibid., 78.

p. 34 'In the afternoon': diary entry dated 30 November 1662.

p. 36 'the Jew, the Mahometan': Voltaire, *Letters Concerning the English Nation* (1773), Letter VI, 'On the Presbyterians'.

p. 36 They termed themselves: Peter Renton, *The Lost Synagogues of London* (London, 2000), 30.

p. 38 His own likeness: diary entry dated 9 January 1662.

p. 39 'as well done as ever I saw': diary entry dated 15 February 1667.

p. 39 'punching my sister . . . half-crowne': quoted in Richard S. Westfall, *The Life of Isaac Newton* (Cambridge, 1994), 17.

p. 40 'a fit person': John Giuseppi, *The Bank of England: A History from its Foundation in 1694* (London, 1966), 47.

p. 41 'I have Been so Unfortunate': Deidre Palk (ed.), *Prisoners' Letters to the Bank of England 1781–1827* (London, 2007), vol. XLII, vii.

p. 41 'architectural crime': quoted by Jonathan Glancey in *Lost Buildings* (London, 2008), 65.

p. 42 'Mahometan gruel ... tasting not unlike it': R. Bradley, *The Virtue and Use of Coffee* (London, 1772), 12.

p. 43 Just how important: James Walvin, *Fruits of Empire: Exotic Produce and British Taste, 1660–1800* (London, 1997), 39.

p. 43 'the Coffee-man ... Customers to read': George S. McCue, 'Libraries of the London Coffeehouses', *The Library Quarterly*, vol. 4, no. 4 (October, 1934), 624.

p. 45 'whose great ambition': Ned Ward, *London Spy*, 299.

p. 46 'for the Lyons ... very tame': diary entry dated 11 January 1660.

p. 46 'they should take as much care': Ned Ward, *London Spy*, 236.

p. 47 'Cats of the mountains ... Jackall': Daniel Hahn, *The Tower Menagerie: Being the Amazing True Story of the Royal Collection of Wild and Ferocious Beasts* (London, 2003), 125.

p. 47 'They say': The papers of Gertrude Savile, Nottinghamshire Archives: DD/SR/212/10-11.

p. 47 'The wild creatures ... in his den': *Curiosities in the Tower of London* (London, 1741), 31.

p. 48 Surveys conducted: Christopher Plumb, 'Exotic Animals in Eighteenth Century Britain' (PhD thesis in Museology, submitted to the University of Manchester's Faculty of Humanities, 2010), 60–61.

p. 48 'perfect strangers': Edward Turner Bennett, *The Tower Menagerie (comprising the natural history of the animals contained in that establishment, with anecdotes of their characters and history* (London, 1829), 128.

p. 48 'their limbs and tails ... asleep': ibid., 153.

p. 48 'heave anything ... a surprising Degree': *An Historical Description of the Tower of London and its Curiosities* (London, 1753), 23.

p. 48 'one of them having torn': the 1810 Tower guidebook, quoted by Hahn in *The Tower Menagerie*, 191.

p. 49 'wisdom ... intoxicating articles': Bennett, *The Tower Menagerie*, 174.

p. 49 'The subject of the present article': James Wilson, 'Essays on the Origin and Natural History of Domestic Animals', *The Quarterly Journal of Agriculture*, vol. 2 (November 1829–February 1831), 64.

2: The Margins

p. 50 'got a great way': Edward Brayley, quoted in Rowland Dobie, *The History of the United Parishes of St Giles in the Fields and St George's Bloomsbury* (London, 1829), 183.

p. 50 'pestered with . . . strangers': John Stow, *Survey of London* (London, 1598), 47.

p. 51 'where old clothes': footnote by William Roscoe to *The Dunciad* in *The Works of Alexander Pope* (London, 1824), 100.

p. 51 'There is no expressing': Thomas Pennant, *An Account of London* (London, 1790), 286.

p. 51 'Jews used to go': John Sherren Brewer, *English Studies; or Essays in English History and Literature* (London, 1881), 427.

p. 51 'between two and three miles': Henry Mayhew, *London Labour and the London Poor: a cyclopaedia of the condition and earnings of those that will work, those that cannot work, and those that will not work: Volume II* (London, 1851), 10.

p. 52 'dead dogges': Stow, quoted in Weinreb, Hibbert, Keay and Keay, *The London Encyclopedia* (London, 2008), 417.

p. 52 'On lines stretched': W. Denton, *Records of St Giles' Cripplegate* (London, 1883), 104–6.

p. 53 'dull, narrow, uninviting': Walter Thornbury, 'Whitefriars', *Old and New London: Volume 1* (London, 1878), 182–99.

p. 55 'Lewdly Given . . . gallery Maids': rules and regulations for hospital staff, extracted from Minutes of Bridewell and Bethlem Governors (20 June 1756). See also Jonathan Andrews and Andrew Scull, *Undertaker of the Mind: John Monro and Mad-Doctoring in Eighteenth-Century England* (Berkeley, California, 2001).

p. 56 'Madness is a distemper': *Remarks on Dr. Battie's Treatise of Madness by John Monro* (London, 1758).

p. 56 'experts . . . Air Loom': quoted in John Haslam, *Illustrations of Madness* (London, 2003), xxxii.

p. 57 'motley assemblage . . . by botchers': John Thomas Smith, *Nollekens and his Times: Volume I* (London, 1829), 213.

p. 57 'jobbing tailors': Denton, *Records of St Giles'*, 104.

p. 58 'as it was a Screen . . . unguarded Youth': quoted in Rictor Norton,

Mother Clap's Molly House: The Gay Subculture in England 1700–1830 (Stroud, 2006), 126.

p. 58 At noon on Thursday 8 February: the account of the London earthquake is from T. D. Kendrick's *The Lisbon Earthquake* (London, 1957).

p. 58 'natural explanation . . . of earthquakes': John Wesley, *The Cause and Cure of Earthquakes* (London, 1750).

p. 59 'a lunatic lifeguardsman': Horace Walpole quoted in Kendrick, *The Lisbon Earthquake*, 11.

p. 59 '730 coaches': ibid., 13.

p. 61 'with slow and gradual majesty . . . spectators': Rose Macauley, *The Minor Pleasures of Life* (London, 1936), 90.

p. 61 'the harbour of the skies': as recounted by the curator in the Strawberry Hill tour, from material in the Yale archive.

p. 61 In 1800, it was the site: as reported in *The Albion* of July 1800.

p. 62 'ye poets, ragged and forlorn': see Jonathan Swift's poem of 1726, 'Advice to the Grub Street Verse-Writers'.

p. 63 'Mercury-woman': Paula McDowell, *The Women of Grub Street: Press, Politics, and Gender in the London Literary Marketplace 1678–1730* (Oxford, 1998), 55.

p. 63 'through Seas of Scurrility . . . of a Woman': ibid., 217.

p. 65 In 1798: David R. Green, *Finsbury: Past, Present & Future* (London, 2009), 6.

p. 65 'All manner of gross': Old Bailey Proceedings Online (www.old-baileyonline.org, accessed 4 February 2012), trial of Margaret Clap (July 1726), t17260711-54.

p. 66 'typical homosexual': Norton, *Mother Clap's Molly House*, 19.

p. 67 'sly reforming hirelings': Ned Ward, *The Field Spy* (London, 1714), 16.

p. 68 'marrying room . . . blessed': Old Bailey Proceedings Online, trial of Margaret Clap.

p. 68 'I was no stranger . . . my own Body': ibid. (accessed 18 January 2012), trial of William Brown (July 1726), t17260711-77).

p. 68 'Though the earth': *The Works of John Locke: Volume 2* (London, 1727), 166.

p. 70 'Four beds . . . part of the coterie': *The Phoenix of Sodom; Or the Vere Street Coterie* (London, 1813), 12–13.

p. 71   'A vast concourse': *The Annual Register or a View of History, Literature and Politics for the Year 1811* (London, 1811), 28.

p. 71   'in an improper': *The trial of Josiah Phillips for a libel on the Duke of Cumberland and the proceedings previous thereto, in 1810* (London, 1833), 9.

p. 72   'He was a prodigy': the story of Chatterton's life is taken from Linda Kelly, *The Marvellous Boy: The Life and Myth of Thomas Chatterton* (London, 1971); Nick Groom, 'Thomas Chatterton Was a Forger', *The Yearbook of English Studies*, vol. 28 (Eighteenth Century Lexis and Lexicography, 1998), 276–91.

p. 74   'it is wonderful': James Boswell, *Life of Samuel Johnson* (London, 1833 edition), 68.

p. 74   'affords in its central enclosure': Edward Walford, 'Lincoln's Inn Fields', *Old and New London: Volume 3* (London, 1878), 44.

p. 75   'who disabled himself': Richard Steele, *Spectator*, no. 6 (7 March 1711).

p. 75   'Rich gay': Thomas Dibden, *The London Theatre* (London, 1815), 3.

p. 76   'common bricklayer . . . for fame': Timothy Hyde, 'Some Evidence of Libel, Criticism, and Publicity in the Architectural Career of Sir John Soane', *Perspecta*, vol. 37 (Famous, 2005), 144–63.

p. 76   'I presume': *Morning Post*, 30 September 1812.

p. 76   'glaring impropriety . . . modern works': quoted in David Watkin, *Sir John Soane, Enlightenment Thought and the Royal Academy Lectures* (Cambridge, 1996), 76.

p. 77   'adapted for spectacle': John Britton, *The Union of Architecture, Sculpture and Painting* (London, 1827), 44.

p. 77   'in perpetuity . . . a megalomaniac': John Summerson, 'Change, Decay and the Soane Museum', *Architectural Association Journal* (October 1949), 50.

p. 78   'talked with a vivacity': James Boswell, *Life of Samuel Johnson* (London, 1833 edition), 292.

p. 78   'the art of addressing a jury': *Edinburgh Review*, vol. 16 (1810), 109.

p. 79   'of the most determined integrity': Edward Foss, *The Grandeur of the Law: Or, the legal peers of England: with sketches of their professional career* (London, 1843), 138.

p. 79   'Old Mother Shipton': Walter Thornbury, 'Fleet Street: General

Introduction', *Old and New London: Volume 1* (London, 1878), 32–53.

p. 79 They drank heavily: Dan Cruickshank, *The Secret History of Georgian London: How the Wages of Sin Shaped the Capital* (London, 2009), 181.

p. 80 'unable to speak': *Philosophical experiments and observations of the late eminent Dr. Robert Hooke, F.R.S.* (London, 1726), 210.

p. 80 'Little White Alley': Old Bailey Proceedings Online (www.oldbaileyonline.org, accessed 18 January 2012), Ordinary of Newgate's account (November 1744), OA17441107.

p. 80 'luscious . . . and Temple': Hallie Rubenhold, *Harris's List of Covent Garden Ladies* (London, 2005), 48–9.

3: Westminster and St James's

p. 82 'why so wretched': John Gwynne, *London and Westminster, Improved* (London, 1766), 8.

p. 82 'Gentleman Schollars . . . Youth and Quality': Old Bailey Proceedings Online (www.oldbaileyonline.org, accessed 18 January 2012), Ordinary's account (August 1679), o16790827-1.

p. 84 'a stately veneer . . . and crime': Cardinal Wiseman, *An Appeal to the Reason and Good Feeling of the English People on the Subject of Catholic Hierarchy* (London, 1850), 30.

p. 85 On a Saturday in 1762: Tim Hitchcock, *Down and Out in Eighteenth-Century London* (London, 2004), 32.

p. 85 'so called from a mill': Edward Walford, 'The City of Westminster: Introduction', *Old and New London: Volume 4* (London, 1878), 1.

p. 86 'the evening is devoted': John Pinkerton, *A General Collection of the Best and Most Interesting Voyages and Travels in all Parts of the World: Volume 2* (London, 1808), 92.

p. 88 'I was ashamed': Old Bailey Proceedings Online (www.oldbaileyonline.org, accessed 18 January 2012), trial of John Loppenberg (October 1740), t17401015-66.

p. 88 In the hard winter months: Lynn MacKay, 'A Culture of Poverty? The St Martin in the Fields Workhouse, 1817', *Journal of Interdisciplinary History*, vol. 26, no. 2 (Autumn 1995), 214.

p. 89 The women made up: ibid., 221.

p. 89 St Sepulchre's installed: Hitchcock, *Down and Out*, 139.

p. 90 Martin's Mendicity Studies: ibid., 3–7.

p. 90 Quasi-charitable bodies: *The Reports of the Society for the Suppression of Mendicity, established in London, 1818* (London, 1821).

p. 91 'the ancient Horse-ferry': Thomas Pennant, *An Account of London* (London, 1790), 57.

p. 91 Around half the money: details of this story taken from Peter Cameron: 'Henry Jernegan, the Kandlers and the client who changed his mind', *The Silver Society Journal* (Autumn 1996).

p. 92 'designed and made a silver cistern': quoted in C. L'Estrange Ewen, *Lotteries and Sweepstakes: An Historical, Legal and Ethical Survey of Their Introduction, Repression and Establishment in the British Isles* (London, 1932), 142.

p. 92 'a very great ornament . . . into the river': *The Gentleman's Magazine* quoted in 'Westminster Bridge', *Survey of London, Volume 23. Lambeth: South Bank and Vauxhall* (London, 1951), 67.

p. 92 'was to prevent the suicide': Pennant, *An Account of London*, 91.

p. 93 On one visit: Giacomo Casanova, *History of My Life: Volume 9* (Baltimore, Maryland, 1997 edition), 319–23.

p. 93 'Mademoiselle Charpillon': Ian Kelly, *Casanova* (London, 2008), 266.

p. 93 'was formerly made use of': *A New View of London* (London, 1708), 68.

p. 93 'length is . . . *gothic*': Pennant, *An Account of London*, 83.

p. 94 'It is said': William John Loftie, *The Inns of Court and Chancery* (London, 1895), 123.

p. 94 Waghorn's had: see the print by Edward Pugh (1763–1813) 'The Houses of Parliament with the Royal Procession'.

p. 94 She accused fellow prisoners: Old Bailey Proceedings Online (www.oldbaileyonline.org, accessed 4 February 2012), trial of Edward Wooldridge and John Nichols (March 1720), t17200303-43.

p. 95 In the 1757 trial: ibid., trial of Daniel Lackey (April 1757), t17570420-42.

p. 95 Throughout the eighteenth century: Antony Simpson, 'Vulnerability and the age of female consent: legal innovation and its effect on prosecutions for rape in eighteenth-century London', in G. S.

Rousseau and Roy Porter (eds.), *Sexual Underworlds of the Enlightenment* (Manchester, 1987), 181–205.

p. 96 'not to be subject to': John Locke, *Two Treatises on Government* (London, 1821 edition), 206.

p. 96 'a Black . . . dare not say criminal': *The Diary and Letters of his Excellency Thomas Hutchinson (1711–1780)* (Boston, 1884), 276.

p. 97 '*Fiat justitia* . . . heavens fall': William M. Wiecek, 'Somersett: Lord Mansfield and the Legitimacy of Slavery in the Anglo-American World', *The University of Chicago Law Review*, vol. 42, no. 1 (Autumn 1974), 102.

p. 97 'ingenious Africans . . . as a Slave': Donna T. Andrew (ed.), *London Debating Societies 1776–1799* (London, 1994), 221.

p. 97 When he died: Ruth Paley, 'Imperial Politics and English Law: The Many Contexts of "Somersett"', *Law and History Review*, vol. 24, no. 3 (Fall 2006), 663.

p. 97 'the negroe cause': this phrase originated with 'Considerations on the Negroe Cause Addressed to Lord Mansfield', in 1773, by Samuel Estwick, Assistant Agent to the Island of Barbados, printed in Pall Mall.

p. 97 'unsuccessful contest at cribbage': www.brycchancarey.com/sancho/letter2.htm.

p. 98 He was a prolific letter writer: details of the letters of Ignatius Sancho are from Vincent Carretta (ed.), *Unchained Voices: An Anthology of Black Authors in the English-Speaking World of the Eighteenth Century* (Kentucky, 1996).

p. 98 'the Extraordinary Negro': Joseph Jekyll, *The Letters of the late Ignatius Sancho, an African, to which are prefixed memoirs of his life* (London, 1782), i.

p. 98 'A man can never be great': *The North Briton*, issue no. 144.

p. 102 'How is it that we hear': James Boswell, *Life of Samuel Johnson* (London, 1833 edition), 204.

p. 102 'were, and are, all mad . . . capering pig': Christopher Hibbert, *King Mob: The Story of Lord George Gordon and the Riots of 1780* (London, 1958), 1.

p. 103 'occupying every avenue': *The Life and Times of Frederick Reynolds, Written by Himself, in Two Volumes: Volume 1* (London, 1827), 124.

p. 104   'Popish birds': Hibbert, *King Mob*, 61.

p. 104   'London seemed a second Troy': William Cowper, 'Table Talk' in *Poems* (London, 1782) , l. 323.

p. 104   'Such a time of terror': quoted in Hibbert, *King Mob*, vi.

p. 105   'the effect of Accident': *London Courant*, 26 August 1780.

p. 106   'She gets out of her carriage': Cecil Faber Aspinall-Oglander and Frances E. G. Boscawen, *Admiral's Widow: Being the Life and Letters of the Hon. Mrs Edward Boscawen from 1761 to 1805* (London, 1943), letter dated 12 April 1784.

p. 106   'sitting cross-legged': John Hogg, *London As It Is: Being a series of observations on the health, habits, and amusements of the people* (London, 1837), 41.

p. 106   'Have the people': quoted in Andrew, *London Debating Societies*, 177.

p. 107   'ye dwellings of Noble men': 'St James's Square: General', *Survey of London, Volumes 29 and 30. St James Westminster, Part 1* (London, 1960), 56.

p. 107   'a man of pleasure': Arthur Irwin Dasent, *The History of St James's Square and the Foundation of the West End of London, with a Glimpse of Whitehall in the Reign of Charles the Second* (London, 1895), 4.

p. 107   'the most impertinent slut': as recorded by Samuel Pepys in his diary entry dated 14 January 1668.

p. 107   'Those who have offices': Don Manuel Gonzales, Portuguese merchant, quoted by John Pinkerton in *A General Collection of the Best and Most Interesting Voyages and Travels in all Parts of the World: Volume 2* (London, 1808), 90.

p. 108   'a dirty barrow-bunter': Tobias George Smollett, *The Expedition of Humphry Clinker* (London, 1771), 145.

p. 108   He was treated brutally: Old Bailey Proceedings Online (www.oldbaileyonline.org, accessed 27 January 2012), trial of Richard Albridge, alias Alder (December 1732), t17321206-5.

p. 109   'Is not the cohabitation': quoted in Andrew, *London Debating Societies*, 11.

p. 109   'as a remedy for': François de La Rochefoucauld, *A Frenchman in England, 1784* (Cambridge, 1933 edition), 51.

p. 110   'morbid propensity': John Cordy Jeafferson, *The Real Lord Byron* (London, 1883), 63.

p. 110   'I maintain that': Marguerite Blessington, *A Journal of Conversations with Lord Byron* (London, 1869), 345.

p. 111   'it was remarked': W. G. Constable, 'The Foundation of the National Gallery', *The Burlington Magazine for Connoisseurs*, vol. 44, no. 253 (April 1924), 158.

p. 111   'A set of greasy fellows': Revd J. Richardson, *Recollections Political, Literary, Dramatic and Miscellaneous, of the Last Half Century* (London, 1856), 31.

p. 111   'the ladies look'd like': John Ashton, *Social Life in the Reign of Queen Anne: Volume I* (London, 1882), 88.

p. 111   'took its name': Ned Ward, *The London Spy*, first published 1706 (London, 1955 edition), 179–80.

p. 112   'where the women are': Pehr Kalm, *Kalm's Account of his visit to England: on his way to America in 1748*, translated by Joseph Lucas (London, 1892), 62.

p. 112   'the public walk of London': David Piper, *The London Companion* (London, 1964), 144.

p. 112   'not articulate': *The European Magazine, and London Review* (London, 1785), 426.

p. 112   'seemed to hinder . . . frightened me': César de Saussure, *A Foreign View of England in 1725–1729: The Letters of Monsieur César de Saussure to his Family*, translated and edited by Madame Van Muyden (London, 1902), 92.

p. 112   'could not be taught': ibid., 93.

p. 113   'Peter, the Wild Man of Hanover': Thomas Wright, *The Life of Daniel Defoe* (London, 1894), 342.

p. 113   'only three crowns': John Pinkerton (ed.), *Walpoliana* (London, 1800), 7.

p. 113   'no larger than a child's chaise . . . jocose': Edward Wood, *Giantology and Dwarfiana* (London, 1868), 350–51.

p. 113   'gross and obscene . . . their blood': Old Bailey Proceedings Online (www.oldbaileyonline.org, accessed 28 January 2012), trial of Renwick Williams, late of the parish of St James, otherwise called Rhynwick (December 1790), t17901208-54.

p. 114   'the bearers [go] so fast': César de Saussure, *A Foreign View of England*, 104.

p. 115 'the breed of chairs': *The Letters of Horace Walpole, Earl of Orford, in 6 Volumes*, for 1791 (London, 1840), 418.

p. 115 'fine garden and terras': Pinkerton, *A General Collection*, 83.

p. 115 'thus the water . . . royal residence': Hogg, *London As It Is*, 178.

p. 115 'theire ware also': quoted in J. W. Willis Jr, 'European Consumption and Asian Production in the Seventeenth and Eighteenth Centuries', in John Brewer and Roy Porter (eds.), *Consumption and the World of Goods* (London, 1993), 140.

p. 116 'very convenient': James Walvin, *Fruits of Empire: Exotic Produce and British Taste, 1660–1800* (London, 1997), 10.

p. 116 'a hardened and shameless': Boswell, *Life of Samuel Johnson*, 363.

p. 116 'Were they the sons': Jonas Hanway, *Essay on Tea* (London, 1757).

p. 116 As a result, London was inundated: Walvin, *Fruits of Empire*, 26.

p. 116 'with their superiors': John Lettsom, *Natural History of the Tea Trade* (London, 1772), 62.

p. 117 'very severely markt . . . lives of her own children': Lord Wharton (ed.), *The Letters and Works of Lady Mary Wortley Montagu: Volume 1* (London, 1837), 77.

p. 118 'the White Chapple': J. G. Humble, 'Westminster Hospital: The First 250 Years', *British Medical Journal*, vol. 1, no. 5480 (January 1966), 156.

p. 119 'curled wig': ibid., 158.

p. 119 'learnt the value of': see G. R. Cameron, 'Edward Jenner, FRS 1749–1823', *Notes and Records of the Royal Society of London*, vol. 7, no. 1 (December 1949), 43–53.

p. 120 These hymns: Nicholas Temperley, 'The Lock Hospital Chapel and its Music', *Journal of the Royal Musical Association*, vol. 118, no. 1 (1993), 44.

p. 121 The matter was debated: Andrew, *London Debating Societies*, 115–6.

p. 121 'ventured out': *St James's Chronicle*, 11 September 1789.

p. 121 John Hunter had conducted: John Hunter, 'Proposals for the Recovery of People Apparently Drowned', *Philosophical Transactions of the Royal Society of London*, vol. 66, no. 1776, 412–25.

p. 122 For five years before Hunter's: Samuel Bentley, *Literary Anecdotes of the Eighteenth Century* (London, 1814), 182–3.

p. 122 'As proof': Andrew, *London Debating Societies*, 1.

p. 123 'cases of Apparent Death . . . suspended animation': see E. Perman, 'Successful Cardiac Resuscitation with Electricity in the 18th Century?', *The British Medical Journal*, vol. 2, no. 6154 (December 1978), 1770–71.

4: Bloomsbury, Covent Garden and the Strand

p. 125 By the end of the eighteenth century: Rowland Dobie, *The History of the United Parishes of St Giles in the Fields and St George's Bloomsbury* (London, 1829), 137.

p. 125 'The fields . . . desperate characters': ibid., 67.

p. 126 'literary and scientific': Richard Tames, *Bloomsbury Past* (London, 1993), 51.

p. 126 'godless college . . . abundance and perfection': Edward Walford, 'Bloomsbury', *Old and New London: Volume 4* (London, 1878), 480–89.

p. 128 'all manner of Fruites': 'Preface', *Survey Of London, Volume 36. Covent Garden* (London, 1970), vii–viii.

p. 131 'the common Residence . . . dying': quoted in Ruth K. McClure, *Coram's Children: The London Foundling Hospital in the Eighteenth Century* (London, 1981), 19.

p. 132 'the Expressions of Grief': ibid., 50.

p. 133 'four eminent painters': *Vertue Note Books, Volume III, Number 22* (London, 1933), 135.

p. 133 One scathing broadside: pamphlet entitled 'Joyful News to Batchelors and Maids: Being a Song in Praise of the Foundling Hospital and the London Hospital Aldersgate Street', circa 1760, quoted in McClure, *Coram's Children*, 109.

p. 134 The last child: McClure, *Coram's Children*, 114.

p. 134 'so inhuman': ibid., 104.

p. 134 In 1817, the story of the death: evidence taken before the Parliamentary Committee on Climbing Boys, describing the death of Thomas Pitts on 29 March 1813.

p. 135 'a most noisome': Percival Pott, quoted by H. A. Waldron, 'A Brief History of Scrotal Cancer', *British Journal of Industrial Medicine*, vol. 40, no. 4 (November 1983), 390.

p. 135   In 1767, a girl named Mary Clifford: details are taken from Old Bailey Proceedings Online (www.oldbaileyonline.org, accessed 31 January 2012), trial of James Brownrigg, Elizabeth his wife, John their son (September 1767), t17670909-1.

p. 137   'desiring to be informed': McClure, *Coram's Children*, 237.

p. 137   'The parish of St. Giles . . . cats, dogs, &c': descriptions are taken from Edward Walford, 'St. Giles-in-the-Fields', *Old and New London: Volume 3* (London, 1878), 197–218.

p. 140   There were thought to be: Peter Clark, 'The "Mother Gin" Controversy in the Early Eighteenth Century', *Transactions of the Royal Historical Society*, fifth series, vol. 38 (1988), 64.

p. 140   'Gin is sold': *The Trial of the Spirits; Or, Some Considerations upon the Pernicious Consequences of the Gin Trade to Great Britain* (London, 1736), 4.

p. 140   But the government was in a quandary: Jonathan White, 'The "Slow but Sure Poyson": The Representation of Gin and its Drinkers, 1736–1751', *Journal of British Studies*, vol. 42, no. 1 (January 2003), 38.

p. 140   Women were also more prominent: Clark, 'The "Mother Gin" Controversy', 70.

p. 141   'huge sufferings': James Dawson Burn, *Autobiography of a Beggar Boy* (London, 1856), 21.

p. 142   'with three quarts . . . Dirt and all': *Survey of London, 36*, vii–viii.

p. 142   'an easy, and fine-bred gentleman': quoted in T. H. Vail Motter, 'Garrick and the Private Theatres: With a List of Amateur Performances in the Eighteenth Century', *English Literary History*, vol. 11, no. 1 (March 1944), 63–75.

p. 143   'A pause ensued . . . as usual': John Williams, *The Pin-basket to the Children of Thespis* (London, 1797), 41.

p. 143   'Whatever may be': Arthur Murphy, *The Life of David Garrick* (London, 1801), 360.

p. 144   'she was regarded less with admiration': writing in *The Examiner*, 16 June 1816.

p. 144   'remarkably fine . . . a fine girl': Linda Buchanan, 'Sarah Siddons and Her Place in Rhetorical History', *Rhetorica: A Journal of the History of Rhetoric*, vol. 25, no. 4 (Autumn 2007), 431.

p. 145 'Whether the love of fame . . . affirmative': Donna T. Andrew (ed.), *London Debating Societies 1776–1799* (London, 1994), 22.

p. 146 'we sacrifice . . . Apprehending of Robbers': quoted in J. M. Beattie, 'Sir John Fielding and Public Justice: The Bow Street Magistrates' Court, 1754–1780', *Law and History Review*, vol. 25, no. 1 (Spring 2007), 63.

p. 146 'whether brought there': ibid., 74.

p. 147 'of tried courage . . . injustice': ibid., 75.

p. 147 'accost the passengers . . . in the open street': Johann Wilhelm von Archenholz, *A picture of England: Containing a description of the laws, customs, and manners of England* (London, 1789), 193.

p. 147 They were predominantly: Tony Henderson, *Disorderly Women in Eighteenth-Century London: Prostitution and Control in the Metropolis, 1730–1830* (London, 1999), 36–44.

p. 147 'such is the corruption': von Archenholz, *A picture of England*, 193.

p. 148 'strangers to wedded love': quoted in Elizabeth Campbell Denlinger, 'The Garment and the Man: Masculine Desire in "Harris's List of Covent-Garden Ladies", 1764–1793', *Journal of the History of Sexuality*, vol. 11, no. 3 (July 2002), 357–94.

p. 148 'the civil nymph': James Boswell, *London Journal 1762–1763* (London, 1950 edition), 332.

p. 148 'She was ugly . . . gross practice': ibid., 231.

p. 148 'a monstrous big whore': ibid., 240.

p. 149 'The Pimp-General': Hallie Rubenhold, *Harris's List of Covent Garden Ladies* (London, 2005), 15.

p. 149 'an absolute curiosity . . . the back way': ibid., 136–55.

p. 149 'is, indeed, turned of forty': Hallie Rubenhold, *The Covent Garden Ladies: Pimp General Jack & The Extraordinary Story of Harris's List* (London, 2005), 144.

p. 150 'shocking usage . . . shocking manner': *The Gentleman's Magazine*, October 1760.

p. 151 'whereof she did languish': Old Bailey Proceedings Online (www.oldbaileyonline.org, accessed 4 February 2012), trial of Willy Sutton (February 1761), t17610225-18.

p. 151 'soon fell in with a fleet': quoted in Annette Hope, *Londoner's Larder: English Cuisine from Chaucer to the Present* (London, 2005), 120.

p. 152 'besiege(d) with five or six heaps': ibid., 189.

p. 152 'not fill my guts': Ned Ward, *The London Spy*, first published 1706 (London, 1955 edition), 32.

p. 152 'fine inns': François de La Rochefoucauld, *A Frenchman in England, 1784* (Cambridge, 1933 edition), 20.

p. 154 'mostly under the care of': diary excerpt from *The Antiquaries Journal* (1958), 334.

p. 155 'such a size': John Taylor, *The life, death and dissection of the largest elephant ever known in this country and was destroy'd a few days since at Exeter 'Change* (London, 1826), 5.

p. 156 'through the whole flooring': Francis T. Buckland, *Curiosities of Natural History, Volume 1* (London, 1857), 119.

p. 156 'folded his forelegs under him': ibid., 120.

p. 157 'a multitude of obscene prints': Mary Thale (ed.), *The Autobiography of Francis Place, 1771–1854* (Cambridge, 1972), 51.

p. 157 'infested with vermin . . . lap of the mother': ibid., 52.

p. 158 *Lucina* featured: Julie Peakman, *Mighty Lewd Books: The Development of Pornography in Eighteenth-Century England* (Basingstoke, 2003), 23.

5: Soho and Charing Cross

p. 159 'south of Holborn': an abbreviation first recorded in 1641 as So:ho, according to 'General Introduction', *Survey of London, Volumes 33 & 34. St Anne's, Soho* (London, 1966), 1.

p. 160 'is not exactly in anybody's way': Charles Dickens, *Nicholas Nickleby*, first published 1839 (Ware, 1995 edition), 14.

p. 160 'There were few buildings': Charles Dickens, *A Tale of Two Cities*, first published 1859 (Cambridge, 2008 edition), 80.

p. 160 'fitted for business . . . experimental philosophy': 'Soho Square Area: Portland Estate – Nos. 8 and 9 Soho Square: The French Protestant Church', *Survey of London, 33 & 34*, 62.

p. 161 'he is quite my companion': E. Beresford Chancellor, *The Romance of Soho: Being an Account of the District, its Past Distinguished Inhabitants, its Historic Houses, and its Place in the Social Annals of London* (London, 1931), 62.

p. 161 The theme of scientific learning: Thomas Martin, 'Origins of the

Royal Institution', *The British Journal for the History of Science*, vol. 1, no. 1 (June 1962), 49.

p. 161 'that the most extensive': 'Soho Square Area: Portland Estate – Carlisle House: Soho Square', *Survey of London, 33 & 34*, 73–9.

p. 161 'On Saturday last': Chancellor, *The Romance of Soho*, 70.

p. 162 'I concluded she would open': *The Letters of Horace Walpole, Earl of Orford, in 6 Volumes*, for 1771 (London, 1840), 13.

p. 163 'some great Jock': Rictor Norton, 'William Beckford: The Fool of Fonthill', *Gay History and Literature*, 16 November 1999 (www.rictornorton.co.uk/beckfor1.htm).

p. 163 'a desert of magnificence': William Hazlitt, *Sketches of the Principal Picture Galleries of England* (London, 1824), 284.

p. 164 Thomas De Quincey fled his school: all quotes from De Quincey's life are taken from his autobiography *Confessions of an English Opium Eater* (London, 1822).

p. 166 'the Large House . . . SHIPWRECK': *Public Advertiser*, 12 April 1781.

p. 168 'Many parts of this parish': William Maitland, *The History of London from the Romans to the Present Time* (1739), quoted in Henry Benjamin Wheatley and Peter Cunningham, *London Past and Present: Its History, Associations and Traditions*, first published 1891 (Cambridge, 2011 edition), 50.

p. 170 Paul de Lamerie: details of his life are taken from P. A. S. Phillips, *Paul de Lamerie* (London, 1935).

p. 173 Here, treatises on fireworks: Old Bailey Proceedings Online (www.oldbaileyonline.org, accessed 5 February 2012), trial of Robert Jones (July 1772), t17720715-22.

p. 174 'All Englishmen . . . the latest news': César de Saussure, *A Foreign View of England in 1725–1729: The Letters of Monsieur César de Saussure to his Family*, translated and edited by Madame Van Muyden (London, 1902), 64.

p. 174 'a mass of cork': Ronald Paulson, *Hogarth: His Life and Times, Volume I* (London, 1971), 340.

p. 175 'Gentlemen may have': *British Medical Journal*, vol. 1, no. 1799 (June 1895), 1388.

p. 176 'an attitude . . . a mold from him': John Hunter, quoted in Martin

Postle, 'Flayed for Art: The Écorché Figure in the English Art Academy', *British Art Journal*, vol. V, no. 1 (2004), 57.

p. 176 'He who endeavours': Joshua Reynolds, *Seven Discourses on Art* (London, 1769), Discourse 1.

p. 177 'fell into the position': Martin Kemp and Marina Wallace, *Spectacular Bodies: The Art and Science of the Human Body from Leonardo to Now* (Berkeley, California, 2001), 87.

p. 177 'These kind of figures': quoted in Postle, 'Flayed for Art', 60.

p. 177 'a black, a native': Alexander Penrose, *Benjamin Robert Haydon 1786–1846* (London, 1927), 93.

p. 178 Thomas Lawrence was particularly impressed: Wilson's story is taken from Clarke Olney, *Benjamin Robert Haydon, Historical Painter* (Athens, Georgia, 1952).

p. 179 'full tide of human existence': James Boswell, *Life of Samuel Johnson*, recorded for 1775 (London, 1833 edition), 266.

p. 179 'a young woman': 'Trafalgar Square and neighbourhood', *Survey of London, Volume 20. St Martin-in-the-Fields, Part III* (London, 1940), 7–14.

p. 180 'genteelly bred . . . another *erratum*': *Memoirs of the Life and Writing of Benjamin Franklin, written by Himself* (Philadelphia, Pennsylvania, 1818), 45.

p. 181 'were 13 houses': Mary Thale (ed.), *Autobiography of Francis Place, 1771–1854* (Cambridge, 1972), 227.

p. 181 'covered with ballads': ibid., 229.

p. 181 'crazy, tumbledown old house': John Forster, *The Life of Charles Dickens: Volume I* (New York, 1966), 21–2.

p. 182 'mean street': *Johnsoniana; Or, Supplement to Boswell* (London, 1842), 53.

p. 182 'Immediately in front of the Horse Guards': Thale, *Autobiography of Francis Place,* 229.

p. 182 'cross the eastern entrance': *Reports from Committees* (London, 1828), 74.

6: Mayfair

p. 184 Mayfair takes its name: Ben Weinreb, Christopher Hibbert, Julia

Keay and John Keay, *The London Encyclopedia*, third edition (London, 2008).

p. 186 'All the Way through': Daniel Defoe, writing in *Applebee's Weekly Journal*, 17 July 1725.

p. 186 'Man of Taste': the title of William Hogarth's engraving satirizing Lord Burlington and his friends.

p. 188 'one of those edifices': *The Works of Horatio Walpole, Earl of Orford, Volume III* (London, 1798), 487.

p. 188 'half the land': Alexander Pope, 'Summary', *Epistle IV: An Epistle to the Right Honourable Richard Earl of Burlington* (London, 1731), v. 65.

p. 188 'heiress of a scrivener': 'The Acquisition of the Estate', *Survey of London, Volume 39. The Grosvenor Estate in Mayfair, Part I* (London, 1977), 1.

p. 189 What took place there: details of The Tragedy are taken from Charles Gatty, *Mary Davies and the Manor of Ebury* (London, 1921), 54–81.

p. 189 'a wretched attempt': James Ralph, *A Critical Review of the Publick Buildings, Statues and Ornaments of London and Westminster* (London, 1763), 108.

p. 189 The nine-year-old Mozart: Emily Anderson (ed.), *The Letters of Mozart and his Family* (London, 1966), 50–51.

p. 190 At the same time: 'The Social Character of the Estate: A Survey of Householders in *c*.1790', *Survey of London, 39*, 83–6.

p. 190 By the last decade: ibid., 86–9.

p. 190 The magnates: see J. V. Beckett, *The Aristocracy in England, 1660–1924* (London, 1986).

p. 191 'most profligate . . . turf': quoted in 'Grosvenor, Richard, first Earl Grosvenor (1731–1802)', *Oxford Dictionary of National Biography* (Oxford, 2004).

p. 192 'I have wished myself': quoted in 'Stanhope, Philip Dormer, fourth Earl of Chesterfield (1694–1773)', *ODNB*.

p. 192 'Who they are': Philip Dormer Stanhope, *Letters: Volume 1* (London, 1847) Letter LXX, London, May the 15th, O. S. 1749.

p. 192 'Mr. Tollot says': ibid., Letter CXL, London, May the 2nd, O. S. 1751.

p. 193 'I feel a gradual decay': Philip Dormer Stanhope, *Letters: Volume 4* (London, 1847), Letter CCCLXXXVII, London, April 22, 1765.

p. 193 'lively descriptions': Charles Knight, 'Strawberry Hill: Walpole's London', *London: Volume 3* (London, 1851), 159.

p. 195 He began to turn: noted in 'Clive, Robert, first Baron Clive of Plassey (1725–1774)', *ODNB*.

p. 195 'Who is the writer?': Edward Walford, 'Berkeley Square and its neighbourhood', *Old and New London: Volume 4* (London, 1878), 326–38.

p. 196 'Mr Chairman': Percival Spear, *Master of Bengal: Clive of India* (London, 1974), 189.

p. 197 'Primus in India': the inscription on Robert Clive's monument in the Church of St Margaret at Moreton Say.

p. 198 'an excellent carver': *The Somerset House Gazette* (London, 1824), vol. i, 38.

p. 198 'a box with colours': Helena Hayward and Pat Kirkham, *William and John Linnell, Eighteenth-Century London Furniture Makers* (London, 1980), 52.

p. 198 'the central point . . . idiots in my house': quoted in 'Montagu, Elizabeth (Robinson) (1720–1800)', *ODNB*.

p. 200 'infested with': 'Berkeley Square and its neighbourhood', *Old and New London: 4*, 326–38.

p. 200 'they swarmed': William Makepeace Thackeray, *The Virginians* (London, 1859), 296.

p. 201 'If you take a meal': César de Saussure, *A Foreign View of England in 1725–1729: The Letters of Monsieur César de Saussure to his Family*, translated and edited by Madame Van Muyden (London, 1902), 194.

p. 201 'He was a genteel': details of John Parry's life are taken from Old Bailey Proceedings Online (www.oldbaileyonline.org, accessed 5 February 2012), Ordinary of Newgate's account (June 1754), OA17540605.

p. 203 'passing out of the world': Thackeray, *The Virginians*, 296.

p. 203 'You will do . . . very well for me': Robert Chambers, *Book of Days* (London, 1869), entry for 12 January.

p. 203 'Such abundance of choice': Claire Williams, *Sophie in London, 1786* (London, 1933), 87.

p. 204 'silk-bag shop . . . without a groan': 'Piccadilly: Northern tributaries', *Old and New London: 4*, 291–314.

p. 205 'six feet two': Nikolai Tolstoy, *The Half-mad Lord: Thomas Pitt, 2nd Baron Camelford (1775–1804)* (London, 1978), 90.

p. 205 'over the fire ... crest-fallen': quoted in 'Pitt, Thomas, second Baron Camelford (1775–1804)', *ODNB*.

p. 206 'equally replete': Donna T. Andrew (ed.), *London Debating Societies 1776–1799* (London, 1994), 218.

p. 207 'his gaiety': Ian Kelly, *Beau Brummell, The Ultimate Dandy* (London, 2005), 98.

p. 208 'principally assumed ... Poodle': William Jesse, *The Life of George Brummell, Esq., Commonly Called Beau Brummell: Volume I* (London, 1844), 117.

p. 208 'five o'clock on a fine summer's morning': Thomas Raikes, quoted in 'Berkeley Square and its neighbourhood', *Old and New London: 4*, 326–38.

p. 209 'Parliament of Monsters': William Wordsworth, *The Prelude* (London, 1850), Book 7, l. 714.

p. 209 'One gentleman poked': Mrs Matthews, *Memoirs of Charles Matthews, Comedian: Volume 4* (London 1839), 133.

p. 211 'apparently smiling on me': Giovanni Belzoni, *Narrative of the Operations and Recent Discoveries within the Pyramids, Temples, Tombs and Excavations in Egypt and Nubia* (London, 1822), 39.

7: Marylebone

p. 213 'live decently': Johann Wilhelm von Archenholz, quoted by Gordon Mackenzie in *Marylebone: Great City North of Oxford Street* (London, 1972), 94.

p. 215 'the next Entertainment': Bernard Mandeville, 'Of Execution Day, the Journey to Tyburn, and a Word in Behalf of Anatomical Dissections', *An Enquiry into the Causes of the Frequent Executions at Tyburn* (London, 1725), Chapter 3.

p. 215 In 1718, John Price: details of Price's life and death are taken from Old Bailey Proceedings Online (www.oldbaileyonline.org, accessed 6 February 2012), trial of John Price, the quondam Hangman (April 1718), t17180423-24.

p. 216 In 1763, James Boswell watched: details of Paul Lewis's hanging are taken from Old Bailey Proceedings Online, Ordinary of Newgate's account (May 1763), OA17630504, and James Boswell, *London Journal 1762–1763* (London, 1952 edition), 245.

p. 217 'incessant Assiduity': C. E. Wright, 'Portrait of a Bibliophile VIII, Edward Harley, 2nd Earl of Oxford, 1689–1741', *The Book Collector*, vol. 2 (1962), 170.

p. 217 'in very great measure': A. S. Turberville, *A History of Welbeck Abbey and its Owners* (London, 1938), 384.

p. 217 They lodged at: Mackenzie, *Marylebone*, 180.

p. 218 'Saxonic element': Robert DeMaria, *The Life of Samuel Johnson: A Critical Biography* (Oxford, 1993), 114.

p. 218 'the handsomest man': *Extracts from the diary of Thomas Hearne* (London, 1869), entry dated 19 July 1734.

p. 218 'many scarce and valuable': William Curtis, *A Catalogue of the British Medicinal, Culinary, and Agricultural Plants Cultivated in the London Botanic Garden* (London, 1783), ii.

p. 218 'the finest piece': Milo Keynes, 'The Portland Vase: Sir William Hamilton, Josiah Wedgwood and the Darwins', *Notes and Records of the Royal Society of London*, vol. 52, no. 2 (July 1998), 237.

p. 219 'I wish you may soon come': letter dated 5 February 1784, ibid., 239.

p. 219 'a simple woman': *The Letters of Horace Walpole, Earl of Orford, in 6 Volumes*, for 1785 (London, 1840), 6.

p. 221 'we knick-knack men': Susan Jenkins, *Portrait of a Patron: The Patronage and Collecting of James Brydges, 1st Duke of Chandos (1674–1744)* (Aldershot, 2007), 128.

p. 221 'was once standing . . . purposely for him': John Thomas Smith, *Nollekens and his Times: Volume I* (London, 1829), 107–8.

p. 222 Billy grew up in the house: the details of Billy's life are taken from Henry Mayhew, *London Labour and the London Poor: Volume II* (London, 1851), 467–9.

p. 224 'the Dunghill': Henry Whistler quoted in Trevor Burnard, 'European Migration to Jamaica, 1655–1780', *The William and Mary Quarterly*, ser. 3, vol. 53, no. 4 (October 1996), 786.

p. 224 The average white: ibid., 779.

p. 225 'flamboyant eccentric': Lesley Lewis, 'Elizabeth, Countess of

Home, and Her House in Portman Square', *The Burlington Magazine*, vol. 109, no. 773 (August 1967), 450.

p. 225 'known among all': William Beckford quoted in Leo Hollis, *The Stones of London: A History in Twelve Buildings* (London, 2010), 163.

p. 226 'Are there any grounds': Donna T. Andrew (ed.), *London Debating Societies 1776–1799* (London, 1994), 154.

p. 226 'Ought not the Word Obey': ibid., 291.

p. 226 'She diffuses': quoted in David Brandon and Alan Brooke, *Marylebone and Tyburn Past* (London, 2007), 33.

p. 226 'brilliant in diamonds': quoted in Hollis, *The Stones of London*, 179.

p. 229 'the woman clothed': *Leeds Mercury*, 22 October 1803.

p. 230 Yet many hundreds: Jan Bondeson, *The Pig-Faced Lady of Manchester Square & Other Medical Marvels* (Stroud, 2006), 163.

p. 230 'Do Ladies . . . affirmative': Andrew, *London Debating Societies*, 178.

p. 230 By the late eighteenth century: Anne Laurence (ed.), *Women and Their Money, 1700–1950: Essays on Women and Finance* (Oxford, 2008), 14.

p. 231 John Elwes: the details of his life are taken from *The Lives and Portraits of Curious and Odd Characters* (London, 1852), 52–63.

p. 232 'the finest street': quoted in Hollis, *The Stones of London*, 27.

p. 234 'the Best Drawings': Roy Porter and Aileen Ribeiro, *Richard and Maria Cosway: Regency Artists of Taste and Fashion* (Edinburgh, 1995), 20.

p. 234 'Cosway, though a well-made little man': Smith, *Nollekens and his Times*, 325.

p. 235 'the last time I called': Porter and Ribeiro, *Richard and Maria Cosway*, 30.

p. 235 'at the Elder Christie's Picture-Sales': Allan Cunningham, *The lives of the most eminent British painters, sculptors and architects* (London, 1833), 4.

p. 235 'kept [a Florence hotel]': *A Brief Account of the Roads of Italy* (London, 1775), 23.

p. 236 'kept a house in style': 'Recollections of Richard Cosway' in *Library of the Fine Arts or Repertory of Painting, Sculpture, Architecture and Engraving, Volume 4* (London, 1832), 186.

p. 236 'they were not fashionable': William Hazlitt, *The Plain Speaker: Opinion on Books, Men and Things* (London, 1870), 131.

p. 236 He was part of: See Vincent Carretta (ed.), *Unchained Voices: An Anthology of Black Authors in the English-Speaking World of the Eighteenth Century* (Kentucky, 1996).

p. 236 Richard Cosway died suddenly: Smith, *Nollekens and his Times*, 325.

p. 239 Dr Fountain was a friend of Handel: this anecdote and the descriptions of Marylebone Gardens on the following pages are taken from the definitive account by Mollie Sands, *The Eighteenth-Century Pleasure Gardens of Marylebone, 1737–1777* (London, 1987).

p. 241 'the turbulent': Robert Bell, *Description of the Conditions and Manners of the Peasantry of Ireland* (London, 1804), 27.

p. 242 'The extensive waste': Charles Knight, *Passages from a Working Life* (London, 1873), 119.

p. 242 'had then an evil reputation': ibid.

8: The River Thames

p. 243 'took Water . . . Symphonies': *Daily Courant*, 19 July 1717.

p. 243 'In fact, the whole river': Thomas Pennant, *An Account of London* (London, 1790), 281.

p. 244 In Rotherhithe: ibid., 56.

p. 246 'the best mode . . . Maritime Labourers': Patrick Colquhoun, *A Treatise on the Commerce and Police of the River Thames* (London, 1797).

p. 247 Industrial mills: Roy Porter, *London: A Social History* (London, 1994), 196.

p. 247 'They were hospitable': Henry Mayhew, *London Labour and the London Poor: a cyclopaedia of the condition and earnings of those that will work, those that cannot work, and those that will not work: Volume III* (London, 1851), 328.

p. 248 'The pleasantest way': Don Manuel Gonzales, Portuguese merchant, quoted by John Pinkerton in *A General Collection of the Best and Most Interesting Voyages and Travels in all Parts of the World: Volume 2* (London, 1808), 85.

p. 248 'piteously . . . Monsoon Dock': quoted in M. Dorothy George, *London Life in the XVIIIth Century* (London, 1930), 66.

p. 248 'On the river': Ned Ward, *The London Spy*, first published 1706 (London, 1955 edition), 177.

p. 248 'broil'd . . . onions': ibid., 33.

p. 249 'This being the day': A. G. Linney, *Peepshow of the Port of London* (London, 1929), 93.

p. 251 'the Waters': *Philosophical Transactions of the Royal Society 1683–1775*, vol. 26 (1708–9), 454–78.

p. 252 'I remember well': Gordon Home, *Old London Bridge* (London, 1931), 254.

p. 253 'all sorts of Hair . . . Diamonds': ibid., 317.

p. 253 'bridge of wonders': James Howell, *Londonopolis* (London, 1657).

p. 254 Of the 27 people: Home, *Old London Bridge*, 277.

p. 254 'My folly in undertaking . . . and drowned': ibid., 264.

p. 255 'One day Rennie's bridge': G. B. Besant, *London Bridge* (London, 1927), 10.

p. 255 'that nautical hamlet': see Walter Thornbury, 'The Thames Tunnel, Ratcliff Highway and Wapping', *Old and New London: Volume 2* (London, 1878), 128–37.

p. 256 'in use as often': Pennant, *An Account of London*, 282.

p. 256 'Fishermen off Poplar': Linney, *Peepshow*, 80.

p. 256 'being in a ship': James Boswell, *Journal of a Tour of the Hebrides* (London, 1807 edition), 126.

p. 256 'persons who had not any': Richard Thornton, *History of London* (London, 1785), 142.

p. 256 'pestered with women': Admiral John Mennes to Pepys, 19 April 1666, quoted in Suzanne J. Stark, *Female Tars: Women Aboard Ship in the Age of Sail* (London, 1998), 5.

p. 257 'I consider it right': quoted in Stark, *Female Tars*, 20.

p. 257 'in sight and hearing': ibid., 43.

p. 257 'Of all the human race': quoted in Gregory Fremont-Barnes, *Nelson's Sailors* (Oxford, 2005), 48.

p. 257 'between the houses': Pennant, *An Account of London*, 427.

p. 257 'best remembered atrocities': John Timbs, *Romance of London: Strange Stories, Scenes and Remarkable Persons of the Great Town, Volume 2* (London, 1865), 81.

p. 258 'A long narrow street': Pennant, *An Account of London*, 281.

p. 261 'spontaneous gangrene': *Morning Chronicle*, 23 January 1832.

9: Southwark and Lambeth

p. 264 'hideous . . . boat-houses': Edward Walford, 'Lambeth: Waterloo Road', *Old and New London: Volume 6* (London, 1878), 407.

p. 264 'or, as it is called': Thomas Pennant, *An Account of London* (London, 1790), 55.

p. 266 'What folly': quoted in ibid., 56.

p. 266 'savage . . . designing to be present': as reported in *The Loyal Protestant and True Domestick Intelligence*, 7 April 1682.

p. 267 'once more set upon': report collected in *The Gentleman's Magazine*, vol. 86, part I (1816), 207.

p. 267 'a match to be fought': Walter Thornbury, 'Hockley-in-the-Hole', *Old and New London: Volume 2* (London, 1878), 308.

p. 268 'barbarous treatment': William Hogarth, 'Remarks on Various Prints', *Anecdotes of William Hogarth, Written by Himself* (London, 1833), 64.

p. 268 'a fine horse': report collected in *The Gentleman's Magazine*, 86 (I), 207.

p. 268 'the great resort': Thomas Dobson, 'London', *Encyclopedia: Volume X* (Philadelphia, 1798), 263.

p. 269 'balsamic . . . ferment in nature': James Stevens Curl, 'Spas and Pleasure Gardens of London, from the Seventeenth to the Nineteenth Centuries', *Garden History*, vol. 7, no. 2 (Summer 1979), 60.

p. 269 'with Bowling greens . . . fireworks': 'Waterloo Road', *Survey of London, Volume 23. Lambeth: South Bank and Vauxhall* (London, 1951), 25–31.

p. 269 'which had for that purpose': Pennant, *An Account of London*, 32–3.

p. 270 'that substantial': 'Vauxhall Gardens and Kennington Lane', *Survey of London, 23*, 146–7.

p. 270 'Pinery . . . free of Insects': as advertised in the *St James's Chronicle*, 9 September 1775.

p. 271 'splendidly illuminated': from an entry in the *Edinburgh Encyclopedia* of 1830.

p. 274 'this right little': Charles Dickens, *Little Dorrit*, first published 1857 (Ware, 1996 edition) 59.

p. 274 'twenty wards . . . interment': 'Southwark: Old St Thomas's and Guy's Hospitals', *Old and New London: 2*, 89–100.

p. 274 'the patient drink': John Hogg, *London As It Is: Being a series of observations on the health, habits and amusements of the people* (London, 1837), 348.

p. 276 'admitted and discharged': Pennant, *An Account of London*, 52.

p. 276 Thomas Guy was . . . on clothes: see 'Southwark: Old St Thomas's and Guy's Hospitals', *Old and New London: 2*, 89–100.

p. 276 'At the age of . . . and *Mammon*': Pennant, *An Account of London*, 52.

p. 276 '*Resurgam Hommo*': bodysnatcher Joseph Naples' description of himself in his diary.

p. 277 'Great respect': James Blake Bailey, *The Diary of a Resurrectionist 1811–1812, To Which are Added an Account of the Resurrection Men in London and a Short History of the Passing of the Anatomy Act* (London, 1896), 14.

p. 277 Italy's medical students: see Julia Bess Frank, 'Body Snatching: A Grave Medical Problem', *Yale Journal of Biology and Medicine*, vol. 49, no. 4 (September 1976), 399–410.

p. 277 From around 1690: Ruth Richardson, *Death, Dissection and the Destitute* (London, 1987), 39.

p. 277 'it is thereby become necessary': Julia Bess Frank, 'Body Snatching', 400.

p. 278 In 1793, there were 200: ibid.

p. 279 Children under three feet: James Blake Bailey, *The Diary of a Resurrectionist*, 71.

p. 279 'three men . . . into soap': George Smeeton, *Doings in London* (London, 1800), 107.

p. 280 'great timber-yards . . . grains': Pennant, *An Account of London*, 33.

p. 281 The first engine could grind . . . flour and grain: see A. W. Skempton, 'Samuel Wyatt and the Albion Mill', *Architectural History*, vol. 14 (1971), 53–73.

10: Spitalfields, Whitechapel and Stepney

p. 285 'The Lanes were deep': Daniel Defoe, *A Tour Through the Whole Island of Great Britain: Volume II*, first published 1724–6 (London, 1971 edition), 298.

p. 285 Their output: see 'Industries: Brewing' in *A History of the County of Middlesex: Volume 2* (London, 1911), 169.

p. 288 Suzanne de Champagné: the account of her family's escape from France is taken from Carolyn Lougee Chappell, '"The Pains I Took to Save My/His Family": Escape Accounts by a Huguenot Mother and Daughter after the Revocation of the Edict of Nantes', *French Historical Studies*, vol. 22, no. 1 (Winter 1999), 1–64.

p. 289 'This scandalizes': Robin Gwynn (ed.), *Minutes of the Consistory of the French Church of London, Threadneedle Street, 1679–1692* (London, 1994), 146.

p. 289 'members of the congregation . . . refugees': ibid., 134.

p. 290 'They are employed Younger': Robert Campbell, *The London Tradesman* (London, 1747), 258.

p. 290 'undermining': Gwynn, *Minutes of the Consistory*, 332.

p. 291 'if her husband': see Daniel Defoe, *The Complete English Tradesman* (London, 1726), Chapter XXI.

p. 292 'traversed the streets': J. H. Clapham, 'The Spitalfields Acts, 1773–1824', *The Economic Journal*, vol. 26, no. 104 (December 1916), 460.

p. 293 'They had driven away . . . fancy works': ibid., 463.

p. 294 'The Society met': 'Spitalfields Market Area', *Survey of London, Volume 27. Spitalfields and Mile End New Town* (London, 1957), 135.

p. 294 'it may appear strange . . . at the loom': quoted in Clapham, 'The Spitalfields Acts', 465.

p. 295 'stopped, and looking very gravely': as reported in *The Literary Gazette* (London, 1835), 322.

p. 296 After 1715, the Rector: Walter Thornbury, 'Whitechapel', *Old and New London: Volume 2* (London, 1878), 142.

p. 297 'diverse Lands': 'Mile End New Town', *Survey of London, 27*, 270.

p. 297 '25 Fountains of Lamps': Old Bailey Proceedings Online (www.oldbaileyonline.org, accessed 7 February 2012), trial of James Withy (February 1718), t17180227-11.

11: Hackney and Bethnal Green

p. 299 'Protestant nonconformity': 'Stoke Newington: Growth', *A History of the County of Middlesex, Volume 8: Islington and Stoke Newington parishes* (London, 1985), 143–51.

p. 300 'a shilling for washing': Stephen Burley, *Hackney New College 1786–1796* (London, 2011), 62.

p. 301 'heaps of filth': 'Bethnal Green: Communications', *A History of the County of Middlesex, Volume 11: Stepney, Bethnal Green* (London, 1998), 88–90.

p. 303 In 1751, Bethnal Green village: 'Bethnal Green: Settlement and Building to 1836': ibid., 91–5.

p. 303 From 1800, the construction: 'Bethnal Green: The East: Old Ford Lane, Green Street, and Globe Town', ibid., 117–19.

p. 304 Quaker Francis Trumble: the account of his crime is taken from Old Bailey Proceedings Online (www.oldbaileyonline.org, accessed 7 February 2012), trial of Francis Trumble (July 1739), t17390718-10.

p. 305 'beating & abusing . . . wife's desire': Ruth Paley (ed.), *Justice in Eighteenth-Century Hackney: The Justicing Notebook of Henry Norris and the Hackney Petty Sessions Book* (London, 1991), 2.

p. 307 'though he always appeared': 'Merceron, Joseph (*c.*1764–1839)', *Oxford Dictionary of National Biography* (Oxford, 2004).

p. 309 'disgusting objects': for quotes from the Select Committee reports, see Elaine Murphy, 'A Mad House Transformed: The Lives and Work of Charles James Beverly FRS (1788–1868) and John Warburton MD FRS (1795–1847)', *Notes and Records of the Royal Society of London*, vol. 58, no. 3 (September 2004), 267–81.

p. 310 Carlo earned his living: for details of Carlo's life, see Sarah Wise, *The Italian Boy: Murder and Grave-Robbery in 1830s London* (London, 2004).

p. 311 'two men, named Bishop and May': James Blake Bailey, *The Diary of a Resurrectionist 1811–1812, To Which are Added an Account of the Resurrection Men in London and a Short History of the Passing of the Anatomy Act* (London, 1896), 107.

p. 311 'that they had enticed the boy . . . for twelve shillings': ibid., 109.

12: Islington, Hampstead and Highgate

p. 313 'distempers to which females': quoted by Stephen Remington in 'Three Centuries of Sadler's Wells', *Journal of the Royal Society of the Arts* (July 1982), vol. 130, 473.

p. 314 'swimming and affecting': Michael Hays and Anastasia Nikolopoulou (eds.), *Melodrama: The Cultural Emergence of a Genre* (London, 1998), 171.

p. 315 'every village': *The Letters of Horace Walpole, Earl of Orford, in 6 Volumes*, for 1791 (London, 1840), 324.

p. 315 The walls were made: Pehr Kalm, *Kalm's Account of his Visit to England: On his Way to America in 1748*, translated by Joseph Lucas (London, 1892), 73.

p. 315 'morning and evening . . . at two o'clock': Edward Walford, 'Camden Town and Kentish Town', *Old and New London: Volume 5* (London, 1878), 309–24.

p. 315 'charming old red-brick': Geraldine Edith Mitton, *Hampstead and Marylebone: The Fascination of London* (London, 1902), 15.

p. 315 'Hampstead indeed . . . race of mountaineers': Daniel Defoe, *A Tour Through the Whole Island of Great Britain: Volume II*, first published 1724–6 (London, 1971 edition), 168.

p. 316 'a miserable invalid': Mitton, *Hampstead and Marylebone*, 10.

p. 317 'without any consideration': William Howitt, *The Northern Heights of London* (London, 1862), 127.

p. 317 'oxyde of iron': Samuel Lewis, 'Hampstead – Hampton-Wick', *A Topographical Dictionary of England* (London, 1848), 394.

p. 317 'spa town': see 'Hampstead: Settlement and Growth', *A History of the County of Middlesex, Volume 9: Hampstead, Paddington* (London, 1989), 8–15.

p. 317 By the time he was living in Hampstead: ibid., 3–8.

p. 318 'It is not known': Edward Walford, *Chapters from the Family Chests* (London, 1887), entry for 'Harriet Mellon'.

p. 320 'bury their dead': 'Highgate – Part 2 of 2', *Old and New London: 5*, 405. See also www.highgate-cemetery.org/index.php/faqs.

p. 320 'always at Loggerheads': Maurice Buxton Forman, *The Letters of John Keats* (Oxford, 1947), 41.

p. 321 'drowsed with the fume': John Keats, poem 'To Autumn' (London, 1819), l. 17.

p. 321 'ever be a weaver's boy': Forman, *The Letters of John Keats*, 360.

p. 321 'Cockney . . . blackguard': in a letter to his publisher, John Murray, dated 18 November 1820.

p. 321 'That drop of blood . . . unfortunate': William Michael Rosetti, *Life of John Keats* (London, 1887), 42.

p. 322 'the fairy lamplighter': Sidney Colvin, *Keats* (London, 1887), 205.

p. 322 'Now you must be firm': Joseph Severn, quoted in W. Jackson Bate, *John Keats* (Cambridge, Massachusetts, 1963), 695.

p. 322 'I am broken': Sue Brown, *Joseph Severn, A Life: The Rewards of Friendship* (Oxford, 2009), 111.

p. 323 'the kindest act': Forman, *The Letters of John Keats*, lxiii.

p. 323 '4 & 5 ounces': quoted in Earl Leslie Griggs and Seymour Teulon Porter, 'Samuel Taylor Coleridge and Opium', *Huntington Library Quarterly*, vol. 17, no. 4 (August 1954), 361.

p. 323 'I mean to exert': R. B. Litchfield, *Tom Wedgwood, the first photographer: An account of his life, his discovery and his friendship with Samuel Taylor Coleridge, including the letters of Coleridge to the Wedgwoods and an examination of accounts of earlier photographic discoveries* (London, 1903), 45.

p. 323 'I was seduced': ibid., 54.

p. 324 'I have in this one dirty business': Earl Leslie Griggs (ed.), *Collected Letters of Samuel Taylor Coleridge, Volume I, 1785–1800* (Oxford, 1966), xxxiv.

p. 324 'note for a Porter . . . literary labour': quoted in Richard Holmes, *Coleridge: Darker Reflections, 1804–1834* (London, 1999), 421.

p. 324 'loose, slack, not well-dressed': Colvin, *Keats*, 347.

p. 324 'a white-aproned youth . . . misery of my Existence': Porter quoted in Griggs, 'Samuel Taylor Coleridge and Opium', *HLQ* 17 (4), 362.

p. 325 'peculiar room . . . summer day': Thomas Carlyle, *The Life of John Sterling* (Boston, 1851), Chapter VIII: extract of memories of Samuel Taylor Coleridge.

Afterword

p. 327 'two entire miles': Roy Porter, *London: A Social History* (London, 1994), 224.

Select Bibliography

Books

An Historical Description of the Tower of London and its Curiosities (London, 1753)

Andrew, Donna T. (ed.), *London Debating Societies 1776–1799* (London, 1994)

Andrews, Jonathan and Scull, Andrew, *Undertaker of the Mind: John Monro and Mad-Doctoring in Eighteenth-Century England* (Berkeley, California, 2001)

Archenholz, Johann Wilhelm von, *A Picture of England: Containing a description of the laws, customs, and manners of England* (London, 1789)

Bailey, James Blake, *The Diary of a Resurrectionist 1811–1812, To Which Are Added an Account of the Resurrection Men in London and a Short History of the Passing of the Anatomy Act* (London, 1896)

Baker, Daniel, 'One Warning More' (London, 1660)

Bell, Robert, *Description of the Conditions and Manners of the Peasantry of Ireland* (London, 1804)

Belzoni, Giovanni, *Narrative of the Operations and Recent Discoveries within the Pyramids, Temples, Tombs and Excavations in Egypt and Nubia* (London, 1822)

Bentley, Samuel, *Literary Anecdotes of the Eighteenth Century* (London, 1814)

Blessington, Marguerite, *A Journal of Conversations with Lord Byron* (London, 1869)

Bondeson, Jan, *The Pig-Faced Lady of Manchester Square & Other Medical Marvels* (Stroud, 2006)

Boswell, James, *London Journal 1762–1763* (London, 1950 edition)

Bradley, R., *The Virtue and Use of Coffee* (London, 1772)

Brandon, David and Brooke, Alan, *Marylebone and Tyburn Past* (London, 2007)

Brewer, John and Porter, Roy (eds.), *Consumption and the World of Goods* (London, 1993)

Brown, Sue, *Joseph Severn, A Life: The Rewards of Friendship* (Oxford, 2009)

Burley, Stephen, *Hackney New College 1786–1796* (London, 2011)

Burn, John Southerden, *History of the Fleet Marriages* (London, 1846)

Campbell, Robert, *The London Tradesman* (London, 1747)

Carlyle, Thomas, *The Life of John Sterling* (Boston, 1851)

Carretta, Vincent (ed.), *Unchained Voices: An Anthology of Black Authors in the English-Speaking World of the Eighteenth Century* (Kentucky, 1996)

Casanova, Giacomo, *History of My Life* (Baltimore, Maryland, 1997 edition)

Chambers, James, *Building St Paul's* (London, 2007)

Chater, Kathleen, *Untold Histories: Black People in England and Wales During the Period of the British Slave Trade, c1660–1807* (Manchester, 2009)

Colquhoun, Patrick, *A Treatise on the Commerce and Police of the River Thames* (London, 1797)

Cruickshank, Dan, *The Secret History of Georgian London: How the Wages of Sin Shaped the Capital* (London, 2009)

Curiosities in the Tower of London (London, 1741)

Dasent, Arthur Irwin, *The History of St James's Square and the Foundation of the West End of London, with a Glimpse of Whitehall in the Reign of Charles the Second* (London, 1895)

Davis, Dorothy, *A History of Shopping* (London, 1966)

Defoe, Daniel, *A Journal of the Plague Year* (London, 1722)

Defoe, Daniel, *A Tour Through the Whole Island of Great Britain* (London, 1724–6)

Defoe, Daniel, *The Complete English Tradesman* (London, 1726)

DeMaria, Robert, *The Life of Samuel Johnson: A Critical Biography* (Oxford, 1993)

Denton, W., *Records of St Giles' Cripplegate* (London, 1883)

Dobie, Rowland, *The History of the United Parishes of St Giles in the Fields and St George's Bloomsbury* (London, 1829)

Dodd, George, *The Food of London: A Sketch of the Chief Varieties, Sources of Supply, Probable Quantities, Modes of Arrival, Processes of Manufacture, Suspected Adulteration, and Machinery of Distribution, of the Food for a Community of Two Millions and a Half* (London, 1856)

Earle, Peter, *The Making of the English Middle Class: Business, Society and Family Life in London, 1660–1730* (London, 1989)

Egan, Pierce, *Life in London, Or, the day and night scenes of Jerry Hawthorn, Esq.: and his elegant friend Corinthian Tom, accompanied by Bob Logic, the Oxonian, in their rambles and sprees through the metropolis* (London, 1904)

Ewen, C. L'Estrange, *Lotteries and Sweepstakes: An Historical, Legal and Ethical Survey of Their Introduction, Repression and Establishment in the British Isles* (London, 1932)

Forman, Maurice Buxton, *The Letters of John Keats* (Oxford, 1947)

George, M. Dorothy, *London Life in the XVIIIth Century* (London, 1930)

Giuseppi, John, *The Bank of England: A History from its Foundation in 1694* (London, 1966)

Green, David R., *Finsbury: Past, Present & Future* (London, 2009)

Grundy, Isobel, *Lady Mary Wortley Montagu* (Oxford, 1999)

Gwynn, Robin D., *Huguenot Heritage: The History and Contribution of the Huguenots in Britain* (Sussex, 2001)

Gwynne, John, *London and Westminster, Improved* (London, 1766)

Hahn, Daniel, *The Tower Menagerie: Being the Amazing True Story of the Royal Collection of Wild and Ferocious Beasts* (London, 2003)

Ham, Elizabeth, *Elizabeth Ham by Herself* (London, 1792)

Hands, A. P., *French Protestant Refugees Relieved Through the Threadneedle Street Church, London, 1681–1687* (London, 1971)

Hanway, Jonas, *Essay on Tea* (London, 1757)

Harvey, Gideon, *The City Remembrancer* (London, 1769)

Harvey, Karen, *Reading Sex in the Eighteenth Century: Bodies and Gender in English Erotic Culture* (Cambridge, 2004)

Hayward, Helena and Kirkham, Pat, *William and John Linnell, Eighteenth-Century London Furniture Makers* (London, 1980)

Hazlitt, William, *Sketches of the Principal Picture Galleries of England* (London, 1824)

Henderson, Tony, *Disorderly Women in Eighteenth-Century London: Prostitution and Control in the Metropolis, 1730–1830* (London, 1999)

Hibbert, Christopher, *King Mob: The Story of Lord George Gordon and the London Riots of 1780* (London, 1958)

Hitchcock, Tim, *Down and Out in Eighteenth-Century London* (London, 2004)

Hogg, John, *London As It Is: Being a series of observations on the health, habits, and amusements of the people* (London, 1837)

Hollis, Leo, *The Phoenix: The Men Who Made Modern London* (London, 2009)

Hollis, Leo, *The Stones of London: A History in Twelve Buildings* (London, 2010)

Home, Gordon, *Old London Bridge* (London, 1931)

Hone, William, *The Every-day Book* (London, 1826)

Hope, Annette, *Londoner's Larder: English Cuisine from Chaucer to the Present* (London, 2005)

Howell, James, *Londonopolis* (1657)

Jackson, Peter, *London Bridge: A Visual History* (London, 2002)

Jenkins, Susan, *Portrait of a Patron: The Patronage and Collecting of James Brydges, 1st Duke of Chandos (1674–1744)* (Aldershot, 2007)

Jesse, William, *The Life of George Brummell, Esq., Commonly Called Beau Brummell, Volume 1* (London, 1844)

Kalm, Pehr, *Kalm's Account of his Visit to England: On his Way to America in 1748*, translated by Joseph Lucas (London, 1892)

Kelly, Ian, *Beau Brummell, The Ultimate Dandy* (London, 2005)

Kelly, Ian, *Casanova* (London, 2008)

Kelly, Linda, *The Marvellous Boy: The Life and Myth of Thomas Chatterton* (London, 1971)

Kemp, Martin and Wallace, Marina, *Spectacular Bodies: The Art and Science of the Human Body from Leonardo to Now* (Berkeley, California, 2001)

Kendrick, T. D., *The Lisbon Earthquake* (London, 1957)

Kent, Henry, *The Shopkeeper's and Tradesman's Assistant* (London, 1768)

Larwood, Jacob, *English Inn Signs (being a revised and modernized version of History of Signboards)* (London, 1951)

Laurence, Anne (ed.), *Women and Their Money, 1700–1950: Essays on Women and Finance* (Oxford, 2008)

Lettsom, John, *Natural History of the Tea Trade* (London, 1772)

Linney, A. G., *Peepshow of the Port of London* (London, 1929)

Lippincott, Louise, *Selling Art in Georgian London: The Rise of Arthur Pond* (New Haven, Connecticut, 1983)

Litchfield, R. B., *Tom Wedgwood, the first photographer: An account of his life, his discovery and his friendship with Samuel Taylor Coleridge, including the letters of Coleridge to the Wedgwoods and an examination of accounts of alleged earlier photographic discoveries* (London, 1903)

Longstaffe-Gowan, Todd, *The London Town Garden, 1740–1840* (New Haven, Connecticut, 2001)

Lynch, Jack, *Deception and Detection in Eighteenth-Century Britain* (Aldershot, 2008)

McClure, Ruth K., *Coram's Children: The London Foundling Hospital in the Eighteenth Century* (London, 1981)

McDowell, Paula, *The Women of Grub Street: Press, Politics, and Gender in the London Literary Marketplace 1678–1730* (Oxford, 1998)

McEwan, Joanne and Sharpe, Pamela (eds.), *Accommodating Poverty: The Housing and Living Arrangements of the English Poor, c1600–1850* (Basingstoke, 2011)

Mack, Maynard, *Alexander Pope: A Life* (New Haven, Connecticut, 1985)

Mackenzie, Gordon, *Marylebone: Great City North of Oxford Street* (London, 1972)

Mayhew, Henry, *London Labour and the London Poor, Volumes I, II & III* (London, 1851)

Megarry, Sir Robert, *Inns Ancient and Modern: A Topographical and Historical Introduction to the Inns of Court, Inns of Chancery, and Serjeants' Inns* (London, 1972)

Mitton, Geraldine Edith, *Hampstead and Marylebone: The Fascination of London* (London, 1902)

Monro, John, *Remarks on Dr. Battie's Treatise of Madness by John Monro* (London, 1758)

Nicholls, James, *The Politics of Alcohol: A History of the Drink Question in England* (Manchester, 2009)

Norton, Rictor, *Mother Clap's Molly House: The Gay Subculture in England 1700–1830* (Stroud, 2006)

Olney, Clarke, *Benjamin Robert Haydon, Historical Painter* (Athens, Georgia, 1952)

Olsen, Kristin, *Daily Life in 18th-Century England* (Westport, Connecticut, 1999)

Paley, Ruth (ed.), *Justice in Eighteenth-Century Hackney: The Justicing Notebook of Henry Norris and the Hackney Petty Sessions Book* (London, 1991)

Palk, Deidre (ed.), *Prisoners' Letters to the Bank of England 1781–1827* (London, 2007)

Palmer, Susan, *The Soanes At Home: Domestic Life At Lincoln's Inn Fields* (London, 1997)

Paulson, Ronald, *Hogarth: His Life and Times* (London, 1971)

Peakman, Julie, *Mighty Lewd Books: The Development of Pornography in Eighteenth-Century England* (Basingstoke, 2003)

Peakman, Julie (ed.), *Sexual Perversions, 1670–1890* (Basingstoke, 2009)

Pennant, Thomas, *An Account of London* (London, 1790)

Penrose, Alexander, *Benjamin Robert Haydon 1786–1846* (London, 1927)

Percival, Milton, *Robert Walpole, Earl of Orford, 1676–1745* (Oxford, 1916)

Phillips, P. A. S., *Paul de Lamerie* (London 1935)

Pinkerton, John (ed.), *Walpoliana* (London, 1800)

Pinkerton, John, *A General Collection of the Best and Most Interesting Voyages and Travels in all Parts of the World: Volume 2* (London, 1808)

Porter, Roy, *London: A Social History* (London, 1994)

Porter, Roy and Mulvey, Marie (eds.), *Pleasure in the Eighteenth Century* (Basingstoke, 1996)

Porter, Roy and Ribeiro, Aileen, *Richard and Maria Cosway: Regency Artists of Taste and Fashion* (Edinburgh, 1995)

Ralph, James, *A Critical Review of the Publick Buildings, Statues and Ornaments of London and Westminster* (London, 1763)

Renton, Peter, *The Lost Synagogues of London* (London, 2000)

Reynolds, Frederick, *The Life and Times of Frederick Reynolds, Written By Himself, in Two Volumes: Volume I* (London, 1827)

Reynolds, Joshua, *Seven Discourses on Art* (London, 1769)

Richardson, Ruth, *Death, Dissection and the Destitute* (London, 1987)

Rochefoucauld, François de La, *A Frenchman in England, 1784* (Cambridge, 1933 edition)

Rogers, Pat, *Grub Street: Studies in a Subculture* (London, 1972)

Rosetti, William Michael, *Life of John Keats* (London, 1887)

Rousseau, G. S. and Porter, Roy (eds.), *Sexual Underworlds of the Enlightenment* (Manchester, 1987)

Rubenhold, Hallie, *The Covent Garden Ladies: Pimp General Jack & The Extraordinary Story of Harris's List* (London, 2005)

Rugg, Thomas, *The Diurnal of Thomas Rugg, 1659–1660* (London, 1961)

Sands, Mollie, *The Eighteenth-Century Pleasure Gardens of Marylebone, 1737–1777* (London, 1987)

Saussure, César de, *A Foreign View of England in 1725–1729: The Letters of Monsieur César de Saussure to his Family*, translated and edited by Madame Van Muyden (London, 1902)

Smith, J. R., *The Speckled Monster: Smallpox in England, 1670–1970* (Chelmsford, 1987)

Smith, John Thomas, *Nollekens and his Times; and memoirs of contemporary artists from the time of Roubiliac, Hogarth and Reynolds to that of Fuseli, Flaxman and Blake* (London, 1829)

Smollett, Tobias George, *The Expedition of Humphry Clinker* (London, 1771)

Spear, Percival, *Master of Bengal: Clive of India* (London, 1974)

Spence, Craig, *London in the 1690s: A Social Atlas* (London, 2000)

Stanhope, Philip Dormer, *Letters* (London, 1847)

Stark, Suzanne J., *Female Tars: Women Aboard Ship in the Age of Sail* (London, 1998)

Steele, Valerie, *The Corset: A Cultural History* (New Haven, Connecticut, 2001)

Tames, Richard, *Soho Past* (London, 1994)

Thale, Mary (ed.), *The Autobiography of Francis Place (1771–1854)* (Cambridge, 1972)

The European Magazine, and London Review (London, 1785)

The Lives and Portraits of Curious and Odd Characters (London, 1852)

The Phoenix of Sodom; Or the Vere Street Coterie (London, 1813)

The Trial of the Spirits; Or, Some Considerations upon the Pernicious Consequences of the Gin Trade to Great Britain (London, 1736)

Thornbury, Walter, *Old and New London: Volumes 1 & 2* (London, 1878)

Thornton, Richard, *History of London* (London, 1785)

Timbs, John, *Clubs and Club Life in London: With anecdotes of its famous coffee-houses, hostelries, and taverns, from the seventeenth century to the present time* (London, 1872)

Tolstoy, Nikolai, *The Half-mad Lord: Thomas Pitt, 2nd Baron Camelford (1775–1804)* (London, 1978)

Voltaire, *Letters Concerning the English Nation*, Letter VI 'On the Presbyterians' (London, 1733)

Walford, Edward, *Old and New London: Volumes 3–6* (London, 1878)

Walford, Edward, *Chapters from the Family Chests* (London, 1887)

Walpole, Horace, *Vertue Note Books, Volume III, Number 22* (London, 1933)

Walvin, James, *Fruits of Empire: Exotic Produce and British Taste, 1660–1800* (London, 1997)

Ward, Ned, *The London Spy Compleat* (London, 1706)

Ward, Ned, *The Field Spy* (London, 1714)

Watkin, David, *Sir John Soane, Enlightenment Thought and the Royal Academy Lectures* (Cambridge, 1996)

Werrett, Simon, *Fireworks: Pyrotechnic Arts and Sciences in European History* (Chicago, Illinois, 2010)

Wharton, Lord (ed.), *The Letters and Works of Lady Mary Wortley Montagu: Volume 1* (London, 1837)

Williams, Claire, *Sophie in London, 1786* (London, 1933)

Williams, John, *The Pin-basket to the Children of Thespis* (London, 1797)

Wise, Sarah, *The Italian Boy: Murder and Grave-Robbery in 1830s London* (London, 2004)

Wood, Edward, *Giantology and Dwarfiana* (London, 1868)

Wright, Thomas, *The Life of Daniel Defoe* (London, 1894)

Periodicals

Beattie, J. M., 'Sir John Fielding and Public Justice: The Bow Street Magistrates' Court, 1754–1780', *Law and History Review*, vol. 25, no. 1 (Spring 2007), 61–100

Buchanan, Linda, 'Sarah Siddons and Her Place in Rhetorical History', *Rhetorica: A Journal of the History of Rhetoric*, vol. 25, no. 4 (Autumn 2007), 413–34

Burnard, Trevor, 'European Migration to Jamaica, 1655–1780', *The William and Mary Quarterly*, ser. 3, vol. 53, no. 4 (October 1996), 769–96

Cameron, G. R., 'Edward Jenner, FRS 1749–1823', *Notes and Records of the Royal Society of London*, vol. 7, no. 1 (December 1949), 43–53

Clapham, J. H., 'The Spitalfields Acts, 1773–1824', *The Economic Journal*, vol. 26, no. 104 (December 1916), 459–71

Clark, Peter, 'The "Mother Gin" Controversy in the Early Eighteenth Century', *Transactions of the Royal Historical Society*, fifth series, vol. 38 (1988), 63–84

Constable, W. G., 'The Foundation of the National Gallery', *The Burlington Magazine for Connoisseurs*, vol. 44, no. 253 (April 1924), 158–72

Curl, James Stevens, 'Spas and Pleasure Gardens of London, from the Seventeenth to the Nineteenth Centuries', *Garden History*, vol. 7, no. 2 (Summer 1979), 27–68

Denlinger, Elizabeth Campbell, 'The Garment and the Man: Masculine Desire in "Harris's List of Covent-Garden Ladies", 1764–1793', *Journal of the History of Sexuality*, vol. 11, no. 3 (July 2002), 357–94

Frank, Julia Bess, 'Body Snatching: A Grave Medical Problem', *Yale Journal of Biology and Medicine*, vol. 49, no. 4 (September 1976), 399–410

Humble, J. G., 'Westminster Hospital: The First 250 Years', *British Medical Journal*, vol. 1, no. 5480 (January 1996), 156–62

Hunter, John, 'Proposals for the Recovery of People Apparently Drowned', *Philosophical Transactions of the Royal Society of London*, vol. 66, no. 1776, 412–25

Keynes, Milo, 'The Portland Vase: Sir William Hamilton, Josiah Wedgwood and the Darwins', *Notes and Records of the Royal Society of London*, vol. 52, no. 2 (July 1998), 237–59

Lewis, Lesley, 'Elizabeth, Countess of Home, and Her House in Portman Square', *The Burlington Magazine*, vol. 109, no. 773 (August 1967), 443–53

MacKay, Lynn, 'A Culture of Poverty? The St Martin in the Fields Workhouse, 1817', *Journal of Interdisciplinary History*, vol. 26, no. 2 (Autumn 1995), 209–31

Murphy, Elaine, 'A Mad House Transformed: The Lives and Work of Charles James Beverly FRS (1788–1868) and John Warburton MD FRS (1795–1847)', *Notes and Records of the Royal Society of London*, vol. 58, no. 3 (September 2004), 267–81

Perman, E., 'Successful Cardiac Resuscitation with Electricity in the 18th Century?', *British Medical Journal*, vol. 2, no. 6154 (December 1978), 1770–71

Postle, Martin, 'Flayed for Art: The Écorché Figure in the English Art Academy', *British Art Journal*, vol. V, no. 1 (2004), 55–63

Skempton, A. W., 'Samuel Wyatt and the Albion Mill', *Architectural History*, vol. 14 (1971), 53–73

Summerson, John, 'Change, Decay and the Soane Museum', *Architectural Association Journal* (October 1949), 50–53

Temperley, Nicholas, 'The Lock Hospital Chapel and Its Music', *Journal of the Royal Musical Association*, vol. 118, no. 1 (1993), 44–72

Waldron, H. A., 'A brief history of scrotal cancer', *British Journal of Industrial Medicine*, vol. 40, no. 4 (November 1983), 390–401

White, Jonathan, 'The "Slow but Sure Poyson": The Representation of Gin and its Drinkers, 1736–1751', *Journal of British Studies*, vol. 42, no. 1 (January 2003), 35–64

Wright, C. E., 'Portrait of a Bibliophile VIII, Edward Harley, 2nd Earl of Oxford, 1689–1741', *The Book Collector*, vol. 2 (1962), 158–74

Index